The Nutmeg's Curse

The Nutmeg's Curse

PARABLES FOR A PLANET IN CRISIS

Amitav Ghosh

The University of Chicago Press

The University of Chicago Press, Chicago 60637
Published 2021
Paperback edition 2022
Printed in the United States of America

31 30 29 28 27 26 25 24 23 22   1 2 3 4 5

ISBN-13: 978-0-226-81545-9 (cloth)
ISBN-13: 978-0-226-82395-9 (paper)
ISBN-13: 978-0-226-81546-6 (e-book)
DOI: https://doi.org/10.7208/chicago/9780226815466.001.0001

Library of Congress Cataloging-in-Publication Data

Names: Ghosh, Amitav, 1956– author.
Title: The nutmeg's curse : parables for a planet in crisis / Amitav
   Ghosh.
Description: Chicago : University of Chicago Press, 2021. | Includes
   bibliographical references and index.
Identifiers: LCCN 2021012764 | ISBN 9780226815459 (cloth) | ISBN
   9780226815466 (ebook)
Subjects: LCSH: Imperialism. | Climatic changes. | Equality. | Social
   history.
Classification: LCC JC359 .G464 2021 | DDC 363.738/74—dc23
LC record available at https://lccn.loc.gov/2021012764

♾ This paper meets the requirements of ANSI/NISO Z39.48-1992
(Permanence of Paper).

In memory of
Anjali Ghosh,
Barbara Bernache Baker,
and
Jeffrey J. W. Baker

Contents

List of Figures · ix

1 A Lamp Falls · 5

2 "Burn Everywhere Their Dwellings" · 21

3 "The Fruits of the Nutmeg Have Died" · 31

4 Terraforming · 49

5 "We Shall All Be Gone Shortly" · 63

6 Bonds of Earth · 73

7 Monstrous Gaia · 85

8 Fossilized Forests · 99

9 Choke Points · 105

10 Father of All Things · 121

11 Vulnerabilities · 133

12 A Fog of Numbers · 147

13 War by Another Name · 163

14 "The Divine Angel of Discontent" · 173

15 Brutes · 183

16 "The Falling Sky" · 205

17 Utopias · 217

18 A Vitalist Politics · 235

19 Hidden Forces · 245

Acknowledgments · 259

Notes · 261

Bibliography · 297

Index · 327

Figures

1   *The East Indies* (1689) · 2–3
2   *The Banda Islands* (ca. 1749–1755) · 4
3   "Banda Islands Nutmeg" (1619) · 10
4   Clove-topped Monument · 113
5   Gunung Api · 246
6   Bandanese Memorial · 247

The Nutmeg's Curse

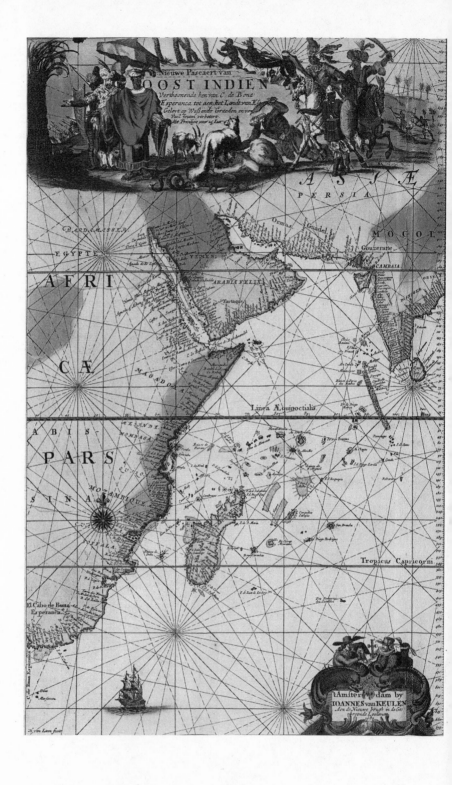

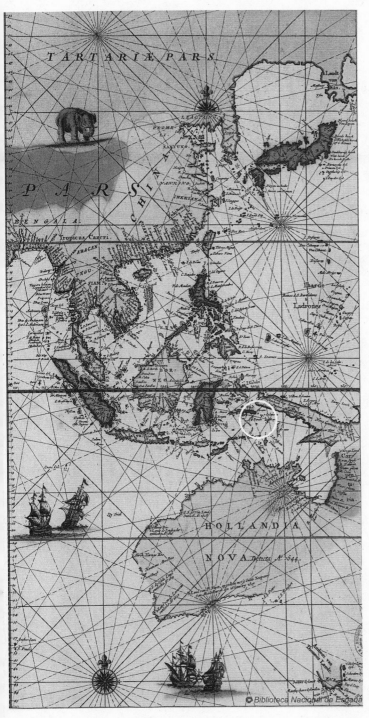

FIGURE 1. Johannes van Keulen, *The East Indies* (1689). Biblioteca Digital Hispánica. Photograph: Wikimedia Commons. (The Banda islands appear in the white circle.)

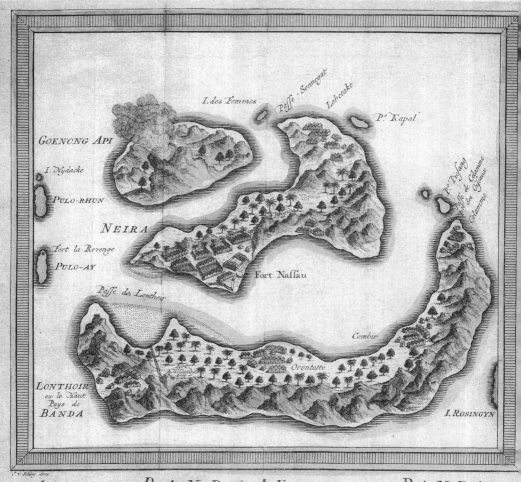

Goenong Api

I. des Femmes

Passe Sonnegat

Labetake

P.e Kapal

I. Nydacke

PULO-RHUN

P.e Defarej
Passe de Calanne
Isle des Defarej
Calanne

NEIRA

Fort la Revenge

PULO-AY

Fort Nassau

Passe de Lonthoir

Combir

A. Hollandia

Orontatte

LONTHOIR
ou le Haut
Pays de
BANDA

I. ROSINGYN

T.V. Schley direx.

ISLES DE BANDA. | EYLANDEN VAN BANDA.

FIGURE 2. Nicolas Bellin, *The Banda Islands* (ca. 1749–1755). Copper plate engraving.

1

A Lamp Falls

To this day nobody knows exactly what transpired in Selamon on that April night, in the year 1621, except that a lamp fell to the floor in the building where Martijn Sonck, a Dutch official, was billeted.

Selamon is a village in the Banda archipelago, a tiny cluster of islands at the far southeastern end of the Indian Ocean.[1] The settlement is located at the northern end of Lonthor, which is also sometimes referred to as Great Banda (Banda Besar) because it is the largest island in the cluster.[2] "Great" is a somewhat extravagant epithet for an island that is only two and a half miles in length and half a mile in width—but then, that isn't an insignificant size in an archipelago so minute that on most maps it is marked only by a sprinkling of dots.[3]

Yet here is Martijn Sonck, on April 21, 1621, halfway around the world from his homeland, in Selamon's *bale-bale*, or meeting hall, which he has requisitioned as a billet for himself and his counselors.[4] Sonck has also occupied the settlement's most venerable mosque—"a beautiful institution," made of white stone, airy and clean inside, with two large urns of water positioned at the entrance for congregants to wash their feet before stepping in. The elders of the village haven't taken kindly to the seizure of their mosque, but Sonck has brusquely brushed aside their protests, telling them they have plenty of other places to practice their religion.

This is of a piece with everything else that Sonck has done in the short while that he has been on Lonthor Island. He has seized the best houses for his troops, and he has also sent soldiers swarming over the village, terrifying the inhabitants. But these measures are mere preliminaries, intended only to lay the groundwork for what Sonck actually has in mind: he has come to Selamon under orders to destroy the village and expel its inhabitants from this idyllic island, with its lush forests and sparkling blue seas.

The brutality of this plan is such that the villagers have not, perhaps, been able to fully comprehend it yet. But the Dutchman, for his part, has made no secret of his intentions; to the contrary, he has made it perfectly clear to the elders that he expects their full cooperation in the destruction of their own settlement and the expulsion of their fellow villagers.

Nor is Sonck the first Dutch official to deliver this message to Selamon. The villagers, and their fellow Bandanese, have already endured several weeks of threats and shows of force, always accompanied by the same demands: that they tear down the village's walls, surrender their arms and tools—even the rudders of their boats—and make preparations for their imminent removal from the island. The demands are so extreme, so outlandish, that the villagers have, no doubt, wondered whether the Dutchmen are in their right minds. But Sonck has been at pains to let them know that he is in earnest: his commanding officer, none other than the governor-general himself, has run out of patience. The people of Selamon will have to obey his orders down to the last detail.

· · ·

HOW MUST IT FEEL to find yourself face-to-face with someone who has made it clear that he has the power to bring your world to an end, and has every intention of doing so?

Over the preceding couple of decades the people of Selamon, and their fellow Bandanese, have resisted the Dutch to the best of their abilities; on occasion they have even been able to drive the Europeans away. But they have never had to face a force as large and as well-armed as the one that Sonck has brought with him. Outmatched, they have tried hard to appease Sonck to the best of their ability: while some villagers have fled into the neighboring forests, a good many have stayed on, perhaps hoping that a mistake has been made and that the Dutch will leave if they manage to hold out.

Those who have remained, many of whom are women and children, have taken care not to give the Dutchmen any excuse for violence. But Sonck has a mission to carry out, one to which he is not particularly well suited—he is a revenue official, not a soldier—and he is probably beset by a feeling of inadequacy. In the villagers' quiescence he senses a seething anger, and he wishes, perhaps, that they would give him an excuse, some pretext for what he needs to do next.

On the night of April 21, when Sonck retires to Selamon's commandeered meeting house with his counselors, his state of mind is very precarious. There is so much tension in the air that the silence seems to augur a seismic eruption.

The atmosphere is such that for someone in Sonck's state it is impossible, perhaps, to see the falling of an object as an ordinary mishap—it has to be a sign of something else, betokening some sinister intent. So when the lamp falls, Sonck jumps instantly to the conclusion that it is a signal, intended to trigger a surprise attack on himself and his soldiers. He and his panicked counselors snatch up their firearms and begin shooting at random.

It is a dark night, "as dark as only an Indies night without moonlight can be." In such conditions, when nothing is visible, it is easy to imagine the seething presence of a ghostly army. Sonck and his counselors keep unloosing barrage after barrage at their invisible enemy, startling even their own guards, who have seen no sign of an attack.

. . .

THE BANDA ISLANDS sit upon one of the fault lines where the Earth shows itself to be most palpably alive: the islands, and their volcano, are among the offspring of the Ring of Fire that runs from Chile, in the east, to the rim of the Indian Ocean, in the west. A still active volcano, Gunung Api ("Fire Mountain"), towers above the Bandas, its peak perpetually wreathed in plumes of swirling cloud and upwelling steam.

Gunung Api is one of a great number of volcanoes in this

stretch of ocean; the surrounding waters are dotted with beautifully formed, conical mountains that surge majestically out of the waves, some of them rising to heights of a thousand meters or more. The very name of the region, Maluku (which gave birth to the English toponym "Moluccas"), is said to derive from *Molòko*, a word that means "mountain" or "mountain island."[5]

The mountain islands of Maluku often erupt with devastating force, bringing ruin and destruction upon the people who live in their vicinity. Yet there is also something magical about these eruptions, something akin to the pain of childbirth. For the eruptions of Maluku's volcanoes bring to the surface alchemical mixtures of materials which interact with the winds and weather of the region in such a way as to create forests that teem with wonders and rarities.

In the case of the Banda Islands the gift of Gunung Api is a botanical species that has flourished on this tiny archipelago like nowhere else: the tree that produces both nutmeg and mace.

The trees and their offspring were of very different temperaments. The trees were home-loving and did not venture out of their native Maluku until the eighteenth century. Nutmegs and mace, on the other hand, were tireless travelers: how much so is easy to chart, simply because, before the eighteenth century, every single nutmeg and every shred of mace originated in, or around, the Bandas. So it follows that any mention of nutmeg or mace in any text, anywhere, before the 1700s automatically establishes a link with the Bandas. In Chinese texts those mentions date back to the first century before the Common Era; in Latin texts the nutmeg appears a century later.[6] But nutmegs had probably reached Europe and China long before writers thought to mention them in texts. This was certainly the case in India, where a carbonized nutmeg has been found in an archaeological site that dates back to 400–300 BCE. The first reliably dated textual mention (which is actually of mace) followed two or three centuries later.[7]

Of this there can be no doubt, at any rate: nutmegs had traveled thousands of miles across the oceans long before the first Europeans reached Maluku.[8] It was these journeys that ultimately brought European navigators to Maluku; they came because plant products like nutmegs had already traveled in the other direction, long before them.[9]

As they made their way across the known world, nutmegs, mace, and other spices brought into being trading networks that stretched all the way across the Indian Ocean, reaching deep into Africa and Eurasia.[10] The nodes and routes of these networks, and the people who were active in them, varied greatly over time, as kingdoms rose and fell, but for more than a millennium the voyages of the nutmeg remained remarkably consistent, growing steadily in both volume and value.

Apart from their culinary uses, nutmegs, cloves, pepper, and other spices were valued also for their medicinal properties.[11] In the sixteenth century, the value of the nutmeg soared when doctors in Elizabethan England decided that the spice could be used to cure the plague, epidemics of which were then sweeping through Eurasia.[12] In the late Middle Ages, nutmegs became so valuable in Europe that a handful could buy a house or a ship.[13] So astronomical was the cost of spices in this era that it is impossible to account for their value in terms of utility alone. They were, in effect, fetishes, primordial forms of the commodity; they were valued because they had become envy-inducing symbols of luxury and wealth, conforming perfectly to Adam Smith's insight that wealth is something that is "desired, not for the material satisfactions that it brings but because it is desired by others."[14]

Before the sixteenth century nutmegs reached Europe by changing hands many times, at many points of transit. The latter stages of their journey took them through Egypt, or the Levant, to Venice, which, in the centuries leading up to the voyages of Christopher Columbus and Vasco de Gama, ran a tightly controlled monopoly on the European spice trade.[15] Columbus himself hailed from Venice's archrival, Genoa, where the Serene Republic's monopoly on the Eastern trade had long been bitterly resented; it was in order to break the Venetian hold on the trade that the early European navigators set off on the journeys that led to the Americas and the Indian Ocean.[16] Among their goals, one of the most important was to find the islands that were home to the nutmeg. The stakes were immense, for the navigators and for the monarchs who financed

FIGURE 3. Anon., "Banda Islands Nutmeg" (1619). Engraving. Rijksmuseum. Photograph: Wikimedia Commons.

them: the spice race, it has been said, was the space race of its time.[17]

Little wonder then that the nutmeg tree had brought Dutchmen like Sonck halfway around the world to the island of Lonthor.

Taking a nutmeg out of its fruit is like unearthing a tiny planet.

Like a planet, the nutmeg is encased within a series of expanding spheres. There is, first of all, the fruit's matte-brown skin, a kind of exosphere. Then there is the pale, perfumed flesh, growing denser toward the core, like a planet's outer atmosphere. And when all the flesh has been stripped away, you have in your hand a ball wrapped in what could be a stratosphere of fiery, crimson clouds: it is this fragrant outer sleeve that is known as mace. Stripping off the mace reveals yet another casing, a glossy, ridged, chocolate-colored carapace, which holds the nut inside like a protective troposphere. Only when this shell is cracked open do you have the nut in your palm, its surface clouded by matte-brown continents floating on patches of ivory.

And should you then break the nut open, you will see inside

something akin to a geological structure—except that it is composed of the unique mixture of substances that produces the aroma, and the psychotropic effects, that are the nut's very own superpowers.

Like a planet, a nutmeg too can never be seen in its entirety at one time. As with the moon, or any spherical (or quasi-spherical) object, a nutmeg has two hemispheres; when one is in the light, the other must be in darkness—for one to be seen by the human eye, the other must be hidden.

THE ISLAND OF LONTHOR is shaped like a boomerang, and it adjoins two other islands: Gunung Api and Banda Naira, a tiny islet that was already, in 1621, the seat of two massive Dutch forts. The three islands are themselves the remnants of an exploded volcano, grouped around its now-submerged crater.[18] Between them lies a stretch of sheltered water that is deep enough to accommodate oceangoing ships. Anchored there on the night of April 21 is the fleet that has brought Martijn Sonck to the Banda Islands.

On still nights sounds carry easily across this stretch of water. The rattle of agitated musket fire on Lonthor is clearly heard on the *Nieuw-Hollandia*, the flagship of the commander who has brought this fleet to the Bandas: Governor-General Jan Pieterszoon Coen.

An accountant by training, Coen, at the age of thirty-three, has served as the governor-general of the East Indies for three years already. A man of immense energy, competence, and determination, he has risen through the ranks of the Dutch East India Company like a jet of volcanic ash. Known, behind his back, as De Schraale ("Old Skin and Bones"), he is a blunt, ruthless man, not given to mincing his words.[19] In a letter to the Seventeen Gentlemen who preside over the Company, Governor-General Coen once observed: "There is nothing in the world that gives one a better right than power."[20]

Now the most powerful proconsul of the world's mightiest commercial company, Coen is no stranger to the Banda Islands.[21] He was here twelve years earlier, as a member of a Dutch force that came to negotiate a treaty with the Bandanese.[22] During the negotiations a part of that force was ambushed on the shores of Banda Naira and forty-six Dutchmen, including the leading officer, were slaughtered by the Bandanese.[23] Coen was among those who got away with his life, but his memories of this episode have shaped his view of the Dutch mission in the Banda Islands.[24]

Ever since the first Dutch ships came to the archipelago it has been the aim of the venerable East India Company—the Vereenigde Oostindische Compagnie, or VOC—to impose a trade monopoly on the Bandanese.[25] But this goal has proved elusive because the concept of a trading monopoly, although common in Europe, is completely foreign to the commercial traditions of the Indian Ocean.[26] In these waters entrepôts and maritime states have always competed with each other to attract as many foreign merchants as possible. It was in this spirit that the Bandanese welcomed the first party of Europeans to visit their islands: a small Portuguese contingent that included Ferdinand Magellan. That was back in 1512; in the years since, the Bandanese have discovered (to their cost) that the Europeans who come to their shores, no matter of what nationality, all have the same thing in mind: a treaty granting them an exclusive right to the islands' nutmegs and mace.[27]

But such a right is impossible for the Bandanese to grant. How can they refuse to trade with their accustomed business partners, from shores near and far? The islanders depend on their neighbors for food and much else.[28] Besides, the Bandanese are themselves skilled traders, and many of them have close links with other merchant communities in the Indian Ocean; they can hardly turn their friends away empty-handed.[29] Nor would that make commercial sense, since the Europeans often don't pay as well as Asian buyers. And the Bandanese, like most Asians, don't find European goods particularly desirable: what are they, with their warm climate, to do with woolen cloth, for instance?[30]

It would have been easier for the Dutch if the Bandanese had had a powerful ruler, a sultan who could be coerced into compliance, as had happened on other islands in Maluku.[31] But the Banda Islands have no single ruler who can be threatened and bullied into forcing his subjects to obey the foreigners' demands.[32] "They have neither king nor lord" was the conclusion of the first Portuguese navigators to visit the islands, "and all their government depends on the advice of their elders; and as these are often at variance, they quarrel among themselves."[33]

This is not the whole truth, of course. The Bandanese have aristocratic lineages, as well as merchant families that possess great wealth and many servitors. It is a combative society, divided into walled settlements that sometimes fight pitched battles against each other.[34] But no single settlement or family has ever subdued the entire archipelago; the islanders seem to have a deep-seated distaste for centralized, unitary rule.

Bandanese tradition has it that the islands were once ruled by four kings.[35] But by the time the first Dutch ships came to the archipelago, the only figures of authority there were a few dozen elders and *orang-kaya*, which means literally "men of wealth."[36] A few of these elders carry the title of harbormaster, or Shahbandar, but neither they nor any of the *orang-kaya* possess the political authority to enforce a treaty on the entire archipelago, tiny though it is.[37]

Yet the Europeans—first the Portuguese and Spanish, and then the Dutch—have for more than a hundred years insistently pursued the goal of establishing a monopoly over the islanders' most important products: nutmeg and mace.[38] The most relentless of all are the Dutch; they have sent fleets to the islands again and again, with the intention of forcing treaties on the inhabitants.[39] The islanders have resisted as best they could, often accepting help from other Europeans.[40] But the Bandanese are too few in number—there are only about fifteen thousand of them altogether—to fight the world's most powerful navy.[41] With great reluctance their elders have signed several treaties, sometimes without knowing what they said (the documents were in Dutch).[42] But covertly they have continued to trade with other merchants, and whenever possible they have also resisted with arms, as they did in 1609, when they ambushed the party of Dutchmen that included the future governor-general, Jan Pieterszoon Coen.[43]

In the aftermath of that slaughter Coen has come to believe—as had some of his predecessors—that *die Bandaneezen* are incorrigible and that the Banda problem needs a final solution: the islands must be emptied of their inhabitants. Unless that is accomplished the VOC will never be able to establish a monopoly on nutmeg and mace. Once the Bandanese are gone, settlers and slaves can be brought in to create a new economy in the archipelago. This will be a departure from the usual Dutch practice, which is to focus on trade and avoid territorial acquisitions.[44] But since the nutmeg trade is synonymous with the Bandas, it can't be helped.[45] And the sooner it's done, the better: the English, who have been snapping at the heels of the Dutch from the Americas to the East Indies, have recently established a toehold in the Bandas, on a tiny island called Run.[46] Coen is determined not to allow them to expand their footprint in the archipelago.

Writing to the directors of the VOC, Coen has noted: "It would be best in my opinion to completely chase all the Bandanese from the land"—and it is with exactly this in mind that he has come to the Banda Islands now.[47] To get the job done as efficiently as possible he has added a contingent of eighty Japanese mercenaries to his forces: they are *ronin*, or masterless samurai. Not only are they cheaper and hardier than European soldiers, they are also professional swordsmen and highly skilled executioners, experts in the arts of decapitation and dismemberment.[48]

. . . .

THE MYSTERY OF Selamon's lamp probably wouldn't have taken hold of my mind to the extent that it did, if it were not for an uncanny intersection between human and nonhuman forms of agency.

I began writing this chapter in early March of 2020, at just the time when a microscopic entity, the newest coronavirus, was quickly becoming the largest, most threatening, and most inescapable presence on the planet. As cars and people vanished from the streets of Brooklyn, where I live, a peculiar sense of dislocation set in. Reading the notes I had made on my visit to the Banda Islands in November 2016, I sometimes had the eerie sense of having returned incorporeally to the archipelago.

On that visit I had stayed in a hotel built by a man called Des Alwi, who had once been known as the Raja of the Bandas. A member of one of the most prominent families in the islands, Alwi, who died in 2010, is remembered by everyone who knew him as an unusually charismatic, larger-than-life presence. An author and diplomat, he had established a foundation dedicated to the preservation of the islands' heritage. Apart from restoring many crumbling colonial buildings, the foundation had also printed a few books and pamphlets, among them an introduction to the history of the islands written by a friend of Des Alwi's, an American historian called Willard A. Hanna. It was in this book, titled *Indonesian Banda: Colonialism and Its Aftermath in the Nutmeg Islands*, that I first read about the lamp that fell in Selamon on the night of April 21, 1621.

The detail was mentioned only in passing, but it haunted me. Why had such a simple, everyday mishap caused so much panic amongst Sonck's contingent of Dutch soldiers?

During the stillness of those Brooklyn nights, when the silence was broken only by the sirens of speeding ambulances, it was possible to imagine that a sudden and unexpected sound might remind everyone of the invisible nonhuman presences that surround us, intervening in everyday life in ways that completely transform the meaning of ordinary events.

Not far from my house is one of Brooklyn's largest hospitals. At that time Covid-19 was claiming so many lives that the bodies of the dead were being stacked outside, in refrigerated trucks. When I stepped out of my house I could sense fear seething in the streets around me, and this induced a sense of kinship with the terror-struck villagers of Selamon, as they lay huddled in their homes, wondering if the fall of the lamp was a portent of worse things to come.

I wanted to know more about the fall of that lamp. But how? The difficulties of throwing light on a moment four centuries in the past become vastly greater when the setting is a place as remote and forgotten as the Banda archipelago. Few indeed are the scholars who have written about the Bandas, so the events of 1621 are shrouded in obscurity, skimmed over even in most histories and ethnographies of the region.[49] Where then had Hanna found this detail? As I combed through his book, it became clear that his main source was a monograph called *De Vestiging van het Nederland-sche Gezag over de Banda-Eilanden (1599–1621)* (The establishment of

Dutch rule over the Banda Islands). The author's name was J. A. van der Chijs, and the book was published in Batavia (Jakarta) in 1886.

At this point in New York City's lockdown I, like many others, was in a somewhat dazed, fugue-like state. In the preceding months, propelled by the spiraling acceleration of the Before-Covid Time, I had been traveling constantly. The sudden cessation of movement had created a sensation of breathlessness, as though a speeding car had been brought to a screeching halt on an expressway.

My wife, Debbie, who is known to her readers as Deborah Baker, was away in Charlottesville, Virginia, researching a book and spending time with her family. Earlier in the year, in January 2020, the same month in which we had celebrated our thirtieth anniversary, she had lost her ninety-year-old mother, Barbara. The loss had sent her eighty-nine-year-old father into a downward spiral, so she needed to be in Virginia for a while. I had meant to follow but changed my mind when infection rates in New York suddenly began to soar; the risk of carrying the contagion with me made it seem irresponsible to venture out of the city. Nor, in that disorienting moment, did I feel much inclined to leave the familiarity of Brooklyn, where my son and daughter also live. So it happened that an uncanny conjunction of circumstances ensured that I was on my own, spending even longer hours in my study than I usually do.

If it were not for the strangeness of that locked-down time, I don't think I would have done what I did next: I searched the internet for a pdf of Van der Chijs's book—and to my surprise one turned up! I downloaded it unthinkingly; I don't know why because I don't read Dutch. But there it was in front of me, a treasure trove of secrets, and all I could do was stare at it, as though it were a rune-stone or petroglyph.

One day, while waiting for New York's daily 7 p.m. ritual of thanking the city's first responders by clapping, cheering, and (in my case) banging pots, I started to scroll randomly through the text of Van der Chijs's book. Soon enough I came to some familiar names and words—the word "lamp," I discovered, has the same meaning in Dutch and English. On an impulse I typed a Dutch sentence into a widely used online translation app—and somewhat to my surprise, it produced a string of words that made sense: "About midnight from the 21st to the 22nd of April [1621], a lamp fell in the *bale-bale*, where Sonck slept with his counselors, an insignificant event [but] enough to cause panic among the Europeans, who were always and everywhere seeing treason."[50]

After that it was impossible to stop. I forgot about the pot-banging ritual and instead began to feed Dutch sentences into the app, one after another—and there were just enough glimmers of sense behind the often-garbled results to draw me deeper and deeper into the text.

I quickly discovered that I had been lucky with that first sentence: with some passages the app's results were complete gibberish. But those chunks of nonsense had one thing in common: most of them were within quotes. It was these passages that seemed to confound the app, which was clearly built to translate modern Dutch.

Putting two and two together, I realized that much of Van der Chijs's account consisted of direct quotations from seventeenth-century sources. I would learn later that Van der Chijs had worked as the *landsarchivaris*, or head archivist, of the Dutch colonial administration in Batavia; he therefore had direct access to all the relevant seventeenth-century documents, and it was on these that he had based his book—which was fortunate, since many of those documents have since disappeared.[51]

As I puzzled over the strings of nonsense that the translation app was churning out, I began to wonder whether the spellings of certain common Dutch words might have changed since the seventeenth century—as is the case, for instance, with the English words "hath" and "has."

I happen, fortunately, to be acquainted with one of the great Dutch historians of Asia, Dirk Kolff, whose knowledge of seventeenth-century Dutch archives, especially those of the VOC, is unmatched. I wrote to him explaining my dilemma, and he very kindly sent me a list of changed spellings. The list worked like magic: when I gave seventeenth-century words their modern spellings, the app's renditions became much clearer.

So, with more and more ambulances shrieking past the window

of my study, in what had once been the Dutch village of Breukelen, I began to type entire pages into the app, sentence by sentence, paragraph by paragraph. Soon it was as if two nonhuman entities, the internet and the coronavirus, both operating at a planetary scale, had come together to create a ghostly portal to transport me, through the spirit of a long-dead Dutchman, to the Banda Islands on the night of April 21, 1621.

WHAT POSSIBLE BEARING could the story of something as cheap and insignificant as the nutmeg have on the twenty-first century?

After all, what happened in the Banda Islands was merely one instance of a history of colonization that was then unfolding on a vastly larger scale on the other side of the Earth, in the Americas. It might be said that the page has been turned on that chapter of history: that the twenty-first century bears no resemblance to that long-ago time when plants and botanical matter could decide the fate of human beings. The modern era, it is often asserted, has freed humanity from the Earth, and propelled it into a new age of progress in which human-made goods take precedence over natural products.

The trouble is that none of the above is true.

We are today even *more* dependent on botanical matter than we were three hundred years (or five hundred, or even five millennia) ago, and not just for our food. Most contemporary humans are completely dependent on energy that comes from long-buried carbon—and what are coal, oil, and natural gas except fossilized forms of botanical matter?

As for the circulation of goods, in that too fossil fuels vastly outweigh any category of human-made goods. In the words of two energy economists: "Energy is the most important commodity in the world today. And by almost any metric, the energy industry is impossibly large. Yearly energy sales at over 10 trillion dollars dwarf expenditures on any other single commodity; trade and transport of energy is immense with over 3 trillion dollars in international transactions driving product deliveries through 2 million kilometers of pipelines and 500 million deadweight tons of merchant shipping; 8 of the 10 largest global corporations are energy companies; and a third of the global shipping fleet is occupied shipping oil. Given these figures it may not be surprising that world energy consumption takes the energy equivalent of over 2800 barrels of oil per second to quench."[52] If we were to add up the sum total of all goods that were moving along the sea and land routes of the Middle Ages, we would probably find that manufactured articles, like porcelain and textiles, accounted for a greater proportion of trade then than they do now.

If we put aside the myth-making of modernity, in which humans are triumphantly free of material dependence on the planet, and acknowledge the reality of our ever-increasing servitude to the products of the Earth, then the story of the Bandanese no longer seems so distant from our present predicament. To the contrary, the continuities between the two are so pressing and powerful that it could even be said that the fate of the Banda Islands might be read as a template for the present, if only we knew how to tell that story.

2

"Burn Everywhere Their Dwellings"

The fleet that Jan Coen has brought with him is the largest ever to come to the Bandas; it consists of more than fifty vessels, including eighteen Dutch ships, and more than two thousand men.[1] Although Coen has come fully prepared for bloodshed, he begins his campaign of expulsion by trying to persuade the Bandanese to leave their homes peacefully. To that end Dutch soldiers and officials are sent from village to village, to order the inhabitants to quietly surrender their arms, demolish their fortifications, and submit to deportation.

But the plan doesn't go smoothly; instead of surrendering, large numbers of islanders flee into the forests.[2] The business of flushing them out drags on for weeks, adding to the expenses of the expedition. The delay brings Coen to a fine edge of frustration, and he decides to ratchet up the pressure: he appoints Sonck governor of Lonthor, and sends him to Selamon to explain to the elders that they have run out of time; if they fail to comply now they will themselves be treated as enemies.

On the night of April 21, when the sound of ragged gunfire reaches Coen on his flagship, he immediately assumes that Sonck and his party have met with an ambush, like the one he himself survived on his first visit to the Banda Islands. He loses no time in ordering four companies of soldiers to rush to Sonck's aid on Lonthor.

By the time the reinforcements reach Sonck the next morning, the tensions of the night have subsided in Selamon. But the sudden arrival of the musketeers creates panic in the village, and fighting breaks out. Some villagers flee to the adjoining slopes with musketeers in hot pursuit. But the terrain is difficult, with steep paths winding through dense forests. The Dutch party is forced to turn back.

In the meantime, Coen decides to speak to the Bandanese elders himself. A number of them are brought to his flagship, where he subjects them to a long rant, reminding them of broken treaties, the ambush of 1609, and many other acts of resistance. After he finishes, he is answered in fluent Dutch by one of the Bandanese elders, the Shahbandar of Lonthor, who goes by the name of Joncker Dirck Callenbacker and is probably of mixed ancestry.[3] Callenbacker explains to the *Heer Generael* that he and the other *orang-kaya* cannot be held responsible for all Bandanese, because they are not rulers as such, but merely respected men. Besides, he reminds the governor-general, the Dutch have not always kept their word about how much they would pay for nutmeg and mace, so the islanders have sometimes had no option but to sell to other partners. As for past hostilities, when blood was spilled it was in clashes where both sides were fighting for what they believed to be right.

Having said all this, the Shahbandar then tries to strike a conciliatory note, and offers the elders' most sincere apologies, assuring Coen that they will do their best to meet his demands. But this is not enough for Coen, who insists on a further surety: he demands that the elders surrender their sons to his forces, to ensure that they will keep their word. The elders accept these terms and comply with his last demand as soon as they are allowed to leave. A boatload of their male children are sent over from Lonthor to a warship called the *Dragon*.

The next day Callenbacker and some of the other elders go to Selamon and gather together a large party of men, women, and children. They too are sent to the *Dragon* to prove that the elders are now ready to evacuate their village.

But Coen remains unconvinced; he still does not believe that the

Bandanese will keep their word and leave their islands peacefully. On April 24, two days after his meeting with the Bandanese elders, he announces to his council that he has learned that the people of Lonthor have decided to perish rather than surrender, so it is now necessary to consider whether to "ruin the remaining places, remove the people from the land, catch them and [do] whatever we like with [them]."[4] The council gives its unanimous agreement; a resolution is passed and signed by twenty-one members, declaring that Dutch forces will be sent "to burn everywhere their dwellings, to take away or destroy their remaining boats and to leave the Bandanese no choice but to come to us or depart from the country."[5]

After this, for a week, the records fall silent; no accounts exist of what happened over the following days, and of exactly how the Bandanese were left with "no choice but to come to us," as ordained by the council's resolution. Subsequent events prove, however, that the directions issued by Coen and his council have been carried out to the letter, and that Dutch forces have systematically destroyed villages and settlements across the islands, capturing as many of their inhabitants as they could and killing the rest. The captives — old men, women, and children alike — are enslaved and sent to Java; they include 789 members of the families of the *orang-kaya*. Some of the slaves end up as far away as Sri Lanka.[6]

IN THE ABSENCE of written firsthand accounts, it is impossible to know how the events of that fateful week unfolded in the Bandas — but a phrase in the Council's resolution, "burn everywhere their dwellings," provides a clue. It suggests a tactic, burning peasant villages to the ground, that was widely used during the Thirty Years' War in the Netherlands. Known as *brandschattingen* in Dutch, the tactic was the military practice that was most feared by the farmers of the region.[7]

A very large number of the soldiers who fought in the Low Countries during the Thirty Years' War — between a quarter and almost a third — were English mercenaries.[8] Many of these soldiers went on to fight in America, and they took the tactic of *brands-*

chattingen with them, turning it into a means of eliminating entire tribes. Incendiary attacks figured prominently, for instance, in the Pequot War of 1636–1638, which was fought between the English settlers of New England and the Pequot, an Algonquian tribe of what is now Connecticut. The conflict has been described as "the first deliberately genocidal war conducted by the English in North America."[9]

The Banda Islands may be on the other side of the planet from Connecticut, but in the seventeenth century the two locations were, in fact, closely linked to each other, as the two farthest poles of the Dutch seaborne empire. Although the Dutch played no part in the Pequot War, the site of the worst massacre—Mystic, Connecticut—lay right upon the border of New Netherland, the Dutch colony that had its seat in New Amsterdam, on the island of Manhattan; the Dutch too had extensive dealings with the Pequot, and competition over trade was one of the factors that precipitated the conflict.[10]

The massacre at Mystic occurred in 1637, when a company of English soldiers and their Indian allies used the cover of night to attack a fortified Pequot settlement while hundreds of people were asleep inside. The attack was directed by two English soldiers who had both served as mercenaries in the Netherlands: John Mason and John Underhill (the latter was actually born in Holland and had a Dutch wife). John Mason led the attack, and it was he who had the idea of burning down the settlement, with a torch that he had seized from a Pequot dwelling.

John Mason and John Underhill both wrote accounts of the attack, and their descriptions are vivid enough to convey a sense of what might have happened in the Bandas during that fateful week. The passage below is from John Mason's *A Brief History of the Pequot War*.

The Captain [Mason himself] said WE MUST BURN THEM; and immediately stepping into the *Wigwam* where he had been before, brought out a Fire-Brand, and putting it into the Matts with which they were covered, set the *Wigwams* on Fire . . . and when it was thoroughly kindled, the *Indians* ran as Men most dreadfully Amazed. . . .

And indeed such a dreadful Terror did the ALMIGHTY let fall upon their Spirits, that they would fly from us and run into the very Flames, where many of them perished . . . many of them gathering to windward, lay pelting at us with their Arrows; and we repaid them with our small Shot: Others of the Stoutest issued forth, as we did guess, to the Number of *Forty*, who perished by the Sword. . . . Thus were they now at their Wits End, who not many Hours before exalted themselves in their great Pride. . . . But GOD was above them, who laughed at his Enemies and Enemies of his People to Scorn, making them as a fiery Oven: thus were the Stout Hearted spoiled, having slept their last Sleep, and none of their Men could find their Hands: Thus did the LORD judge among the Heathen, filling the Place with dead Bodies.[11]

This is John Underhill's account of the same event:

Captain Mason entering into a Wigwam, brought out a fire-brand, after he had wounded many in the house, then he set fire on the West-side where he entered, my self set fire on the South end with a train of Powder, the fires of both meeting in the center of the Fort blazed most terribly, and burnt all in the space of half an hour . . . there were about four hundred souls in this Fort, and not above five of them escaped out of our hands. Great and doleful was the bloody sight to the view of young soldiers that never had been in Warre, to see so many souls lie gasping on the ground so thick in some places, that you could hardly pass along.[12]

The two near-contemporary massacres, one in the Bandas and one in what is now Connecticut, are linked by haunting continuities. Both occurred in the context of heightened Anglo-Dutch rivalries, and against the wider backdrop of the wars of religion that were then raging in Europe. In both, large numbers of captives were enslaved and transported overseas to work on plantations; and both these massacres were intended to extinguish the existence of a people.[13] In the case of the Pequot, their extinction was made official by the treaty that ended the war: the survivors were forbidden to use the very name "Pequot."[14] Celebrating this triumph, a Puritan historian wrote: "the name of the Pequots (as of Amalech) is blotted out from under heaven, there being not one that is, or (at least) dare call himself a Pequot."[15]

If the victors assumed that they had the right to formally extinguish a tribe, it was because European doctrines of empire had indeed evolved in that direction. These doctrines found their fullest articulation in the work of the philosopher, polemicist, and Lord Chancellor of England, Sir Francis Bacon. In his *An Advertisement Touching an Holy War*, which was written around the time of the Banda massacre and published shortly before the Pequot War, Bacon lays out in some detail the reasons why it was lawful, in his view, for Christian Europeans to end the existence of certain groups: "For like as there are particular persons outlawed and proscribed by civil laws of several countries; so are there nations that are outlawed and proscribed by the law of nature and nations, or by the immediate commandment of God." These wayward countries, Bacon argues, are not nations at all, but rather "routs and shoals of people, as have utterly degenerated from the laws of nature." Such being the case, it was both lawful and godly for any nation "that is civil and policed . . . [to] cut them off from the face of the earth."[16] This doctrine was formalized by Emer de Vattel, one of the jurists who codified international law in the late eighteenth century: "nations are justified," he ruled, "in uniting together as a body with the object of punishing, and even exterminating, such savage peoples."[17]

This argument effectively conferred on Christian Europeans a God-given right to attack and extinguish peoples who appeared errant or monstrous in their eyes. It is in this "crucial thought," argue Peter Linebaugh and Marcus Rediker, that "genocide and divinity cross. Bacon's advertisement for a holy war was thus a call for several types of genocide, which found its sanction in biblical and classical antiquity."[18]

Bacon's reasoning may appear archaic, but it continues to animate the workings of empire to this day. In essence he was making the argument that a well-governed country ("any nation that is civil and policed") has an absolute right to invade countries that are "degenerate" or in violation of the "laws of nature and nations." This is, of course, the fundamental doctrine of "liberal interventionism," and it has been invoked many times in recent decades to justify "wars of choice" launched by Western powers.

· · ·

THE MASSACRE ORDERED by Coen was so effective that within seven days it was declared, at a council meeting on his flagship, that "all towns and fortified places of Banda had, by God's grace been taken, erased, burned down and about 1200 souls caught."

On May 6, Coen reported to his superiors, with no little satisfaction, that his forces had "utterly destroyed and burned down" the major settlements of Lonthor, and that the remnants of the islands' population had fled into the mountains, where they had been joined by fugitives from other parts of the archipelago. "In this way all towns and places of the whole of Banda were taken (possession of) and destroyed."[19]

Yet, on the heights of Lonthor Island, where thousands of Bandanese had taken shelter, the resistance continued. The steep terrain and bad weather made it difficult for the Dutch to subjugate them; Dutch attacks were repulsed several times. This caused even greater annoyance to Coen, who was now impatient to be gone but did not want to leave until he had brought "complete tranquility" to the islands.

In the meantime, as people were being butchered and enslaved across the islands, Jan Coen was still intent on uncovering the meaning of the fallen lamp. To that end the hostage sons of the *orang-kaya* were subjected to interrogations that probably included a form of torture that was much in favor amongst the VOC's functionaries: called the water torture, it was a prototype of what is now known as waterboarding. It involved repeatedly pouring water over a suspect's cloth-bound head, bringing him close to suffocation. Another method was to place a cone "around the victim's neck above his mouth and nose; water was then poured in, forcing him to gulp water to avoid drowning, which not only choked him but caused his tissues to swell out of all proportion from excess water in the body, causing severe agony; this torture was supplemented in some cases by burning the victim's armpits, feet, and hands with a candle or pulling out his fingernails."[20]

The intention was to expose a conspiracy, and the methods did not fail to bear fruit: a "confession" was duly extracted from a boy, a nephew of Dirck Callenbacker's, who said that he had been present at a meeting of elders where it was decided that a surprise attack would be launched on the Dutch on the night when the lamp fell; the ultimate intention, the confession went, was to kill Sonck, and Coen himself.

It seems never to have occurred to either Coen or Sonck that if the Bandanese were planning an attack they would hardly have spoiled the surprise by signaling their intent with a falling lamp. Nor do they seem to have asked how an inanimate object could be made to fall from afar, at a precisely timed moment.

Once the boy's forced testimony had been recorded, Jan Coen set up a tribunal with three members, Sonck being one, to ascertain whether the "confession" was valid or not. On the orders of the tribunal several dozen elders were brought to the *Dragon*, and to another ship called the *Zuiderzee*, for questioning. They were then tortured so "rigorously" that two of them died on the rack, and a third jumped overboard and drowned.

According to a Dutch officer who later wrote an anonymous account of these events, none of the Bandanese elders admitted to a conspiracy; they all protested their innocence. Coen, on the other hand, would claim that they had indeed admitted to plotting an attack. The truth was irrelevant anyway, for a guilty verdict was a foregone conclusion.

The elders were taken into custody and orders were given for the construction of a circular enclosure, with bamboo stakes, a little way beyond the grim stone walls of Fort Nassau, on Banda Naira. On May 8, 1621, forty-four elders were led into this enclosure with their hands tied.[21] Eight of them "who were the most guilty according to the judges" were placed apart, while the others milled about in confusion "like a flock of sheep."

It was raining hard that day. In the midst of the downpour the elders were read the sentence of their execution, for conspiracy, and for violating their treaties with the Dutch. Then six Japanese swordsmen were sent into the enclosure to carry out the sentence.

The first to be butchered were the eight elders who had been singled out as the ringleaders of the conspiracy. They were beheaded and then quartered. None of them resisted, although one elder, perhaps Callenbacker, was heard to say, in Dutch: "Sirs, have you no mercy then?"

No mercy was shown: the remaining thirty-six elders were also beheaded and quartered. The severed heads and dismembered body parts were impaled on stakes.

According to local tradition, the remains of the forty-four elders were later thrown into a nearby well.

JAN COEN LEFT the Bandas two months after he had arrived, leaving behind a large force under Sonck's command. Their orders were to suppress all resistance and to ensure the removal of all remaining Bandanese.

Over the next couple of months the Dutch forces continued to encounter pockets of resistance, especially along the heights of Lonthor, where groups of Bandanese were still holding out. Some fugitives even managed to escape, in hidden boats or in rescue vessels sent from neighboring islands like Seram and Kei. But hundreds also died at sea while trying to escape, and thousands perished of starvation and disease in the forests of Lonthor.[22]

Some two months after the start of the butchery, a Bandanese runaway surrendered to the Dutch and told them that the remaining fugitives had no gunpowder or ammunition and were starving. The informant then led Sonck and a force of several hundred Dutch soldiers to the fugitives' encampment in the mountains. The Bandanese had only stones and spears to defend themselves with and were quickly defeated. This marked the end of the resistance. The remaining villages surrendered quietly and their inhabitants were taken captive and deported, to be sold as slaves.

In short, within a few months of the falling of that lamp, the

Bandanese, once a proud and enterprising trading community, had ceased to exist as a people. Their world had been brought to an end in a span of less than ten weeks.

. . .

MANY YEARS AFTER the Bandanese had been "cut off from the face of the earth," Anglo-Dutch rivalries would once again link the fate of the Bandas to New Netherland. In 1667, the Treaty of Breda transferred the island of Run "permanently to the Dutch as part of a wider settlement that also included the handing over of the Dutch colony of New Amsterdam (later New York) to the English."[23] This bargain may be forgotten in the United States, but the few dozen people who live on tiny, sunbaked Run still take pride in being the inhabitants of the island that was exchanged for Manhattan.

The handing over of Run ended the first and last English territorial claim in Maluku. From then on English territorial ambitions in Asia would be focused mainly on the Indian subcontinent.

3

"The Fruits of the Nutmeg Have Died"

The horror of the story of the Bandanese lies, in no small part, in the fact that the narrative of their elimination from their land revolves around a tree, a species of incomparable value, gifted to the islanders by the region's volcanic ecology.

Yet, what can be said about the role of the nutmeg tree in this story? It is certainly true that the history of the archipelago cannot be narrated without reference to the tree—but it cannot for that reason be said that the tree authored or decided the fate of the Bandanese. There were, after all, other islands in the region where, in similar circumstances, people were able to avoid extermination. That was the case, for example, with another Malukan archipelago, a few hundred kilometers to the north of the Bandas. This cluster of islands, of which the best known is Ternate, also possessed an enormously valuable botanical species—the tree that produces cloves, a spice that was just as valuable as nutmeg and mace. As with the nutmeg, the clove tree brought immense wealth, as well as great suffering, on the people of the Ternate; yet they somehow managed to escape the fate that befell the Bandanese.

How and why was this so? Was it because Ternate and its sister island, Tidore, were both sultanates, each the seat of its own empire, with vastly larger populations than the Banda Islands?[1] Or was it just chance and happenstance, merely a matter of chains of events that unfolded differently? Or did the specific character of the clove tree, and the volcanoes that nurtured them, also play a part in this story?

These questions bring us to the limits of a certain way of telling stories about the past. The empirical, documentary methods of historical scholarship—the methods that allowed me to construct a timeline of what happened in the Bandas in 1621—depend critically on language, literacy, and writing. The evidence for those methods comes primarily from written records. In the stories they tell, entities that lack language figure only as backdrops against which human dramas are enacted. Nutmegs, cloves, and volcanoes may figure in these stories, but they cannot themselves be actors in the stories that historians tell; nor can they tell stories of their own.

For Malukans, on the other hand, as for many others who live in seismic zones, volcanoes are makers of history as well as tellers of stories. Indeed the oldest living story told by humans comes from a volcano: Budj Bim, in Australia's Victoria State. For the Gunditjmara, the Indigenous people of the region, who developed the world's earliest aquaculture system, the volcano is a founding ancestor.[2] Their creation myth tells of four giant beings coming to the southeastern shores of the continent. Three of them dispersed to other parts of the land, but one stayed in place, crouching, and his body became the volcano, Budj Bim, and his teeth became the lava that erupted out of it.

"There is little doubt," writes Heather Builth, an archaeologist, "that local Aboriginal groups had been witness to volcanic activity. . . . In 1870 the Portland *Guardian* published a Gunditjmara local oral history that revealed witness of volcanic activity and the associated tsunami that was said to have drowned most of the people."[3]

Scientists have determined that Budj Bim last erupted about 30,000 years ago, so this would be the event witnessed by the ancestors of the Gunditjmara.[4] That would make this the oldest story to be passed down to modern times, superseding Indigenous Australian myths about sea level rise, which are thought to reflect events that occurred 7,000 years ago. Those were once believed to be humanity's oldest extant stories; the story of Budj Bim, if the dating is correct, would be many times older.[5] Yet, even from that distant past, the magic of the volcano has continued to touch upon the lives of the Gunditjmara: the story of Budj Bim, passed down over thousands of generations, played a major part in this community's reclamation of some of their ancestral lands in 2007.[6]

Nowhere is the living lore of volcanoes more extensive than across the islands of Indonesia, with their multitudes of soaring cones and smoking craters. In this archipelago a volcano is almost always "a spiritual as well as a geothermal entity—a vengeful and angry geospirit."[7] For scientists and disaster experts these stories are something of a nuisance. "Javanese people often share a deeply devout relationship with volcanoes," writes a team of Earth scientists, in barely concealed disapproval. "In Java, volcanoes are considered connected to human society to achieve a universal harmony between society, nature, and the cosmos. . . . Although most Javanese people are aware of scientific explanations for natural phenomena, they usually prefer to draw on explanations that relate natural events to their social world."[8]

The Indonesian reverence for volcanoes is a matter of frustration also for Islamic and Christian fundamentalists, who regard such beliefs with abhorrence. Yet volcanoes continue to be intricately knit into the lives of Indonesians, not just culturally and spiritually, but also politically. Before elections, for instance, it often happened that Javanese politicians would visit the spiritual guardian of Mount Merapi, on the slopes of that dangerously active volcano.[9]

Maluku's volcanoes are especially rich in stories, and none more so than the great volcano of Ternate, Mount Gamalama. In *The Original Dream*, a contemporary novel by Nukila Amal, who is herself from Ternate, Mount Gamalama speaks to a shaman who climbs up to the crater and stands with "her two feet flat on the ground, hair blowing in the wind. Her eyes were near black, near umber, near earth. They closed tight, sensing the arrival of something. Something rose silently from the earth beneath her feet. An utterance, a near whisper, entered her body through the soles of her feet, rising louder and more tumultuously, then came screaming out of her through the crown of her head. . . . She slumped to the ground, her tears spilled. Eyes moist, she felt the earth. Little by little, her fingers gathered up the earth around her feet, until her hands were full. She clutched the handfuls of earth, cupped them in her lap, and shed tears on them. Blessing. Or curse."[10]

Towering above the Banda Islands, Gunung Api too was believed to have the gift of producing omens and portents. That was why there was much misgiving on the islands when the volcano erupted, after a long period of dormancy, on the very day when a Dutch ship came to the archipelago for the first time, in 1599. People recalled a prophecy made by a Muslim mystic, shortly before, that a group of White men, from a place far away, would come to invade the islands one day.

To this day the descendants of those who escaped the Banda massacre use a word for "history," *fokorndan*, that comes from *fokor*, which means "mountain"—or rather "Banda Mountain," that is to say Gunung Api.[11]

This is a way of thinking about the past in which space and time echo each other, and it is by no means particular to the Bandanese. Indeed, this form of thought may well have found its fullest elaboration on the other side of the planet, among the Indigenous peoples of North America, whose spiritual lives and understanding of history were always tied to specific landscapes. In the words of the great Native American thinker Vine Deloria Jr., a shared feature of Indigenous North American spiritual traditions is that they all "have a sacred center at a particular place, be it a river, a mountain, a plateau, valley, or other natural feature. . . . Regardless of what subsequently happens to the people, the sacred lands remain as permanent fixtures in their cultural or religious understanding."[12]

Developing this argument, Deloria contrasts modes of thought that take their orientation from terrestrial spaces with those that privilege time. For the latter, the crucial question in relation to any event is "*when* did it happen?" For the former, it is "*where* did it happen?" The first question shapes the possible answers in a determinate way, locating the event within a particular historical period. The second question shapes the possible answers in a completely different way, because it accords a degree of agency to the landscape itself, and all that lies within it, including the entire range of nonhuman beings. The result, in Deloria's words, is that "the [Indian] tribes confront and interact with a particular land along with its life forms. The task or role of the tribal religions is to relate the community of people to each and every facet of creation as they have experienced it."

For many Indigenous groups, landscapes remain as vividly alive today as they ever were. "For Indian men and women," writes the anthropologist Peter Basso, of the Western Apache of Arizona, "the past lies embedded in features of the earth—in canyons and lakes, mountains and arroyos, rocks and vacant fields—which together endow their lands with multiple forms of significance that reach into their lives and shape the ways they think."[13] Stories about the past, built around familiar landmarks, inform every aspect of Apache life. Through these stories features of the landscape speak to people just as loudly as the human voices that historians bring to life from documentary sources.

THE MODERN GAZE sees only one of the nutmeg's two hemi-spheres: that part of it which is *Myristica fragrans*, a subject of science and commerce. The other half eludes it because it will only manifest itself in songs and stories. And in today's stories and songs there is no place for the nutmeg; it is merely an inert object, a planet that contains no intrinsic meaning, and no properties other than those that make it a subject of science and commerce.

For the Bandanese, too, the nutmeg was an object of horticulture and commerce, both of which demanded considerable technical and practical skills. But for them the nutmeg also had other properties, hidden in the hemisphere that recedes from the modern gaze.

On the Malukan island of Kai, not far from the Bandas, there are a few villages that are, to this day, populated mainly by descendants of the survivors of the genocide of 1621.[14] The names of these villages evoke the lost homeland, and their inhabitants still speak *turwandan*, the Banda language; their songs and stories still bring to life not just the "Banda mountain," but also its blessing (or curse), the nutmeg.

we weep and weep
when, on what day
"get on your way"
we, pearls of wisdom
the fruits of nutmeg have died
she sends a letter so we may speak
pearls of wisdom
fruits of nutmeg have died . . .
pearls of wisdom
the nutmegs have died
there is no faith here
there is no blessing inside this island.[15]

FOR THE BANDANESE, the landscapes of their islands were places of dwelling that were enmeshed with human life in ways that were imaginative as well as material; the land did not exist solely to produce nutmeg and mace. It was not land but Land, which is, in the words of the Indigenous scientist and thinker Max Liboiron, "the unique entity that is the combined living spirit of plants, animals, water, humans, histories, and events. . . ."[16]

For Jan Coen and the VOC, on the other hand, the trees, volcanoes, and landscapes of the Bandas had no meaning except as resources that could be harnessed to generate profit.[17] This outlook reflected a metaphysic that was then emerging in Europe, in which matter was seen as "brute" and "stupid" and hence deserving of conquest "with the most destructive of technologies with nothing but profit and material wealth as ends. . . ."[18] For Coen and his ilk the trees that were woven into the songs and memories of the Bandanese contained nothing beyond their utility; as for the idea that a volcano could make meaning, that would have been, for them, merely "superstition," or even "idolatry." Nor, in the eyes of Dutch colonists, was there any intrinsic connection between the Bandanese and the landscape they inhabited—they could simply be replaced by workers and managers who would transform the islands into a nutmeg-producing factory.

This was a radically new way of envisioning the Earth, as a "vast machine made of inert particles in ceaseless motion."[19] Even in Europe, the mechanistic vision of the world had only just begun to take shape, and then too, only among elites that were directly or indirectly involved in the two great European projects of the time: the conquest of the Americas and the trade in enslaved Africans. It was the rendering of humans into mute resources that enabled the metaphysical leap whereby the Earth and everything in it could also be reduced to inertness. In that sense men like Coen, Sonck, and their predecessors were not just colonists but also philosophers; it was their violence, directed at "natives" and the landscapes they inhabited, that laid the foundations of the mechanistic philosophies that would later be attributed to their contemporaries, like Descartes and Mandeville, Bacon and Boyle.

Above all, it was the subjugation, and repopulating, of the Americas that enabled educated, upper-class European men to think of themselves as the subduers of everything they surveyed, even in their own countries, and especially within that domain they conceived of as "Nature"—an inert repository of resources, which, in order to be "improved," needed to be expropriated, no matter whether from Amerindians or from English or Scottish peasants.[20] But European peasants too did not take kindly to the expropriation of common lands through fences and enclosures; nor were they amenable to the suppression of their ways of thinking about the Earth. At that time, the great majority of Europeans, like common people everywhere, also believed the universe to be a living organism, animated by many kinds of unseen forces.[21] When poor Europeans resisted the dual suppression of their rights to land and of the sacredness of their landscapes, they too were subjected to forms of violence that were intimately linked with colonial conquest.

This is particularly evident in the case of witch-hunting, which literally demonized huge numbers of generally poor European women, with tropes drawn from colonialist perceptions of Amerindians as devil worshipers. European images of witches grilling dismembered human body parts, for example, derived directly from representations of the supposedly cannibalistic rituals of the Tupinamba, a Caribbean tribe in whose culinary culture the grill was a central element.[22]

The temporal overlap between European witch-burnings and the "Great Dyings" of the Americas did not come about by coincidence; it has been said, with good reason, that the collective mind of Europe at this time was "beset by Christian heretics, alien Jews and American Indians who committed unspeakable crimes involving the use of human flesh and blood."[23] These conjoined processes of violence, physical and intellectual, were all necessary for the emergence of a new economy based on extracting resources from a desacralized, inanimate Earth.

Over centuries of suppression, non-mechanistic and vitalist modes of thought were pushed to the margins of Western culture, but they did not disappear; they were kept alive on the one hand by those who lived close to the European continent's soils, forests, and seas; and on the other by celebrated intellectuals like Paracelsus, Swedenborg, and Schopenhauer, as well as the writers of what has been called "the radical Enlightenment"—Hölderlin, Goethe, Blake, Shelley, William Morris, Whitman, Thoreau, and so on.[24] Many European farming communities have clung to their vitalist beliefs to this day, despite the ceaseless denigration, and even active persecution, visited on them by urban elites.[25] Indeed, not only did the vitalist metaphysic stay alive in the West—it could even be said to have gathered strength as it metamorphosed into an always repressed yet always resurgent subterranean current, a counterculture "without which the public elite culture cannot be fully understood and out of which any number of popular cultural movements have sprung, usually in direct or indirect opposition to the reigning public and elite orthodoxies."[26]

Those elite orthodoxies, in turn, were the product not just of the subjugation of human "brutes and savages," but also of an entire range of nonhuman beings—trees, animals, and landscapes. Indeed, "subdue" was a key word in these conquests, recurring again and again in reference not just to human beings but also to the terrain. Out of these processes of subduing and muting was born the idea of "Nature" as an inert entity, a conception that would in time become a basic tenet of what might be called "official modernity."[27] This metaphysic, fundamentally an ideology of conquest, would eventually become hegemonic in the West, and is now shared by the entire global elite: within its parameters the idea that a volcano can produce meaning, or that the nutmeg can be a protagonist in history, can never be anything other than a delusion or a "primitive superstition."

To envisage the world in this way was a crucial step toward making an inert Nature a reality. As Ben Ehrenreich observes: "Only once we imagined the world as dead could we dedicate ourselves to making it so."[28]

WHEN WORD OF Coen's attack on the Banda Islands got back to Holland, it was the killing of the elders, rather than the elimination of the Bandanese, that made the greatest impression, earning the governor-general some mild words of reproof from the "Seventeen Gentlemen" who presided over the VOC. But later, after taking stock of the full extent to which Coen's actions would enrich the VOC, and realizing that their own share of the spoils would allow them to fill their houses with all the tulips, porcelain, and paintings their hearts desired, the Gentlemen backtracked and voted to reward the *Heer Generael* with a gratuity of three thousand guilders.[29] Later, statues of Coen arose in towns and cities across Holland.

The VOC's monopoly on the spices of the East Indies made the Dutch famous across Europe for their enterprise and commercial prowess. "The prodigious increase of the Netherlands," wrote one of the founders of the English East India Company, "is the envy of the present and may be the wonder of future generations."[30] The French encyclopedist Denis Diderot echoed this sentiment: "It is to Holland that the rest of Europe goes for everything it lacks. Holland is Europe's commercial hub. The Dutch have worked to such good purpose that, through their ingenuity, they have obtained all of life's necessities, in defiance of the elements."[31]

The monetary returns on spices were astronomical, amounting on occasion to more than 400 percent of the initial investment on a voyage.[32] Profits like these helped to underwrite the remarkable flourishing of the arts that occurred in Holland in the seventeenth century, a period that came to be known as the Dutch Golden Age. Spices would sometimes figure in the artwork of this era, especially in "still lifes," a genre of painting that became immensely popular at this time. These paintings, which depict "mute assemblages of ready comestibles," perfectly reflect the colonial envisioning of "nature" as a vast mass of inert resources—an enframing that is made even clearer by the French name for the genre: *Nature Morte*.[33]

The violence that reduced "nature" to this state of inertness never figures in the art of the Dutch Golden Age. "As the history grew more egregious," writes the art historian Julie Berger Hochstrasser, "the still lifes seem to become more adamantly opulent."[34] There are innumerable books on the art of the Dutch Golden Age; few indeed are those that mention the Banda genocide.

But the events of 1621 did not vanish from memory, either of the descendants of the Bandanese survivors or of European colonists in Asia. Albert Bickmore, an American scholar who visited the Bandas in the mid-nineteenth century, was evidently regaled with stories about the island's history by his Dutch hosts. In a book published in 1868, he summed up the events of 1621 in a few short, matter-of-fact lines: "The Dutch then began a war of extermination, which lasted eighteen years, and was only brought to an end by a large expedition from Java, conducted by the governor-general in person. . . . All [the Bandanese] who were left alive fled to the neighboring islands, and not a vestige of their language or peculiar customs is known to exist at the present time."[35]

This passage leaves no doubt that it was well known to Westerners that the Dutch campaign against the Bandanese was indeed a war of extermination. Bickmore doesn't present his conclusion as being in any way controversial or out of the ordinary. To his readers the phrase "war of extermination" would have told its own story: this was a narrative that drew upon innumerable different strands of Western history, science, and (not least) literature. It needed neither explanation nor narration; it was a story that told itself.

For the contemporary reader that story can be summarized by a word that did not exist when Bickmore was writing: "genocide." But to use the word in this context is to raise the question of whether it fits what happened in the Bandas in 1621. The Bandanese were not, after all, totally eliminated. Some survived by escaping to other parts of Maluku, including the only part of the Bandas that was under English control: the islet of Run. In years to come the Bandanese survivors would even launch armed raids on the people who were brought in by the VOC to repopulate the Bandas.[36]

It is not known for sure how many Bandanese survived the massacre of 1621. Coen himself believed that no more than a few hundred fugitives escaped from the Bandas. In a letter to the VOC's directors he wrote: "So far we have not heard of more than 300 Bandanese who have escaped from the whole of Banda."[37] But even if Coen were wrong, and a thousand or more Bandanese managed to get away with their lives, this would still mean that more than 90 percent of the population of the archipelago was either killed, captured, or enslaved.[38]

Does this qualify as a genocide? Even under its strictest definition, the word "genocide" does not require the total extermination of a population. The 1946 UN convention on genocide, for example, defines it as "acts committed with intent to destroy, in whole or in part, a national, ethnical, racial or religious group, as such." Raphael Lemkin, the Polish Jewish jurist who coined the term after the Second World War, wrote: "The crime of genocide should be recognized therein as a conspiracy to exterminate national, religious or racial groups." This would certainly apply to the decisions that were taken by Jan Coen and his council prior to the massacres.

A further question hinges on how the killing was done. There are no figures on how many Bandanese were slaughtered with arms and armaments, but the indications are that the majority managed to escape into the mountains. It was there that they perished of starvation, disease, exposure, and mass suicide. This outcome was ensured by the destruction of the material basis of their lives — their settlements, houses, food stocks, tools, even their boats. In the broadest possible sense, the elimination of the Bandanese was brought about not just by targeted killings of humans, but by destroying the entire web of nonhuman connections that sustained a certain way of life. This was exactly what was intended when the council instructed its forces "to burn everywhere their dwellings, to take away or destroy their remaining boats and to leave the Bandanese no choice but to come to us or depart from the country."

The Banda massacre thus followed the pattern of most early colonial "exterminations," because the technology of the time did not permit industrial-scale mass killings. Usually people were eliminated through the destruction of crucial elements in the web of life that sustained them: for example, by deforestation, or the mass killing of animals that were essential to their diet.

A great deal hinges on the intent that lay behind these interventions; in the case of the Banda Islands, Jan Coen's dispatches leave little doubt that he did indeed intend to depopulate the archipelago. This was recognized very early by Dutch writers and historians, who, to their great credit, began to develop a critical perspective on their country's colonial history at a time when the elites of the Anglosphere and the Francosphere were near unanimous in their support for imperialism.[39] It was in 1860 that the writer Eduard Douwes Dekker, who wrote under the name "Multatuli," published *Max Havelaar*, his forceful indictment of Dutch colonialism in the East Indies. By the late nineteenth century, Jan Coen had already become a target of harsh criticism in the Netherlands.[40] "There is blood on his name," wrote J. A. van der Chijs in 1886, "and if his statue had not already been erected, I doubt very much if it would now be done."[41]

That Coen intended to eliminate an entire population is so clear that in 2012 two experts, writing in the *Journal of Genocide Research*, concluded that "the almost total annihilation of the population of the Banda Islands in 1621 [was] a clearly genocidal act committed under the direction of Governor-General Jan Pieterszoon Coen in enforcing the Dutch spice trade monopoly. . . ."[42]

Given all of this, it is hard to think of a persuasive reason to avoid using the word "genocide" in relation to the Dutch conquest of the Bandas.

· · ·

"THERE CAN BE NO trade without war," Jan Coen once famously said, "and no war without trade."[43] The VOC's capital in the Maluku region, Amboyna (now Ambon), was a city that embodied this dictum, being both a market and a military outpost ordered around strict racial hierarchies, with laws and procedures of its own. Amboyna was thus the earliest of the VOC's "company towns," another iteration of which, halfway around the planet, was the Dutch colony of New Amsterdam, on the island of Manhattan.[44]

In 1623, two years after the VOC's conquest of the Bandas, Amboyna was the site of an event that decided the course of European imperialism in Asia. In March of that year a member of the VOC's contingent of Japanese *ronin* was accused of participating in an English conspiracy to take over Amboyna by overthrowing the Dutch. Under torture the *ronin* admitted to the plot and implicated some of the city's English residents.[45] The Englishmen were then tried and tortured as well, after which a verdict of treason was passed on them by the Dutch governor and his council. This led to the beheading of ten Englishmen, nine Japanese *ronin*, and a Eurasian man probably of mixed Bengali and Portuguese descent.[46]

Thanks largely to the efforts of the East India Company, these executions would soon assume an extraordinary salience in the English national imagination.[47] Putting on a virtuoso display of the propaganda skills that would remain for centuries one of the greatest assets of the British Empire, the Company succeeded in turning a tissue of "lies, half-truths, exaggerations, prevarications . . . and calumny" into a "half-cocked, implausible, naïve, self-serving and vindictive" story that nonetheless became an "origin myth of empire," one that would be used again and again as a warrant for British expansion and aggression.[48]

Essential to the creation of the myth was a Company-financed pamphlet entitled *A True Relation of the Unjust, Cruell, and Barbarous Proceedings against the English at Amboyna*. Published in both English and Dutch in 1624, the pamphlet included gory illustrations of Englishmen being tortured by the agents of the VOC.

In the Company's telling, the story of Amboyna was a narrative of English innocence and victimhood in which blameless English traders were subjected to a "massacre." This story "tainted all the Dutch," writes the historian Alison Games, "with the deaths at Amboyna, and not a decade passed for over 300 years without Amboyna appearing in a British pamphlet, poem, periodical, play, novel, history, schoolbook, essay, or illustration." The poet John Dryden wrote a play called *Amboyna; the State of Innocence* in 1673; Jonathan Swift, Daniel Defoe, and innumerable other authors incorporated the myth into their work.[49] The Company may have invented the myth, but it was the intensely chauvinistic nature of English literary culture that gave the story its longevity and reach.

In her fascinating study, *Inventing the English Massacre: Amboyna in History and Memory*, Alison Games shows that the word "massacre" was itself instrumental in the creation of the myth. The word was then relatively new in English, a recent borrowing from the French, in which it had originally referred to a butcher's block. But during the sixteenth century the word came to be used for sectarian mass killings, like the St. Bartholomew's Day massacre of Protestants in France in 1572. The East India Company's contribution to the connotations of the word "massacre" was to paint a halo of religious martyrdom around the execution of its officials. Through this framing the Company "created a new and distinctive type of English massacre," in which commercial rivalries were fused with religious victimhood.

"Massacre," in this sense, referred to White, Christian martyrdom; it was not used for mass killings in which Europeans slaughtered others, as was then happening across the Americas and elsewhere. Although several English traders knew, and disapproved, of the Banda killings of 1621, they did not describe that indiscriminate slaughter as a "massacre." Yet, two years later, they were quick to apply the word to the judicial execution of Englishmen at Amboyna. Subsequently, the fact that nine Japanese *ronin* and one Bengali-Portuguese man had also been executed at Amboyna would be erased from the myth. "By the twentieth century, these non-European accomplices had vanished altogether in British histories of the incident" (6).

So it happened that in the Anglosphere's understanding of history the execution of ten Englishmen at Amboyna in 1623 became an event of world historical significance, while the slaughter of thousands of Bandanese men, women, and children vanished from memory. Instead, through constant reiteration over centuries, the Amboyna executions became a pivotal element in the British conception of their imperial project: "As a turning point of empire [Amboyna] put English innocence at the center of a national fiction that disguised and distorted the violence that was the hallmark of Britain's own imperial aggression" (194).

In this "national fiction" of British victimhood, Amboyna provided the model for the framing of a string of other events, the most notable being the "Black Hole of Calcutta" in 1756, and the uprisings that convulsed the Indian subcontinent in 1857. The "Massacre at Amboyna" even served to create another connection between Maluku and Manhattan: in 1664, the story was used to stir up New Englanders against the Dutch colony of New Netherland, and those resentments ultimately led to the takeover of New Amsterdam and its surroundings by the English.

The legend's success was due in no small part to the disruptive power of new technologies of communication—in this instance, print. It is worth recalling that books, booklets, and printed illustrations played a major role also in inciting the European witch craze, which was at its peak when the Company's Amboyna pamphlet appeared. Much like the even more powerful communications technologies of our own times, print was instrumental in generating vast amounts of "fake news" that served to stir up waves of mass hysteria. Images and illustrations have always been especially effective in this regard, and are more so now than ever before.

The technology of print also played a crucial part in spreading the myth of Amboyna across the English-speaking world. Books and pamphlets about Amboyna found their way into libraries across the British Empire, from Calcutta to the Caribbean and Virginia: Thomas Jefferson possessed several books about the incident. The emergence in the 1880s of history as an academic discipline put another stamp of approval on the myth, with a string of supposed English martyrdoms being linked back to Amboyna by professional imperial historians.

The poisonous legacies of these fantasies of innocence and martyrdom have never been more clearly visible than they are now, as myths of White, Anglo victimhood surface again in forms that are powerful enough to rock the political systems of the United States and Great Britain.

. . .

IN THE FOLLOWING centuries Ambon, with its history of both seismic and social upheavals, would become an embodiment of the paradoxes of volcanic landscapes, with all their blessings and curses. During the Second World War, Ambon was the scene of a major Allied defeat. More than a thousand Australian, Dutch, and American soldiers surrendered to the Japanese at Ambon, and around half were confined in a prisoner of war camp on the island. Terrible atrocities were committed at this camp, and 329 soldiers, most of them Australian, died there.[50] After the war Ambon became the setting of one of the largest ever war crimes trials: ninety-three Japanese officers were tried, and four were sentenced to execution.

Five years later, on the brink of Indonesian independence, Ambon became a battleground again when a group of Christian separatists declared independence in the name of the Republic of South Maluku. The declaration was prompted by the fear that the Christians of southern Maluku, who then constituted a majority of the population, would be marginalized in Muslim-majority Indonesia.

Within a few months, South Maluku was forcibly reincorporated into Indonesia, but religious tensions surfaced again in 1999 when a paroxysm of violence, sparked by gangland conflicts in faraway Jakarta, erupted across Maluku, pitting Christians and Muslims against each other.[51] "[A] trivial fight between thugs in a market," writes the Malukan novelist Nukila Amal, "led to dire consequences. Islands fell, one by one, like dominoes in a game played by unseen hands. Religious conflicts flared up and escalated . . . white sandy-beached islands turned coal black, black as the dead of night. Villages along the coast and in the interior became desolate ruins, blanketed in soot left behind by the flames. The rains dragged on, the winds wounded."[52]

The violence lasted several years, and was not contained until 2005. For a long time afterwards visitors and tourists were not allowed into Maluku. When I visited the islands in 2016, the restrictions had only recently been loosened, but reminders of the violence remained, not just in the form of blackened and gutted buildings, but also in the atmosphere: there was a tautness in the air that was all too familiar to me from my own memories of religious violence in India.

4

Terraforming

Renaming was one of the principal instruments with which colonists erased the prior meanings of conquered landscapes. In New England, soon after the Puritans had exterminated the Pequot, they applied themselves to the task of cutting off, in John Mason's words, "the Remembrance of them from the Earth" by erasing the tribe's name. To that end the General Assembly of Connecticut decided that the survivors would not be allowed to call themselves Pequots; that the Pequot River would become the Thames; and that the village known as Pequot would be renamed New London—in "remembrance," the legislators declared, "of the chief city in our dear native country."[1]

In such acts of renaming, the adjective "New" comes to be invested with an extraordinary semantic and symbolic violence. Not only does it create a *tabula rasa*, erasing the past, but it also invests a place with meanings derived from faraway places, "our dear native country."

Sometimes the erasure of meaning that accompanied the remaking of the Americas springs unexpectedly out of the landscape. So it did for me, many years ago, when I pulled off a highway to take a look at the Four Corners—a monument that marks the only spot in the US where four states meet: Arizona, Colorado, New Mexico, and Utah.

The monument lies off Route 160, which traverses some of the most beautiful landscapes on Earth. The mountains, canyons, and

deserts it passes through are so luminous that it is easy to understand why the landscape came to be invested with a metaphysical
significance for its Native inhabitants, the Diné (Navajo). For them
this was Dinétah, the land into which the First Beings had climbed,
from the Underworld. "It is here," writes the Diné historian Jennifer Nez Denetdale, "that many of the events related in the creation
narratives took place, beginning with the emergence from the
lower worlds into the present world, the Glittering World."[2]

The Glittering World is not far from the Four Corners monument, but there might as well be an ocean between them. There
is nothing of interest near the monument, no eye-catching rock,
or gulch, or canyon: utterly indifferent to its surroundings, the
marker sits upon a stretch of featureless, scrub-covered desert "like
a thumbtack on a map."[3] It consists of two straight lines, marked
upon a concrete plinth.

Nothing could be less dramatic than this structure—and yet,
the crossing of the lines generates an uncanny power. The visitors who line up to see it are endlessly inventive in finding ways
to make contact with the precise point where the lines intersect.
Some stand on it to be photographed, some balance on it on tiptoe,
and some spread their limbs along the lines while trying to place
their belly buttons directly on the point of intersection, as if to
symbolically mark the spot as a navel of the Earth—an *omphalos*,
as Delphi was to the Greeks.

There is a kind of enchantment in the air, but it has nothing to
do with the landscape; it derives rather from Euclidean geometry
and the lines that Europeans drew upon the globe as they set out to
conquer the world. One of them is a line of longitude that takes its
base measure from faraway Greenwich, England, thereby invoking
the imaginary homeland of the settlers who drew it. For them the
meaning of this landscape derived ultimately from "our dear native
country," no matter how distant.

For the Diné, on the other hand, every feature of the landscape
was imbued with meaning. The nineteenth-century Diné leader
Barboncito once explained his people's attachment to their land
with these words: "When the Navajo were first created, four
mountains and rivers were pointed out to us, inside of which we

should live, that was to be our country, and was given us by the first woman of the Navajo tribe."[4] These stories, and the landmarks to which they are tied, serve as a kind of scripture for the Navajo: mountains are their cathedrals; their outcrops and arroyos are the equivalent of stained-glass windows.[5]

Yet the Diné's attachment to their homeland did not prevent their being driven out of it in 1864, by Colonel Kit Carson and the US Army. Burning food stocks, cutting down orchards, and exterminating livestock, Carson and his soldiers defeated the Diné by eradicating the web of life that sustained them.[6] Beggared and helpless, thousands of Diné were force-marched to Bosque Redondo in New Mexico, a patch of country where nothing grew. Hundreds died during the march; thousands more perished during the Diné's captivity.[7]

Years later, when the Diné were finally allowed to return to a part of their homeland, one of their chiefs literally longed to speak to the land: "We felt like talking to the ground," he said, "we loved it so."[8]

That landscapes are alive has been reiterated again and again, throughout Native American history.[9] In 1855, for instance, an Indian chief, a leader of the Cayuse of what is now Oregon, refused to sign a treaty because he felt that it excluded the voice of the Earth: "I wonder if the ground has anything to say?" he asked. "I wonder if the ground is listening to what is said?"[10]

For him, as for the Bandanese, the Earth could and did speak.

Kit Carson, who has many memorials, parks, and streets named after him in that part of the world, harbored no personal ill will toward the Navajo. After driving them out of the Glittering World, he said: "I've seen as much of 'em as any white man livin', and I can't help but pity 'em. They'll all soon be gone anyhow."[11]

Kit Carson's commanding officer, General James H. Carleton, expressed the same thought in loftier language: "In their appointed time [God] wills that one race of men—as in races of lower animals—shall disappear off the face of the earth and give place to another race. . . . The races of the Mammoths and Mastodons, and great Sloths, came and passed away: the Red Man of America is passing away."[12]

These words were uttered at about the same time that Albert Bickmore was writing his account of the extermination of the Bandanese. Both passages express sentiments that were then very widely held among educated Westerners; it was considered foolish sentimentalism at that time to doubt that the lesser races would disappear, as had the mammoths and mastodons.

Yet what was once considered a certainty by Western scientists and administrators, educators and intellectuals, has not come to pass; neither the Pequot, nor the Diné, nor the Bandanese have disappeared. Having lived through the ending of their worlds, they have found ways not merely to survive, but even, in some instances, to flourish.

THE PREVALENCE OF the word "New" in maps of the Americas and Australia points to one of the most important aspects of European expansion: ecological and topographic transformation. It was this aspect of European colonialism that the pioneering ecological historian Alfred Crosby sought to highlight when he coined the term "Neo-Europes" to describe the changes that were wrought upon the flora, fauna, demography, and terrain of Australia and the Americas (and also of islands like the Canaries and New Zealand).[13]

At the time Crosby was writing, in the 1980s, it would have seemed far-fetched to imagine that changes in terrestrial landscapes might also have had an impact on the atmosphere of the entire planet. But that possibility no longer seems improbable, in an era when the intricate connections between various Earth systems are becoming increasingly evident. Indeed, what seems unlikely today is that transformations of such a magnitude could have occurred *without* any planetary consequences.

That the planet went through a century and a half of cooling has long been known; this period, which was at its peak from the late sixteenth to the mid-seventeenth century, is often referred to as the "Little Ice Age." It is also well known that during this time there was a sudden drop in atmospheric carbon. But these anomalies are generally attributed to "natural" factors like variations in solar and seismic activity; it was long thought to be merely a coincidence that they occurred at a time when Europe was tightening its grip on North and South America. But recent research suggests another possibility: that the catastrophic decline in the population of the Americas that started with the European onslaught might have contributed in some degree to the drop in global mean temperatures that occurred in the Little Ice Age.[14] So many Amerindians perished in the sixteenth and seventeenth centuries—estimates vary between 70 and 95 percent of the population of the two continents—that vast tracts of land that had once been used to grow food reverted to forest (which is why cities and temple complexes are still being discovered in the jungles of South and Central America).[15] The hypothesis goes that the sudden burgeoning of greenery in the two continents created a reverse-greenhouse effect, sequestering huge amounts of carbon dioxide and thus contributing to the fall in global mean temperatures.

This hypothesis is by no means proven.[16] But if it is indeed the case that the Little Ice Age was brought about even in part by human activity, then it would establish yet another connection between the seventeenth century and our own era of human-induced climatic perturbation.

· · ·

THE EXPRESSION "TERRAFORMING" is generally thought to have been coined by the science fiction writer Jack Williamson, who used it in a novella published in 1942. Williamson's neologism joins "terra" or "land" with "forming" in the sense of "making" or "molding," hence it could be glossed as "land-making" or "land-molding." There is no intrinsic reason, then, why the concept of "terraforming" should not be applicable to planet Earth—indeed, in Latin, "terra" is exactly "earth" in the sense of "land." But in contemporary English the word is almost always used in relation to other planets. This is implicit also in the term's formal definition, for example, in the *Oxford English Dictionary*, which glosses it as "planetary engineering designed to enhance the capacity of an extraterrestrial planetary environment to sustain life."

The idea of terraforming, however, far predates the birth of the neologism: H. G. Wells's novel *War of the Worlds*, in which extraterrestrials attack the Earth with the intention of adapting the planet for their own use, is premised on a version of it. The inspiration for the novel is said to have come from one of the better known colonial "wars of extermination"—the conflict that eliminated the Indigenous people of Tasmania after the island's colonization by the British.

What Wells does in *War of the Worlds* is reverse the colonial perspective: the metropolitan heartland of the world's biggest terrestrial empire is itself threatened with colonization by an advanced race of aliens, whose intention is to do to the inhabitants of the planet Earth what the British have done to countless others—wipe them out, seize their land, and adapt it for their own use. "The shock effect of Wells's fiction," writes the historian Christopher M. Clark, "derived not from the novelty of such destruction, which was already familiar from the European colonial past, but from its unexpected relocation to a white metropolitan setting."[17]

The science-fictional concept of terraforming is thus an extrapolation from colonial history, except that it extends the project of creating neo-Europes into one of creating neo-Earths. Consequently, narratives of terraforming draw heavily on the rhetoric and imagery of empire, envisioning space as a "frontier" to be "conquered" and "colonized." The concept's deep roots in the settler-colonial experience may explain why it has such wide appeal in the English-speaking world, not just among fans of science fiction, but also among tech billionaires, entrepreneurs, engineers, and so on.[18] It suggests an almost poignant yearning to repeat an ancestral experience of colonizing and subjugating not just other humans, but also planetary environments.

Colonization and conquest are, of course, as old as human history itself. Even settler colonialism was neither new nor particular to the Americas. It had been practiced in the Canary Islands, in Ireland, and in parts of the Chinese Empire, which had its own parallel forms of settler colonialism. What makes the European colonization of the Americas distinctive, however, is the sheer scale and the rapidity of the environmental transformations that accompanied it, radically altering more than a quarter of the Earth's land surface in a few hundred years. That these transformations may even have contributed to planet-wide climatic disruptions suggests something of the scale and speed at which the changes occurred. In this history the colonization of North America by the English again occupies a special place: it was there that processes of terraforming were applied most intensively, and with greatest success, in the sense that large tracts of land were reengineered to resemble European models so that they would suit European ways of life.

To remake immense stretches of terrain to suit the lifestyles of another continent inevitably entailed the undermining and elimination of the ways of life of those who had inhabited those lands for many thousands of years. The project of terraforming was therefore fundamentally conflictual; it was in itself a mode of warfare, of a distinctive kind.

Through most of human history wars have been fought between human adversaries, with human-made weapons. But terraforming required a different kind of war in which environmental interventions and nonhuman entities played a central part. This aspect of the colonial project loomed large in early accounts of the European conquest. Girolamo Benzoni, the Italian-born conquistador whose *History of the New World* was published in 1565, described Indigenous perceptions of Europeans with these words: "They say that we have come to this earth to destroy the world. They say . . . that we devour everything, we consume the earth, we redirect the rivers, we are never quiet, never at rest, but always run here and there, seeking gold and silver, never satisfied, and then we gamble with it, make war, kill each other, rob, swear, never say the truth, and have deprived them of their means of livelihood."[19]

Wars of terraforming were thus biopolitical conflicts in which entire populations were subjected to forms of violence that included massive biological and ecological disruptions. In his *Democracy in America*, Alexis de Tocqueville captures the nature of this kind of conflict, which was fought primarily not with guns and weapons, but by means of broader environmental changes:

> From the day when a European settlement rises in the neighborhood
> of territory occupied by the Indians, the wild game takes fright . . .
> the moment the endless noises of European industrial activity are

heard in any place, the animals begin to flee. . . . A few European families, by settling in widely separated locations, finally drive away the wild animals from all the intervening land for ever. The Indians who had lived there up to that time in some sort of abundance find it difficult to survive and more difficult still to acquire the necessary articles of barter. Driving away their game is the equivalent of turning our farmers' fields into barren wastes. Soon they lose, almost entirely, the means of subsistence. Then these doomed people are seen roaming like hungry wolves through their deserted forests.[20]

De Tocqueville understood very well the aims of this kind of conflict, but he did not recognize it as war. For him as for other Europeans, war (properly speaking) was a formalized affair, fought between states, with armies and armaments. These other conflicts were different: they began without formal declarations and never really ended, unfolding over decades and centuries. Conflicts of this kind have been variously described as "irregular wars," "*petites guerres*," and as America's "first way of war." The defining characteristic of this form of warfare was an enormously elevated level of violence in which neither women nor children were spared. "From both military necessity and hands-on experience," writes John Grenier, a military historian and serving Air Force officer, "successive generations of Americans, both soldiers and civilians, made the killing of Indian men, women and children a defining element of their first military traditions and thereby part of a shared American identity."[21]

It need hardly be said that Native Americans had fought wars in precolonial times as well; in many Indian communities warfare and warriors were greatly valorized, and both were often invested with spiritual meaning. But precolonial wars in North America were a form of ritualized conflict, fought mainly between men. Women and children were rarely killed, and the extermination of enemy groups was never the aim of war-making, as it was, for instance, in the Pequot War. In that conflict, as was almost always the case in colonial wars, colonists had a number of Indian allies. But those Indians were so horrified by the savagery of the colonists' violence that they strove to restrain them, and when their efforts failed, they quietly melted away.[22]

The normalizing of the killing of noncombatants was taken a step further when English colonies began to offer bounties for the scalps of Indian men, women, and children. Not only did their embrace of scalp-hunting serve to commercialize war; it also legitimized the killing of noncombatants. The practice thus became "a permanent feature of both the colonial frontier economy and Americans' way of war."

These wars followed an unvarying pattern. As Jill Lepore notes, over three centuries Europeans and Native Americans "would fight uncannily similar wars over and over again."[23] Nor were these wars fought only by soldiers; entire populations, races, cultures, worldviews, and indeed ecosystems were pitted against each other: "total war" and "total mobilization" occurred in the Americas long before they came to Europe.[24]

So all-encompassing were these colonial conflicts that the participants found it difficult even to find a name for them. Thus William Hubbard, a seventeenth-century chronicler of King Philip's War, decided to call his account of the conflict "a narrative" rather than a history, because it was too "barbarous" to be called a war.[25] Present-day historians too are divided about what to call King Philip's War, because, as Jill Lepore notes, "what took place in New England in 1675 and 1676 was simply too nasty to 'deserve the Name of a War.'"[26]

Nineteenth-century writers, however, would not have lacked for a term to describe this kind of warfare: these are exactly the conflicts that Westerners had in mind when they spoke of "wars of extermination." Wars of extermination were precisely biopolitical wars, in which the weaponization of the environment was a critical element of the conflict.

In this lies a fundamental difference between settler-colonial conflicts and the colonial wars fought by Europeans in Asia and Africa. The wars waged by the British in India, for example, conformed to the usual patterns of Eurasian warfare: soldiers fought each other with human-made weapons, and the wars were usually limited in duration.

Settler-colonial conflicts were of a completely different order of warfare. Indigenous peoples faced a state of permanent (or "forever") war that involved many kinds of other-than-human beings and entities: pathogens, rivers, forests, plants, and animals all played a part in the struggle.

The nonhuman enmeshments of these conflicts are so extensive that they confound the accustomed categories of "history" and "politics," both of which are imagined, in the modern sense, as domains of exclusively human activity. The absolute distinction between the natural and the human that is so central to Western ways of thinking leaves no room for other-than-human beings to figure as protagonists in history or politics; at best, they can be treated as inert elements in particular ecological settings.[27]

Yet even though Europeans did not recognize nonhumans of any kind as protagonists in human affairs, settlers were, of course, perfectly well aware of the role that "nature" played in their conflicts with Native Americans. "Ideas about nature," writes Joyce Chaplin, "were the foundation of English colonization because they defined the terms by which the English believed in their conquest of America. To their minds material forces explained displacement of the aboriginal population, a natural process that required less definitive use of military action than had been the case with the Spanish."[28]

In other words, English settlers believed that they were less cruel than their Spanish counterparts because instead of military violence, they were using "material forces" and "natural processes" to decimate Indigenous peoples. This belief is so extraordinary that it requires a moment's reflection: in effect it simultaneously acknowledges that nonhuman forces are being used as weapons while also asserting that settlers bear no blame for the impacts because they are unfolding in the domain of "Nature," through "material forces." This conjuration neatly effaces the role human actions play in setting environmental changes in motion; it is as if they occur independently of human intentions. In this framing biopolitical warfare is strictly distinguished from other human conflicts. Indeed, it is not recognized as conflict at all; it is assigned to some other, supposedly independent, natural order. The Western idea of "nature" is thus the key element that simultaneously enables and conceals the true character of biopolitical warfare. Echoes of this history can still be heard, as for example when

American climate denialists claim that fluctuations in climate are "natural," and are therefore impervious to human intervention.

THESE DISTINCTIONS LIE at the core of the scholarly debates that surround the question of what caused the "Great Dying" of Indigenous peoples during the colonization of the Americas. A large, and still dominant, branch of scholarship emphasizes the role of forces that appear to have acted independently of human agency, the most important of them being disease.[29] Early European colonists (so the argument goes) had acquired immunities to the diseases they brought with them; since Native Americans lacked these immunities, the diseases fell on "virgin soil" and decimated Indigenous populations independently of the intentions of the colonists.

Others have argued that there is little "substantial evidence to back up what are essentially intuitive assertions about Indian immunity."[30] In fact, studies of "virgin soil" populations in Amazonia have found that Amerindian immune systems do not function in a markedly different way from those of other groups.[31] Why then did Native Americans succumb in such vastly disproportionate numbers? Quite possibly it was because their susceptibility to disease was greatly increased by the multiple kinds of structural violence that accompanied European colonization, such as: "overwork in mines, frequent outright butchery, malnutrition and starvation resulting from the breakdown of Indigenous trade networks, subsistence food production and loss of land, loss of will to live or reproduce (and thus suicide, abortion and infanticide)."[32] When faced with similarly stressful conditions, White settlers also fell prey to disease in large numbers, as happened in Jamestown, Virginia, in 1607.[33]

In an article titled "Virgin Soils Revisited," David Jones writes: "Although unprecedented in their widespread severity, virgin soil epidemics may have arisen from nothing more unique than the familiar forces of poverty, malnutrition, environmental stress, dislocation, and social disparity that cause epidemics among all other populations."[34] Similarly, the historian Paul Kelton, in a detailed study of sixteenth- and seventeenth-century epidemics in the

American Southeast, found that "English-inspired commerce in Native slaves was the element of colonialism most responsible for making indigenous peoples across the region vulnerable to newly introduced diseases."[35]

Why, then, did the virgin soil theory find such widespread acceptance? Jones attributes its popularity not to the persuasiveness of the research behind it, but rather to the fact that "immunological determinism can still assuage Euroamerican guilt over American Indian depopulation, whether in the conscious motives of historians, or in the semiconscious desires of their readers."[36]

Clearly, there were many factors at work in the "Great Dyings," and the precise weightage of each will probably never be settled; as Jones observes, European and Amerindian populations have over the last five hundred years become so mixed that the "opportunity for further research on first contact populations remains remote."[37]

What is striking about the debate, however, is that it hinges upon differences in the way the relationship between humans and other-than-humans is envisioned: for one side, disease is seen to exercise its effects independently of what humans intend; for the other, it is seen as being enmeshed with other forms of human violence. In that sense the scholarly debate reflects the differences between settler and Indigenous conceptions of the conflicts they were engaged in.

Since Indigenous Americans did not subscribe to the distinctions that European drew between the natural and the social, the human and the nonhuman, they understood perfectly well that behind the increasing derangement of the air, the landscape, and the bodies of those who inhabited it there lay a viscerally human conflict.

As early as the sixteenth century, soon after the founding of the first English colonies in Virginia, the Native Americans of the region began to represent diseases as weapons of war, speaking of them as "invisible bullets."[38] In some stories diseases were represented as the settlers' kinsmen and allies. In 1767, a British superintendent was told that the people of the Potawatomi tribe believed that "the great Number they lost of their People at & returning from Lake George in 1757, was owing to ye English poisoning the Rum, & giving them the Small Pox, for which they owe them an everlasting ill will."[39] Around 1770, a group of Ojibwa were presented with a contaminated flag by some traders as a mark of friendship; after it was unfurled an epidemic broke out. This episode remained in Ojibwa memory for centuries. In 1928 a medical historian wrote: "The Indians to this day are firmly of the opinion that the small-pox was, at this time, communicated through the articles presented to their brethren by the agent of the fur company at Mackinac."[40]

In a Kiowa legend the tribe's mythic hero comes upon a stranger dressed like a missionary and asks him who he is. "I'm smallpox," says the stranger. "I come from far away, across the Eastern Ocean. I am one with the white men—they are my people as the Kiowas are yours. Sometimes I travel ahead of them sometimes I lurk behind. But I am always their companion and you will find me in their camps and in their houses."[41]

As for European settlers, there is plenty of evidence to show that they knew very well that pathogens were their most effective allies. On June 24, 1763, in the thick of the Indian uprising known as Pontiac's Rebellion, two Lenape emissaries were in Fort Pitt, Pennsylvania, for a parlay. When it came time for them to leave they were given some parting gifts that had been issued and signed for by the fort's commanding officer. Later, a British trader called William Trent would note in his journal, "We gave them two Blankets and an Handkerchief out of the Small Pox Hospital. I hope it will have the desired effect." And so it did: an epidemic broke out in Ohio, coinciding "closely with the distribution of infected articles by individuals at Fort Pitt."[42]

In the meantime, the same idea had occurred also, at about the same time, to the commander of the British forces in New York, Sir Jeffrey Amherst. In a memorandum sent to Col. Henry Bouquet, in Philadelphia, he wrote: "Could it not be contrived to Send the *Small Pox* among those Disaffected Tribes of Indians? We must, on this occasion, Use Every Stratagem in our power to Reduce them." Bouquet answered with alacrity: "I will try to Innoculate the Indians by means of Blankets that may fall in their hands, taking care however not to get the disease myself." To this Amherst responded: "You will Do well to try to Innoculate the Indians by means of Blanketts, as well as to try Every other method that can serve to Extirpate this Execrable Race."

In a prize-winning essay titled "Biological Warfare in Eighteenth-Century North America," the historian Elizabeth Fenn notes that the exchange between Amherst and Bouquet was not anomalous: "Evidence from other fields of battle indicates that in the minds of many, smallpox had an established, if irregular, place in late-eighteenth-century warfare." She notes also that as a weapon of war, smallpox had another advantage: "unlike rape, pillage, and other atrocities in which the intent and identity of the perpetrator could be made clear, the propagation of smallpox had the advantage of deniability." Native Americans weren't the only people against whom the British deployed disease; they used this form of warfare also against White Americans, during the Revolutionary War.[43]

In the nineteenth century, White settlers sometimes used vials of smallpox and cowpox (which they carried with them for inoculation) quite literally as weapons. One such instance, from 1805, appears in the published account of the Lewis and Clark expedition: "The Sioux had it in contemplation to . . . murder us in the spring, but were prevented from making the attack, by our threatening to spread the *smallpox*, with all its horrors."[44] Sometimes the spread of disease would be helped in other ways—for instance, by herding Indigenous people into camps where mortality rates would skyrocket. Or settler communities would simply withhold treatment from their Indigenous neighbors, and allow "nature" to run its course. Over the centuries this became a lasting pattern in the Americas: the substandard medical care and inadequate nutrition that is sometimes provided to Indigenous peoples today by government agencies is itself a form of withholding; it jeopardizes lives not by direct action, but by inaction.

5

"We Shall All Be Gone Shortly"

Ecological interventions were not just an incidental effect of European settlement in the Americas; they were central to the project, the explicit aim of which was to turn territories that were perceived to be wastelands into terrain that fitted a European conception of productive land. Indeed, the settlers' very claims to the territories were based on an idea that was essentially ecological: the notion that the land was "savage," "wild," and vacant, because it was neither tilled nor divided into property. The seventeenth-century Puritan leader John Winthrop, for instance, argued that Indians had no rights of ownership in the land "for they inclose no ground, neither have they cattle to maintain it, but remove their dwellings as they have occasion."[1] It was by planting, and creating "plantations," that the settlers claimed the land. The right to terraform was thus an essential part of settler identity; their claim of ownership was founded on the notion that they were "improving" the land by making it productive in ways that were recognizable as such by Europeans.[2] As the historian William Cronon notes, "European perceptions of what constituted a proper use of the environment . . . thus became a European ideology of conquest."

But of course the land was neither unproductive nor wild, in the sense of being free of human interventions, before the arrival of Europeans. It was just that the potential of American ecosystems was harnessed in a fashion that was completely different from the European way.[3] These ecosystems were so bountiful that sixteenth-

and seventeenth-century Europeans were often amazed by the stature and good health of Native Americans. But their well-being required extremely careful husbandry, not just of agricultural land but also of forests, where fire was used as an essential technology to control the undergrowth and create park-like habitats that facilitated hunting.[4] Contrary to the colonists' perceptions, Indians were not just helping themselves to the bounty of the land; rather, "they were harvesting a foodstuff which they had consciously been instrumental in creating." But for settlers these ways of tending the land were not recognizable as forms of cultivation or "improvement," and they used Indian hunting practices to condemn them as "lazy savages" and to deny that they "had a rightful claim to the land they hunted."[5]

For many settlers, the environment of New England was, in the words of an early colonial leader and minister, "a hideous & desolate wilderness, full of wild beasts & wild men."[6] Subduing this wild land meant changing it ecologically, and remaking it in the image of Europe, which was then itself undergoing the most extensive terrestrial transformations in its history.[7] This project was explicitly acknowledged and celebrated by the colonists. "As early as 1653, the historian Edward Johnson could count it as one of God's providences that a 'remote, rocky, barren, bushy, wildwoody wilderness' had been transformed in a generation into 'a second England for fertilness.'"[8]

The differences between European and Indian conceptions of living on the land have never been more eloquently summarized than by the Oglala Lakota chief Standing Bear: "We did not think of the great open plains, the beautiful rolling hills, and winding streams with tangled growth as 'wild.' Only to the white man was Nature a 'wilderness' and only to him was the land 'infested' with 'wild' animals and 'savage' people. To us it was tame. Earth was bountiful and we were surrounded with the blessings of the Great Mystery."[9]

These contrasting conceptions, suggests the Native American botanist Robin Wall Kimmerer, were ultimately founded on radically different stories about the world, like those of Skywoman and Eve:

On one side of the world were people whose relationship with the living world was shaped by Skywoman, who created a garden for all. On the other side was another woman with a garden and a tree. But for tasting its fruit, she was banished from the garden. . . . That mother of men was made to wander in the wilderness and earn her bread by the sweat of her brow, not by filling her mouth with the sweet juicy fruits that bend the branches low. In order to eat, she was instructed to subdue the wilderness into which she was cast.[10]

BECAUSE NATIVE AMERICANS saw the Earth as bountiful, they did not immediately recognize that the settlers' way of relating to the land—by clear-cutting trees, setting up permanent settlements, and building fenced enclosures—would make their own ways of life ecologically untenable.[11] Only when the settlers' ecological interventions began to disrupt their food chains did the Indians begin to see them "as sources of permanent disequilibrium."[12]

Many kinds of nonhumans were instrumental in creating this state of disequilibrium. Most disruptive of all were the settlers' "companion species": cows and pigs, which required pastures and fences, and which often strayed into forests. The ecological impacts of the colonists' domestic animals were far-reaching: they worsened the effects of erosion, eliminated native grasses, consumed resources that native fauna depended on, contributed to shifts in microclimates, and helped to convert forests into farmland. In short, they were a major factor in compounding the problems that confronted Indians as a result of colonization.[13]

For English settlers, domestic animals were yet another means of "improving" the land along European models. But the demands of survival in early America were such that the settlers were unable to tend to their livestock in the manner of European farmers. Instead they allowed their animals to roam free, which had disastrous consequences for Indians: cows and pigs strayed everywhere, destroying Native cornfields and trampling over cultivated land. Not surprisingly, domestic animals became a recurrent source of conflict between settlers and Indians.

By the mid-seventeenth century the Algonquians knew that

they were facing the destruction of the entire web of life that sustained them. In 1642, when the Narragansett sachem Miantonomi sought to create an anti-colonial alliance, he placed the environmental changes effected by English settlers at the heart of his appeal to other Algonquian tribes.[14] Speaking to the Montauk of Long Island, he said: "We shall all be gone shortly, for you know our fathers had plenty of deer and skins, our plains were full of deer, as also our woods, and of turkies, and our coves full of fish and fowl. But the English having gotten our land, they with scythes cut down the grass, and with axes fell the trees; their cows and horses eat the grass, and their hogs spoil our clam banks, and we shall all be starved."[15]

It was not till 1675 that an alliance of Algonquian tribes took up arms against settlers in New England, in the conflict that has come to be known as "King Philip's War." The war lasted three years and was savagely fought, with both sides dismembering enemies, taking body parts as trophies, and sparing neither women nor children. The savagery of the conflict is often attributed to cultural differences and religious zeal—yet the conflict was also, in the most visceral way, an environmental struggle. On both sides the violence was directed not just at human bodies, but also at the ecological underpinnings of the adversaries' divergent ways of life. The Algonquians specifically targeted the structures that were most representative of the incipient Europeanization of the terrain. They attacked the settlers' towns, villages, and houses—not with the intention of occupying or making use of them, but in the hope of literally expunging them from the landscape, with fire. Nor did the settlers fail to perceive that it was their attempted Europeanization of the land that was under attack. "Colonial writers understood the destruction of their houses," writes Joyce Chaplin, "as a blow not only to their property but also to the very Englishness of the landscape."[16] When settlers attacked Algonquian settlements, they too put dwellings and granaries indiscriminately to the torch, as if to obliterate the Indigenous way of dwelling in the landscape.

Another striking feature of the environmental aspects of King Philip's War was the targeting, by Algonquians, of domestic animals. This followed a pattern that went back to at least 1609, when conflicts between settlers and Indians in Virginia led to the slaughter of six hundred hogs.[17] From a Native point of view cows and pigs were vermin, just as Indigenous species, like wolves and coyotes, were for settlers: during King Philip's War, cattle came under relentless attack. "Nor have our Cattle escaped the Cruelty of these worse than Brute and Savage Beasts," wrote a Puritan chronicler. "For what Cattle they took they seldom killed outright: or if they did, would eat but little of the Flesh, but rather cut their Bellies, and letting them go several Days, trailing their Guts after them, putting out their eyes, or cutting off one Leg, etc."[18] Altogether 8,000 head of cattle were killed in the course of the war.[19]

Over the following centuries cattle would repeatedly precipitate conflicts between settlers and Native Americans. In the eighteenth century, the Yamasees of Virginia entered into an alliance with the English, only to find that the settlers' cows and pigs were driving away the deer on which they were dependent. In 1715 the Yamasees took up arms against the settlers and were quickly annihilated: "Scalp hunters, armed black slaves, and Iroquois proxies preyed upon Yamasees as if they were animals in the woods," writes John Grenier. He adds: "It was a powerful example of the first way of war in action."[20]

In the nineteenth century the wagon trains that crossed the Great Plains were accompanied by herds of cattle that depleted the grazing lands of the buffalo on which many Indigenous groups depended. Sometimes cows would stray into native lands, sparking deadly outbreaks of violence.

Conflicts over cattle have remained to this day a constant feature of the terraforming of the Americas. One of the main reasons why the deforestation of the Amazon is still accelerating is that settlers—and giant agribusiness corporations—are pushing to expand cattle farming in Brazil. Now, as in seventeenth-century New England, this requires large-scale deforestation and the creation of pasturage; now, as then, this entails the destruction of Indigenous life-worlds.

In a 1983 meeting of some Indigenous Amazonian groups, the activist and writer Ailton Krenak spoke in a vein that was strikingly similar to Miantonomi's: "We need to speak together against those who want to take over our land. Otherwise we will disappear, like our ancestors before us. . . . These *fazendeiros* (squatter farmers) want to chase us off the land where our ancestors lived by claiming that it belongs to them now! We are surrounded by their barbed wire and their cattle."[21]

This is yet another instance of the astonishing continuities that place the current planetary crisis within a centuries-old history of terraforming.

. . .

THE LONG-TERM IMPACTS of disease, livestock, and land clearances manifested silently, and invisibly: they represented, so to speak, a passive front of conflict, in which destruction was effected in a mediated fashion, through nonhuman beings and forces. On this front it was not intentional action but *inaction* that was a key factor. The conflict had another front, of active ecological interventions—but there too the violence was mediated through nonhumans, in the sense that the immediate targets were not human bodies but rather critical elements in the webs of life that sustained them. One example of this was the extermination of the buffalo herds of the Great Plains. This strategy was adopted by the US Army when it became clear that the highly mobile warriors of the Lakota-Cheyenne-Arapaho alliance could not be defeated in conventional battles.[22] It was then, writes the Lakota scholar and activist Nick Estes, that "the frontier army sanctioned the mass slaughter of buffalo to shatter the will to resist by eliminating a primary food supply." Between 1865 and 1883 American soldiers and hunters killed between 10 and 15 million buffalo, leaving only a few hundred alive. "'The Indian problem,'" writes Estes, "was also a 'buffalo problem' and both faced similar extermination processes, as much connected in death as they were in life. The destruction of one required the destruction of the other."[23]

In the late nineteenth century, a Kiowa woman, describing the elimination of her people's way of life, said:

When the white men wanted to build railroads, or when they wanted to farm or raise cattle, the buffalo still protected the Kiowas. They tore up the railroad tracks and the gardens. They chased the cattle off the ranges. The buffalo loved their people as much as the Kiowas loved them. . . . There was war between the buffalo and the white men . . . the white men hired hunters to do nothing but kill the buffalo. Up and down the plains those men ranged, shooting sometimes as many as a hundred buffalo a day. . . . Sometimes there would be a pile of bones as high as a man, stretching a mile along the railroad track. . . . The buffalo saw that their day was over. They could protect their people no longer.[24]

In the ensuing decades what remained of the material basis of Indigenous life in the upper Great Plains was destroyed again and again by processes of terraforming, most of all through the diversion and damming of rivers. "The building of dams," writes Dina Gilio-Whitaker, "has historically delivered some of the most devastating blows to Native communities. Flooding caused by dams dislocated entire towns and destroyed fishing sites, contributing to starvation and poverty inflicted by US policies."[25]

The most extensive environmental intervention in the upper Missouri region occurred in the 1940s and 1950s, with the building of a network of dams under the Pick-Sloan Plan.[26] The dams were so sited that they flooded some of the only fertile stretches of land on the reservations that had been created after the elimination of the buffalo. Vine Deloria Jr. describes the building of these dams as "without a doubt, the single most destructive act ever perpetrated on any tribe by the United States."[27]

Each of these, and many other interventions, displaced large numbers of people, who were then, through military means and acts of legal exclusion, pushed beyond a notional border into zones of containment. Yet even these zones were never stable; further interventions and acts of exclusion often forced already displaced populations to move again and again. As Patrick Wolfe has observed, invasion was not an event but a structure.[28]

Over time some of these places of relocation became "sacrifice zones" where the inhabitants were forced, as their ancestors had been, to deal with massively disrupted environments. So, for instance, fifty years after the massacre at Wounded Knee, in 1890, the Oceti Sakowin (Sioux) peoples were once again confronted by the might of the US military when the federal government seized 342,000 acres of the Pine Ridge reservation and turned them into a bombing range for the Air Force: those lands are now so strewn with ordinance as to be unusable.[29]

"While Native peoples have been massacred and fought, cheated, and robbed of their historical lands," writes Winona LaDuke, "today their lands are subject to some of the most invasive industrial interventions imaginable. According to the Worldwatch Institute, 317 reservations in the United States are threatened by environmental hazards, ranging from toxic wastes to clearcuts."[30]

Thus, for example, sites in the southwestern desert that were sacred territories for the Western Shoshone and Southern Paiute were turned into nuclear testing sites because military leaders decided that the land "really wasn't much good anyway."[31] Much of the uranium for the weapons that were tested at the site also came from Native American lands, with the result that the Navajo Nation is now "home to more than 1,000 abandoned uranium mines and four former uranium mills."[32]

The Laguna writer Leslie Marmon Silko, who grew up in the region, writes in her memoir, *The Turquoise Ledge*: "Clouds of radio-active particles from the Nevada atomic test site passed over us every time they 'tested' a bomb. We were 'down-winders' with all the other 'expendable' people who became guinea pigs."[33] Among the "expendable" there are many Black groups as well, including the people who live in Louisiana's "chemical corridor," where "many large petrochemical factories dump dangerous chemicals into the air, water and ground." The corridor is located largely on the premises of former plantations and is "surrounded by traditionally black villages and hamlets."[34] It is no accident that many of these sacrifice zones have been disproportionately affected by the planetary crisis in its many guises: the Navajo Nation, for instance, was besieged by wildfires at the height of the Covid-19 pandemic, in July 2020.[35]

IN BEARING WITNESS to the profound environmental changes that were unfolding around them, American Indians drew their own conclusions about where colonial terraforming would lead. In 1855 the Duwamish chief Seattle, after whom the city is named, wrote a letter to President Franklin Pierce in which he said: "Continue to contaminate your bed, and you will one night suffocate in your own waste. When the buffalo are all slaughtered, the wild horses all tamed, the secret corners of the forest heavy with the scent of men, and the view of the ripe hills blotted by talking wires, where is the thicket? Gone. Where is the eagle? Gone. And what is to say goodbye to the swift and the hunt, the end of living and the beginning of survival?"[36]

Now, as humanity faces the possibility of a future in which living will indeed have turned into a battle for survival, it is becoming increasingly clear that Indigenous understandings of terraforming were, in fact, far more sophisticated than those of today's techno-futurists. Indeed, this long-ago lament by an anonymous Omaha man is uncannily similar to many of the elegies of loss that are being written today about the current age of extinctions:

When I was a youth, the country was very beautiful. Along the rivers were belts of timberland, where grew cottonwood, maple, elm, ash, hickory, and walnut trees, and many other kinds. Also there were many kind of vines and shrubs. And under these grew many good herbs and beautiful flowering plants.

In both the woodlands and the prairie I could see the trails of many kinds of animals and could hear the cheerful songs of many kinds of birds. When I walked abroad, I could see many forms of life, beautiful living creatures which Wakanda [the Great Spirit] had placed here; and these were, after their manner, walking, flying, leaping, running, playing all about.

But now the face of all the land is changed and sad. The living creatures are gone. I see the land desolate and I suffer an unspeakable sadness. Sometimes I wake in the night, and I feel as though I should suffocate from the pressure of this awful feeling of loneliness.[37]

6

Bonds of Earth

The project of terraforming enframes the world in much the same way that the Banda Islands came to be seen by their conquerors: this is the frame of world-as-resource, in which landscapes (or planets) come to be regarded as factories and "Nature" is seen as subdued and cheap.[1]

In principle there is no reason why reducing any particular terrain to a resource should lead to its depletion, in terms of either meaning or productivity. It should be possible, after all, to "use" that terrain rationally, matching ends and means.

And yet that is not what happens. It would seem that there is an inherent instability to the framework of world-as-resource that impels it to devour that which it enframes. That is what happened in Maluku: even after fulfilling their ambitions in the region, the officials of the VOC were never satisfied with their spice monopoly.

There was a certain inevitability to this, for the paradox of value was bound to claim its due once the supply of nutmegs, mace, and cloves had become regular and predictable: when spices ceased to be rarities, their prices began to decline. Their provenance too stopped working in their favor, once they came to be associated not with the glamour that attaches to magical, faraway lands, but with colonies peopled by "lesser races."

In addition, tastes had begun to change in Europe. Anxieties about sexuality led to the shunning of dietary items that were thought to overstimulate the body and create propensities for the "solitary vice."[2] The poet Percy Bysshe Shelley denounced spices as well as the spice trade as "harmful to the moral fibre" of the body and the nation.[3] Upper-class Europeans, who had once relished spicy food, now began to take pride in the blandness of their cuisine.

The fall in the value of spices was a source of great concern to the VOC, which responded with a number of countermeasures, among them a campaign of extermination, directed this time not at people but at trees—the very trees that had brought them to Maluku. In order to limit the supply of spices on the global market, the VOC decreed that nutmeg trees would be grown only on the Bandas, and clove trees only on Ambon Island.[4] Every clove and nutmeg tree on every other island—and there are more than a thousand islands in Maluku—was to be extirpated.[5] Thus was launched the policy of eradication, or extirpation (*exterpatie*), in accordance with which the Sultan of Ternate—the island that had for centuries been the center of the clove trade—was forced to sign a treaty, in 1652, pledging to destroy every clove tree on the island.[6] The clove, like the nutmeg, had become the bearer of a "resource curse," an affliction that would consume much of the planet in the centuries ahead.

The VOC had set itself a monumental task: on island after island, spice trees were found to be growing in unexpected places.[7] Yet the extirpation policy was pursued for over a century with an obsessiveness that appears, in retrospect, distinctly unhinged.

In 1686 a Dutch governor, writing from Ternate, struggled to explain to his superiors in Amsterdam what he was up against:

Your Lordships would find it difficult to comprehend how many [spice trees] there are on most of the islands in this area. If we truly intend to uproot these trees, we must do it with hundreds of men divided into groups and spread out through the forests. For this we must have people who have the desire and inclination to carry out the work since the forests are so thick that a man can barely raise his head. Moreover, they are often full of thorns and bushes which tear to shreds whatever a man is wearing and damage his legs, hands, and face. . . . The places are many, and the uprooting [of spice trees] appears to be nearly an impossible task. It is the most difficult and exhausting work that one can imagine. Sometimes [the spice trees] are so inaccessible that one must push up the [thorny] rattan vines in order to get to them. There is also the danger of breaking a leg. Sometimes the spice trees are surrounded by so many other trees and bushes that one cannot see them. . . . Over half come back sick or incapacitated from these expeditions.

Evidently, the terrain was fighting back.

"It is very difficult and unpleasant to get to [the spice trees]," wrote another Dutch official, in 1697. "Often we have to crawl on our hands and feet, which results in damage to our hands and so many pricks from thorns that we do not dare to go forward. The difficult paths, swollen rivers, daily rains, and the extreme cold have resulted in only five of the seven soldiers with me at present being able to be used to search for these vexatious plants."[8]

The VOC was the embodiment of early capitalism; it was run by stolid burghers who prided themselves on their rationality, moderation, and common sense.[9] Yet they pursued a policy that perfectly illustrates the unrestrainable excess that lies hidden at the heart of the vision of world-as-resource—an excess that leads ultimately not just to genocide but an even greater violence, an impulse that can only be called "omnicide," the desire to destroy everything. This impulse was often on display during the conquest of the Americas. "If a man had need of one pig," wrote a Spanish conquistador in 1553, "he killed twenty; if four Indians were wanted, he took a dozen. . . . [T]hey thought no more of killing Indians than if they were useless beasts."[10]

It was this same incubus of excess that took possession of the burghers who ran the VOC. "By the middle of the eighteenth century," writes the historian Leonard Andaya, "the Company was obsessed by the eradication campaign. Official reports are devoted almost exclusively to the results of these expeditions."[11]

But the Company was up against a formidable opponent—trees, which measure time on a scale completely different from humans. Against the scythes and axes of the VOC's minions, the trees deployed a far more powerful weapon: their ability to propagate. Their seeds, smuggled out by French and English plant-hunters, took root on other islands, where they flourished in such numbers that in time the memory of their connections with Maluku was almost forgotten: it was Barbados that would boast of being the "Nutmeg Island," and it was Connecticut that would eventually come to be known as the "Nutmeg State."

If trees could savor *schadenfreude*, then the nutmegs of Maluku wouldn't have had very long to wait; at the end of the eighteenth century, hollowed out by decades of corruption, and weakened by a changing geopolitical order, the VOC collapsed.[12]

· · ·

THE TREE OF the Bandas may have flourished in other lands; but nowhere on Earth, other than Maluku, do people still sing about the nutmeg and weave it into their memories of their ancestors and their lost homeland. Everywhere else the nutmeg is just a commodity, a resource; it has no meaning in excess of its utility. Nobody sings songs about the nutmeg in Barbados or Connecticut.

In this too, the tiny planet-shaped nut has something to teach us about the Earth. The nutmeg's travels, and its strange career, perfectly illustrate the loss of meaning that is produced by the vision of world-as-resource. To see the world in this way requires not just the physical subjugation of people and territory, but also a specific idea of conquest, as a process of extraction. This is another legacy of European expansion, and particularly of the settling of North America, which produced metaphors and imagery on a scale to match its violence. "Settlers 'pursued nature to her hiding places,'" writes the historian Greg Grandin, "and as they did, they created a new set of commandments: Establish 'power over this world, everywhere naturally a wilderness.' 'Subdue nature.' 'Go forth.' 'Conquer a wilderness.' 'Take possession of the continent.' 'Overspread.' 'Increase.' 'Multiply.' 'Scour.' 'Clear.'"[13]

Once conquest is achieved, the conquered object gives the impression of being supine and inert. Having succumbed to mastery, it holds no more mysteries; the challenge it once posed to the conqueror's imagination is exhausted.

Exhaustion is a metaphor that occurs often in science fiction stories about terraforming. Swarms of aliens go off to conquer another planet because their own is "exhausted." It is the same presumption that impels billionaires to plan the conquest of Mars, now that the Earth is "exhausted."

But it bears asking: of what exactly is the Earth "exhausted"? The planet's riches may be depleted, but they are very far from being completely spent. And in any case, the imagining of the Earth's exhaustion occurred long before the absolute depletion of its resources was even distantly envisaged as a possibility.

Which is only to say that what the Earth is really exhausted of is not its resources; what it has lost is *meaning*. Conquered, inert, supine, the Earth can no longer ennoble, nor delight, nor produce new aspirations. All it can inspire in its would-be conqueror's mind is the kind of contempt that arises from familiarity.

Over time this contempt has come to be planted so deep within cultures of modernity that it has become a part of its unseen foundations.

CONSIDER, FOR EXAMPLE, these lines from a poem that has become an American monument in its own right:

> Oh, I have slipped the surly bonds of earth
> And danced the skies on laughter-silvered wings.

The lines are from "High Flight," a poem written in 1941 by John Gillespie Magee, a young Canadian American pilot. Magee was killed shortly after he wrote "High Flight," but because of this one poem, he was almost instantly canonized as *the* American poet of World War II. The lines have appeared on innumerable headstones across the country, and they have entered American popular culture in a way that is almost unique. Orson Welles made a recording of "High Flight" in 1942, and according to the Library of Congress, "In the 1950s and through at least the early 1980s, the poem was included in many television stations' 'sign-offs' before going off the air, carving out a place in the imaginations and memories of several generations of Americans." A copy of "High Flight" was even deposited on the moon in 1971.

Today, the poem is perhaps best remembered for President Ronald Reagan's speech in January 1986, following on the *Challenger* disaster. The last sentence of the speech linked the first and last lines of the poem: "The crew of the space shuttle *Challenger*," said President Reagan, "honored us by the manner in which they lived their lives. We will never forget them, nor the last time we saw them, this morning, as they prepared for their journey and waved good-bye and 'slipped the surly bonds of earth' to 'touch the face of God.'"

Few poems have lodged themselves as securely at the heart of American culture as "High Flight." And the poem is, without a doubt, a moving and beautiful piece of verse. Such is its power that it finesses the implications of what is indisputably its most arresting image: "the surly bonds of earth." Rarely does anyone stop to ask: what exactly is "surly" about the Earth's bonds? Or why should the planet be thought of as a home from which humans would be fortunate to escape?

What can be said of such a view except that it spills over from mere contempt for the Earth into an active hatred for it?

It could be said that "High Flight" is merely a celebration of aviation, a new and exciting technology. But the truth is that the ideas that are central to the poem were woven into the fabric of European culture even before the invention of aviation. Traces of them can be found, although expressed differently, in the work of many writers and poets, including that of Alfred, Lord Tennyson, who was perhaps the most celebrated English poet of the late nineteenth century.

One of the reasons Tennyson was so greatly admired by his peers was that he was considered the most scientifically informed poet of his time; like many Victorian writers, he took a keen interest in science and was profoundly influenced by Charles Lyell, Charles Darwin, and the other eminent scientific thinkers of his era.

In Tennyson's work this influence expresses itself in verses that are meditations on evolution, as well as on the birth and destiny of Mankind. Here is one such passage from one of his most famous poems, *In Memoriam*:

The solid earth whereon we tread
In tracts of fluent heat began,

And grew to seeming-random forms,
   The seeming prey of cyclic storms,
Till at the last arose the man;

Who throve and branch'd from clime to clime,
   The herald of a higher race. . . .

As time passes, the poem continues, it falls upon Man to

Move upward, working out the beast,
And let the ape and tiger die.

The wording is carefully neutral, almost until the end. Man's rise is the work of "Time"; but having been granted a higher place, he proves that he can himself "shape and use" the passage of time so as to "move upward," ridding himself of all that is bestial in his being. Only in the last lines—"And let the ape and tiger die"—is it revealed that for man to "move upward" many other species must perish. Tennyson does not exactly celebrate this, but he doesn't bemoan it either: it seems merely inevitable.

When I use the word "species" here, I don't mean only animals. When Victorian writers used the word "Man," they were not necessarily referring to the entirety of the taxonomic category *Homo sapiens*—"the wise ape"—that was invented by Linnaeus in 1758. Even though all members of the class *Homo sapiens* are a single species according to the Linnaean definition, Linnaeus himself also divided the species into various subspecies, according to geography, physical attributes, and so on.[14] In this schema there were many intermediary forms between primates and civilized man, such as gorillas and "savages." It was assumed that the working of evolutionary processes would only broaden the gap between different kinds of men. So, as Darwin wrote in *The Descent of Man*: "At some future period not very distant as measured in centuries, the civilized races of man will almost certainly exterminate and replace throughout the world the savage races."[15]

It is important to note that Darwin did not advocate this outcome, nor did he see it as being in any way desirable. He was famously a liberal, and a passionate abolitionist. At a time when theories that posited different origins for different races were gaining in influence, Darwin was uncompromising in his insistence that all humans shared a single origin.[16] But the destiny of a theory cannot necessarily be decided by its originator, and the fact remains that strands of Darwin's thought did come to be woven into the fabric of a certain kind of racial supremacism that remains influential to this day.[17] Nor can there be any doubt that Darwin shared the belief, then widespread among educated Westerners, that certain human groups were doomed to extinction because of processes that were outside the purview of human agency.[18]

Darwin's views are immaterial, however, because they had no bearing on Tennyson's vision of the ascent of Man. The remarkable thing about Tennyson's poem is that it was written *before* Darwin had published his theory of evolution: *In Memoriam* was completed in 1849, ten years before the publication of *The Origin of Species*. Tennyson was grappling with ideas that were already in circulation among educated Westerners at that time—theories that proposed that species could be transmuted by the impersonal functioning of natural laws, operating without divine intervention. In his poem Tennyson was addressing the challenges that the findings of science would pose for literal, evangelical understandings of the Bible. Science and faith were reconciled in the poem, precisely through the ideas of transmutation and evolution: Man moves "thro' life of lower phase" to become

> . . . a closer link
> Betwixt us and the crowning race

What distinguishes this "crowning race" is that in its hands Nature is "like an open book"; "no longer half-akin to brute," this race is a species that is closer to God:

> That God, which ever lives and loves,
>   One God, one law, one element,
>   And one far-off divine event,
> To which the whole creation moves.

This figuration is hauntingly similar to the image invoked by the young airman Magee, who wrote his poem almost a hundred years later: that of an airman slipping the "surly bonds of earth" to "touch the face of God." But Tennyson extends this line of thinking much further. He sees the ascent of his "crowning race" as coming about by the severing of every kind of earthly tie, through the overcoming of everything that links humanity to other creatures and animals. He even proposes what we might call an "end of history" or an "end of the world":

[a] far-off divine event,
To which the whole creation moves.

This is Man's final ascent, when all creation ends and he is united with God.

THE VIOLENCE CONTAINED in these ideas is almost beyond comprehension. Is it really possible, we can only wonder in disbelief, that the most prominent lyric poet of the Victorian age envisioned the extinction of apes and tigers as a positive step toward Man's evolution into a species that would be a "crowning race"?

What is puzzling about these ideas is that they are counterintuitive. Shouldn't the theory of evolution, and the knowledge that humans are linked to other life-forms by close ties of kinship, have created a sense of familial fellow feeling? Shouldn't the discovery that all humans are descended from shared ancestors have created a sense of fraternal solidarity? While this did happen for some, for many others the idea of evolution did exactly the opposite: it reinforced a belief in the absolute exceptionalism and supremacy of one kind of human—White, Western Man. Evolution came to be seen as an inevitable process of elevating this "crowning race" over all other beings, human and nonhuman.

A belief in human exceptionalism is not by any means unusual. Premodern Christians, Muslims, and many others believed that Man was a species favored by God. Yet none of them ever embraced the idea that Man's advancement should entail the wholesale eradication of other species, and indeed of most humans. Yet by the late nineteenth century these ideas were accepted as mere common sense by a great number of liberal, progressive Westerners.[19] This was particularly true of the classes that happened also to hold the power to implement their beliefs and theories in the real world, through state policy.

It would be idle to deny that some of these ideas are still widely prevalent, and not just in the West. Underlying them is a conception of the world, and of historical time, that sees the Earth not as a nurturer or a life-giver, but as a dead weight whose enveloping ties must be escaped if Man is to rise to a higher stage of being. It is a vision in which genocide and ecocide are seen to be not just inevitable, but instruments of a higher purpose. Indeed, this worldview goes much further than either ecocide or genocide: it envisions and welcomes the prospect of "omnicide," the extermination of everything—people, animals, and the planet itself. The end of the world is seen, as Tennyson puts it, as the "far-off event" that allows Man to realize his true self, as pure Spirit, disencumbered of all fleshly and earthly ties.

These ideas may appear deranged, but they continue to constitute a vital substrate of contemporary imaginaries. Signs of this substrate are everywhere around us: in the evangelical Christian idea of the "Rapture"; in the apocalyptic visions of ecofascists; in the dreams of those who yearn for a world "cleansed" of humanity; and in the fantasies of the billionaires who, having grown tired of this surly Earth and its sullen inhabitants, aspire to create a tamer version of it by terraforming some other planet.[20] Their dream may be wrapped in futuristic cladding, but it is in fact nothing but an atavistic yearning to put in motion once again the processes of terraforming by which settler-colonials turned large parts of the Earth into "neo-Europes."

THE BELIEFS, VISIONS, and projects I have referred to here are all connected by a single, powerful thread: the assumption that planets are inert; that they have no volition and cannot act; that they exist only as resources to be used by those humans who are strong enough to conquer them. These foundational philosophical premises also underlie many academic disciplines and practices, which assume that entities and "resources" are fundamentally inert and possess no agentive properties of their own. Traces of these underpinnings can be detected even in Alfred Crosby's notion of "neo-Europes." Crosby appears to have taken for granted that the transformation of the ecologies of Europe's colonies was a finished project, and that the stability of those landscapes, in their reinvented forms, was assured for the indefinite future.

But is this actually the case?

Today, as we look at the floods, wildfires, and droughts that afflict some of the most intensively terraformed parts of the Earth—Florida, California, the American Midwest, southeastern Australia, and so on—it is hard not to wonder whether those landscapes have now decided to shrug off the forms imposed on them by European settlers.

As we watch the environmental and biological disasters that are now unfolding across the Earth, it is becoming ever harder to hold on to the belief that the planet is an inert body that exists merely in order to provide humans with resources. Instead, the Earth's responses are increasingly reminiscent of the imaginary planet after which the Polish science fiction writer Stanislaw Lem named his brilliant novel, *Solaris*: when provoked by humans Solaris begins to strike back in utterly unexpected and uncanny ways.

In any event it is increasingly clear that the Earth can, and does, act, except that its actions unfold over scales of time that shrink the four-hundred-year gap between 1621 and 2021 to a mere instant, like that which separates the slipping of a boulder on a mountain slope from the landslide that follows. From that perspective the climatic changes of our era are nothing other than the Earth's response to four centuries of terraforming, during which time the project, in its neoliberal guise, has come to be universally adopted by global elites.

These developments are making it ever more evident that many "savage" and "brutish" people understood something about landscapes and the Earth that their conquerors did not. This, perhaps, is why even hardheaded, empirically minded foresters, water experts, and landscape engineers have begun to advocate policies that are based on Indigenous understandings of ecosystems. Experts even have a name, and an acronym, for this now—"Traditional Ecological Knowledge" (TEK).[21] Yet the very name is suggestive of a fundamental misunderstanding: it assumes that Indigenous understandings are usable "knowledge" rather than an awareness created and sustained by songs and stories.

You cannot relate to Gunung Api as the Bandanese did unless you *know* that your volcano is capable of producing meanings; you cannot relate to Dinétah as the Diné did unless the Glittering World glitters for you too.

The planet will never come alive for you unless your songs and stories give life to all the beings, seen and unseen, that inhabit a living Earth—Gaia.

7
Monstrous Gaia

The story of how the Gaia hypothesis got its name has been told many times, and by none other than the man who chose the name: James Lovelock. The story's setting is a bucolic English village called Bowerchalke, in Wiltshire, where Lovelock was living in the late 1960s when the hypothesis was still in gestation. One of Lovelock's neighbors in the village was the writer William Golding, author of that perennial schoolroom favorite, *Lord of the Flies*.

Lovelock would sometimes run into the novelist on his way to the village post office, and on occasion these encounters would turn into long walks, during which he would explain his ideas to Golding. On one such walk Lovelock happened to mention that he was having trouble finding a name that would do justice to his idea of the Earth as a living entity, in which atmospheric, oceanic, and many other systems interacted dynamically.

Golding thought about this for a few days and then suggested that Lovelock name his hypothesis after Gaia, the Greek goddess of the Earth. By his own account Lovelock misheard Golding's suggestion; he thought Golding had said "gyre," meaning a whorl or vortex. But upon being provided with an explanation, Lovelock seized upon "Gaia" with great enthusiasm.

In the ensuing decades Lovelock would develop the Gaia hypothesis in close collaboration with Lynn Margulis, a microbiologist, and eventually their work would bring about a paradigm shift in the Earth sciences. But initially the idea that the Earth is a living entity in which "life maintains the conditions for life" aroused skepticism and even hostility within the scientific community. The very name Gaia was considered objectionable by some.

Lovelock, for his part, probably expected this reaction: in a short essay called "What Is Gaia?" he makes it clear that the name was intended as a provocation.

> Long ago the Greeks . . . gave to the Earth the name Gaia or, for short, Ge. In those days science and theology were one and science, although less precise, had soul. As time passed this warm relation-ship faded and was replaced by the frigidity of schoolmen. The life sciences, no longer concerned with life, fell to classifying dead things and even to vivisection. . . . Now at least there are signs of a change. Science becomes holistic again and rediscovers soul, and theology, moved by ecumenical forces, begins to realize that Gaia is not to be subdivided for academic convenience and that Ge is much more than a prefix.[1]

But Lovelock's provocation was not intended only for the sci-entific community: by calling for the rediscovery of "soul" (*anima* in Latin) in material objects and earthly forces he was conjuring up the specter of "vitalism," or even "animism"—the belief that humans are not the only ensouled beings.[2] And to do this is to vio-late one of the most powerful taboos of official modernity.

The modern conception of matter as inert—or "as an inanimate object of inquiry"—emerged out of several intersecting processes of violence: between Catholics and Protestants; between various Protestant sects; between elite European men and poor women; and, perhaps most significantly, between European colonizers and the Indigenous peoples of the Americas, many of whom believed that earthly forces and material entities of all kinds had innate powers and agency.[3] The struggle over these diametrically opposed views was a metaphysical conflict that mirrored the violence of the terrestrial wars that were then being fought between settlers and natives. The aim of eradicating "the belief that spirit existed in all matter" thus came to be seen as "a final stage of English conquest—over nature, and over those who had improper views of nature."[4]

As the ideologies of modernity were rising to dominance, the war against vitalism would go hand in hand with the expansion of European projects of colonialism and conquest. An essential element of these projects was the idea that only "savages" and "primitives" believe that the Earth—or earthly entities like forests and volcanoes—have qualities that elude human perception. To be "civilized" was to accept that the Earth is inert and machine-like, and that no aspect of it, in principle, can elude human knowledge. A defining characteristic of "savagery," on the other hand, was the "belief in the vitality of natural and celestial objects."[5]

Thus spake John Wesley Powell, the late nineteenth-century geologist, soldier, and explorer after whom Utah and Arizona's Lake Powell is named. Powell, whose views had a lasting influence on American policy toward Native Americans, was so convinced that vitalism and civilization were mutually exclusive that he also said: "Next to teaching them [Indians] to work, the most important thing is to teach them the English language. Into their own language there is woven so much mythology and sorcery that . . . the ideas and thoughts of civilized life cannot be communicated to them in their own tongues."[6]

As this passage makes clear, for eminent men of science like Powell, to believe that the Earth was anything more than an inanimate resource was to declare oneself a superstitious savage—and that, in turn, was tantamount to placing oneself on the waiting list for extinction or extermination. Vitalism, savagery, and extinction were a series in which each term implied the next. Thus in 1883, in a country where freedom of religion was a foundational creed, the US Department of the Interior instituted a Code of Indian Offenses that essentially banned the practice of native religions.[7] Not till the passage of the American Indian Religious Freedom Act, in 1978, were native beliefs legalized.[8]

It is against this background that Lovelock's provocation must be judged: for here he was, a fully paid-up scientist, engineer, and Westerner, threatening to undermine a monumental, centuries-long project of suppression by naming his theory after a goddess—Gaia![9]

WHO WAS GAIA?

The Gaia of the Greeks was by no means the kind of figure that we tend to imagine when we think of an Earth goddess: she was neither a figure of nurture nor a benevolent, motherly deity like the Kichua's Pachamama.[10] In the *Theogony*, the account of the world's beginnings written by Hesiod, Homer's great contemporary, there are many epithets attached to Gaia's name, such as "wide-bosomed," "wide-pathed," "boundless," "bounteous," and "holy." But another epithet that recurs often is "monstrous."[11] Gaia is one of four original beings, a member of a quartet that includes Chaos (the chasm), Tartaros (the depths of the Earth), and Eros, "the most beautiful among the immortal gods."

Gaia gives birth to Uranos and then mates with him, producing many children, all of whom "hated their father from the beginning." And well they might, for no sooner are Gaia's children born than Uranos hides them under her so that they cannot come forth into the light. Gaia tires of this and finally, "groaning within," she conceives a "cunning, evil trick."[12] She makes a serrated sickle out of an indestructible element, adamant, and shows it to her children, saying:

> My children, with a reckless father; if only you agree
> to obey me. We would avenge the evil outrage of this father
> of yours, for he first devised unseemly deeds.

The prospect of angering their father terrifies all of Gaia's off-spring except one—Kronos, "of crooked counsel," who agrees to serve as her accomplice:

> Mother, I promise that I will bring to completion
> this deed, since I do not care for that ill-named father
> of ours. For he first devised unseemly deeds.

On hearing these words, "monstrous Gaia" laughs loudly in her heart and hides Kronos, armed with the adamantine sickle, in a place where he can ambush his father. When Uranos next comes to lie with Gaia, Kronos reaches out with the sickle and cuts off his father's genitals.

But once enthroned, Kronos proves to be no less voracious than his sire: having learned from Gaia that it is his fate to be overthrown by his son, he devours each of the children that his wife, Rheia, bears until at last Gaia intervenes again, and spirits away the last of them, Zeus, who does indeed, with Gaia's counsel, overthrow Kronos and establish himself as the most powerful of the gods.

Gaia, then, is sometimes a wily schemer, almost a trickster, except that her deeds are vast in their scale. But Gaia also suffers, for she is the battleground upon which men and gods act out their strife, leaving her groaning and screaming as the forests burn and the oceans boil.

> And monstrous Gaia was burning all over
> with an ineffable blast and melted like tin heated
> beneath the skill of craftsmen in bellowed crucibles
> or iron, which is the strongest of all things,
> being subdued in the mountain glens by blazing fire,
> melts in the shining earth beneath Hephaestos' hands.
> In this way, Gaia was melting from the flame of the blazing fire.

It is as though Hesiod had an inkling of what was to come.

. . .

ANOTHER LEGEND IN which Gaia plays a trickster-like role is that of the Golden Apples.

The legend goes that when Zeus married Hera, Gaia came bearing a branch of Golden Apples. Hera was so captivated that she begged Gaia to plant the apples in her own garden, in the far west. Once they had been planted, Hera chose the clear-voiced Hesperides to guard them. But as insurance she also appointed another caretaker—Ladon, who is variously described as a dragon or a serpent.

From Gaia's Golden Apples are born the seeds of strife; they are a source of unending temptation and discord. It is this property that gives them the power to intervene in the course of human history; it is a Golden Apple that sets in motion the chain of events that leads to the Trojan War.

In the legend, when Peleus, king of Phthia, marries the sea nymph Thetis, Zeus throws a banquet to which the goddess Eris, or Discord, is not invited. In revenge Eris steals a golden apple from Hera's garden and throws it into the festivities, inscribed with the words: "To the fairest of all."

Three goddesses—Hera, Athena, and Aphrodite—claim the apple and ask Zeus to be the judge. But Zeus refuses and decrees instead that the contest will be judged by a mortal who is famed for his sense of fairness: Paris, son of Priam, King of Troy. So, guided by Hermes, the three goddesses go down to bathe in the spring of Ida before approaching Paris, who is on the slopes of Mount Ida. When Paris is unable to choose between the goddesses on their looks alone, all three try to bribe him with gifts: Hera offers to make him king of Asia and Europe; Athena offers him wisdom and the gift of martial valor; and Aphrodite promises him the most beautiful woman in the world, Helen, wife of Menelaus.

Thus begin the events that lead to the destruction of Troy and the expulsion of the Trojans from their homeland. Behind all of it lies a miraculous fruit—one of Gaia's Golden Apples.

IN THE BIBLE a fruit—which many would come to believe was an apple—is the instrument of humanity's fall from a state of grace.

There are parallel elements in the stories of the Fruit of Knowledge and the Golden Apples: both feature a garden, a serpent, and, of course, an irresistibly tempting fruit. In the biblical story too, the fruit, and the tree that bears it, creates a web of entanglements that spill over from the Earth into human history.

That there was an analogy between the biblical tree of knowledge and the trees of Maluku was evident to Bartolomé Leonardo de Argensola, a seventeenth-century Spanish historian: "The clove," he wrote, ". . . is the precious Commodity which gives Power and Wealth to . . . Kings and causes their wars. This is the fruit of Discord . . . for it there has been, and still is, more fighting than for the Mines of Gold."[13]

In the Indian epic tradition, flowers rather than fruit are objects of overwhelming desire. In the *Mahabharata*, Draupadi comes upon a lotus of miraculous beauty and asks Bhima to fetch her the plant. The resulting quest takes Bhima to the magical mountain of Gandhamadana, where he has a revelatory encounter with Hanumana. This is by no means the only such quest in the *Mahabharata*. Plants, flowers, herbs, and trees recur again and again as objects of desire and admiration.

WHAT ALL THESE stories have in common is that they see humanity as being so closely entangled with the products of the Earth that the past cannot be remembered without them. In modern, scholarly histories, on the other hand, cloves, nutmegs, mace, tobacco, sugarcane, and so on are all resources or commodities, and their fate depends entirely on humans; in other words, they are inert and have no world- or history-making powers of their own.

This approach has many strengths: by reducing all commodities to comparable metrics, a discipline such as economic history, for example, can reveal a great deal about the behavior of prices, consumers, and so on. But the procedures of scholarly history, revelatory though they often are, can sometimes also serve to obscure the extraordinarily complicated ways in which apparently inert resources are enmeshed with human lives and human history. A case in point is opium, a commodity the Dutch began to trade in at about the same time that they were trying to establish monopolies over cloves and nutmegs.

That opium can alleviate pain and induce euphoria has been known since antiquity, and small quantities of the drug have been in circulation for millennia. But it was not till the seventeenth century that opium began to be traded in significant quantities. Once again, the pioneers were the Dutch, who started a commercial traffic in the drug by using it to pay for spices from the Malabar Coast and the East Indies.[14] The VOC's opium operation quickly became one of its chief sources of revenue, enriching many of its highest officials and even the Dutch royal family.[15]

It was the British who took the next step, scaling up the cultivation of opium in India to industrial dimensions, and using it to pay for the East India Company's tea purchases in China. The profits from opium essentially financed the British Raj, while also enriching many British, Indian, and American traders, including a large number of those who came to be known as Boston Brahmins.[16]

The bulk trade in opium was thus a distinctly modern, industrial-age phenomenon—yet ironically, the European and American traders who trafficked in it thought of it as a relic of the "Oriental" past. To them it was a thing that had no relationship with their own age of quickening progress. In their eyes the use of opium was a sign of the degeneracy of "lower" and "fallen" races, people who were on their way to being left behind by history.

Through much of the twentieth century too, opium was stigmatized as an archaism, a thing that belonged to a closed chapter of the past. Synthetic substitutes were sure to replace this plant-based substance, it was assumed; and when that happened, opium would simply disappear into the mists of time, as had other once-valuable resources like gambier and indigo.

But it would seem that opium has a mind of its own, for it has consistently defied these expectations. The current opioid crisis in the US shows that opium is very much with us to this day: it is the proverbial genie that can't be put back in the bottle. Like a virus, opium can change and mutate; and just as viruses have receptors, so does opium: the portals through which it enters history are human greed and pain, despair and misery. The morphine molecule, common to all opiates, seems to actively rebel against attempts to expel it from the human body, inflicting great suffering on those who attempt to do so. How exactly this happens is still unknown, because, as one pharmacologist puts it, opium "just doesn't follow the rules."[17]

The peculiar nature of opium's enmeshment with human life shows that it possesses a power that exceeds its materiality: that it can enter history and have effects upon the world in ways that are not determined by human beings. "Uncanny" is the only word that comes close to describing the inexplicable aspects of the poppy's enmeshment with human life. These enmeshments cannot be accounted for either through the language of resources or by the chemical properties of the flower that goes by the scientific name of *Papaver somniferum*.

"NAMES," WRITES THE Native American botanist Robin Wall Kimmerer, "are the way we humans build relationships, not only with each other but with the living world."[18] The power to name, or rather rename, was thus one of the greatest privileges of empire, because it created the scaffolding of what is now the dominant mode of relating to the living world.

The task of assigning new names to all things began in earnest at about the time that Maluku was being absorbed into the Dutch Empire. While the naming of places was done by European explorers and navigators, the naming of all other things was left to a motley phalanx of "natural philosophers," virtuosi, physicians, and collectors of curiosities that followed on the heels of empire builders like Jan Coen.[19] It was by cataloging, classifying, and (not least) naming the environmental endowments of empires that these specialists made it possible for imperial policy-makers in Europe to decide how best to make use of those resources. It is in this sense that, historically speaking, "science and empire are cause and effect of one another."[20]

The naturalist who would come to be most closely identified with Maluku arrived in Ambon in 1653, thirty-two years after the Banda massacre. He was half German and half Dutch, and his original name was Georg Eberhard Rumpf—although it was under the Latinate honorific Rumphius that he would gain lasting fame.[21]

Rumphius came to Ambon when he was only twenty-six years old; he would spend the rest of his life there, serving the VOC in various capacities, as a soldier, merchant, administrator, advisor, and finally as a naturalist.[22] As with other European naturalists of that era, Rumphius's work was made possible by collaborations with local savants.[23] In the East Indies, these savants were often local women, and in the case of Rumphius his collaborator was his wife, Susanna, whom he met and married a few years after his arrival in Ambon.[24] She was a native-born Ambonese, possibly Eurasian or half Chinese, and was deeply versed in Malukan botanical lore. By all accounts their marriage was a happy one, and they had two daughters and a son together.

But the years of felicity were short for Rumphius; he had not long been married when he was struck by the first of the many misfortunes that would bedevil his life. At the age of forty-three he went blind, possibly because of narrow-angle glaucoma.[25] Then, four years later, in 1674, Susanna and the couple's youngest daughter were killed by a devastating earthquake that struck Ambon on the day of the Chinese New Year. The two women had gone out for a stroll, to observe the festivities in the town's Chinese quarter. They were in a friend's house when the earth began to shake; they tried to run but were killed by a falling wall. "It was full piteous," says an entry in the official register of Ambon's Fort Victoria, "to see that man [Rumphius] sit next to these his corpses, as well as to hear his lamentations concerning both this accident and his blindness."[26] Rumphius would later name an orchid after his wife: *Flos susannae*, which was later given the Linnaean name *Pecteilis susannae*.[27]

The two-term Linnaean system of nomenclature did not yet exist in Rumphius's lifetime, so he followed his own idiosyncratic system of naming. This does not seem to have detracted from the scientific value of his work; the accuracy of his descriptions of the flowers, plants, and sea creatures of Maluku have been vindicated time and again.[28] Indeed, the lack of jargon gives Rumphius's work an unusually poetic, even magical (or vitalist) quality: "His writings have a spirit of sympathy, a fellowship often absent in post-Linnaean indexers."[29]

Would Rumphius have taken kindly to the Linnaean system had it been introduced in his lifetime? It cannot be taken for granted that he would have. Even though the system is now synonymous with "nature" itself, its rise to dominance was by no means natural or uncontested. Indeed, some of its fiercest critics were scholars based in the imperial periphery, as was the case with Rumphius.[30]

The Linnaean system is, without a doubt, a marvelously elegant method of categorization, almost miraculous in its expansiveness. But it was not because it was Nature's twin that it triumphed over its competitors; it was because of a decisive intervention by the Spanish Empire, which ordained, in the mid-eighteenth century, that Linnaeus's binomial system would be adopted by all its botanical expeditions so that they would have common terms and a consistent language.[31] Through the process of consistent naming, all things were to be made comparable so that they could be turned into "useful resources."[32]

Blessed by empires, Linnaeus's system became the foundation of a way of knowing that would claim, from very early on, a monopoly on truth, discounting all other knowledge systems and their methods. Yet, secretly, Western science was often dependent on other ways of knowing. The history of the nutmeg tree includes many stories of such collaborations.

The scientific name of the nutmeg tree, *Myristica fragrans* Houtt., was picked not by Rumphius but by another Dutch botanist whose surname remains connected to it to this day: Martinus Houttuyn. But even after its naming, the identity of the tree, of which there are at least sixteen varieties, continued to confound European botanists.[33] When specimens were smuggled out of Maluku, in 1754, to the French colony of Mauritius (then known as the Isle de France), the question of whether the trees were "true" nutmegs sparked off a series of near-operatic clashes between two rival French botanists and their cliques. Even the metropolitan authorities in faraway Paris were unable to settle the matter.[34] Nor did the botanists in Mauritius have an easy time of keeping the plants alive: nutmeg trees are of two sexes, male and female, and in that era French botanists had complicated feelings about plant sexuality. In the end the trees were saved not by superior European botanical knowledge, but by the practical expertise of an enslaved Bengali gardener by the name of Charles Rama.[35]

Charles Rama's collaboration with French botanists, like countless other similar collaborations between European naturalists and non-Western savants and adepts, shows that different forms of expertise, and different ways of knowing, need not exclude each other; indeed, they can complement and even augment each other. The great Indian mathematician Srinivasa Ramanujan—"the man who knew infinity"—had very little early education in mathematics, and much of it came from his mother, who was a traditional numerologist. This may have contributed to his uncanny affinity with numbers.[36] To this day, Indian physicists and mathematicians have no difficulty in switching between their scientific work and traditional rituals. The same is true of some Native American scientists like Kimmerer, whose *Braiding Sweetgrass* skillfully weaves together different ways of relating to plants—as objects of scientific inquiry *and* as subjects of songs and stories.

Kimmerer tells a story about a plant scientist who goes into the rain forest with an Indigenous guide whose ability to accurately identify various plants is so impressive that the scientist is moved to compliment him on his knowledge. "'Well, well, young man, you certainly know the names of a lot of these plants.' The guide nods and replies with downcast eyes. 'Yes, I have learned the names of all the bushes, but I have yet to learn the songs.'"[37]

The story is not intended to imply that scientists are indifferent to the poetry and wonder of what they observe; quite the contrary. "The practice of doing real science," writes Kimmerer, "brings the questioner into an unparalleled intimacy with nature fraught with wonder and creativity as we try to comprehend the mysteries of the more-than-human world. Trying to understand the life of another being or another system so unlike our own is often humbling and, for many scientists, is a deeply spiritual pursuit."[38]

Yet, even the most sensitive of scientists are prevented, by the conventions of their disciplines, from seeing their objects of study as protagonists in their own right, fully capable of generating forms of narrative and meaning. And in the absence of meaning it sometimes becomes impossible, even for those who are so inclined, to imagine a productive relationship between humans and the world around them.

Another story Kimmerer tells is about a survey she once con-

ducted in her General Ecology class, amongst a group of advanced
students who had learned a great deal about pollution, climate
change, and habitat loss. Many of them had even opted for careers
in environmental protection. Yet when asked for examples of interactions between people and land that were positive rather than
negative, most of them could not think of even *one*.

"I was stunned," writes Kimmerer. "How is it possible that in
twenty years of education they cannot think of any beneficial relationships between people and the environment? Perhaps the negative examples they see every day—brownfields, factory farms, sub-
urban sprawl—truncated their ability to see some good between
humans and earth. As the land becomes impoverished so too does
the scope of their vision."

Reflecting on this, Kimmerer notes: "How can we begin to move
toward ecological and cultural sustainability if we cannot even
imagine what the path feels like?"[39] She adds: "Our relationship
with land cannot heal until we hear its stories. But who will tell
them?"

A NECESSARY FIRST STEP toward telling a story about, say, nutmegs is to leave behind a monoculture of naming that is intended
to make all things comparable: a story in which the principal character is called *Myristica fragrans* Houtt. is never going to take wing.

For the enslaved gardener Charles Rama, as for all Bengali
speakers, the word for nutmeg would have been *jâyaphal*, which
is a contraction of the Sanskrit *jâti-phala*. The precise meaning of
jâti is uncertain, but some scholars believe that it refers to "jas-
mine," or more generally "fragrant flower."[40] There is no doubt at
all, however, about the second element, *phala*, which means "fruit"
(hence "fragrant fruit"). The Sanskrit term *phala* is the root also of
the word for nutmeg in Bandanese, Bahasa Indonesia, and other
Malay languages: *pala*. By contrast, the Dutch word for nutmeg is
nootmuskaat, which, like the English word, comes from the Latin
words for "nut" and "musk" (hence "fragrant nut"); it is the Dutch
word for "mace," *foelie*, that is derived from the Sanskrit *phala*, by
way of Bandanese and Malay.

When I look at a *pala* lying in my palm and think of it as a *jâyaphal*, it is no great stretch to think of it as a tiny planet, or as a maker of history, or as something that hides within itself a vitality that endows it with the power to bless or curse. This possibility is not foreclosed even when I think of it as a "nutmeg" or *nootmuskat*. It is only when I think of it as *Myristica fragrans* Houtt. that those thoughts evaporate and the nut becomes subdued and muted—reduced, as was intended by the Linnaean system, to the status of an inert resource. To think of it then as anything but a commodity seems childlike and fantastical, almost savage.

To imagine that other aspect of the *pala*'s being, in which it enters history as a potent force and a protagonist in songs and stories, it becomes necessary to remember that nutmegs have a hidden side, which always eludes the eye. It is there that songs, poems, and stories reside. If this hemisphere withers, then the other too will eventually lose the meanings that give this tiny planet a place in the webs of life that sustain humanity.

8

Fossilized Forests

Of all commodities none are better suited to being treated as "resources" than those compacted remains of primordial forests that we call "fossil fuels." This is due in no small part to the fact that fossil fuels lend themselves exceptionally well to enumeration, not just in terms of quantity but also because of what they produce: energy. Exactly how many kilowatts a certain quantity of coal, oil, or natural gas will produce can be determined with great precision; exactly how much carbon dioxide will be emitted in the production of that kilowatt can also be determined, with equal precision. It is known, moreover, that the same wattage can be generated *without* producing a similar quantity of greenhouse gases. Since science has established, beyond any doubt, that greenhouse gases pose a dire threat to humanity, it seems self-evident—to me, and to all others who are concerned about this threat—that every effort should be made to move, with the greatest possible urgency, from fossil fuels to renewable sources of energy.

Nor does a changeover to renewable energy seem unachievable: innumerable pathways to such a transition have been charted, and it is perfectly clear now that energy from renewable sources could meet enough of the world's needs to bring about a substantial reduction in global greenhouse gas emissions. Not only is such a transition technically feasible; it could also bring many other benefits, such as new jobs. It has even been suggested that a transition could lead to a new, Earth-friendly industrial revolution.

Yet the fact remains that progress toward a transition has been painfully slow and erratic. Indeed, instead of declining, as is required by the climate emergency, fossil-fuel consumption has kept rising through the first two decades of the new millennium, with only occasional dips. It was not till 2020 that there was a sharp decline—and even this downturn was brought about not by policies or economic considerations, but by a virus that sprang out from the edges of a forest in a remote fastness within boundless Gaia.

Clearly the world has every incentive to phase out fossil fuels and move toward a "greener" economy. Why, then, has it been so slow in advancing along that path?

This question, so essential to the world's future, has been addressed at length by many important thinkers. In general their answers tend to point toward economic systems, especially capitalism and the profit motive: the argument goes that a small number of corporations and individuals, who have reaped vast profits from fossil fuels, are determined to prevent a transition to a less carbon-intensive economy, so that they can go on making money, even if this should entail the destruction of the world. Naomi Oreskes, Erik Conway, Michael C. Mann, and many others have shown that energy corporations have wielded their enormous financial and political power to undermine scientific research on climate change.[1] Nathaniel Rich has shown, similarly, that in the 1970s and 1980s, when American environmental movements were gaining ground, oil corporations used their political power to prevent the US government from adopting policies that would have discouraged the growth of the fossil-fuel industry.[2]

Naomi Klein has gone further, arguing that the problem is capitalism as a global system, especially in its neoliberal avatar.[3] She and many others have demonstrated that the free market, left to itself, will never make a concerted push for the adoption of renewable energy: the profits from fossil fuels are so great as to create enormous incentives for Big Oil and Big Coal to resist such a change.

These arguments are persuasive and well grounded. There is no doubt whatsoever in my mind that capitalism and neoliberalism are powerful obstacles to an energy transition. But it is also clear to me that an exclusive focus on the economy can obscure certain obstacles to an energy transition that are harder to identify because they are not easily enumerable or quantifiable. In order to recognize these obstacles, it is necessary to step outside the framework in which fossil fuels are regarded as resources that are, in principle, similar to other resources that produce energy. In other words, it becomes necessary to identify the properties that make a kilowatt produced by fossil fuels *different* from the same quantity of energy generated by solar panels and windmills. For it isn't only because they produce energy that fossil fuels have come to be established at the core of modern life: it is also because the energy they produce interacts with structures of power in ways that are specific to fossil fuels. In this lies their uncanny vitality.

IT WAS PRECISELY because fossil fuels possess the property of reinforcing structures of power that they triumphed over other sources of energy in the nineteenth century. This is clear from the work of the historian Andreas Malm, who has shown that the standard narrative of the Industrial Revolution—that the invention of coal-powered steam engines by James Watt in 1776 kicked off a rapid transition to a carbon economy in Britain—is simply not true. Through much of the Industrial Revolution, water remained the main energy source for British and American industry.

The reason why coal-powered mills began to edge out their water-powered competitors in the early nineteenth century was not that coal was cheaper or more efficient. Water-powered mills were just as productive, and far cheaper to operate than coal-fired mills. It was for *social* rather than technical reasons that steam-powered machines prevailed: because, for example, coal-mills allowed mill owners to locate their factories in densely crowded cities, where cheap labor was easily available. "The [steam] engine," writes Malm, "was a superior medium for extracting surplus wealth from the working class, because, unlike the waterwheel, it could be put virtually anywhere."[4]

. . .

THE MATERIAL CHARACTERISTICS of oil make it even more potent than coal in its ability to reinforce structures of power. For the ruling classes, coal had one great drawback, which was that it had to be extracted by large numbers of miners, working in conditions that ensured their radicalization; this was why miners were at the forefront of the world's labor movements through the late nineteenth and early twentieth centuries. As Timothy Mitchell has shown, this was one of the reasons why Anglo-American elites decided to engineer a transition from coal to oil as the world's main source of energy. Unlike coal, the extraction and transportation of oil does not require large numbers of workers.[5] It frees capital from local entanglements and allows it to roam the world at will.

In short, fossil fuels have from the start been enmeshed with human lives in ways that tend to reinforce the power of the ruling classes. This dynamic is perfectly expressed by the dual meaning of the English word "power," which combines the idea of energy, "as in a force of nature," with "'power' as in a relation between humans, an authority, a structure of domination."[6]

Energy derived from sources like the sun, air, and water, on the other hand, is imbued with immense liberatory potential. In principle every house, farm, and factory could free itself from the grid by generating its own power. No longer would long power lines and gigantic, leak-prone tankers be needed for the transportation of energy; no longer would workers have to toil in underground mines or in remote deserts and rough seas; there would be no need for the long supply chains required by fossil fuels.

These virtues were evident even in the early nineteenth century. In 1824, the visionary hydraulic engineer Robert Thom advocated water-powered manufacturing for the Scottish town of Greenock with these words: "Here you would have no steam-engines vomiting forth smoke and polluting earth and air for miles around; but on the contrary, the pure 'stream of the mountain,' flowing past in ceaseless profusion, carrying along with it freshness, health and vigor."[7]

For Thom, as for many environmentalists today, green energy was the stuff of utopian dreams—and that, it turns out, was precisely the problem. Andreas Malm's research shows that one of the reasons why steam engines won out over water-powered machines is that water rights were goods of the commons, and mill owners had to enter into complicated negotiations to acquire them. These dealings required "*emotional energy* from which steam power users were entirely free."[8] In contrast, "with engine and boiler the mill-owner could do as he pleased, virtually without let or hindrance."[9]

For mill owners, then, one of the great advantages of steam engines over water-powered machines was that their source of energy—coal—could be acquired for exclusive use in a way that water could not. Since rivers, and the wind, were perpetually circulating through the landscape, they could not be cut up, carted away, and stored as private property.[10]

In short, steam, and thus coal, won out over water precisely because it empowered the dominant classes and was better suited to their favored regime of property.

· · · · ·

THE LIBERATORY POTENTIAL of renewable energy has a very important international dimension as well: if adopted at scale it could transform, indeed revolutionize, the current global order. No longer would countries have to be dependent on unpredictable petro-states; no longer would they have to set aside huge portions of their annual budgets for oil payments; no longer would they have to worry about their energy supplies being disrupted by wars or revolutions in faraway countries; and, perhaps most importantly, no longer would they have to rely on superpowers to keep open the sea channels through which oil tankers must pass.

Why, then, is the world so reluctant to embrace this prospect? To whom might these developments be unwelcome?

Petro-states like Saudi Arabia and Brunei obviously have a clear interest in the continuation of the global fossil-fuel economy, for the simple reason that their own economies are tied to it. But like coal, oil by its very nature has come to be enmeshed with global hierarchies of power in other, more elusive ways, creating vested interests that are neither economic nor enumerable. This has come about because of another aspect of the materiality of petroleum — the simple fact that it must be moved, by ship or pipeline, from its point of extraction to other places. Out of this arises a geopolitical dynamic that leads directly back to the conflicts that revolved around cloves and nutmegs.

9

Choke Points

The fact that Gaia, in her monstrous avatar, decided to distribute fossil fuels very unevenly across the Earth has been central to the emergence of the world's current geopolitical order. From a vitalist point of view, it could be said that the wars of the twentieth century were won as much by the fossilized energy of botanical matter as by particular groups of humans.

In the First World War Germany's lack of oil put it at a huge disadvantage against the Allies, more or less ensuring its defeat. The shortage of oil effectively canceled the technological advantages Germany enjoyed at the start of the war: despite having a large fleet, for instance, it was unable to use its navy effectively because its coal-burning ships needed to refuel every eleven days. Conversely, the assured supply of American oil conferred so great an advantage on Britain and France that "it could be fairly stated that the war was won for the Western allies by tankers."[1] Not for nothing was it said of the First World War that Britain, France, and the United States floated "to victory on a sea of oil."[2]

In the Second World War the shortage of oil was even more critical to the defeat of the Axis powers. The German Luftwaffe was forced to rely on synthetic fuels derived from coal, and these could not provide the high-octane energy that was necessary for high-compression aero engines: "it was largely due to the inferior engines in German aircraft that the Luftwaffe lost the Battle of Britain."[3] The shortage of oil also dictated Germany's war strategy:

it was in order to seize the oilfields of the Caucasus that the German army pushed eastward into the Soviet Union in 1942, leading to a defeat at Stalingrad from which it never recovered. Japan's invasion of the Dutch East Indies was similarly forced by its lack of oil.[4]

In short, over the course of the twentieth century access to oil became the central focus of global geopolitical strategy: for a Great Power, to be able to ensure or hinder the flow of oil was to have a thumb on the jugulars of its adversaries. In the first part of the twentieth century the guarantor of the flow of oil was Britain. After the Second World War, the baton was passed, along with a string of British naval bases, to the United States. The role of guarantor of global energy flows is still crucial to US strategic dominance and to its position as global hegemon.

Today, as Elizabeth DeLoughrey has pointed out, "US energy policy has become increasingly militarized and secured by the Navy, the largest oceanic force on the planet."[5] In the words of the historian Michael Klare, the Iraq War of 2003 marked the transformation of the US military into "a global oil protection service, guarding pipelines, refineries, and loading facilities in the Middle East and elsewhere."[6]

It is important to note that the strategic value of controlling oil flows is only tangentially related to the US's energy requirements. The period in which the American military was turning into "a global oil protection service" was one in which the US was well on its way to reducing its dependence on imported oil. The fact that the US is now self-sufficient in fossil fuels has in no way diminished the strategic importance of oil as an instrument for the projection of power—it is the ability to *deny* energy supplies to rivals that is strategically of central importance.

THE GEOPOLITICAL ARCHITECTURE of oil supports another important American asset: the petrodollar system, which has been described as the "second pillar" of American dominance in the world, and as "the hidden hand of American hegemony."[7]

The petrodollar emerged out of the geopolitical turmoil of the postwar years and the strategic struggles of the Cold War. In 1974, a group of Arab nations imposed an oil embargo in retaliation for the US's support of Israel in the Yom Kippur War. In response President Richard Nixon sent his Treasury Secretary, William Simon, to Saudi Arabia on a vitally important mission. Simon was to offer security guarantees as well as preferential access to American Treasury bonds, in return for which Saudi Arabia would undertake to conduct all its sales of oil in dollars. The mission succeeded, and because of Saudi Arabia's heft in the global oil market, every other oil-producing nation also had to conduct its sales in dollars from then on. As a result, every country that buys oil must first buy dollars, and this cycle has become one of the foundations of the contemporary American economy.

The petrodollar system undergirds the US economy in another very important way: Saudi Arabia helps to finance the federal government's debt by buying vast amounts of Treasury bonds. Exactly how much US debt is in Saudi hands is still unknown, because in the course of the 1974 negotiations King Faisal succeeded in extracting a promise that the figure would be kept secret. But the amount is probably in the region of a trillion dollars: in 2016 the Saudi government threatened to sell 750 billion dollars' worth of Treasury bonds if Congress passed a bill that would have allowed the kingdom to be held liable for the attacks of September 11, 2001. Needless to say, the bill did not pass.

It has been said that the petrodollar regime "is in many respects more important than US military superiority."[8] It is hardly surprising, then, that the US government has repeatedly shown that it will be vigorous in defending the petrodollar regime. Not the least of Saddam Hussein's offenses was that he had begun to trade oil in currencies other than the dollar. Venezuela, under Hugo Chavez, also strayed from the petrodollar regime. That may explain why the US has been so persistent in trying to bring about regime change in that country.

In short: a weakening of the petrodollar regime would mean the loss of an irreplaceable American strategic and financial asset.

THE FACT THAT oil is unevenly distributed, and needs to be conveyed across the oceans, means that its flow can be controlled with relative ease by exerting pressure on a few maritime choke points. And, as it happens, the most important of these choke points are in the Indian Ocean—because one of Gaia's quirks, not unlike that which prompted her to give Maluku its volcanoes and forests, also led her to submerge much of the area around the Persian Gulf under a shallow sea that periodically expanded and contracted in a manner that was perfect for the depositing of plant matter.[9]

As a result, this region now holds the world's largest oil and gas reserves: just as the forests of the Indian Ocean basin produced some of the most valuable commodities of the early modern era, their precursors, in their fossilized forms, continue to undergird the world economy to this day. Of the world's top-ten oil export-ing nations, five are in this region. In order to reach consumers, their energy exports must pass through a handful of maritime choke points. The most important of these are the Strait of Hor-muz (through which flow 40 percent of the world's oil exports), and the Strait of Malacca, which is vital for the transportation of oil to China, South Korea, Japan, and Taiwan—a region that accounts for a larger segment of the world economy than either Europe or North America. Two other locations that are of great strategic importance, because of their position athwart major maritime routes, are the southern tip and the Horn of Africa.

It is surely no coincidence that these are the exact locations that European colonial powers fought over when the Indian Ocean's most important commodities were cloves, nutmeg, and pepper. The Portuguese understood very early that trade in this region could be controlled by seizing the channels where the veins of the Indian Ocean narrow into pulse points. By the middle of the sixteenth century they had their thumbs poised near all of them, with bases in Hormuz, Malacca, Socotra, the tip of Africa, and also Macau, which overlooks another strategically crucial channel: the entrance to the Pearl River. Portugal's Asian capital, Goa, was like the center of a spider's web, connected to every outpost by an in-visible filament.

Building on these foundations, the Dutch seized Malacca and Hormuz, and established a major colony at the Cape of Good Hope, in the seventeenth century. Over the next two centuries the British further tightened the Western grip on the Indian Ocean by colonizing India, Aden, the Malay Peninsula, South Africa, and Hong Kong. With every transition there were minor adjustments of location—Singapore replaced Malacca, and Hong Kong replaced Macau as the port that controlled the Pearl River—but on the whole, the geopolitical continuities created by Gaia's quirky shaping of the Indian Ocean have remained remarkably consistent over time.

None of the Indian Ocean's choke points are under direct Western control today—Hong Kong was the last of them. But they are no longer absolutely necessary, for it is the US military that now watches over the choke points of the region, from an "Empire of Bases" that stretches from Guam and Diego Garcia to a dense patchwork of installations in the Middle East.[10]

This empire may be under American control today, but it is the product of centuries of combined Western effort, going back to the 1500s. What would happen to this vast strategic structure if there were to be a quick, worldwide transition to forms of energy that do not need to be transported across oceans? The answer is obvious: its value would be hugely diminished. China, India, Japan, and other large Asian economies would not need to worry about the Strait of Hormuz or Malacca—they would generate their power on their own soil. One of the great blessings of renewable energy, from an ecological point of view, is that it does not need to be transported across the oceans. But that aspect of its materiality is precisely its greatest shortcoming from a strategic point of view: renewable energy does not flow in a way that makes it vulnerable to maritime power.

The possibility of India or China being able to meet all their energy needs from renewables is distant, at best. Yet both countries clearly have strategic as well as economic reasons for moving in that direction as fast as possible. This, no doubt, is one of the reasons why China has been so quick to establish itself as the world leader in this sector: it is today by far the world's largest oil importer, and in the long run this is its greatest strategic vulnerability.[11]

The same logic applies in reverse to the world's dominant maritime powers—that is to say, the US and its close allies in the Anglo-sphere. If the geopolitical implications of the petroleum economy have created incentives for India, China, and many others to move toward renewables, then they have also created specifically strategic (as opposed to economic) vested interests in the fossil-fuel economy for the world's dominant powers. Simply put, fossil fuels are the foundation on which the Anglosphere's strategic hegemony rests.

The net result is a world turned on its head. Five centuries of history—going back to geopolitical rivalries over the control of cloves, nutmegs, and pepper—have given the world's most "advanced" countries a strategic interest in perpetuating the global fossil-fuel regime. Conversely, this history has given rising powers like China and India an important strategic incentive to move to renewables.

TERNATE AND TIDORE, the islands that were for millennia the centers of the world's clove trade, are both dominated by beauti-fully shaped, conical volcanoes that rise to heights of over a thou-sand meters. From the air, flying over the narrow channel that sep-arates Ternate from Tidore, the two islands present a breathtaking sight, with their twin volcanoes soaring above the turquoise blue water, their towering craters encircled by halos of cloud. The dense greenery of their slopes is broken only by dark streaks of solidified lava and the rust-red roofs of the picturesque little settlements that cling to the skirts of their volcanoes.

The islands' idyllic appearance is not the least of the reasons why it is difficult to think of them as being pivotal to world history; at first sight they seem to be untouched by the grimy workings of time.

Then there is the matter of their remoteness. In an age of shrunken distances, Ternate and Tidore are still difficult to get to. They are separated from Indonesia's capital by two time zones and some 3,500 kilometers. To reach them by sea, from Jakarta, takes weeks. Flights are few, and most of them require a change of planes in northern or southern Sulawesi, in either Manado or Makassar.

If ever there were a periphery, far removed from the great global centers of history, where would it be if not here?

Yet these spice islands exercised such a powerful hold on the Western imagination that every European navigator of the early modern era had their sights trained on them. The Portuguese reached Ternate in 1512, and it was there that they built Maluku's first European fort, in 1522. Originally named São João Baptista de Ternate, it is now known as Benteng [Fort] Kastella.

Through the sixteenth century, the fort of São João Baptista de Ternate would be one of the pivots of global geopolitics. A string of European luminaries passed through its walls: St. Francis Xavier arrived by way of Goa, in 1547, and one of his converts, a rebel queen called Nukila, became a figure of legend not only in the Moluccas (where she is known as Rainha Buki Raja) but also in Europe: the Jacobean dramatist John Fletcher was inspired to write a play about her in 1647 titled *The Island Princess*. Another visitor who came to Ternate by way of Goa was Luis de Camões, author of the Portuguese national epic, *The Lusiads*, in which the islands' names are invoked in these lines:

Tidore see! Ternate, whence are roll'd
(Holding black Night a Torch) thick Plumes of Fame![12]

The power of the clove, and the geopolitical importance of Maluku in the sixteenth and seventeenth centuries, is evident also in the ruined fortifications that lie scattered all over Ternate and the surrounding islands. Quite possibly there is no corner of the Earth that contains so dense a concentration of castellations from the early modern era.[13] Built by the Portuguese, Spanish, and Dutch, the remnants of these forts bear eloquent witness to the astonishing energies that were once generated by the rivalry for spices.

The picturesqueness of these ruins belies the purpose for which they were built: to reduce the islands to what Giorgio Agamben calls "states of exception." Over the centuries, wave after wave of violence flowed out of these forts, engulfing the islands' inhabitants. Ternate's Fort Kastella is, to this day, indelibly associated with a killing that occurred in 1570, when the Portuguese lured the then-reigning Sultan of Ternate into the fort and murdered him. The infuriated islanders then besieged the fort for five years and ultimately forced the withdrawal of the Portuguese.

Today, those events are commemorated by a monument that stands at the center of the ruined fort. The monument's plinth has four sides, each of which has a mural etched on it: one depicts the Sultan being stabbed in the back by a Portuguese soldier; in another a row of Portuguese soldiers bow their heads before the islanders' swords.

The most striking part of the monument, however, is the figure that sits atop the tall plinth: a pink and yellow sculpture of a clove.

The structure seems bizarre at first, so rare is it for a historical memorial to be dominated by a botanical icon. But the overall effect is strangely moving precisely because of its unexpectedness: in raising the clove above the human scenes depicted on the plinth, the monument places a nonhuman entity squarely at the center of Ternate's history. It is an acknowledgment of the role of botanical products in shaping the history of the Indian Ocean.

· · ·

THE GEOPOLITICAL IMPORTANCE of the Indian Ocean basin is due in no small part to the concentrations of population that surround it: roughly three out of every five people in the world live in a country that adjoins these waters. The situation was probably similar in the sixteenth and seventeenth centuries. Indeed, in all likelihood the only era in which the global distribution of population was differently weighted was when Europe was going through a period of phenomenal demographic expansion, during the long nineteenth century.

The Indian Ocean basin was also, historically, the main theater of the world's economic activity. Again, as with the distribution of population, this was not the case in the nineteenth century, and much of the twentieth, when the planet's economic center of gravity moved to the Atlantic. But that began to change in the late twentieth century, and the Indian Ocean is now once again the

FIGURE 4. Clove-topped monument at Fort Kastela, Ternate Island. Photograph by the author.

principal theater of the world's economic activity: "one-third of the world's bulk cargo, 50% of the world's container traffic and 70% of crude and oil products pass through Indian Ocean sea lanes."[14]

But manufacturing was also historically concentrated in this region, especially in India and China. In this too the world is now reverting to the historical norm, and this has created some striking parallels between the early modern era and the present day, especially in regard to geopolitics and trade. Consider, for example, the phenomenon known as the "logistics revolution."[15]

Originally a military concept, logistics has now become so central to business practices that it has taken the fusion between trade and war to an entirely new level. The logistics revolution was set in motion by the invention of the shipping container, an American military innovation of the Second World War. Containers passed into commercial use in the 1950s, and in the ensuing decades they were a critical factor in generating a staggering expansion in transoceanic trade. In 1973 ships transported 4 million standardized containers; in 2010 that figure had risen to 560 million. Today 90 percent of all global trade, and 95 percent of US-bound cargo, moves by ship.

These developments have been accompanied by equally dramatic changes in processes of production: no longer located at single sites, factories now consist of supply chains that extend across the planet and are logistically coordinated from minute to minute, so that they can respond instantaneously to fluctuations in demand. Not for nothing does a leading courier company trumpet the slogan: "Logistics is the force that enables the modern economy."

But these long supply chains also make the modern economy much more vulnerable to disruption. In turn, this has generated security imperatives that have come to be centered on so-called "logistics cities," after a model pioneered by Dubai.

The "logistics city" typically consists of a highly securitized distribution hub with a tightly controlled labor force. Thus Dubai Logistics City, which opened shortly after the start of the US-led "War on Terror," offers a militarized cocoon of safety to corporations while at the same time denying its workers even the most basic rights—all in the name of security.

Basra Logistics City provides an even better example of this new kind of urban space. The city is located near Iraq's only deep-water port, Umm Qasr, which has long been a site of great strategic significance. After the start of the second Iraq War, in 2003, this port became the funnel through which US forces were supplied. It was also the site of Camp Bucca, which was in many ways the forerunner of Abu Ghraib: at one time it was the largest US military detention center in Iraq, with 22,000 detainees.

Camp Bucca was gifted to Iraq in 2010 and was rebranded soon afterwards as "Basra Logistics City." Today this city is one of the world's largest petroleum hubs, run by an American corporation that has been exempted from all corporate taxes and fees. The corporation is also entitled to employ an entirely foreign workforce, few of whom enjoy any rights. The city is of course heavily fortified and closely guarded, and (as is the case with most logistics cities) its protection is provided by private security corporations.

The model of the logistics city is now increasingly being adopted in North America: workers in major logistics hubs like Oakland and Vancouver also have to go through very extensive (and racially slanted) processes of security screening and are forced to sign away many of their rights. In effect, wherever they exist, logistics cities are "states of exception" outside the normal rule of law. Ironically, many of these cities—like Dubai, Basra, Singapore, and Oakland— are also exceptionally vulnerable to climate change.

Modern "logistics cities" may be new in appearance, but they are, of course, directly descended from the slave forts, trading posts, and "company towns" of the Dutch and English East India Companies. They are in fact the very apotheosis of Jan Coen's dictum: "No war without trade, no trade without war." In effect, the state of exception that was imposed on the islands of Maluku by European colonists is now slowly spreading across the globe.

It is no accident that the logistics city was pioneered in Asia; over the last three decades, the Indian Ocean region has witnessed a phenomenal rise in both trade and conflict. It takes only a glance at a map to see that most of the world's deadliest conflicts are clustered around the shores of the Indian Ocean.[16] Many of today's fastest-growing militaries are also in the Indian Ocean region—for example, those of Saudi Arabia, India, Oman, and Indonesia.

Even more striking is the list of countries that spend the most on their militaries in relation to their means: the list is topped by Oman, and includes several other countries of the Indian Ocean basin. Nor is the military expansion within the region restricted to the countries that are located there. The US has many bases in these waters, and China too is rapidly expanding its presence there. In effect this region has become both battlefield and sweatshop — and sadly, the processes that have created this condition are only likely to intensify in years to come.

It is hard to escape the conclusion that the Indian Ocean basin is now the chief theater of the planetary crisis.

THE DISCUSSION OF climate change, as of every other aspect of the planetary crisis, tends to be dominated by the question of capitalism and other economic issues; geopolitics, empire, and questions of power figure in it far less. One reason for this is that the modern citizen has become, almost unconsciously, *Homo economicus*: "Not only has the influence of Economy spread throughout the world," writes the philosopher of economics Jean Dupuy, "it has taken over our very ways of thinking about the world."[17]

The hold of the economy on the modern imagination has progressed to the point that capitalism has come to be seen as the prime mover of modern history, while geopolitics and empire are regarded as its secondary effects. Yet it is a simple fact that the era of Western military conquests predates the emergence of capitalism by centuries. Indeed, it was these conquests, and the imperial systems that arose in their wake, that fostered and made possible the rise to dominance of what we now call capitalism. "The genocide of Amerindian peoples," it has been said, "was the beginning of the modern world for Europe: without the despoiling of the Americas, Europe would never have become more than the backyard of Eurasia, the home continent of civilizations that were much richer. . . . No pillage of the Americas, no capitalism, no Industrial Revolution, thus perhaps no Anthropocene either."[18]

As this passage makes clear, colonialism, genocide, and structures of organized violence were the foundations on which industrial modernity was built. "War is the father of all things," said Heraclitus, and there is plenty of evidence to show that this was true also of the Industrial Revolution, a major driver of which was the British weapons industry.

Because of its insatiable appetite for weaponry and warships the British government played a "major role in the creation and employment of arguably the most iconic developments of the industrial revolution, including the steam engine, copper sheathing, and interchangeable-parts manufacturing."[19] Armaments manufacturers with close connections to the state also played a critical role in promoting technological change: many key innovations were incubated in their factories, and they even provided the funds for the work of innovators like Priestley, Boulton, Watt, and Keir.[20]

The vital connection between war and trade was of course perfectly well understood by early empire builders like Jan Coen. Not till the eighteenth century did this connection come to be obscured by a liberal myth in which war and conquest were seen as aberrations that had nothing to do with what we now call the economy. In fact, as the historian Priya Satia notes: "Violence committed abroad, in service of imperial expansion, was central to the making of capitalist modernity."[21] The forever wars of today show that not much has changed.

Another of the deeply rooted myths that surround capitalism is the belief that the essential features of the market economy arose out of historical developments that were endogenous to the core regions of Europe. Equally deeply embedded is the idea that capitalism represents a radical break with Europe's feudal past, being founded on free rather than coerced labor—hence its potential for progress and innovation.

The evisceration of these assumptions is one of the most important achievements of what Cedric J. Robinson identified as the Black Radical Tradition. Starting with W. E. B. Du Bois, the thinkers of this tradition have repeatedly shown that colonial conquest, slavery, and race were essential to the emergence of capitalism as a system. As Robinson saw it, the mass enslavement of Amerindians and Africans that started in the sixteenth century was actually an amplification of the preexisting practices of states like Venice, Genoa, Portugal, and England, which had long traded in slaves from the peripheries of Europe—Ireland, eastern Europe, the Caucasus, the Slavic lands, and so on. With the conquest of the Americas those patterns of enslavement mutated into far larger, more complex, and more brutal systems, engulfing principally Amerindians and Africans: it was their labor, forcibly extracted within the confines of mines and plantations, that produced the precious metals and commodities—sugar, alcohol, tobacco, cotton, and so on—that made the emergence of capitalism possible in the eighteenth and nineteenth centuries. "From whatever vantage point one chooses," writes Robinson, "the relationship between slave labor, the slave trade, and the weaving of the early capitalist economies is apparent. Whatever were the alternatives, the point remains: historically, slavery was a critical foundation for capitalism."[22]

The term that Robinson used to describe this global, racially inflected system of production was "racial capitalism," and the VOC's remaking of the Banda Islands after the massacre of 1621 illustrates, with an instructive clarity, the appropriateness of this term.[23]

Of the fundamentally capitalist nature of the VOC there can be no doubt: it was one of the world's first limited-liability, joint-stock corporations; it had a highly developed system of accounting and was quick to adopt new technologies; it was, in every way, an entity driven by capitalist forms of rationality in its pursuit of profit.[24] The Company's refashioning of the economy and society of the Bandas was completely consistent with its role as a pioneer of capitalism: the system that it put in place in the archipelago was an early form of industrialized agriculture, "combining capital, land, labor, and technology in a rationalized mix, with the purpose of achieving large-scale, profitable agricultural production."[25]

Yet this form of economic rationality was predicated on armed conquest, the elimination of natives, and the creation of a racialized social structure similar to that of European colonies in the Americas, with a dominant Euro-descended minority ruling over a majority of enslaved Asians. In no way can the role of unfree labor in the functioning of this otherwise rationalized economy be explained away as an archaism or a holdover from the past; not only was it a foundational aspect of the project—it was a sign, precisely, of its modernity. The Banda version of "racial capitalism" would change over time, as the dominant minority became more hybrid, but its basic structure lasted for almost two and a half centuries, well into the modern era—that is to say, until 1868, when slavery was banned in the Dutch East Indies.[26]

The history of the Banda Islands serves as an important reminder of the place of conquest and geopolitical dominance in the history of capitalism. Early joint-stock corporations like the VOC and the EIC were entities that combined the functions of warfare and trade in accordance with Jan Coen's famous dictum. This combination of functions was reinforced when capitalism developed a formal economic doctrine in the ideology of "Free Trade." This complex of ideas is as much a geopolitical as an economic ideology: it has served as a rationale for war from the time of the First Opium War, and continues to do so to this day. Its advocates see no contradiction between their belief in the absolute autonomy of free markets and their embrace of state intervention in the form of war. Capitalism is, and has always been, a war economy, repeatedly rescued from collapse by geopolitical conflagrations, as was the case after the Great Depression.

In short, capitalism was never endogenous to the West: Europe's colonial conquests and the mass enslavement of Amerindians and Africans were essential to its formation. Nor was it based mainly on free labor—not even in the nineteenth and twentieth centuries, when many of the raw materials required by Western factories were produced by non-White workers under conditions of coercion, if not outright slavery. In the final analysis, it was the military and geopolitical dominance of the Western empires that made it possible for small minorities to exercise power over vast multitudes of people: over their bodies, their labor, their beliefs, and (not least) their environments. In that sense it was capitalism that was a secondary effect of empire, as is so clearly visible in the VOC's remaking of the Banda Islands.

Why then does capitalism so often come to be abstracted from its wider geopolitical contexts? Cedric Robinson suggests, obliquely, that "the preoccupation of Western radicalism with capitalism as a system" is a way of avoiding the real "nastiness." The implication, I think, is that Western intellectual and academic discourse is so configured that it is easier to talk about abstract economic systems than it is to address racism, imperialism, and the structures of organized violence that sustain global hierarchies of power.[27]

Robinson's diagnosis bears directly on the rapidly growing body of literature that places capitalism at the center of the planetary crisis: this is, in a sense, a new iteration of a Western radical tradition that has long assumed, in Cedric Robinson's words, that "all the social and historical processes that matter" are endogenous to the West.[28] Thus, for instance, it is often said that "it is easier to imagine the end of the world than the end of capitalism."[29] It is telling that this aphorism has now attained the status of received wisdom—because it takes only a moment's reflection to realize that it is patently untrue. The majority of the world's population did not live in capitalist societies for much of the twentieth century. Even in the West the normal functioning of capitalism was suspended for years, during the two world wars. What has never been suspended, since the sixteenth century, are the dynamics of global empire; indeed, they were at the root of both world wars. Imperial powers, even as they fought each other in Europe, would often collaborate in the colonies to ensure that European dominance would continue afterwards.

That which is really harder to imagine than the end of the world is the end of the absolute geopolitical dominance of the West. Yet it is precisely this prospect that now looms, adding a further dimension of uncertainty to the planetary crisis.

10
Father of All Things

The role that fossil fuels play in war-making is another, mon-strously vital, aspect of their enmeshment with structures of power and forms of violence.

That modernity established a directly transitive relationship between economic growth and fossil fuels is often acknowledged. What tends to pass unremarked is that exactly the same equa-tion holds true for fossil fuels in relation to war-making.[1] In other words, a country's ability to project military force is directly con-nected to the size of its carbon footprint—and this has been true since the early nineteenth century.

This transitivity was established early in the nineteenth century, and it gave the British Empire an insuperable advantage, especially on the seas. The British expeditionary force that set sail for China in 1840, at the start of the First Opium War, was insignificant in size, consisting of a couple of dozen warships and around 4,000 fighting men. But this small force was able to inflict a series of resounding defeats on the army and navy of the Qing Empire. This was made possible, in no small part, by a secret weapon: a steam-powered battleship called the *Nemesis*, the first of her kind to venture into the Indian Ocean. The steamer lived up to her name in battle after battle, destroying entire fleets with ease. That the Chinese navy was badly led and ill-equipped was immaterial; the greatest admirals of the age of sail would have fared no better: "Drake, De Ruyter and Nelson, with all their skill or experience," it has been observed, "could have done nothing against one steam man-of-war."[2]

The *Nemesis* was one of the harbingers of a new era in which fossil fuels would become central to warfare and the projection of military power. Since then the use of fossil fuels in war-making has risen in a steep curve. During the Second World War the American military's consumption of petroleum amounted to one gallon of petroleum per soldier per day; during the first Gulf War this rose to four gallons per soldier per day; in the recent wars in Iraq and Afghanistan, the rate of consumption surged to sixteen gallons per soldier per day.[3]

Today the Pentagon is the single largest consumer of energy in the United States—and probably in the world.[4] The US military maintains vast fleets of vehicles, ships, and aircraft, and many of these consume huge amounts of fossil fuels. A non-nuclear aircraft carrier consumes 5,621 gallons of fuel per hour; in other words, these vessels burn up as much fuel in one day as a small midwestern town might use in a year. But a single F-16 aircraft consumes a third as much fuel in one hour of ordinary operations—around 1,700 gallons. If the plane's afterburners are engaged, it consumes two and a half times as much fuel per hour as an aircraft carrier—14,400 gallons.[5] The US Air Force has around a thousand F-16s, and they are but a small part of the air fleet. Needless to add, battle tanks, armored cars, Humvees, and so on also require large amounts of fuel. Nor are these machines idle in peacetime; many of them are in constant use, not just for purposes of training and maintenance, but also because the US's nine hundred domestic military installations need to be connected to its network of around a thousand bases in other countries.[6]

In the 1990s the three branches of the US military consumed approximately 25 million tons of fuel per year. This was more than a fifth of the country's total consumption, and "more than the total commercial energy consumption of nearly two thirds of the world's countries."[7] During the years of the Iraq War, the US military was consuming around 1.3 billion gallons of oil annually for its Middle Eastern operations alone. That was more than the annual consumption of Bangladesh, a country of 180 million people.[8] These activities come with other environmental costs as well, because the operation of military equipment requires the use of many kinds of toxic chemicals like thinners, solvents, pesticides, and so on. As a result, the Department of Defense "generates 500,000 tons of toxic waste annually, more than the top five US chemical companies combined, and it is estimated that the armed forces of the major world powers produce the greatest amount of hazardous waste in the world."[9]

This does not include the emissions and waste products that are generated in the process of constructing weapons, warships, and warplanes. Nor does it take account of the rapid expansion of another sector of the military: defense contractors, whose presence is growing quickly around the globe.

But the US Department of Defense is by no means the only military establishment that is dependent on vast quantities of fossil fuels. This is true also of every major and minor power around the world. The armed forces of China, Saudi Arabia, Russia, Turkey, and India are expanding very rapidly, and they are all spending huge amounts of money on energy-intensive systems.

It is instructive, in this regard, to compare the world's military expenditures with its spending on climate change mitigation. At the UN climate summit in Copenhagen in 2009, it was agreed that wealthy countries would channel $100 billion a year to poorer nations, to help them cope with the impacts of climate change. But the Green Climate Fund set up by the UN succeeded in raising only $10.43 billion and is now running out of money: it never came close to being funded at the level envisaged at the summit.[10] In that same period the world's annual military expenditure has risen from slightly above $1.5 trillion to almost $2 trillion.[11] The total costs of the US's post-9/11 wars have been estimated as over $6 trillion.[12]

"Militarization," it has been said, "is the single most ecologically destructive human endeavor."[13] Yet the subject is so little studied that, according to three leading scholars in the field, "research on the environmental impacts of militarism [is] non-existent in the social sciences."[14] Of the scholars who do study the subject, several are associated with the so-called "treadmill of destruction" school of sociology.[15] One of the consistent findings of this school is that while the "military-industrial complex" is, of course, closely connected to the economy, it is by no means subordinate to it, because it generates its own imperatives and follows its own logic.[16] Indeed, not only is the military itself a major driver of the economy; it forms the protective outer shell that allows capitalism to function.

As far back as 1992, the Union of Concerned Scientists warned that humanity faced a stark choice between spending its resources on war and violence, or on preventing catastrophic environmental damage. The report was signed by 1,700 scientists, including the majority of Nobel Prize winners in the sciences.[17] In 2017 the warning was reissued, and this time it was signed by more than 15,000 scientists: it concluded that the state of the world was even worse than before.

The first UCS report attracted a good deal of attention; the second one passed almost unnoticed.

THAT THE GLOBAL CLIMATE is changing because of human activity is not a matter of dispute for the military establishments of the West; they have all incorporated climate disruptions into their planning for the future. They have also commissioned innumerable studies and reports on the subject, with the Pentagon leading the way. Nor did the Pentagon show any signs of wavering in its acknowledgment of the reality of climate change, even under intense political pressure from the Trump administration.[18]

That this should be so is hardly surprising, since much of the early evidence for climate change came from scientific institutions funded by the US Department of Defense: the first ice-core samples, for instance, were taken from the Arctic by the US military early in the Cold War. The impetus for the founding of many other important meteorological, geological, and oceanographic institutions also came from the Cold War; the same is true for the funding of the supercomputers that are now essential to climate science.[19] The US military was thus well ahead of other organizations in its understanding of the threat of climate change.

As America's largest employer and real estate owner, the US Department of Defense has long been directly exposed to the impacts of global warming—perhaps more so than any other institution on the planet. Many of its bases are situated on coastlines and islands, and are therefore threatened by rising sea levels and intensifying storms. The US Navy's East Coast hub at Norfolk, Virginia—the largest naval station in the world—is already prone to flooding, and much of it will be submerged before the end of the century; the nearby Air Force base at Langley is similarly expected to be subject to almost daily flooding in years to come.[20] Some crucial US bases overseas are also likely to be swamped in the coming decades, the most important of them being the naval station on the low-lying island of Diego Garcia, in the Indian Ocean.

Sea-level rise is by no means the only climate threat confronting the US military; many inland bases are also dealing with other climate-related problems. In 2018 Hurricane Michael struck the Tyndall Air Force base in Florida with great force, damaging seventeen jets, each worth a third of a billion dollars. Other inland bases face threats that include permafrost melt, rain bomb events, wildfires, heatwaves, and prolonged drought. So extensive are these threats that in 2019 the Department of Defense reported that dozens of its installations were already being affected by climate change: 53 had been hit by recurrent flooding, 43 by drought, 36 by wildfires, and 6 by desertification.[21]

A threat of a different sort lies in the military's massive operational dependence on fossil fuels. During the recent wars in Afghanistan and Iraq, large convoys of trucks had to wind their way along dangerous desert roads to supply bases in the interior with fuel. It was these extended supply lines that made the "improvised explosive device" so lethally effective: a cheap, easily made weapon, assembled from the detritus of industrial civilization, the IED was able to tie down the world's most powerful and technologically advanced army.

Among military planners these attacks have deepened long-standing anxieties about the operational vulnerabilities that result from a heavy dependence on hydrocarbons. Because of these concerns, the Pentagon has long been a leader in funding research and development in alternative energy technologies; it has also been quick to adopt solar and wind power whenever possible. Yet even though the Department of Defense has, at times, succeeded in lowering its total consumption of fossil fuels, it has not found a way of severing the primal bond between fossil fuels and military power that came into being in the early nineteenth century: every time the Pentagon fights a war, its consumption of hydrocarbons surges. Nor is it easy to conceive of that bond being broken without the invention of a new means of powering helicopters and supersonic jets: in some years no less than 70 percent of the Pentagon's operational energy use is for jet fuel.[22]

Indeed, the predicament of the US Department of Defense is a refraction of the quandary that now confronts the world's status quo powers: how do you reduce your dependence on the very "resources" on which your geopolitical power is founded? How do you reduce the fossil-fuel consumption of a gargantuan military machine that exists largely to serve as a "delivery service" for hydrocarbons?

The US military's positive response to the findings of climate science is sometimes welcomed by those who regard the denialism of the political sphere as the primary obstacle to mitigatory action on global warming. But this is to mistake the disease for the cure. The job of the world's dominant military establishments is precisely to *defend* the most important drivers of climate change—the carbon economy and the systems of extraction, production, and consumption that it supports. Nor can these establishments be expected to address the unseen drivers of the planetary crisis, such as inequities of class, race, and geopolitical power: their very mission is to *preserve* the hierarchies that favor the status quo. No one has ever stated this more clearly than George Kennan, one of the architects of the postwar strategic order: "We have about 50 percent of the world's wealth," he told the leaders of the US in 1948, "but only 6.3 percent of its population. In this situation, we cannot fail to be the object of envy and resentment. Our real task in the coming period is to devise a pattern of relations which will permit us to maintain this position of disparity. To do so, we will have to dispense with all sentimentality and day-dreaming; and our attention will have to be concentrated everywhere on our immediate national objectives."[23]

At the same time, it is also true that American institutions produce the bulk of the global research on climate change. Moreover, the US is home to more environmental organizations and activists than any other country. Surveys also show that a growing majority of Americans are concerned about climate change. These counterbalancing factors suggest that significant change is possible, even on geopolitical issues. One possible model could be the 1963 Limited Test Ban Treaty, which was signed by the US and the USSR at the height of the Cold War. This pact, it is worth recalling, was simultaneously "the first arms control agreement as well as the first environmental treaty."[24]

THE REDUCTION OF greenhouse gas emissions is at best a minor issue for military planners in relation to climate change. A senior officer once expressed this succinctly at a community hearing in Virginia: "We are in the business of protecting the nation, not the environment."[25]

The military's climate-related plans are mainly oriented toward dealing with the conflicts that global warming will create or exacerbate: for instance, struggles over water; regional wars; terrorism; and mass movements of people caused by hurricanes and desertification, droughts and flooding.

Reading these plans (there are many posted on the internet) is an instructive exercise.[26] The most striking thing about them is that they take the acceleration of climate change as a given, more or less assuming that there will be no concerted mitigatory action in regard to global greenhouse gas emissions. They assume also that the effects of climate change as a "threat multiplier" will only continue to grow more severe, requiring more and more military interventions.

The list of climate-related security threats is very long, partly because it includes many issues that would not, until recently, have been considered military matters at all.[27] Dealing with migrants and refugees, for instance, was once squarely within the sphere of civilian governance. Today, whether in the waters around Australia, or in the Mediterranean, or along the US's southern border, or on India's border with Bangladesh, migration is largely in military and paramilitary hands.

Dealing with natural disasters was also once largely in the realm of civil society. There was a time, not so long ago, when the people who were first on the scene after earthquakes and cyclones were volunteers from charities, religious organizations, and relief groups, and of course civilian officials and police officers. It is only in the last couple of decades that military and paramilitary personnel have come to be thought of as "first responders." This has advanced to the point where civilian volunteers are sometimes explicitly barred from entering disaster-hit areas in the US, as happened after Hurricane Katrina.

Not only do such disasters provide a rationale for military intrusions into new spaces; they also supply a new humanitarian justification for military expansion in general. Military planners have even begun to co-opt the language and tactics of social movements, for purposes of recruitment and in order to expand their policy reach.[28]

It may seem natural today that military and paramilitary personnel should lead the response to disasters. But there is no intrinsic reason why this should be so: civil society organizations like Médecins sans Frontières, Oxfam, and many others have all the necessary skills to act as first responders. If they lack aircraft and ships, it is only because no international mechanisms exist for making such resources available to them. It is because of a political choice, then, that disasters are being militarized, a choice that derives ultimately from a wider process whereby many societies have become saturated with militarism.[29]

That disaster relief is increasingly provided by organizations with massive carbon footprints is more than an irony: it creates a chain of consequences whereby disasters will accelerate disasters. It also ensures that disaster relief will itself become an arena for military competition. This dynamic was already on display in 2013, during the world's response to Typhoon Haiyan, when more than two dozen countries sent military contingents to the Philippines.

The largest military presence by far was the American: the US Navy deployed an aircraft carrier, a naval strike group, 66 aircraft, and some 13,400 personnel there. This is, no doubt, a forerunner of things to come, especially in the Indian Ocean basin, with its dense concentrations of population and its susceptibility to disasters.

Was humanitarian concern the only reason for the huge military deployments after Typhoon Haiyan? Or was projection of power also a factor? It is worth recalling that when a similar disaster occurred in 2017, when Hurricane Maria devasted Puerto Rico—an American territory—the US military's response was on a much smaller scale than it was for Typhoon Haiyan. Nor does the US consider humanitarianism a sufficient reason to allow foreign disaster-relief contingents to enter its own territories, even at times when its forces are unable to deliver sufficient quantities of aid to the victims, as happened after Hurricane Katrina and Hurricane Maria.

Climate-related disasters are expanding the military footprint in other ways as well. After Hurricane Katrina, for instance, President George W. Bush and other American politicians frequently compared the disaster to a nuclear attack. Through this framing, the event came to be absorbed into a much older nuclear discourse that has long been used to increase military expenditure, even as funding for public welfare was declining.[30]

In effect climate-related disasters have themselves become a contributing factor in the steep increase in military spending that is under way around the world.

To look these facts in the face is to recognize that it is a grave error to imagine that the world is not preparing for the disrupted planet of the future. It's just that it's not preparing by taking mitigatory measures or by reducing emissions: instead, it is preparing for a new geopolitical struggle for dominance.

IT IS INCREASINGLY CLEAR today that a transition, albeit partial, in energy regimes is not only possible but inevitable. It is hardly surprising, then, that a great deal is being written about the economic and technological implications of this transition. By contrast, there is far less discussion (at least in public) of the geopolitical repercussions of this transition, although they will also be momentous. How, for instance, will Washington adjust to the decline of the petrodollar as an instrument for the projection of power? How will Saudi Arabia, Qatar, and the United Arab Emirates, which have amassed enormous influence in Washington through the skillful use of money and diplomacy, respond to the prospect of a diminution in their geopolitical heft? How will the United States reconcile its enormous investments in Middle Eastern military and strategic assets with the shrinking importance of that region's energy exports?

It is difficult, if not impossible, to predict where these long-term processes will lead. What is certain, however, is that a transition in energy regimes will also entail a transition in geopolitical regimes, whereby the status quo powers—most prominently the countries of the Anglosphere and the energy superpowers of the Gulf—will need to adjust to conditions that will tend to dilute their current dominance. How, and indeed if, they will be able to adjust to those changed conditions is one of the great unknowables of the years ahead.

These are not merely abstract questions of foreign policy and strategic decision-making. One of the most important imponderables of the years ahead is whether or not the populations of the status quo powers will be willing, or psychologically able, to adjust to a downward shift in their countries' current geopolitical standing.

Consider, just as an example, an imaginary professor in environmental studies who teaches at a major American university. Because of her intellectual and ethical commitments, the professor has made many lifestyle changes, giving up flying, becoming a vegan, solarizing her house, and so on. She is not only willing, but eager to make every possible sacrifice in order to shrink her carbon footprint. But when asked, "Are you also willing to shrink the geopolitical footprint that is concealed within your carbon footprint?" she dismisses the question as meaningless because she does not conceive of herself as having a geopolitical footprint at all, perhaps because such a notion is not quantifiable. Yet her university does in fact wield significant geopolitical power, and through it, so does she. She plays a role, for instance, in setting the research agenda for innumerable universities around the world: by granting scholarships to overseas students and by issuing invitations to foreign professors; by publishing in, and editing, prestigious American journals; and through her connections with American foundations and think tanks that provide funding for educational institutions in many other countries. Although she may not recognize it, influence of this kind is also linked to the power that lies concealed within the US military's carbon footprint.

Would this professor, eager as she is to make sacrifices to shrink her carbon footprint, be willing to put up with an inversion in her circumstances whereby foreign powers would exercise an influence within her university equivalent to that which she wields in relation to foreign institutions? In other words, would she be willing to sacrifice any part of the power quotient that is hidden within her carbon footprint? I suspect not: her peers' responses to Chinese and Russian attempts to increase their international influence in the spheres of education, information, and media strongly suggest otherwise. Indeed, she would probably be willing to take to the barricades to resist such a change. For her, and for many in her circumstances, making lifestyle sacrifices will be much easier psychologically than adjusting to a significantly altered geopolitical order.

Ultimately, the fate of a global energy transition will not depend solely on technological innovations and the availability of financing. It will also depend, crucially, on whether the populations of the status quo powers are able to accept and adapt to the geopolitical changes that an energy transition will inevitably entail.

11

Vulnerabilities

One constant feature of military and security appraisals of climate change is that they assume that the West will largely be insulated from the worst effects of the planetary crisis: it is taken for granted that countries with a high per capita GDP and advanced infrastructure will continue to be well governed and peaceful, even as poor countries break down under the strain of climate impacts.

These assumptions are superficially plausible, even persuasive. Yet in recent years there have been many instances when this narrative has been turned on its head, the latest of them being the pandemic. There is of course no direct, causal connection between climate change and the Covid-19 pandemic; yet they are not unrelated either. Just as global warming is the result of ever-increasing economic activity, it is clear now that outbreaks of infectious diseases are also a "hidden cost" of economic development, brought about by changing land use and human intrusions upon wildlife habitats.[1] Indeed, both are effects of the ever-increasing acceleration in production, extraction, consumption, and environmental degradation that has occurred in the decades after the Second World War, and especially after 1989.

In that sense climate change events and the Covid-19 pandemic are cognate phenomena, and the paths taken by the pandemic suggest that the planetary crisis too will unfold in surprising and counterintuitive ways. The per capita income of Vietnam, for instance, is a fraction of that of the world's wealthier countries (its position in the global ranking for income is 126 out of 189).[2] Yet, despite sharing a long border with China, Vietnam had very few Covid-19 cases, and that too with a far larger population than the Western countries that did relatively well: Vietnam has fourteen million more people than Germany and ninety-two million more than New Zealand. Sri Lanka is another poor country that has weathered the pandemic exceptionally well.[3]

Among the countries that did not do well, on the other hand, there were many affluent nations, like Italy, Spain, France, Belgium, and, of course, the United Kingdom and the United States. One of the more unfortunate aspects of these outcomes is that they were partly the result of the belief, cherished by Western elites, that their countries' wealth, infrastructure, and vaunted health care systems would insulate them from the worst effects of the pandemic. Beliefs in the intrinsic superiority of the West, along with great power pretensions, also played a part in delaying their adoption of the practices that enabled some East Asian countries to bring the pandemic under control. In an interview with the *New York Times*, a French foreign policy expert observed: "France can't compare itself to South Korea or Taiwan, it can only compare itself to another great power. . . . To compare itself to countries that are not great powers is in some ways unbearable."[4] In less euphemistic language, it could be said that many Western leaders were misled by their own historically rooted prejudices.

· · ·

ON MAY 14, 2020, as I was writing the above paragraph, I was interrupted by news of a gathering storm. A climate scientist friend, Adam Sobel, a leading expert on tropical storms, sent me an email about a potentially dangerous weather system that was then brewing in the abnormally warm waters of the Bay of Bengal; according to several reliable computer models, there was a strong possibility that it would develop into a cyclone and head in the direction of Kolkata, my erstwhile hometown.

The storm could not have come at a worse time, for the country and for my family. Since the start of the pandemic I had been on the phone almost daily with my sister in Kolkata; she and her daughter were living with, and looking after, my eighty-nine-year-old mother, who was very ill with respiratory problems. Arranging her care had been difficult enough before the pandemic; it became even more so when a lockdown of draconian severity made medical supplies difficult to get.

But my family's problems were trivial compared to the disaster the lockdown inflicted on millions of migrant workers across the country. On March 24, when Prime Minister Narendra Modi announced the lockdown, all travel was summarily banned, and railways and airlines were shut down with no prior warning. Evidently the government was unaware that cities like New Delhi, Mumbai, and Bangalore are home to millions of internal migrants, who subsist on daily wages and live hand to mouth in informal settlements and slums; many do not have a proper roof over their heads, let alone access to clean water, food, and health care. No provision was made for these impoverished migrant workers, even though the government had provided planes to evacuate middle-class Indians who were stranded overseas. It was as if a class war had been openly declared.

After the lockdown, workers found themselves stranded in places where they had no support networks and no means of survival. In some cities, those who ventured out into the streets were set upon by the police and brutally beaten. But to remain indoors, in tin-roofed shacks and shanties, in the fierce heat of India's pre-monsoon months, was also impossible. The situation became so bad that many migrants packed up their meager belongings and began to walk to their homes, hundreds of kilometers away, in the burning heat of April and May, suffering all manner of depredations along the way. Every day there were streams of heartbreaking images on the internet: of long lines of people walking along highways with their children on their shoulders; of a boy sobbing in the streets of Delhi after being beaten by a policeman for the crime of being found out of doors; of an infant clinging to the body of her dead mother at a railway station.

Many of those migrant workers were from poverty-stricken areas in the eastern part of the country. A large number were from Kolkata and its surroundings, particularly the Sundarban, the vast mangrove forest to the south of the city, where millions of people had been displaced by earlier cyclones and other climate-related changes in the environment.[5] Those people were now out on the roads, where shelter would be hard to come by. Nor could their safety be ensured even if they managed to reach Kolkata, for the city is itself extremely vulnerable to flooding: much of the urban area lies below sea level, and many neighborhoods are prone to being swamped by the monsoons.

I grew up in one such neighborhood, in the same house where my mother, now critically dependent on respiratory equipment, was being nursed by a couple of attendants who had moved in at the start of the lockdown. She was dependent also on her doctors, who had continued to treat her through the pandemic, bundled up in protective gear. But if the area were to be flooded by a storm surge, it was possible that the house would be completely cut off, and there would be days when no one would be able to get through.

Fortunately, Adam's early warning gave us time to prepare. Over the next few days, as Cyclone Amphan intensified into the most powerful storm ever recorded in the Bay of Bengal, I was constantly on the phone with my sister. We went over the preparations in the minutest detail: how doors and windows were to be secured; how leaks were to be prevented; what kinds of food and medicine were to be stocked; and so on. Knowing that my mother's various respiratory devices would be knocked out if the power failed, we took the precaution of procuring oxygen cylinders.

These preparations made it possible for the house, and everyone in it, to ride out the cyclone without too much difficulty. The power did fail, as expected, but my mother did not have to suffer any great distress, because of the oxygen cylinders. The value of preparedness, at a personal as well as a collective level, was once again vindicated.

In the meantime, the governments of West Bengal and Bangladesh had also made preparations, mounting massive evacuation efforts and moving millions of people away from the coast. As a result, far fewer people died than had been initially feared. This conforms to the general pattern of cyclone impacts in the area over the last couple of decades. As mass evacuations have become more effective, the toll in lives has declined dramatically. The same cannot be said, however, of the impact on people's livelihoods, which is as devastating now as ever—especially for those who live close to the coast.

The day before Amphan struck, I was asked by a newspaper what the effects of the storm would be on the Sundarban. I wrote back to say that recent experience indicated that the people of the Sundarban would probably be very badly hit, despite the evacuations:

> Their villages will be inundated, their dwellings will be swept away, and there will be extensive damage to the embankments that protect the interiors of the islands, where the settlements are. Arable land will be swamped with salt water, and will not be cultivable for years. Fresh water ponds will also be flooded with sea water. Many fishermen will lose their boats and fishing nets. With the cyclone arriving during a pandemic, evacuations themselves may have adverse consequences—it's almost impossible to carry out large scale evacuations while observing social distancing. Nor will it be possible to maintain social distancing in crowded cyclone shelters. On top of that, an untold number of people—many of whom are already suffering from the effects of the lockdown—will lose their livelihoods. A good number of the migrant workers who are now walking back to Bengal, from cities like New Delhi and Mumbai are from the Sundarban. They will arrive to find further devastation. It will be a humanitarian disaster of epic proportions.[6]

Within days it became clear that Cyclone Amphan's impact on the region had indeed been devastating: jobless migrants had trekked home to find their dwellings swept away, their lands saturated with salt water, and their relatives unable to work because of the pandemic. Nor was it easy for residents to avail themselves of the relief funds provided by the government, because much of that money quickly disappeared into the pockets of local politicians and strongmen. Reduced to starvation, many people began to venture into the mangrove forests to forage for food, leading to a steep rise in animal attacks: nineteen people—more than double the number of previous years—were killed by tigers. Yet despite the terrible conditions, there was no violence, looting, or social unrest.

Writing about Amphan, two leading authorities on the Sundarban note: "The vulnerabilities faced by the people of the region are not only due to climate change, nor are they due simply to the lack of infrastructure such as bridges, jetties, hospitals, or brick roads. Instead, they are based on long-term governmental apathy and an utter callousness towards what these islanders are entitled to as citizens."[7]

What Amphan, like the pandemic, exposed was a range of systemic inequities that interact with one another to create extreme vulnerability. It is increasingly clear now that it is these inequities, rather than GDP or per capita income, that will determine how countries are impacted by the planetary crisis.

.   .   .

FOR THE PURPOSES OF military planning, pandemics and climate change are both often treated as "threat multipliers." The usual conclusion is that disasters and outbreaks of new diseases will not only take a terrible toll of lives in poor countries, but will also lead to riots and uprisings that could culminate in the collapse of state structures.

Thinking along these lines, many prominent Western voices predicted a "COVID Apocalypse" for Africa, even as their own hospitals were filling up and dead bodies were being buried in mass graves. But Africa's Covid apocalypse never materialized, and a few sub-Saharan countries, like Senegal, had some of the best outcomes in the world.[8] These outcomes suggest that contrary to received wisdom, the conditions that Western elites have long stigmatized as "backward" and "underdeveloped" may in fact create certain kinds of resilience. It was probably because African leaders had prior experience of infectious diseases, and were therefore well aware of the fragility of their health care systems, that they took prompt and decisive action, while their Western counterparts complacently assumed that the pandemic would pass them by. At least one major American philanthropist is known to have predicted that bodies would be strewn across the streets of African countries—even as the situation was worsening in the US. Commenting on this, the journalists Caleb Okereke and Kelsey Nielsen write: "Indeed, the white gaze knows no rest, even amid a pandemic that has struck the West."[9] In March 2020, war-torn Somalia, one of the world's most beleaguered countries, sent twenty doctors to help Italy with its outbreak of Covid-19.

Nor did the pandemic lead to political upheavals and societal breakdown in poor countries. Contrary to the confident predictions of Western "thought leaders," it was not the poorer and weaker parts of the world that were seized with unrest and violence, but rather the heartlands of the United States, where posse-like mobs, armed with automatic weapons and bedecked with fascist paraphernalia, besieged state capitols; where large numbers of people refused to comply with lockdowns; where doctors and experts were belittled and derided; where violence against people of color continued apace. . . .

IN AN UNCANNY INTERSECTION of words and events, I was drafting the above paragraphs on May 25, when I took a Twitter break and came upon a video clip of a White woman in New York City's Central Park calling the police on a Black birdwatcher who had merely asked her to put her dog on a leash. Later that same day I watched a video clip of a White policeman murdering a Black man by the name of George Floyd by kneeling on his neck for nearly nine minutes.

And then suddenly, overnight, everything changed. It was as though the pandemic, even as it slowed the individual experience of time, had created an enormous acceleration in history. Suddenly the connections between settler colonialism and the planetary crisis were being pointed out by protesters marching on the streets in Brooklyn; suddenly there was an outpouring of articles that drew links between contemporary policing in America and the history of slave patrols leading back to the seventeenth century.

As I write this now, Minneapolis is burning, protests have broken out across America, and reports are coming in about armed

White extremists shooting at demonstrators, most of whom are also White. It is as if the pandemic had intervened directly, to demonstrate that the assumptions and narratives that underlie the judgment of Western strategists are very far from being clear-eyed assessments of what the future holds. They are, rather, products of an "imperial optic," heavily influenced by nineteenth-century ideas of civilizational dominance.[10]

THE UNREST THAT shook America in the ensuing weeks demonstrated, with startling clarity, how systemic inequities can exacerbate the impacts of the planetary crisis. Already by the end of March 2020, it was being reported that the disease was claiming a hugely disproportionate number of victims among Hispanic, Black, and Native American populations. The statistics posted by the Covid Racial Data Tracker presented a grim picture: by early May, in Alabama, almost half the lives claimed by the disease were African American, even though only 27 percent of the state's population is Black.[11] The situation was similar in Mississippi, Tennessee, Colorado, and South Carolina. In Iowa, the percentage of infections among African Americans was four times higher than the percentage of Black people in the state's population. Iowa's Latinos too were facing a grim situation, because they were disproportionately represented in the workforces of meatpacking plants, some of which had become Covid-19 hotspots.

But of all demographic groups, the hardest hit were Native Americans. In some states the rate of infection among them was astronomically higher than it was for the rest of the population: in Wyoming, with less than a 3 percent share of the population, Native Americans accounted for 18.49 percent of the coronavirus cases.[12] In the Southwest, the Navajo Nation reservation had the highest infection rate in the entire United States, higher even than New York, the "epicenter of the epicenter."[13]

These catastrophic outcomes were due, of course, to systemic neglect: the Navajo Nation's health care is provided by a disastrously underfunded government agency, and almost a third of the residents have no running water. Nor did the pattern of governmental neglect change during the pandemic. The writer and activist Julian Brave NoiseCat noted in early May that even though Congress had passed a bill that included $8 billion in relief for Indian Country, Steve Mnuchin, the Treasury Secretary, had held up the funds for six weeks. "By then, reservations like the Navajo Nation had more coronavirus cases per capita than Wuhan at the height of the outbreak in China."[14]

To Mark Charles, a Navajo leader, the connection with the history of colonization was obvious: "It's a problem 250 years in the making," he said, "going back to how this nation was founded. The ethnic cleansing and genocidal policies . . . that's where the problem lies."[15]

But even as the crisis was deepening, many states began to relax their pandemic lockdowns. In Wisconsin, meatpacking plants (where the workers were disproportionately from minority communities) were actually ordered to reopen; the owners of these plants were exempted from legal liabilities while reluctant workers were forced to return under threat of having their welfare payments and unemployment benefits canceled. When these measures were challenged in court, the Chief Justice of the Wisconsin Supreme Court pointed out that the victims of Covid-19 in one badly hit county were merely meat-factory workers, not "the regular folks."[16]

By early May it became clear that publication of the data on racial disparities in the pandemic had had exactly the opposite of the intended effect: far from helping the cause of the worst-affected groups, it had made their situation even worse. "Once the disproportionate impact of the epidemic was revealed to the American political and financial elite," wrote the journalist Adam Serwer on May 8, "many began to regard the rising death toll less as a national emergency than as an inconvenience."[17]

THE COVID-19 PANDEMIC and weather events like Cyclone Amphan and Hurricane Maria have made it amply clear that inequity is a far better predictor of the likely impacts of disasters than aggregate wealth. In general the countries that have fared worst are those that are the most inequitable: the US and Brazil, where class divisions are compounded by race; and India, with its entrenched hierarchies of caste.

Over the last few decades—the very period in which the planetary crisis has been intensifying—the world's wealth has come to be concentrated in the hands of a few dozen billionaires. The same neoliberal policies that enriched them have made the circumstances of many of their compatriots so precarious that more than 60 percent of Americans do not have so much as five hundred dollars set aside for emergencies.[18] During several recent hurricanes, many of the people who stayed home, disobeying evacuation orders, were those who simply could not afford to leave. In that sense it could be said that neoliberal capitalism creates an illusion of wealth while picking the social fabric threadbare, so that it rips apart during disasters and climate shocks.

At no time was this more evident than in 2017, when Hurricane Maria struck Puerto Rico. Hundreds of thousands of people were left without food, supplies, electricity, or access to medical attention. Much of the islanders' suffering, as Naomi Klein has described in detail, was directly caused by neoliberalism: already weakened by a debt crisis, the local government could not afford to get its infrastructure running quickly.[19] A significant part of the relief funds allocated to Puerto Rico by Washington ultimately passed into the hands of bankers and into hedge funds.

Puerto Rico may be poor in relation to the mainland US, but it is much wealthier than most countries in Asia and Africa: its per capita income is three times higher than that of Vietnam. It is also, by standard measurements, vastly wealthier than most of its neighbors, including Cuba. An impoverished country by most measures, Cuba was also hit by Hurricane Maria, but it suffered few fatalities and sustained very little damage. This has been a consistent pattern over decades, simply because Cuba is far better prepared for hurricanes than are its wealthier neighbors. The pattern repeated itself during the Covid-19 pandemic, with Cuba posting a fraction of the fatalities of Puerto Rico. Indeed, at the peak of the crisis, Cuba even sent a team of doctors to Italy to buttress that country's foundering medical system.

There is other evidence to suggest that climate change will

unfold in ways that are complicated and counterintuitive. Italy, for instance, is one of the world's richest countries, yet in recent years it has been hit exceptionally hard by climate change. Before 1999, the figures for severe weather events in Italy, Spain, and the UK were roughly comparable, but since then the numbers have diverged to an astonishing degree, with Italy experiencing many more extreme weather events than the other two countries. Despite its wealth and high living standards, Italy is, in the words of the journalist Stefano Liberti, "in the eye of the cyclone."[20]

Many cities with great concentrations of wealth have also been exceptionally hard-hit by climate disruptions. Houston, which is not only the fourth largest city in the United States but also the hub of the global oil industry, has been repeatedly devastated by flooding, largely because it sits upon a landscape that was once a vast floodplain. Los Angeles is another city where the wealthy have not been insulated from the ravages of wildfires. And in coastal cities, where proximity to the sea is a mark of status—as in Miami or Mumbai—it is likely that the wealthy will actually be the first to feel the adverse effects of climate change.

Phoenix, Arizona, is another city that has attracted large numbers of well-to-do people over the last few decades. But the city sits in the midst of a hot, dry desert, and its very existence is predicated on the vast, complex, and expensive infrastructural systems that keep it supplied with water and with electricity for the air conditioners that make human habitation possible in that landscape. But the area around Phoenix is growing hotter and drier, and even if an unlimited supply of power and water could be ensured in a rapidly warming world, it will still be increasingly difficult to insulate the city's infrastructure from climatic disruptions: a brief breakdown would expose all the fragilities that are intrinsic to the city's location. In Arizona, then, advanced infrastructure, far from being a reliable surety against climate change, has actually helped to create vulnerabilities, in that it has encouraged untrammeled growth in ecologically unsuitable landscapes. The unprecedented wildfires that broke out across the state during the pandemic hold ominous portents for the future.[21]

What Miami, Mumbai, Houston, and Phoenix have in common

is that their growth has been made possible by extensive alterations to their surroundings. These alterations are now precisely the causes of their vulnerabilities. This may well be an indicator of how climate change will unfold: the locations that will be most adversely affected are those that have been most intensively interfered with—"terraformed," in other words. And of course, most of those locations are in wealthy countries, or in the wealthiest regions of poor countries, as is the case with Mumbai. It is as if climate change were goading the terrain to shrug off the forms imposed on it over the last centuries. This is quickly becoming one of the distinctive features of the planetary crisis: the wildfires in California and southeastern Australia, the repeated flooding of Houston, and the increasing unruliness of the Missouri River all suggest that the planetary crisis will manifest itself with exceptional force in those parts of the Earth that have been most intensively terraformed to resemble European models. Essentially, these landscapes are throwing off the forms that settlers imposed on them, as a preliminary to switching to some new, unknown state.

THE DIRECTION TAKEN by the Covid-19 pandemic also suggests that future events may take some unexpected turns. Before 2020, respected experts placed the US and the UK at the very top of a list of "Countries Best Prepared to Deal with the Pandemic."[22] China was relegated to fifty-first place on the list, and a cluster of African countries were lumped together at the bottom. In the event, the assessment could not have been more misleading—the actual outcomes were startlingly at odds with those predictions. While the Trump administration's incompetence was no doubt responsible to some degree for the US's handling of the pandemic, the effects of other, longer-term trends also contributed to the many stumbles and failures. The US's Centers for Disease Control, for instance, is widely held to be the best institution of its kind in the world—yet in the decades before Covid, it had been disastrously slow also in responding to America's opioid epidemic.

Underlying all of this is another disquieting long-term trend, toward a form of governance that the anthropologist Joseph Masco has described as "suicidal" because it "privileges images of catastrophic future events" while being unable to respond to immediate challenges. Because of this "the American public can simultaneously know the United States to be an unrivaled military, economic, and scientific superpower, a state with unprecedented capacities, agencies, and resources, and yet feel completely powerless in the face of failed US military, financial, and environmental commitments."[23]

Military and security assessments of climate change fit this pattern perfectly in the sense that they project images of catastrophe into the future in a fashion that negates the possibility of confronting climate change in the present day.

12
A Fog of Numbers

What percentage of the world's greenhouse gas emissions derives from military uses of energy? I have no idea, for this is one area—perhaps the only one—in which the literature on climate change is mysteriously deficient in numbers. This may be because the numbers are impossible to ascertain with any accuracy, since the military's presence is ubiquitous also in many spheres of civilian life: as Joseph Masco has pointed out, in the US there are now very few social institutions or infrastructural systems that are *not* "embedded within the larger U.S. counterterror state apparatus."[1]

But one fact of which there is no doubt whatsoever is that military-related emissions have never figured in international climate negotiations. This is because a decision was taken, at the behest of the US, that emissions related to military activities would be excluded from the negotiations for the 1997 Kyoto Protocol. Ever since then the Intergovernmental Panel on Climate Change has continued "to treat national military emissions, specifically international aircraft and naval bunker fuels, differently than other emission types."[2]

This is not, however, the only reason why the military and geopolitical enmeshments of fossil fuels rarely figure in the public discussion of global warming. It is also because climate change has come to be thought of, especially in the West, as a phenomenon that pertains mainly to technology and economics. Inasmuch as issues of geopolitics figure within this frame, they are usually represented as being determined by economic factors or by the broader workings of capitalism.

Because of this techno-economic framing, the subject of climate change has come to be enclosed within a vast palisade of scientific and academic expertise: indeed, the very phrase "climate change" has come to refer not just to a process that is unfolding in the world, but also to a highly specialized field of knowledge, one that extends across a wide swath of learned disciplines, ranging from the atmospheric sciences to engineering, law, economics, and so on. This large and growing field is located squarely within Western institutions of learning: whether we speak of paleobotany, renewable energy, carbon taxes, or climate economics, the great bulk of the research on these subjects is produced by colleges, universities, and think tanks in the global North. Not only is the credentialed work on these subjects produced in such institutions; those credentials also set the agenda for the discussion of the phenomenon itself. The people who sit on UN panels and government committees are usually the very people who produce credentialed work on climate change.

In other words, the phenomenon of climate change and the research that surrounds it have come to be almost totally identified with each other. Arguably, there exists no other sphere of contemporary life in which there is so great an overlap between a phenomenon and the credentialed literature that frames it. In discussions of the economy, for instance, it is not assumed that only economists or academic experts can speak of the subject. It is generally accepted that workers, shopkeepers, factory managers, stockbrokers, and others who have no acquaintance with the expert literature may have valid perspectives of their own.

Climate change is a much vaster phenomenon than the economy, yet the voices and perspectives of those who are affected by it—farmers, fisherfolk, migrants, and so on—very rarely figure in the discussion. And when they do, it is usually merely as victims, whose voices fill the blanks in a script that has already been written by specialists.

It goes without saying that if it were not for experts, the world would not be talking about global warming at all. The causes and impacts of the atmospheric changes that are now unfolding across the planet could not have been investigated without climate science; it is the work that climate scientists do that has uncovered the interconnections of various Earth systems and the feedback loops they create. Some of these scientists have persevered heroically in the teeth of death threats, harassment, and opposition, not just from governments but also from energy corporations. The world owes them a great debt of gratitude for their work; I personally have nothing but admiration for their courage and persistence.

Yet it needs to be recognized that even if climate scientists had *not* done this invaluable work, climate change itself would not disappear, any more than the economy would disappear in the absence of economists. It is not primarily through the work of economists, after all, that workers, businessmen, and bankers are alerted to fluctuations in prices and salaries. Indeed, in some instances bankers, trade unionists, and shopkeepers may know more about the phenomenon that we call "the economy" than economists do.

Nor is it the case that humans and human societies are incapable of comprehending and responding to climatic disruptions in the absence of modern science. During the Little Ice Age of the seventeenth century, Japan's rulers understood that something was awry in their environment and acted accordingly, imposing a range of economic and political controls, limiting consumption, fostering frugality, compelling farmers to adopt a series of prudential measures, and so on.[3] As a result, while many parts of the world suffered greatly, Japan's well-being was such that a contemporary chronicler boasted: "In this age, there are none even among peasants and rustics, no matter how humble, who have not handled gold and silver aplenty. Our empire enjoys peace and prosperity; on the roads not one beggar or outcast is to be seen."[4]

So while there is every reason to be grateful to climate scientists and other specialists for the work they do, this should not obscure the fact that academically credentialed experts are by no means the only diviners of climate change. People who make their living from the land, or the forest, or the sea have also known, for a while, that the Earth's physical realities are changing dramatically.

For those who observe their surroundings carefully, the indications of long-term change can come from unexpected sources. For an Indigenous group of central Australia, warnings of a changing climate came from the flooding of a site associated with initiation rites that had never been flooded before. For other Indigenous Australians, the signs lay in the behavior of plants and animals: "Bottlebrush is not flowering at the right season, the grunters [fish] are not biting . . . used to be when wattle tree flowering we get barramundi, not always that way anymore."[5]

In his book *Wisdom Sits in Places*, the anthropologist Keith H. Basso writes about an elder of the Western Apache, Charles Henry, for whom the clues to the changes in his environment lay in place-names: he noticed, for instance, that water no longer flows at what was once a spring called *Tłiish Bi Tú'é* ("Snakes' Water"), or at another place called "Bird's Water." Henry saw that the plants from which some places took their names no longer grew there — for instance, a place called "Stand of Arrow Cane" no longer had that species of cane, which needs moist conditions to thrive. These places are all tied to stories that describe how they got their names: "Snakes' Water," for instance, was once owned by snakes, and people had to ask their permission before they could drink there.[6] The discrepancies between the names, the stories, and the realities of the present day made it obvious to Charles Henry that this part of Arizona was getting drier: "The names do not lie. . . . They show what is different and what is still the same."[7]

Steeped in the lore of the land, a man like Charles Henry observes his surroundings with a closeness of attention that is made possible by the very fact of his distance from mainstream culture. The same pattern replicates itself across the globe: those who are most attentive to environmental change are, more often than not, people who are at the margins, people whose relationships to the soil, or the forest, or the water are minimally mediated by technology. The farmer who is most likely to pay attention to a prolonged drought is one who cannot afford an electric pump or chemical inputs; the fisher who is most likely to observe changes in the marine environment is one who does not have sonar equipment to locate schools of fish; the woman who is most likely to notice rainfall deficits is one who does not have access to piped water and must walk to ever more distant wells. But such people are generally poor and do not have access to the networks through which information is disseminated; they are, in fact, located at the opposite end of the social spectrum from the majority of the world's scientists and academics.

Experts are not at fault, of course, for the skewed way in which the world gathers information; they can hardly be held responsible for the social contexts in which they work. But it is nonetheless important to recognize that the reason our first messages about climate change came from scientists, rather than from marginal farmers, or women who fetch water, is not that scientists were the only people to notice what was under way: it was because scientists were more visible within the circles that wield power in the world. Sadly, they were themselves too much on the margins of those circles to be visible enough.

THE FOG OF NUMBERS that surrounds climate change offers many opportunities for the manipulation of public opinion. The notion of the per capita carbon footprint is a good example. This measure, which is calculated by dividing a nation's total carbon emissions by the sum of its population, has found very wide currency: there are thousands of graphic representations of it on the internet, and many of these draw on American data. They invariably attribute the size of an American's per capita footprint to intensive consumption, in the form of gas-guzzling cars, wasteful usage of domestic energy, meat-heavy diets, and so on. In this framing climate change becomes a matter of individual responsibility and consumer choice.

What these graphs and charts exclude, of course, are institutional emissions, like those related to the US military and to the projection of American power. That entire reality is simply conjured away by a graphic that makes climate change a matter of personal responsibility. It is as if ordinary Americans contributed nothing to defense expenditure—even though a significant part of their taxes are earmarked precisely for that purpose.

But these colorful little charts and graphs did not appear out of nowhere. They were introduced by a $100 million–plus per year advertising campaign financed by the energy giant BP. The aims of this huge branding and advertising campaign were to assign "responsibility for climate impact to the individual" and to promote "a view of climate change not so much as a present reality but rather as a future threat."[8]

There can be no denying that the BP campaign succeeded spectacularly in embedding both of these perceptions deep within Western popular culture. And that success was due in no small part to the rhetorical power this age of enumeration accords to numbers, graphs, and charts: the campaign achieved its effects by relying on the hypnotic effect of numbers, and by taking advantage of preexisting perceptions that had already framed climate change in terms of economics, science, and technology.

ALL BODIES OF knowledge are shaped and marked by the circumstances from which they emerge. Since the bulk of the literature on climate change comes out of Western universities, it is inevitably marked by the methods and practices of those institutions.

The methods of scientists, in particular, have profoundly shaped the way climate change is imagined and thought about. Take, for instance, a procedure that is in widespread use among climate scientists: that of using models to make projections in relation to a future date. Using this method a scientist might predict, for example, that sea levels will rise by so many meters over the next thirty, or eighty, or one hundred years. An unintended consequence of this practice is that it reinforces a perception that abstracts climate change from the past and projects it in the opposite direction, toward the future. This perception has come to color most of the thinking that goes into climate change, especially in the West: no matter whether in economics, or law, or indeed fiction, global warming is almost always imagined in relation to the future. As one historian has ruefully noted: "If you search the Intergovernmental Panel on Climate Change's 2007 synthesis report . . . you will not find the words 'history' or 'historical.'"[9]

To be sure, historians have not neglected to provide historical contexts for global warming.[10] But theirs is bound to be a minority view in a field where the pinpointing of what is new and unprecedented is crucial to the identification of the phenomenon itself. Consider, for example, a method that is often used to ascertain whether or not a weather event has been influenced by human activity: to do this scientists often proceed by comparing contemporary heatwaves and hurricanes to those of the past. If a heatwave can be shown to have no precedents in the historical record, then the likelihood of its having been impacted by human activity rises: the unprecedented nature of the event is itself evidence that it has been impacted by human activity.

For climate scientists, this is an exceptionally valuable method. However, the method also casts a long shadow outside the sciences, making it easy to lose sight of the fact that while an event may be unprecedented, the human activities that have left their fingerprint on it may actually be embedded in long and enduring patterns of history. Since the events are unprecedented, and therefore new, it seems almost self-evident that the era of climate change is itself radically new, separated from preceding ages by a clean break—and thanks to the academic practice of assigning dates to geological periods, we may even soon be provided with a date for when the world tipped over into a new era, the "Anthropocene."[11]

In imagining this era as radically new, it becomes easy also to imagine that the break with the past has created many other phenomena that are completely different from those that existed before: hence "climate justice" takes on a coloring that sets it apart from "justice" in general; and "climate migration" takes on a hue that makes it seem different from other, more familiar forms of displacement. It becomes tempting to imagine that this new era is suffused with phenomena that are waiting to be identified as unprecedented and utterly novel.

IT WAS WITH exactly these assumptions in mind that I began to follow the so-called European "migration crisis" that started in 2015. The images that began to circulate at that time—of refugees crossing the Mediterranean in rickety boats, or trekking across mountains with their children clinging to their backs—were so powerful that I could not wrench my eyes away from them.

But as I combed through this material I gradually became aware of a striking discrepancy. In newspaper reports the refugees were described, more often than not, as being from war-torn parts of Asia or sub-Saharan Africa: Afghanistan, Iraq, Syria, Somalia, Sudan, Eritrea, and so on. Rarely, if ever, was there any mention of refugees from South Asia. Yet, in picture after picture of boats in the Mediterranean and of people crossing the Balkans, I could see faces that were recognizably South Asian. Indeed, it seemed to me that a good number of those refugees were from the very part of the world where my own roots lie: the Bengal Delta.

Digging into the official statistics from Italy—the country that was, along with Greece, then receiving the largest number of refugees—I discovered that I was right: many Bengalis, most of them young men, were indeed making these difficult and dangerous journeys. The statistics showed that in some months Bangladeshis were among the largest groups of refugees crossing the Mediterranean to seek shelter in Italy.[12] I discovered, to my astonishment, that at times Bangladeshis far outnumbered Iraqis, Afghans, or Somalis. This confounded me, because Bangladesh, while it may have its problems, can hardly be described as a "war-torn country." Nor is the country's economy in dire straits: Bangladesh has actually been one of the top performers globally for the last several years, and its growth rate surpassed India's in 2018. Indeed Bangladesh's performance has been so impressive that a leading economist recently observed that the country is "on a path that would have been unimaginable just two decades ago: toward becoming an Asian success story."[13]

Why then, I began to wonder, were so many Bangladeshis undertaking these hazardous journeys across West Asia and North Africa to Europe? That climate change might hold the answer seemed obvious. Climate migration is, after all, a recognized phenomenon, and people who have been displaced by environmental impacts are often described as "climate migrants" or "climate refugees." These terms have been embraced by many displaced people, and are now in wide use among advocacy groups. Indeed, Italy has had its own self-described climate refugees since 1951, when a catastrophic flood left 180,000 people homeless in the Polesine region of the Po Delta.[14]

That Bangladesh, and the Bengal Delta more generally, is exceptionally vulnerable to climate change is a well-known fact: much of the country lies less than one meter above sea level, and it has already lost a good deal of land to the rising waters.[15] In 2005 the partial sinking of a single island led to the displacement of more than half a million people.

Scientists have long predicted that flooding and saltwater intrusion will displace millions more from the low-lying plains of the Bengal Delta. Was it possible, I wondered, that some of the refugees who were crossing the Mediterranean on those rickety boats were "climate migrants" displaced by the impacts of global warming? Surely that had to be the case; how could it not be so?

To find answers to these questions at secondhand was all but impossible, since South Asians rarely figured in media reports on the migration crisis. At a certain point it became clear to me that I would have to talk directly with the refugees themselves. So, in 2016, with the help of a number of organizations that work with refugees, I traveled across Italy, visiting holding camps and other facilities, and especially seeking out South Asians who had recently crossed the Mediterranean by boat. It was my intuition, from the start, that speaking to refugees in their own languages would provide fresh perspectives, and in this I was amply vindicated.

IN PARMA, THROUGH the good offices of a voluntary organization called "Escapes," I met a thirty-something Bengali refugee who had recently crossed the Mediterranean: I'll call him Khokon. He had grown up in a village in Bangladesh's Kishoreganj district, in a family of farmers. As a boy, Khokon had worked on his father's land while also attending a local school.

Khokon remembered a time when the land had borne good harvests of rice, sustaining the whole family. But the environment had begun to change as he was growing up. There were sudden and catastrophic inundations, caused sometimes by heavy rains and sometimes by the release of huge volumes of water by dams upstream, in India. In 1998 Khokon's family's land was flooded for six months. The incidence of other weather-related disasters began to increase as well: there were prolonged dry spells, violent hailstorms, and unseasonal downpours. As the environmental disruptions accelerated, the political situation also began to deteriorate. Members of the ruling party seized some of Khokon's family's land, and the family was unable to get it back. "The conditions in the district are lethal now," Khokon told me. "Before it was just oppression; now on top of the oppression there's disaster after disaster."

In the end Khokon's father decided that the family's best hope lay in selling a part of their land and using the proceeds to pay a *dalal*, or agent, to send Khokon abroad. So the land was sold, and the money enabled Khokon, then in his twenties, to travel to France—but to no avail, for he was soon deported back to Bangladesh. He stayed home for seven months but was unable to find any employment, so his family sold the rest of their land and paid another agent to send him abroad again. Dubai was Khokon's chosen destination, and he paid accordingly; but the agent cheated him and he ended up in Libya instead. For the next several years he had to endure enslavement, beatings, extortion, and torture. But somehow he managed to save up enough money to pay traffickers to send him from Libya to Sicily in a ramshackle boat.

The journey was a nightmare. Those who paid extra were accommodated on the boat's upper deck; Khokon was down below, near the engine, packed in with dozens of others in suffocating heat. A man who vomited was thrown overboard; many others died as well. By the time the journey ended, at the Italian island of Lampedusa, Khokon was traumatized. But various support groups for refugees gave him shelter and he eventually traveled to Parma, where he had relatives, and found a job at a warehouse.

AFTER HEARING KHOKON OUT, I thought: if ever there was a story of climate migration, then this is surely it. Khokon himself was well able to see that environmental disruptions had played a major part in setting him off on his journey: he was knowledgeable about global warming, as is often the case with people from Bangladesh, where climate-related information is widely disseminated by the government and by nongovernmental organizations. Khokon was certainly well aware that sea levels are rising and that rainfall is growing more erratic because of broader changes in the global climate. But when I asked him whether it would be accurate to describe his journey as an instance of "climate migration," he flatly disagreed. No, he insisted, there were many other reasons for his departure: political violence, the employment situation, family disagreements, and aspirations to a higher standard of living. There was also the additional factor of communications technology: as is often the case with migrants today, Khokon's travels were intricately connected to the internet, which is the primary medium for making payments to traffickers and for receiving instructions from their networks.

Elsewhere in Italy I would meet many other migrants whose journeys seemed to be self-evidently instances of climate migration. Many of them were also well informed about climate change—yet none of them believed that their journeys had been driven primarily by environmental disruptions.

In the face of this refusal, I was tempted to assume that these migrants were unwilling, for one reason or another, to acknowledge the reality of their predicament: because it might put them at a disadvantage in relation to Italian officialdom; or because of some sort of psychological blockage, rooted perhaps in personal pride. In any event, it seemed beyond dispute to me that these men were climate migrants, whether they knew it or not; I persuaded myself that I understood their stories better than they did themselves, because I had access to more authoritative information.

It was not till much later that I began to understand that the difference between the migrants' thinking and mine was that for them climate change was not a thing apart, a phenomenon that could be isolated from other aspects of their experience by a set of numbers or dates. Rather, their experience was formed by sudden and catastrophic intersections of many different factors, of which some were undoubtedly new, like smartphones and changes in the weather. But some other factors were not new at all, being rooted ultimately in deeply entrenched structures of exploitation and conflict.

Viewed from this perspective, climate change is but one aspect of a much broader planetary crisis: it is not the prime cause of dislocation, but rather a cognate phenomenon. In this sense climate change, mass dislocations, pollution, environmental degradation, political breakdown, and the Covid-19 pandemic are all cognate effects of the ever-increasing acceleration of the last three decades. Not only are these crises interlinked—they are all deeply rooted in history, and they are all ultimately driven by the dynamics of global power.

WHEN ISSUES LIKE climate migration and climate justice are discussed by experts in international conferences, one of the guiding assumptions is that the negotiations are intended to produce fair and just outcomes. Another such assumption, common to what is known as the "liberal world order," is that structures of governance, national and international, exist to promote people's welfare and to advance the causes of equality, security, and justice.

What migrants like Khokon know, on the other hand, is that every aspect of their plight is rooted in unyielding, intractable, and historically rooted forms of class and racial *in*justice. They know that if they were wealthy or White they would not have to risk their lives on rickety boats. They know that the processes that have displaced them are embedded in very old and deeply entrenched social relationships of power, national and international. From that point of view, forms of governance, national and international, exist not to promote justice or welfare but precisely to *protect* the systemic inequalities and historic injustices that produce the displacement of refugees.

It is largely in affluent countries, then, and mainly among the more privileged, that climate change is perceived as a techno-economic concern oriented toward the future; for the have-nots of the world, in rich and poor countries alike, it is primarily a matter of justice, rooted in histories of race, class, and geopolitics. From this perspective, climate negotiations are not just about emissions and greenhouse gases; they hinge precisely upon issues that are not, and can never be, discussed—issues that are ultimately related to the global distribution of power.

.   .   .

AS WITH THE NUTMEG, the clove was very picky in choosing where to grow; everything had to be "just so" in order for it to flourish. On the slopes of Ternate's Mount Gamalama, clove trees found a home that perfectly suited them, just as nutmegs had found their ideal home in the low-lying islands of the Bandas: "it is said that nutmeg trees must be able to smell the sea, whereas clove trees must be able to see it."[16]

Only on these clusters of islands did a number of different factors fall into alignment in such a way as to create perfect homes for these gifts of the Earth. But what the Earth gives, it can also take away. This became shockingly clear to me at the first clove garden I visited in Ternate. Overlooked by the island's volcano, Mount Gamalama, the garden was in a wonderfully scenic location. A few clove trees were in flower, their leaves dotted with clusters of delicate yellowish-pink buds: these are the unblossomed buds that become cloves once dried.

But that day only a handful of the garden's trees were budding; the others were dead or dying, their branches devoid of leaves and their trunks the color of ash. This was happening all over the island, I was told, and the farmers I spoke to were unanimous about the cause: the climate has changed in recent years, they said; there is less rain and it falls more erratically. This in turn has led to the spread of blights and disease. The prolonged drought has also caused forest fires of unprecedented intensity: earlier that year a wildfire had raged for three days on the slopes of Mount Gamalama, a phenomenon new to the islanders' experience.

In other words, the delicate balance of the island's environmental conditions has been upset; no longer is their alignment precisely poised to nurture the clove. And Ternate has itself contributed to these changes, although in a very small way. Indonesia is one of the world's fastest-growing countries, and the hum of its accelerating economy can be clearly heard on the island's streets, which are lined with neat, brightly painted houses and well-stocked shops and markets. A grand new waterfront mosque, with soaring minarets, crowns the island's main thoroughfare, which also winds past busy wholesale bazaars, several large modern malls, and at least one immense "hypermarket." The island has fast internet connectivity, many ATMs, good roads, and plenty of cars and motorcycles. Remote and idyllic as Ternate is, it is by no means a stranger to the forms of acceleration that are ultimately the cause of the decline of its fabled trees.

Often, while visiting Ternate's graying clove orchards, I would ask those who worked in them: "Since climate change is killing your trees, do you think the people of Ternate, and Indonesia in general, should make an effort to reduce their consumption and cut back their carbon emissions?"

Almost always the answer was some variant of the following: "Why should *we* cut back our consumption and our emissions, when they are still far below Western levels? Wouldn't that be unjust to us? The West enriched itself at our expense when we were weak and powerless. It's our turn to catch up now."

Words like these came as no surprise to me; I have heard their like many times, not just in Indonesia, but also in India, China, and elsewhere. Across much of the global South these beliefs are held with a strength of conviction that belies the idea that the planetary crisis can be addressed merely by "fixing" capitalism. At the heart of the crisis lie geopolitical problems, and inequities of power, inherited from the era of colonization: those issues cannot be wished away.

It may seem that this makes the planetary crisis all the more intractable—and so indeed it does, in some ways. But it also opens up some grounds for hope. Because the conception of wealth that underlies this framing of justice and equity is fundamentally mimetic: "Until I have what the Other has, I am poor"; or "Not till I have what the Other has will justice be served." It follows then that this conception of wealth is founded on the Other's conception of the Good Life, as a standard to be aspired to. Hence, if the Other's conception of the Good Life were to change, then the resonances would be felt everywhere.

In this lies the importance of movements like Occupy, and Extinction Rebellion, and documents like Pope Francis's encyclical *Fratelli Tutti*: embedded in them all is a radically different conception of the Good Life.

· · ·

ON MAY 30, 2020, there was a big Black Lives Matter protest in Charlottesville, Virginia, where three years earlier a coalition of White supremacists had staged a rally that ended with the death of Heather Heyer, an antiracism protester. Debbie was at the BLM protest, and the stream of pictures she sent me gave me a sense of almost being there.

That evening, during a Skype dinner, Debbie told me that her father had stopped eating and was very downcast. His doctor had said that there was nothing wrong with him as such; it was just a case of "failure to thrive."

Tall and skinny, Jeff bore a passing resemblance to Abraham Lincoln, whose style of beard he had adopted. A former professor of biology, he had authored a well-known textbook on the subject, and he had strong views on the importance of science in promoting public welfare. But after losing his wife, Barbara, in January, he had lost the will to live: through more than fifty years of marriage, his life had revolved around his vivacious, charming, and energetic wife. Her death had left him reeling, and he was now mostly in a fugue state, talking about seeing his parents and asking when he could go home.

Jeff had asked several times when I would come down to Virginia, and in any other circumstance I would have lost no time in going to see him. From the day we first met, Jeff, Barbara, and I had taken a great liking to each other, and over the years that affection had grown into a deep attachment. It was wrenching not to be able to go, but New York's Covid-19 numbers were peaking at that time, while central Virginia was still "virgin soil." The possibility that I might carry the infection with me if I went, and perhaps even infect someone who was already enfeebled, was too chilling to contemplate. I remained in Brooklyn.

Three days later, on June 3, around noon, Debbie called to say that Jeff was gone; he had died peacefully in the loving presence of two of his children.

In those days the papers were filled with stories about people dying alone in hospitals, with nurses holding up cellphones to give their families a last glimpse of their loved ones. The times were such that my first thought was that Jeff had been lucky to go as he had, lying in the same bed that he had been born in, at home in a tranquil woodland, with three of his children and several grand-children nearby.

I thought of the day I met Jeff and Barbara, which was also the day I met Debbie—Easter Sunday, 1988. I was then on my first visit to the United States, at the invitation of the University of Virginia. I also remembered how, two years later, Jeff and Barbara had come to Calcutta for our wedding, and Jeff, dressed in a white dhoti and kurta, had sat cross-legged before the fire-altar, on the roof of my family home, and recited Sanskrit *shlokas* with the officiating *purohit*. Everyone had marveled at the clarity of his pronunciation.

I remembered also innumerable stories I had heard from migrants in Italy, of not being able to go home to visit ailing loved ones because of delayed documents. Often, I had tried to imagine myself in their place. Now I no longer had to imagine it: monstrous Gaia had found a way of putting me in their shoes.

13

War by Another Name

In the last week of May 2020, at the height of the Covid pandemic, when the whole world seemed to be frozen in place, two decrepit fishing boats set sail from Libya, heading for Italy. Both capsized and dozens of refugees drowned.

Later that same week, twenty-six Bangladeshis and four Africans were shot dead by human traffickers in western Libya, in a desert town called Mizbah.[1] That name was familiar to me because of conversations I had had with Bengali migrants in Italy, four years earlier. A couple of men I spoke with had passed through the city; they had described being held in cramped, warehouse-like "connection houses," with very little food and water. At the start of their journeys, their *dalals* had charged them a fortune in Bangladeshi money—between $8,000 and $10,000 US dollars—giving them to understand that the sum would be enough to take them all the way through Libya to the Mediterranean coast. But upon arriving in Mizbah, their traffickers had demanded further payments. They were told to call their families back home, to ask them to deposit more money with their *dalals*. Not to do so was to risk being beaten or tortured.

It was a situation of this kind that led to the killings of May 28, in Mizbah. The traffickers had asked the migrants for extra payments, and a fight had broken out in which a Libyan had died. His family had taken revenge by opening fire and killing thirty migrants.[2] The shootings went almost unnoticed in the international press, even though Libya was then frequently in the news because of a sudden escalation in its years-long civil war.

The reason the civil war caught the attention of the international press while the shootings did not was the presence of uniformed soldiers, command structures, and political factions: this made the civil conflict identifiable as a war.[3] When a refugee drowns in the Mediterranean there is no immediate conflict to point to as the cause of their death. Their plight seems to be the outcome, rather, of some larger, impersonal process—maybe poverty, or climate change, neither of which is immediately identifiable as a conflict or a war.

Yet the refugees' experience of the planetary crisis is exactly that of a war: they experience its violence in crossing the border into Turkey; in the slave camps of Libya or the Sinai; in the rickety boats that bring them across the Mediterranean; in the barrages of gunfire that greet them when they try to cross borders; and in the surgical facilities where their organs are harvested to be sold for thousands of dollars on the international market.[4]

IT IS OFTEN SAID that climate change should be tackled as though it were a war. What refugees like Khokon know is that climate change already *is* a war. But it is not the kind of war that climate activists have in mind, like the First and Second World Wars, when Britain and the United States mobilized to confront and defeat a human enemy. Environmental changes and nonhuman entities do not typically play a significant part in wars of that kind.

The war contemporary refugees experience is different; it is in fact more akin to the biopolitical conflicts of the sixteenth and seventeenth centuries. Like the biopolitical conflicts of the past, today's "forever wars" are not events, with a defined beginning and end (like the Second World War); they are ongoing conflicts, in which the violence sometimes ebbs and sometimes crests, but is never completely in abeyance. The wars being fought on the many fronts that the US military often describes as "Indian country"—Afghanistan, northern Pakistan, Iraq, Somalia, and so on—are similarly not events, but rather "structures of invasion." Many of the refugees who end up risking their lives on the Mediterranean are, of course, escaping from those conflicts. As they flee, they find themselves drawn deeper and deeper into new badlands like Libya, countries that have also been destabilized by Western "forever wars."

As with the biopolitical conflicts of the past, the episodic violence of the forever wars is joined to another axis of conflict, a front where "slow violence" unfolds because of inaction.[5] Just as, in the seventeenth and eighteenth centuries, innumerable Indigenous groups were displaced by gradual environmental changes like the disappearance of deer, increased flooding, and the encroachments of livestock, so too are people like Khokon being forced from their land by inexorably rising seas, or by catastrophic floods or desertification. The acceleration of these processes too is the result of the slow violence of inaction.

Just as the Lakota, repeatedly displaced by wars and the rising of dammed waters, were herded into ever-shrinking reservations, so too are the refugees of today's biopolitical wars being forced into zones of containment in North Africa, the Sahara, Mexico, Central America, and islands like Nauru. They too are casualties in a conflict that is not recognizable as war, in the sense defined by Western legal theorists. Yet the parallels with the biopolitical wars of the past are perfectly clear to many Indigenous peoples—thus the title of Nick Estes's powerful account of the environmental struggles of the Lakota and their kin: *Our History Is the Future*.

· · ·

UNCANNY INDEED ARE the similarities between the current planetary crisis and the environmental disruptions that destroyed the life-worlds of innumerable Amerindian and Australian peoples. Now, as before, the devastation of livelihoods and habitats is being effected by apparently impersonal Earth systems; now, as then, it is occurring largely out of sight of those who are most responsible for animating those forces—and by "those who are most responsible" I mean not only affluent Westerners, but also the urban elites and middle classes of countries like India, China, Indonesia, and so on.

Another striking continuity between the biopolitical wars of the past and the ecological disruptions of today lies in the way that human agency is masked by "material forces" and "natural processes." When an island is lost to the rising seas, when a wildfire sweeps in at blinding speed, when a rain bomb explodes over an unprepared city, it is difficult to connect the catastrophe to a human conflict: it seems like an altogether different category of phenomenon. But it was exactly this kind of environmentally mediated conflict that accompanied the colonization of the Americas. For Indigenous peoples it was as if the very elements had become the agents of their undoing. Then too, much of the destruction occurred far from those who had set the processes in motion; advancing settlers would stumble upon overgrown cornfields and depopulated villages. "I have been assured," wrote de Tocqueville, "that [the] effect of the approach of the white man was often felt up to five hundred miles from their frontier. Their influence is thus exerted over tribes whose names they hardly know and who suffer from the evils of invasion long before they know the perpetrators."[6]

Often it was noise that was the cause of long-range environmental disruption. "Colonial farms and villages could probably be heard before they could be seen. The sounds of trees crashing to the ground, saws and axes shaping timber into planks and boards, hammers rapping on the beams and clapboard of houses, and men grunting while digging postholes for fences all announced colonists' occupation of another tract of land."[7] The sheer volume of sound would have been enough to clear the surrounding countryside of the game on which Indians depended.

More often than not there was no settler in sight when disaster overtook an Indian village; the carriers of the calamity were usually other-than-human—clouds of mosquitoes, swarms of rats, plagues of all-devouring sheep and cows, vanishing topsoil, floods caused by deforestation, and of course disease.[8] The trader or missionary who had gone around a village shaking hands would be long gone by the time the contagion he had brought with him began to spread, felling people already weakened by hunger.

Then too, the conflict was accompanied by an extended treaty-making process, with declarations of goodwill on all sides. Often these treaties were negotiated by people of good intention, and were signed in good faith. Yet, all sides understood that the treaties, no matter how lofty their language, could and would be torn up when they clashed with what the dominant parties saw as their vital interests. The resemblance to global climate negotiations is by no means accidental.

Now, as before, the fact that the devastation is being effected by nonhuman, "natural" forces makes it possible for many people, especially in the West—and especially in countries with settler-colonial histories—to claim that climate change is occurring independently of human intentions and agency. The grounds for this claim lie precisely within the gap that modernity created between nature and culture, human and nonhuman.

Now, as before, the idea that the laws of nature operate outside the domain of human agency makes it possible to justify inaction. In this sense inaction is itself a strategy of conflict that pits people with high per capita greenhouse gas emissions against those whose emissions are much lower. Now, as before, the battle lines are ultimately drawn over a will to power and over irreconcilable differences in ways of life.

From this perspective, as many Indigenous voices have reiterated again and again, the present phase of the planetary crisis is not new at all: rather, it represents the Earth's response to the globalization of the ecological transformations that were set in motion by the European colonization of much of the world.[9] Those processes have now escaped the boundaries of the three colonized continents and have become planetary forces, in no small part because Western settler-colonial culture is no longer confined to the settler colonies. Since the adoption in 1989 of the Washington Consensus, the ideologies and practices of settler colonialism have been actively promoted, in their neoliberal guise, by the world's most powerful countries, and have come to be almost universally adopted by national and global elites. It is those settler-colonial practices that are now being implemented by China, in Xinjiang; by Indonesia, in Papua; and by India, in Kashmir and in many of its forest regions.

·   ·   ·

IT HAS OFTEN BEEN observed that many Indigenous peoples have already experienced the end, if not of the world, then of *their* worlds.[10] What tends to be forgotten is that the ending of those worlds had another set of witnesses—Euro-descended settlers. What were the lessons that *they* learned from observing those catastrophes?

There is no mystery to this. The conclusion that White settlers came to was that omnicidal war would always work to their advantage. This is the lesson that informs Tennyson's vision of the ascent of the "crowning race." That is also why there are many people in the former settler colonies who do not flinch from the prospect of accelerating, rather than slowing, climate change; indeed, they welcome it, in the belief that they will be protected from its worst effects.

It is impossible to make sense of much that is happening today without acknowledging this. Why is it, for example, that it often happened in recent years that even as the terraformed "neo-Europes" of Australia and the Americas were being devastated by climate disasters, many of those countries' leaders doubled down on expanding the search for fossil fuels?[11] Why is it that very substantial sections of the population of countries like the US, Canada, Australia, and Brazil supported, and continue to support, such policies? Why is it that the slogan "Drill, baby, drill!" gained as much traction as it did in the United States—a country which, along with other Anglophone nations, produces much of the scientific literature on anthropogenic climate change? Is it that the people who support these policies are stupid and cannot understand the rising risks? Or is it because they see those risks differently because of historical memories that are specific to settler colonialism? Is it perhaps because the tactic of conflict through inaction is not new to the places where they live? Or could it be that historical experience has taught them that terraforming is an inherently violent and risky process, but that in the end the odds will be on their side, because of what they imagine to be their biological and technological advantages?

And it is surely no accident that today too there exists a technology of last resort that many believe will ultimately work in favor of the neo-Europes: geo-engineering. Novel as it may seem, geo-engineering is nothing other than terraforming carried literally into the stratosphere: it should by rights be called "strato-forming." Today some of the richest and most powerful people, and institutions, in the West are openly promoting geo-engineering. Their enthusiasm makes it impossible to forget that "from the mid-eighteenth century onward, modern science explicitly supported empire, defining strategies for colonization."[12]

.   .   .

THE BELIEF IN the inherent biological advantages of the White body is, of course, a recurrent theme in American history. Joyce Chaplin, in her excellent book *Subject Matter*, demonstrates that for English colonists in America, the belief in the superiority of their own bodies actually preceded their conviction of the superiority of their technology. Already in the seventeenth century, she writes, the English had "concluded that the truly inferior material entities in the Americas were the bodies of its native peoples. . . ."[13] This conviction was founded mainly on the settlers' observations of "the Great Dying" that occurred among Native Americans as a result of the introduction of new diseases.[14]

Over the centuries those beliefs were repeatedly reinforced by epidemics that killed staggeringly disproportionate numbers of Native and African Americans. Among freedpeople after the Civil War, for instance, the mortality rate from epidemics was "uniformly double that of the whites and in many cases three or four times as large."[15] These outcomes were, of course, largely the result of structural factors like poverty, malnutrition, displacement, and violence. Yet they were interpreted as evidence of inherited biological deficiencies. At the time, medical opinion supported and even encouraged such interpretations.[16]

Beliefs about biological differences sometimes dovetailed neatly with narratives of extinction. After the American Civil War, government agencies denied funds and medical resources to freedmen's organizations because they "expected the extinction of the black race." One White politician even warned Congress against providing "federal assistance to freedpeople since their death was inevitable."[17]

The Covid-19 pandemic has made it amply evident that beliefs in biological differences between races are still widespread in America. Every day there is new evidence that certain demographic groups in America believe themselves to be less vulnerable to the disease than others. It is also clear that their ideas are related, in some part, to beliefs about their bodily endowments—that is to say, to their racial profiles. It is surely no coincidence that the push to open the economy, even as the pandemic raged, came from exactly those parts of the US where such beliefs have historically been most entrenched.

All of this is, of course, very well understood by Black Lives Matter protesters of all races. Signs like "Blame racism not race" and "Racism is a Pandemic" made perfectly clear that the protesters perceived the disproportionate tolls of the pandemic as being caused by centuries-old patterns of historical and environmental injustice. In no small part was their anger rooted in the knowledge that political elites had taken a deliberate, but unspoken, decision to sacrifice a large number of lives precisely *because* the dead would be disproportionately non-White.

There is, I think, an important question here for the climate movement. Activists have long sought to appeal to the conscience of the privileged by emphasizing the message that the costs of climate change will largely be borne by the world's poor, mainly Black and brown people. It now needs to be considered whether these appeals to the conscience may not have had exactly the opposite of the intended effect. Is it possible that this message has actually persuaded the privileged to think they need do nothing about climate change because they will be insulated from the worst impacts of global warming by their affluence, and indeed by their bodily advantages? Some may believe that climate change is just another of the periodic challenges of the business cycle; others may have convinced themselves that they will ultimately reap some rewards from climate change, just as their ancestors benefited from the process of continental terraforming.[18]

This is not, actually, a matter of speculation. It is increasingly clear that those who deny the reality of climate change, like the tens of millions of people who supported President Trump and President Jair Bolsonaro of Brazil, believe in inaction, on both climate change and matters of public health, *because* they think that only those who are congenitally weak and vulnerable will suffer. Their solution to both is to push for the expansion of the "sacrifice zones" where the poor and the non-White will bear the brunt of the planetary crisis. This is in fact nothing other than a new iteration of the kind of "conflict through inaction" that was so marked a feature of the biopolitical wars of colonization.

But there are major differences between those times and today. For one thing, the nonhuman "invisible allies" that favored one side over another in those wars are no longer clearly allied with any one side. In some places, where intensively terraformed landscapes seem to be shrugging off their geo-engineered forms, those allies seem to be turning against the victors of the biopolitical wars of the past. Today no group or groups can count on the support of nonhuman allies. Other-than-human beings, forces, and entities, both manmade and earthly, could be pursuing their own ends, of which humans know nothing. Gaia, at once bountiful and monstrous, has now assumed a new avatar: Solaris.

14

"The Divine Angel of Discontent"

When the powerful and the super-rich say they are planning to colonize Mars in order to ensure the survival of the human race, or that they are building underground bunkers in New Zealand, what do they actually mean?[1] What are the unstated assumptions on which such projections are founded?

Clearly the need to ensure the survival of the human race would arise only in the event of the Earth becoming uninhabitable— perhaps because of a "far-off Divine event" that had brought about another Great Dying, on a vastly larger scale than that which followed the European conquest of the Americas. This is so obvious that it need not even be stated; the imminence of this apocalypse has come to be silently assumed, in much the same way that the mass extinction of the "lesser races" was once taken for granted by Western elites.[2] In the past, as now, it was not considered polite to promote extermination publicly; in the past, as now, it was not considered genteel, or necessary, to mention mass mortalities. They merely faded into the background as unstated assumptions.[3]

But of course, not everyone was always polite; there were many who did not mince their words when they spoke of extermination. General William T. Sherman, for instance, wrote in 1873: "We must act with vindictive earnestness against the Sioux, even to their extermination, men, women and children . . . during an assault, the soldiers can not pause to distinguish between male and female, or even discriminate as to age."[4] Nor were soldiers the only advocates of this policy. L. Frank Baum, author of *The Wonderful Wizard of Oz*, once wrote: "The Whites, by law of conquest, by justice of civilization, are masters of the American continent, and the best safety of the frontier settlements will be secured by the total annihilation of the few remaining Indians. Why not annihilation? Their glory has fled, their spirit broken, their manhood effaced; better that they die than live the miserable wretches that they are."[5]

Today too, not everyone is so polite as to skim over the assumed apocalypse. There is a by no means negligible fringe, on the Far Right, which sees another Great Dying (or, as they would put it, "a Malthusian correction") as the only possible solution to the planetary crisis. To them it is immaterial that the carbon footprint of a single American or Australian is equal to that of thirty-three Bangladeshis—so that as far as greenhouse gas emissions are concerned, the population of Bangladesh is not 168 million, but more like 5 million, about half the size of New York City. But this is inconsequential, because what is at issue is not ultimately what is sustainable for the planet; what is at stake is a way of life, founded on high consumption and defended by military power, that can only survive if large numbers of poor, low-emitting people are eliminated.

The purchase of such ideas is wide enough that it is worth asking: Would the elimination of a large number of poor people actually make it possible for the world's affluent to go on living as they are? The answer, actually, is no, because those lifestyles are predicated on metastasis, on endless and ever-increasing growth. This has been the fundamental ideology of the Anglosphere since the dawn of the nineteenth century. To White settlers, one of the most offensive aspects of Native American culture was its incompatibility with the paradigm of ever-growing material desire. In 1896 a leading advocate for the Americanization of Indians wrote, with great urgency, of "the absolute need of awakening in the savage Indian broader desires and ampler wants. To bring him out of savagery into citizenship we must make the Indian more intelligently selfish before we can make him unselfishly intelligent. We need to *awaken in him wants*. In his dull savagery he must be touched by the wings of the divine angel of discontent. . . . Discontent with the teepee and the starving rations of the Indian camp in winter is needed to get the Indian out of the blanket and into trousers,—and trousers with a pocket in them, and with a *pocket that aches to be filled with dollars!*"[6]

It is the "divine angel of discontent" who has metastasized cars into SUVs, and houses into McMansions. Left to itself, the forever discontented lifestyle of contemporary affluence would continue to expand its environmental footprint at an ever-increasing pace, and a time would come when all it would take to fill the shoes of 150 million poor Bangladeshis would be a few thousand wealthy malcontents.

ONLY A RADICAL FRINGE openly embraces the prospect of a Malthusian correction. Yet, Malthusian conceptions implicitly underlie the hardening of borders that is happening across the world. "In much of Europe and the Anglosphere," writes Naomi Klein, "this hardening is already well under way. The European Union, Australia, and the United States have all embraced immigration policies that are variations on 'prevention through deterrence.' The brutal logic is to treat migrants with so much callousness and cruelty that desperate people will be deterred from seeking safety by crossing borders."[7]

An early, and extremely effective, opponent of migration was the right-wing ecological thinker Garrett Hardin, who made his case in an article titled "Living on a Lifeboat." First published in 1974, the article remains influential enough to merit scrutiny.

Hardin's essay begins by highlighting the importance of metaphors in human thought: "Since metaphorical thinking is inescapable it is pointless merely to weep about our human limitations. We must learn to live with them, to understand them, and to control them."[8] The metaphor that Hardin fastens upon is this: "Metaphorically, each rich nation amounts to a lifeboat full of comparatively rich people. The poor of the world are in other, much more crowded lifeboats. Continuously, so to speak, the poor fall out of their lifeboats and swim for a while in the water outside, hoping to be admitted to a rich lifeboat."[9] Since taking the floundering swimmers in would only ensure the death of all, goes the argument, the ethics of the lifeboat demand that those who are on board already should keep others out, in order to ensure their own survival. This argument is an extension of Hardin's other big idea, "the tragedy of the commons," in which he argues that a steadily increasing population of profit-maximizing individuals, within a delimited space, would lead to collapse: "Mutual ruin is inevitable in the commons. This is the core of the tragedy of the commons."[10]

The metaphor of the lifeboat was evidently chosen with great care, for the persuasiveness of the story (and it is exactly that, a story) rests entirely on the image of a few rich lifeboats staying afloat while vast hordes of poor, drowning people clutch at their gunwales. But the analogy on which the argument rests is actually its greatest weakness: all it takes to expose its fallacies is a change of metaphor. What if, for instance, the human predicament were to be represented by a metaphor taken from an actual historical circumstance involving lifeboats: the *Titanic*, where, by common consent, women and children boarded the lifeboats first, rather than the strong and wealthy? Or of a river basin where people decide, by common consent, not to fish during spawning season?

There are, in fact, innumerable examples of people responding to crises by adopting measures that required greater cooperation. The historian Carolyn Merchant, for example, has shown how in Europe, in the twelfth and thirteenth centuries, when populations began to increase, many communities of farmers voluntarily pooled their holdings and ensured that resources were used fairly. "In many regions, therefore, population pressure resulted not in a 'tragedy of the commons' produced by competitive self-interest, but in increased co-operative activity and in group regulation of the eco-system."[11] Indeed, common lands existed everywhere in the world, with no tragic consequences, until Europeans, armed with guns and the ideas of John Locke and his ilk, began to forcefully impose draconian regimes of private poverty. An accurate title for the history of common lands would therefore be "The Tragedy of Enclosure."

The fallacies in Hardin's conception of "the tragedy of the commons" have also been exposed by recent research in heterodox branches of economics. The Nobel Prize–winning economist Elinor Ostrom, for instance, has shown that humans often respond to scarcity and crisis with strategies of cooperation and sharing. Indeed, the ability to cooperate is now regarded by some scientists as a crucial evolutionary advantage.[12] Inasmuch as the ability to cooperate is undermined by extreme attachments to personal freedoms, and by the valorization of the pursuit of individual interests at all costs, these ideas, and the behaviors they generate, could be described as forms of pathological or morbid individualism. The furious growth of Covid-19 cases in those parts of the US where many people regarded masking as an infringement of their individual liberties suggests that it is morbid individualism that turns crises into tragedies.

When the idea that the selfish pursuit of individual interests is a universal feature of human nature is adopted as a basic tenet, it can become a self-fulfilling prophecy. Neoclassical economics, in which that idea is a foundational creed, is a good example. A Cornell study has demonstrated that students of economics are markedly more selfish, more prone to dishonesty, and less willing to cooperate with others than their peers in other fields.[13] What the study demonstrates, in effect, is that selfishness, uncooperativeness, and dishonesty are not "naturally" dominant aspects of the human personality; they become dominant only through processes of indoctrination into certain modes of thought.

English literature too has long been a leading disseminator of the ideology of morbid individualism. William Golding's most famous work, Lord of the Flies, is a good example. The novel tells the story of a group of English schoolchildren who are stranded on a desert island, where their civilizational restraints fall apart, leading to a Hobbesian war of all against all. Empathy and sociability, Golding's narrative suggests, are polite fictions that break down in extreme circumstances, when the primal realities of selfishness and aggression come to the fore, and the "state of nature"—that much-beloved conceit of Western philosophy—takes over.

As it happens, only eleven years after the publication of Lord of the Flies, wide-bosomed Gaia, in her tricksterish way, contrived to create a circumstance in which Golding's view of the world could be tested. In 1965, a group of six teenage schoolboys were stranded on a desert island for fifteen months. But instead of reverting to a state of nature, the boys cooperated, established rules, and looked after each other. "By the time we arrived," writes the sea captain who rescued them, "the boys had set up a small commune with food garden, hollowed-out tree trunks to store rainwater, a gymnasium with curious weights, a badminton court, chicken pens and a permanent fire, all from handiwork, an old knife blade and much determination."[14] But the schoolboys were Tongans, not English, and therefore they presumably did not subscribe to the doctrines of morbid individualism that inform Golding's story. In effect, far from reflecting anything universal, *Lord of the Flies* presents an image of human nature that Western elites *want* to believe because it is a product of the same imaginaries on which their own worldview is founded. That is why the book is taught to schoolchildren to this day.

However, mistaking morbid individualism for a universal human trait is not the most important fallacy in Hardin's story. An even greater misconception lies in the idea that "metaphorically, each rich nation amounts to a lifeboat full of comparatively rich people." To someone who was willing to overlook divisions of class and race, this might once have seemed true. But the intensification of the planetary crisis has made that kind of oversight impossible, by exposing glaring disparities in the human toll of weather-related disasters and, indeed, the pandemic.

If the Covid-19 pandemic has any clear message, it is that no part of the world, rich or poor, will be spared by the planetary crisis— precisely because it is planetary and does not recognize borders. The very nature of this crisis is such that in order to deal with it the world will have to think like a forest; it is those who fail to do so who will be at greatest risk. This is because no country possesses enough lifeboats to save all its people. The supposed safe havens of the United States, for example, consist of a network of walled estates, gated communities, and super-yachts that belong to the ultra-wealthy. Very few indeed will have access to these refuges: the ultimate irony of Hardin's "lifeboat ethics" is that he, who no doubt imagined that he would be seated comfortably in a lifeboat when the world's conditions began to worsen, would stand little chance of boarding the vessels of the super-rich. His own arguments would be used to keep him out.

· · ·

WESTERN IDEAS ABOUT migration are drawn largely from an experience of settler colonialism that involved large numbers of people leaving their European homelands in order to settle permanently in newly conquered territories on distant continents. But this pattern is actually an anomaly in the history of human circulation. Before the European conquest of the Americas, people did not generally move to faraway places with the intention of settling in them permanently. Voluntary movements, as opposed to coerced movements like slavery and bondage, tended to follow patterns of circulation whereby merchants, sailors, and soldiers would move to other places with the intention of spending a few years there before returning to their homelands.[15] These itinerants were sojourners rather than migrants, although some may indeed have never returned to their ancestral lands. This was the dominant pattern of circulation in the pre-sixteenth-century Indian Ocean, where port cities typically had large enclaves of sojourning foreigners (Chinese settlers in Southeast Asia were the exception rather than the rule).

Even after the conquest of the Americas it was by no means easy to persuade Europeans to leave their homelands in order to settle on other continents. In England people were so reluctant to move that a new literary genre of what might be called "migration propaganda" came into being to convince them that they might be better off elsewhere; the genre's pioneers were Richard Hakluyt and Samuel Purchas. Even then the British government eventually had to adopt policies of "transportation," or coerced migration, exporting convicts and other "undesirables" to Australia and other colonies.

It was not till the nineteenth century that Europeans began to leave their mother continent in the tens of millions in order to settle permanently in other continents. Yet, this relatively brief episode in the history of human circulation has molded contemporary ideas about migration so powerfully that it is now assumed that every migrant wants to settle permanently in their destination country. This assumption in turn has become the foundation of policies, and structures of governance, that actually force migrants to settle permanently, sometimes against their inclinations.

It is by no means the case that all, or even most, of the people who leave their homes want to settle elsewhere permanently. This can perhaps best be seen in the case of the single largest category of people who are now on the move across the planet: internal migrants, or those who move within their home countries. In India, for instance, a huge demographic churn has been under way for some time, with enormous numbers of migrant workers moving from the country's poorer eastern regions to the major cities and to other relatively prosperous areas. Internal migration of this kind does not necessarily lead to great material betterment, but it does help to redistribute wealth nationally by providing sustenance for millions of households in poorer parts of the country. Moreover, internal migration has the advantage of preserving family ties by allowing relatives to see each other periodically. The workers who move in this way are mostly "circulatory migrants" rather than settlers; their intention is to make some money over a short period and then go back home.[16]

Even when South Asian workers go abroad, their movements tend to follow the patterns of circulatory migration. Their preferred destinations—the petro-states of the Middle East, and countries like Malaysia and Singapore—are mainly within the region, so they are able to travel back and forth without too much difficulty. In recent years many have also been traveling north to the Central Asian republics, and also to China, where some cities harbor large numbers of foreigners. Guangzhou, for instance, has a population of circulatory migrants from Africa, the Middle East, and South Asia that numbers in the hundreds of thousands.

Circulatory migrants are often willing to put up with a great deal of hardship because they know that their sojourn is not a new life, but a brief phase that will nonetheless radically alter their circumstances when they return to their native villages and towns. If all goes well, they will not only bring back some money, but will also be regarded with respect, not least because they will have many stories to tell.

A science-fictional imagining of a sojourner's journey would feature a harmless and curious extraterrestrial who is stranded on an unfamiliar planet and yearns to go back home (and the great Indian filmmaker Satyajit Ray did indeed write such a script, even before Steven Spielberg made *E.T.*). This is a far cry from the predatory settler-aliens of *War of the Worlds* and *Independence Day*, and it may well provide a better frame for interpreting the long-concealed evidence of extraterrestrial visitations that has been revealed by the US government in recent years.

.   .   .

THE MIGRANTS WHO set off to travel to affluent Western countries are very few in proportion to internal migrants, and for many the journeys do not end well, even when they succeed in reaching their destination. Of the Bengali migrants I spoke to in Italy, many regretted the decision to leave; for some the search for a better life had left them worse off than they had been at home. Although all of them were willing and eager to work, there were no jobs to be had because of the high unemployment rates in Italy. Some were struggling to get by, sharing a room with many others, sleeping in shifts, and eking out a living selling trinkets on street corners while being subjected to constant harassment by the police or right-wing gangs.

Back at home, whatever the hardships, they had at least had the consolation of friends, family, and community; in Europe they were utterly bereft of all human connections. Many would have preferred to return but found themselves trapped in place, either because of asylum laws, or because of the expectations of their relatives back home, or out of the fear of never being able to return. What the great majority of them really aspired to, in fact, was to be circulatory migrants who could earn some money and then go back to their families.

This is now the dominant pattern of migration globally. "International labor migration," writes the German labor economist Klaus F. Zimmermann, "is typically circular, involving non-permanent moves back and forth between home and foreign places of work." Alarmist right-wing narratives about migrants settling permanently in Western countries because of welfare payments are based on a fundamental misunderstanding of contemporary migration: in this hyper-mobile age, that is no longer how people move—even refugees from war zones sometimes adopt circular patterns of travel. "In reality, a large share of migrants move for work-related reasons—and do so on a temporary basis. The movement of labor migrants is therefore often circular: They move back and forth between their homeland and foreign places of work. This circularity suggests the potential of a win-win-win situation for migrants and the sending and receiving countries."[17]

Circulatory migration can admittedly have very damaging effects because it creates circumstances in which workers have no statutory protections and can therefore be brutally exploited. Yet this is the adaptive strategy that huge numbers of people are choosing: in other words, what they are opting for is not total relocation, but a circular pattern of movement that allows them to maintain connections with places that are familiar and where they have support networks. Obviously, this is not a feasible strategy for people who are in danger of losing their lands altogether, like Pacific Islanders. But for those who are losing their livelihoods rather than their homes, this may well be a preferred adaptive strategy: this seems to already be the case not just in South Asia, but also within the European Union and North America. It seems very likely that this will be the adaptive strategy that the majority of displaced people will choose in the future, as climate disruptions intensify.

This being the case, it seems to me that the most humane way forward is to accept this reality and to try and create safeguards and regulatory mechanisms to prevent the blatant exploitation of, say, itinerant agricultural workers, as happens today in India, North America, and parts of the EU.

Adaptive measures, at the individual and the national level, are essential to cope with the deepening crises that loom ahead. Without them, national boundaries will continue to be the primary battlegrounds of the planetary crisis, where growing numbers of people will face an irregular war that condemns them to the fate implicit in the Latin word for "border"—*terminus*. From this derives another word, *extermino*, which means "drive over the border," "exile, banish, exclude." Hence the English word *exterminate*, the exact meaning of which is "to drive over the border to death, banish from life."[18]

15

Brutes

The idea of extermination, and its place within Western culture, has never been explored as insightfully and with as much formal ingenuity as in the work of the Swedish writer and scholar Sven Lindqvist. His books *"Exterminate All the Brutes"* and *Terra Nullius* are narratives of travel in which each step of the journey takes the reader deeper into spaces that are at once terrestrial and imaginative.[1] The first book is framed by a journey across the Sahara, and the second by a road trip in western Australia. Both are explorations of intellectual history that unfold by mapping ideas upon landscapes; their narratives are grounded not in abstractions, but in the ground itself, in the soil of particular places. In that sense, they share a certain kinship with the songs of the Bandanese and the stories told by innumerable Indigenous peoples.

Right at the start of *"Exterminate All the Brutes,"* Lindqvist asserts that his book "is a story, not a contribution to historical research. It is the story of a man traveling by bus through the Saharan desert and, at the same time, traveling by computer through the history of the concept of extermination. In small, sand-ridden desert hotels, his study closes in on one sentence in Joseph Conrad's *Heart of Darkness*: 'Exterminate all the brutes.'"

In Conrad's novella, the sentence "Exterminate all the brutes" comes from the ailing Mr. Kurtz, who is the object of the narrator's search. The words are not uttered aloud by Kurtz; the narrator, Marlow, finds them scrawled across the final pages of a high-minded report that Kurtz has written for the "International Society for the Suppression of Savage Customs." Marlow is mesmerized by that sentence; it blazes at him, "luminous and terrifying, like a flash of lightning in a serene sky: 'Exterminate all the brutes.'"[2]

In Conrad's staging of the scene, the climactic sentence is presented in the guise of a scream of despair, written by a White man who has been driven to the end of his tether by his long exile in the heart of Africa, among the inhabitants of a landscape so primitive that it is "like the earliest beginnings of the world." Kurtz is broken down, as Lindqvist puts it, by "the distances, the climate, and the solitude. . . . Most of all the solitude, for that entails also an inner abandonment. . . . Solitude erased society . . . and left behind fear, mistrust, and violence."[3]

What is curious about this passage is that Lindqvist, insightful as he is, does not notice the dissonance between Conrad's staging of the scene and the intent of his own book, which is precisely to demonstrate that extermination was not an incidental thought that sometimes flashed into the minds of beleaguered White men. What Lindqvist shows is that the idea of extermination was central, not marginal, to Western elite culture; he does this by piling example upon example, quote upon quote. Here, for instance, is an Englishman writing home from what is now Zambia: "Lord Grey's priest, Father Bihler, was convinced that the blacks had to be exterminated. 'He states that the only chance for the future of the race is to exterminate the whole people, both male and female over the age of fourteen,' Grey writes to his wife on January 23, 1897."[4] And here is Alfred Russel Wallace, the "co-discoverer of the theory of evolution," whose "Letter from Ternate," written in 1858, prompted the publication of a seminal article on the theory of evolution: "In his lecture on 'The Origin of Human Races,' Wallace explained in greater detail how he looked on extermination. Quite simply, it was another name for natural selection. Contact with Europeans leads the lower, mentally underdeveloped peoples of other continents to inevitable destruction, says Wallace."[5]

Lindqvist's documentation is so rich that it becomes impossible to doubt that the idea of extermination lay at the core of elite Western culture in the nineteenth century, and even a part of the twentieth century. It was, indeed, naturalized to the point where it informed government policy and was constantly asserted by leading statesmen. Here is Lord Salisbury, Prime Minister of Britain, declaring, as if it were self-evident, in a speech on May 4, 1898: "One can roughly divide the nations of the world into the living and the dying."[6]

The fate that befalls Kurtz, then, bears no resemblance to the destiny of the Europeans who actually carried out exterminations. Men like Jan Coen, John Mason, John Underhill, Jeffrey Amherst, and King Leopold II of Belgium did not die forgotten in miserable huts in the jungle; they were richly rewarded, and their names were commemorated in roads, parks, poems, and history books. John Mason, who massacred the Pequot, would be remembered in Connecticut as one of "the Instrumental Saviours of this Country in the most critical Conjunctures . . . the present and future Generations will for ever be obliged to revere their Memory."[7] Mason's confederate John Underhill, who had many mass killings to his name, would be much celebrated in the late nineteenth century, as another wave of massacres was unfolding in the American West: an ode was written to praise his deeds, and a statue was raised in his honor at a burial ground that was named after him. The statue was dedicated by Theodore Roosevelt, who said on the occasion: "The founder of the family here was a good soldier and a good citizen, and the Underhills have today furnished their full quota of good soldiers and good citizens in their time. If they had not, I would not have been here." Underhill's descendants did indeed count among them many prominent Americans, including Amelia Earhart. Two of contemporary Hollywood's most famous stars are also descended from him; one of them—irony of ironies—has recently been ceremonially adopted by a "Comanche woman and social activist."[8]

As for Jeffrey Amherst, that avid extirpator of Indians, he was one of the most admired figures in England during the period of the American Revolution.[9] In America the reverence for Amherst was so great that his memory remains enshrined in the names of a prominent Massachusetts university town and one of the country's most famous colleges.

Nor were colonial projects of extermination conceived by men who were at the end of their tether. They were in full possession of their faculties when they planned their massacres; indeed, they were often merely implementing official policies that had been drawn up in Europe. This would have been the case, for instance, with Conrad's Kurtz. As for solitude, that played no part in colonial exterminations either: the men who carried them out were never alone, and they almost always acted in the full knowledge that they would have the support not only of their governments, but also of the scientists, writers, poets, and even priests of their countries.

"The idea of extermination," as Lindqvist himself emphasizes, "lies no farther from the heart of humanism than Buchenwald lies from the Goethehaus in Weimar. That insight has been almost completely repressed, even by the Germans, who have been made sole scapegoats for ideas of extermination that are actually a common European heritage."[10]

Yet Lindqvist does not notice something that many non-Westerners intuitively understand: that in making exterminatory violence appear exceptional, as a thought that flashes momentarily through Kurtz's mind, Conrad was in fact concealing the true nature of that phenomenon, and the place it once had within the heart of Whiteness.

Thus the scathing critique of Conrad's novella that Chinua Achebe delivered, ironically, at Amherst, Massachusetts, in 1975.[11]

THROUGHOUT THESE TWO BOOKS Lindqvist's attention is focused on the first term in Conrad's climactic sentence: "extermination." But the sentence includes another term that is no less important: "brutes." What does this word mean? Where does it come from?

The word has an interesting etymology. It entered English by way of French, Latin, and Oscan, an extinct language of southern Italy. It derives from a Proto-Indo-European root, *gréhus*, which had the connotation of "heavy." This word is cognate, curiously enough, with the Sanskrit term *guru*, which is, of course, now a well-entrenched part of the vocabulary of English as well.

In the initial phases of the word's transition, from Latin *brutus*, to French *brut*, to English *brute*, the word generally meant "dull, stupid, insensible" and was mainly used of animals. It was only after the 1530s that the scope of the word "brute" grew broader in English, covering people as well as animals and objects. It became a term that served to merge certain kinds of humans with things whose existence was merely material, insensible.

It is probably no coincidence that the expansion in the meaning of the word "brute" occurred during the most violent period of the conquest of the Americas, which was sometimes presented by Europeans as a "world without humans."[12] The question of whether Amerindians had souls or not, were fully human or not, was one that divided not only soldiers and conquistadores, but also many thinkers and philosophers. In 1550 King Charles V of Spain even summoned a conference at Valladolid to settle the issue. But the participants, who included Bartolomeo de las Casas, failed to come to a decision on the subject; the issue of whether Amerindians were fully human was left unresolved.

It was probably that very lack of resolution that propelled the evolution of the word "brute": how were all these beings, not quite human and not quite animal, to be thought of and referred to? It is easy to see how a word like "brute" would be needed to fill the gap that had grown out of the inability of elite European intellectuals to reach agreement on the question of whether a large part of humanity was, in fact, fully human.

Over time, as the meaning of "brute" broadened, the concept became increasingly assimilated to "Nature"; indeed, the two ideas co-evolved so that it became common to speak of "brute Nature." For Francis Bacon, "bruteness" was a feature of materiality. In his *New Organon* he writes: "The most general principles in nature have to be brute facts."[13] In other words, "bruteness" is that which can be observed in the world; it is exterior to the human.

In this way "brute" evolved into a trans-species term that allowed many human beings—the majority of humankind, in fact—to be assimilated to the rubric of "Nature." Being enmeshed in Nature also meant that this part of humanity was excluded from "History," which was the exclusive domain of the civilized or "historical" nations. But there was a hierarchy even in this. The sociologist and historian Immanuel Wallerstein once reminded his colleagues:

"Ninety-five per cent of all written history before 1945 was that of five historical nations: Great Britain, France, the United States, the Germanies (I choose this formulation deliberately) and the Italies. The other 5 per cent is largely the history of a few less powerful European states, such as the Netherlands or Sweden or Spain. A small percentage was concerned with the European Middle Ages as well as with the presumed founts of modern Europe: ancient Greece and Rome. But not ancient Persia, or even ancient Egypt."[14]

For brutes, time repeated itself endlessly; their past was not worth studying because it had no trajectory and no meaning. As Wallerstein points out, as recently as the 1960s the most eminent British historian of his time, Sir Hugh Trevor-Roper, saw nothing amiss in proclaiming that "Africa had no history." To this day American departments of history devote just 17 percent of their research to regions outside Europe and North America.[15]

The racism implicit in the concept of the "brute" plants a contradiction at the heart of European humanism—which is, after all, founded on the belief that "Man" as a species is exceptional. But the "Man" of European humanism was not, in fact, the human species, since most of Mankind was thought to share in the mute brutishness of "Nature."

Implicit in this is an acknowledgment that humans are actually no different from other beings.

·   ·   ·

LITERATURE'S BEST-KNOWN BRUTE, Shakespeare's Caliban, came into the world just ten years before the massacre of the Bandanese: the play in which Caliban makes his entrance, *The Tempest*, was first performed in 1611.

The Tempest is, of course, famously an allegory of colonialism. The name "Caliban" is probably an anagram for "Cannibal," a word which would originally have referred to a group of Amerindians. "Columbus first recorded the term," writes a literary critic, "in reference to the fifteenth-century inhabitants of Haiti and Cuba, of the Carib tribe, supposedly referring to certain man-eating rituals practiced by some tribal groups on the islands. Because of the affinity between *l, n* and *r*, the tribe has been referred to as *Calib, Carib* and *Canib.*"[16] It is actually highly unlikely that cannibalism was practiced by the Carib—but, as Peter Hulme has pointed out, the alacrity with which the term was "adopted into the bosom of the European family of languages . . . suggests that there had always been an empty place kept warm for it."[17]

In *The Tempest*'s dramatis personae, Caliban is listed as a "savage and deformed slave," and the grotesqueness of his appearance is a recurrent theme in the play. His master, Prospero, describes him as "a freckled whelp," "not honour'd with a human shape"; and frequently reminds him that he is akin to an animal ("thou tortoise") whose existence is purely material, a brute fact ("thou earth").

Yet the essence of Caliban's brutishness does not lie in his external appearance: that is indeed the import of the famous lines in which Prospero reminds Caliban of the most important gift that he has given him:

> . . . I pitied thee,
> Took pains to make thee speak, taught thee each hour
> One thing or other: when thou didst not, savage,
> Know thine own meaning, but wouldst gabble like
> A thing most brutish, I endow'd thy purposes
> With words that made them known.[18]

The essence of Caliban's brutishness lies, then, in his lack of language, in his inability to make meaning, even though he possesses the faculty of speech.

Prospero's words—"I endow'd thy purposes with words that made them known"—go straight to the heart of the European colonizer's framing of the colonized: despite possessing the uniquely human faculty of speech, brutish humans cannot produce meaning; their sounds amount to mere "gabble" until the colonizer gives them words, which endows them at last with the ability to make meaning. Until then, no matter that they have tongues, voices, and languages, brutes are effectively mute, like "Nature" itself, which also makes sounds but produces no meaning. In this view of the world the sounds of Nature are not equivalent to utterances; they are the products of mechanical responses and reactions. The muteness of Nature and the muteness of the brute are reflections of each other.

As a process, then, the muting of a large part of humanity by European colonizers cannot be separated from the simultaneous muting of "Nature." Colonization was thus not merely a process of establishing dominion over human beings; it was also a process of subjugating, and reducing to muteness, an entire universe of beings that was once thought of as having agency, powers of communication, and the ability to make meaning—animals, trees, volcanoes, nutmegs. These mutings were essential to processes of economic extraction—because, as the philosopher Akeel Bilgrami observes, in order to see something as a mere resource, "we first need to see it as brute, as something that makes no normative demands of practical and moral engagement with us."[19]

It is by representing a vast continuum of human and nonhuman beings as "brutes" that the colonizer turns them into "resources," to be used as slaves, servants, and commodities. This entire continuum, not just humans, was represented as being subject to the natural laws that condemn certain species to extinction or extermination.

It is here, I think, that Lindqvist misses a crucial nuance when he interprets the sentence "Exterminate all the brutes" as an exhortation to genocide. Humans are not the only brutes whose extermination is envisaged by Kurtz; there are many others around him—animals, the jungle, indeed the landscape itself.

What Kurtz's scrawled sentence actually expresses, then, is the urge to omnicide.

IT IS VERY RARE today for the word "brute" to be used in the way that it was in the past. Nobody refers to animals as brutes anymore, let alone to people or races; nobody even cries out "you brute!" as characters so often do in Victorian novels.

But even as the original coinage fades from everyday usage, its derivatives, like "brutal" and "brutality," have become ubiquitous—on the internet, in newspapers, and on the signs protesters carry through the streets as they chant "Black Lives Matter!"—for police brutality is, of course, at the heart of the protests.

The current ubiquity of the word "brutality" is an indication of a stunning reversal: no longer is this domain of meaning configured around the savage or the semicivilized; it is centered instead on the repressive machinery of the state, primarily the police. The inversion of meaning establishes an etymological arc that links the planetary crisis directly back to processes of colonization, enslavement, and biopolitical war.

With every passing day—I am writing these words in late July 2020—more and more historical connections are being dragged out of the mists of the past to link, for example, contemporary police violence to the slave patrols of eighteenth- and nineteenth-century plantations. Every day I see references to a date just two years removed from that of the Banda genocide: the year 1619, when the first slave ship was brought to Virginia by English pirates. Every day there is news of statues of slave traders and Confederate generals being toppled.

The outraged commentary in the right-wing media suggests that many are under the impression that the toppling of statues is new, at least in the metropolitan centers of former colonial empires. But it is not. The Dutch began to take down statues of Jan Pietersz. Coen decades ago.

I watch in fascination video clips of a protest in Bristol, England, which ends with the statue of a slave trader responsible for the enslavement of more than 84,000 Africans being thrown into the very waters from which his ships had once set sail. In this, as in most such protests, the participants are mostly young and White.

I watch the beheading of a statue of Christopher Columbus, and am reminded of the omnicidal orgies of the Admiral's second voyage to the Caribbean, when his troops "had gone ashore and killed indiscriminately, as though for sport, whatever animals and birds and natives they encountered, 'looting and destroying all they found,' as the Admiral's son Fernando blithely put it."[20] I remember also that it was this voyage that introduced influenza to the Americas, and that Columbus himself had fallen sick with it, on the island of Hispaniola. While he lay ill his soldiers went on rampages, which, together with the disease, killed more than 50,000 of the island's people.[21] On recovering, Columbus "massed together several hundred armored troops, cavalry and a score or more of trained attack dogs. They set forth across the countryside, tearing into assembled masses of sick and unarmed native people, slaughtering them by the thousands."[22]

On an impulse I look up the number of deaths caused in the US by Covid-19 and find that it has crossed 115,000. I discover also that in the weeks since March 8, when I began to self-isolate, more than 570 people have been killed by mass shootings in the US, and that gun violence has actually increased during the lockdown.[23]

I am mesmerized by video footage of a demonstration, organized jointly by the Black Lives Matter and "Rhodes Must Fall" movements, calling for the removal of a statue of Cecil Rhodes from the premises of an Oxford college. The college authorities had previously dismissed these demands on the grounds that the statue is "a reminder of the complexity of history and of the legacies of colonialism"—an absurd argument, since it is the statue itself that reduces the complexity of history to the image of a colonizer.[24]

The Oxford demonstration is huge, far larger than expected, as are many of the protests that call for the removal of these statues. This seems to puzzle some commentators, even sympathetic ones; they are at a loss to understand how protests against the police have spilled over into the toppling of statues. Why not focus on "policy outcomes" instead? Why bother with relics of the past? How does history matter? Removing a statue, some critics say, will change nothing.

What they don't see is that the struggles over the statues are battles over meaning, and to change the meaning of something is to change everything—precisely because humans are not brutes.

Whatever the Black Lives Matter movement may or may not achieve, it has already succeeded in making manifest the insistent vitality of the past. It has shown that the indifference to history that was once believed to be a prominent feature of American culture was never anything but an elite myth. Native Americans and African Americans were never indifferent to the past, not least because they had to deal with its legacies of violence in their daily lives. Every protest is an assertion that the planetary crisis is rooted in the past and cannot be understood without it.

"History," long used as a tool of subjugation, has spilled out of classrooms and museums and flowed into the streets. Ironically, this has been made possible by the very racism that lay concealed, as Immanuel Wallerstein noted, at the heart of the practice of writing "History." It is precisely because the history of the US, and all the other so-called "historical nations," has been so closely studied that it has become impossible to conceal inconvenient truths. A narrative which began as a chronicle of the triumphant ascent of Western man has provided the tools for its own upending.

I am astonished and moved to see this happening before my eyes, on the streets around me; I had not thought I would see anything like this in my lifetime. It is proof of the human capacity for renewal through empathetic understanding.

I AM AT MY DESK, writing about statues and monuments, when I hear shouts from the street below and see a Black Lives Matter protest going by. I run out to join it, and find myself walking, in the midst of a mainly White crowd, to the monument that towers above Fort Greene Park, the Prison Ship Martyrs monument.

With shouts of "Black lives matter!" ringing through the park, I read the plaque that stands beside the monument. It tells me that the monument was built to commemorate the lives of 11,500 "men, women and children" that were lost in 1776 when the British captured this area from George Washington's Continental army. Thousands of American captives were incarcerated on British prison ships, where they died of "overcrowding, contaminated water, starvation, and disease."

I recall, then, an episode from Indian history that is "probably as well-known in the English-speaking world as the fact that Napoleon was Emperor of France."[25] In 1756, only twenty years before the death of the Prison Ship Martyrs, a hundred twenty-three English prisoners were said to have died, of overcrowding and asphyxiation, in the Indian prison that came to be known as the Black Hole of Calcutta. This story became a "founding myth of empire" and was used for centuries to justify British violence in India.[26]

The trouble is, however, that there is no conclusive proof that the alleged atrocity ever took place. Over more than a century a great many scholars and historians have shown that the evidence for it is flimsy at best, and that if indeed there was a massacre, then the number of fatalities was less than half of what it is alleged to have been. One such scholar, George W. Hartmann, was a professor at Columbia Teachers College. In 1948 he published an article debunking the myth. It began by noting: "Almost every 'educated' adult within the English-speaking world has heard the story of the Black Hole of Calcutta, a minor event supposed to have happened one hot June nearly two hundred years ago in connection with the British conquest of India. Innumerable histories, major and minor, record the short but horrible tale; sober encyclopedias give it the respectable stamp of their authority; and more recently, solid medical, engineering, and psychological textbooks . . . have by their repeated references thereto all but universalized an awareness of this episode."[27]

Monuments had much to do with the perpetuation of the story. In 1902, when the myth of the Black Hole had already been substantially debunked, Lord Curzon, the Viceroy of India, had a monument built, at his own expense, to commemorate the event. "Confidently riding the global wave of high imperialism," writes Partha Chatterjee, "the British rulers once more installed the memory of their early victimhood in India."[28]

The Black Hole of Calcutta thus became the one snippet of India's colonial history that was almost universally known in the English-speaking world. As an experiment, Professor Hartmann asked his students if they had heard of the Black Hole incident: of the 115 students, about one-third said they had, and that they believed the story to be "essentially true."[29] The professor did not ask his students about either Amboyna or the Prison Ship Martyrs. Had he done so, I suspect some would have heard of the former, but very few would have known about the 11,500 Americans who died on British prison ships anchored off the shores of Brooklyn. Even some eminent historians, I have discovered, are unaware of those deaths.

This is but one of many instances in which "History" as related by imperial chroniclers chose to foreground a story that could be turned into a tale of White English victimhood while obscuring another, much deadlier event that did not lend itself to that narrative. Empire, as the historian Priya Satia has remarked, has "made and remade the historical discipline."[30]

THE QUESTIONS OF WHO is a brute and who is fully human, who makes meaning and who does not, lie at the core of the planetary crisis.

At this moment in time, when we look back on the trajectory that has brought humanity to the brink of a planetary catastrophe, we cannot but recognize that our plight is a consequence of the ways in which certain classes of humans—a small minority, in fact—have actively muted others by representing them as brutes, as creatures whose presence on Earth is solely material. It was because of these assumptions that it was taken for granted that the greater part of humanity was intellectually and culturally incapable of industrializing—and that delusion is itself an essential component of the catastrophe that is now unfolding across the planet.

Would the West have embarked on its reckless use of resources if it had imagined that a day might come when the rest of the world would adopt the practices that enabled affluent countries to industrialize, just as the West had itself adopted innumerable non-Western practices and technologies? If this possibility had been acknowledged a century ago, then maybe some thought would have been given to the consequences. But through the nineteenth and much of the twentieth centuries it was an unstated assumption among those who ruled the world that most non-Westerners were simply too stupid, too brutish, to make the transition to industrial civilization on a mass scale. Concealed by abstractions, these assumptions undergirded a range of academic disciplines like development studies, and some branches of economics and sociology, in which poverty was ascribed to "culture," a term that was often laden with racial baggage. These assumptions have penetrated so deep into these disciplines that they can perhaps never be expunged.[31]

It is perhaps only in the last two or three decades that the West has awakened to something that it had not imagined possible:

that the non-West is fully capable of adopting extractive, carbon-intensive economies, and all that goes with them, like scientific and technological research and certain genres of art and literature. Had it been accepted earlier that human beings are, and have always been, essentially mimetic creatures, perfectly capable of learning from one another, then perhaps sustainability would have become an urgent issue much earlier. But this possibility was precluded by long-held elite assumptions until the brutes began to unbrute themselves.

The terrible irony is that the unbruting of the middle classes of the non-West has been achieved precisely by repeating, and even intensifying, the processes of brutalization that were set in motion by Europe's colonial conquests. In India, over the last three decades, the beliefs, practices, and livelihoods of forest peoples have come under attack as never before. In hideous mimicries of the settler-colonial treatment of Indigenous peoples, more and more forest areas have been opened up to the mining and tourism industries, sometimes with the support of exclusionary conservationists, who advocate the removal of forest-dwellers in the name of ecology. Forest peoples' sacred mountains have been desecrated, their lands have been swamped by dams, and their beliefs and rituals have come under attack as "primitive superstitions"—exactly the terms once used by colonial administrators, scientists, and missionaries. The replication of colonial practices extends even to removing tribal children to boarding schools.[32] Similar processes are under way also in China, in relation to the Uighur, and in Indonesia, in relation to Papuans.

The difference is that these mimicries of colonial brutalization have unfolded not over centuries, but over a few decades, going back to 1990: half the greenhouse gases that are now in the atmosphere were emitted in the last thirty years. It is the tremendous acceleration brought about by the worldwide adoption of colonial methods of extraction and consumption that has driven humanity to the edge of the precipice.

It is this compressed time frame that has made sure that non-humans too are no longer as mute as they once were. Other beings and forces—bacteria, viruses, glaciers, forests, the jet stream—have also unmuted themselves and are now thrusting themselves

so exigently on our attention that they can no longer be ignored or
treated as elements of an inert Earth.

. . .

IT IS NOW BEYOND dispute, I think, that the Western scientists,
philosophers, and intellectuals who believed that non-White
peoples were by nature brutish, lacking in sensibility, and effectively mute were profoundly and utterly wrong. What, then, if they
were wrong also about the inertness and brute materiality of what
they called "Nature"? What if it was the people who were regarded
by elite Westerners as brutes and savages—the people who could
see signs of vitality, life, and meaning in beings of many other
kinds—who were right all along? What if the idea that the Earth
teems with other beings who act, communicate, tell stories, and
make meaning is taken seriously?

And why should this be unlikely? The Indian scientist Jagadis
Chandra Bose demonstrated long ago that plants can feel pain and
fear, and even make audible responses to certain kinds of stimuli.
His work was hugely celebrated for a while, but then the agents of
official modernity struck back and silenced him as a "charlatan."

But now the procedures of official modernity have themselves
uncovered communicative abilities in many kinds of nonhumans,
ranging from marine mammals and elephants to trees and forests.[33]
Perhaps the best known of these scientists is the famous primatologist Jane Goodall, who has described instances of communication
with a male chimpanzee that she had named David Greybeard: "His
large and lustrous eyes, set so wide apart . . . seemed somehow to
express his entire personality. David taught me that so long as
I looked into his eyes without arrogance, without any request, he
did not mind. . . . His eyes seemed like windows through which, if
only I had the skill, I could look into his mind."[34]

Today it is possible for Banu Subramaniam, a plant scientist who
studies morning glories, to ask questions that would have been
thought outlandish a few years ago: "Who were the actors in my
morning glory experiments? What of the plant itself? What of its
agency? Its own history?"[35]

Scientists now accept that trees in a forest are able to communicate with each other in certain circumstances—they can send

help, in the form of carbon, to ailing members of their group; and they can warn each other about pestilence and disease.[36] It is now thought that certain plants can even emit sounds that are inaudible to the human ear but are audible to some other living things. So it is only in that they lack language—a human attribute—that trees are mute. But in that humans lack the ability to communicate as trees do, could it not be said that for a tree it is the human who is mute?

It may seem obvious to humans that their ability to destroy trees and forests endows them, and them alone, with the capacity to act. But intentional action can also unfold over completely different scales of time. Trees have inhabited the Earth much longer than human beings, and their individual life spans are, in many cases, far greater than those of people: some live for thousands of years. If trees possessed modes of reasoning, their thoughts would be calibrated to a completely different time scale, perhaps one in which they anticipate that most humans will perish because of a planetary catastrophe. The world after such an event would be one in which trees would flourish as never before, on soil enriched by billions of decomposing human bodies. It may appear self-evident to humans that they are the gardeners who decide what happens to trees. Yet, on a different time scale, it might appear equally evident that trees are gardening humans. They may be the earthly equivalent of the oceanic superorganism of Solaris.

But perhaps this is all wrong? After all, trees and humans are not—or not just—adversaries competing for space. They are also linked by innumerable forms of cooperation. Perhaps what is at fault here is the very idea of a single species.[37] It is now known that the human body contains vast numbers of microorganisms of various kinds; biologists estimate that 90 percent of the human body consists of bacteria, rather than human cells, and one microbiologist has suggested that under a microscope a human body looks like a coral reef, "an assemblage of lifeforms living together."[38] It is known also that microorganisms influence moods, emotions, and the human ability to reason. So if it is true that the human ability to speak, and think, can only be actualized in the presence of other species, can it really be said that these faculties belong exclusively to humans?

Recent research in biology has shown that many species do not evolve singly: bacteria are critical to the survival of animals of all kinds, including humans. "More and more," according to a team of biologists, "symbiosis appears to be the 'rule,' not the exception.... Nature may be selecting 'relationships' rather than individuals or genomes."[39] Many organisms are born without the bacteria that are essential for them to attain adulthood; they must encounter those bacteria in the world—and without those meetings they are unable to fully realize their potential.[40]

Could it not be said of humans too that it is the presence of certain other species, in specific moments of encounter, that has enabled *Homo sapiens* to transcend its limitations? Take for instance that landmark moment in the history of consciousness when the Buddha attained Enlightenment: this event occurred, as is well known, while the Buddha was meditating under a Bodhi tree. Within the Buddhist tradition, for more than two thousand years, the presence of this tree has been inseparable from that moment. This is not to say that the tree transmits illumination, or even that it is an active participant in the process. Nor is it at all the case that everyone who meditates under a Bodhi tree will achieve Enlightenment.

Yet it has long been accepted, by many millions of people, that a trans-species encounter, at a specific historical juncture, was essential to the Enlightenment of one particular human, Prince Siddhartha Gautama. The Buddha himself believed the tree to be essential to his attaining Enlightenment, which is why millions of Buddhists consider the Bodhi tree sacred to this day. In the words of the Dalai Lama:

> Under a tree was the great Sage Buddha born
> Under a tree, he overcame passion
> And attained enlightenment
> Under two trees did he pass in Nirvana.[41]

What does this tell us? It tells us, first of all, that certain kinds of trans-species associations cannot be understood with the methods of science. They are encounters, or events, that occur at specific moments in time and are not repeatable. Such encounters can only be approached historically, by attending to the circumstances in which they occur.

Second, it tells us that an awareness of the possibility of trans-species encounters of this sort has always existed among humans. We need only think of St. Francis of Assisi and the story of how he subdued the man-eating wolf of Gubbio. "Brother wolf," he is reported to have said. "All men cry out against thee, the dogs pursue thee, and all the inhabitants of this city are thy enemies; but I will make peace between them and thee, O brother wolf . . . and neither men nor dogs shall pursue thee any more." This encounter had many witnesses, and tradition has it that the citizens of Gubbio eventually buried the wolf's corpse in a church named after St. Francis. Five and a half centuries later, in 1872, when the church was under repair, a wolf's corpse was found buried under it.

It takes only a moment's reflection to recognize that claims to communications with nonhumans—animals, volcanoes, trees, gods, demons, angels, and indeed God—have been made by innumerable men and women. While many of these claimants may have been frauds and charlatans, some—like St. Francis—were among the most venerated figures of their time: human society and human history would be incomprehensible without these figures. But the claims they made cannot be understood or apprehended through the forms of reasoning that are dominant today, simply because they cannot be replicated or empirically verified. Contemporary reason requires of anyone who makes a claim to communication with nonhumans that they provide evidence of these interactions. That condition necessarily excludes anyone who says: "A nonhuman spoke to me, and only me, just once, when I was in an altered state of mind, and what was communicated by this nonhuman was not something useful, nor something verifiable: it was instead only a story."

Yet most such claims are couched in exactly these terms: They are not repeatable at will; they occur in unique circumstances and often in altered states of mind; and the traces that they leave behind are not observable effects in the real world, but rather stories, which in turn come to be enshrined in texts, icons, and rituals.

So the true question then is not whether nonhumans can communicate and make meaning; rather, we must ask: When and how did a small group of humans come to believe that other beings, including the majority of their own species, were incapable of articulation and agency? How were they able to establish the idea that nonhumans are mute, and without minds, as the dominant wisdom of the time?

AN ESSENTIAL STEP toward the silencing of nonhuman voices was to imagine that only humans are capable of telling stories. This again is not an idea that people have always subscribed to; many, perhaps most, of the world's people still don't. It is essentially another elite idea that gained ground with the onward march of the mechanistic metaphysic. Yet today the idea that humans are the only storytelling animals appears self-evident to those who subscribe to it.

Consider, for instance, this passage from one of the finest portrayals of a landscape in contemporary literature, Graham Swift's superb 1983 novel, *Waterland*. "Only animals," says one of Swift's characters, "live entirely in the Here and Now. Only nature knows neither memory nor history. But man—let me offer you a definition—is the story-telling animal. Wherever he goes he wants to leave behind not a chaotic wake, not an empty space, but the comforting marker-buoys and trail-signs of stories."

This passage serves as the epigraph for a fine article by the environmental historian William Cronon. The article is on the nature of narrative, and Cronon argues that the fundamental difference between a mere succession of events (a "chronology") and a story is that the latter joins events together in a way that invests them with meaning. This, he assumes, is a specifically human ability, hence: "Narrative is a peculiarly human way of organizing reality."[42]

So, once again, what is really at stake is not so much storytelling itself, but rather the question of who can make meaning. Once again the assumption is that nonhumans cannot make, or discern, meaning.

As with so many other attempts to define the exceptionalism of human beings, this idea is tenable only if meaning-making and storytelling are defined in a circular fashion, as being tied to human forms of language. But is it really the case that experiences cannot have any meaning in the absence of language? Clearly this does not obtain for prelinguistic humans: it is well known that even infants understand, and make, many kinds of meaning. So why should it not be possible to connect experiences into meaningful patterns in other ways, through memory, sight, or smell, for instance? Any pet owner knows that a dog understands as meaningful the relationship between the home, the park, and certain times of day. For the dog, is this a "chronology" or a "narrative"? Either way, it is clearly not the case that the dog lives "entirely in the Here and Now"; its experiences are sequential and are understood to unfold in time and space.

The importance of sequencing will be evident to anyone who has ever tried to write a story: a narrative is nothing if not an arrangement of a sequence of events. This is why the sentences that connect one paragraph to another are of such vital importance: they provide the sequential connections between events, and places, out of which a meaningful narrative emerges. This kind of narrative sequencing is analogous to movement through time, as well as space: that is exactly what is meant by the "unfolding" of a story. That may account for why so many of the world's earliest and most powerful narratives are stories that unfold through movement: for example, the *Ramayana*, the *Odyssey*, the Norse Sagas, the *Journey to the West*, and so on.

It is well established now that many animals have long memories and are able to communicate in complex ways. Some of these animals, like elephants, whales, and migratory birds, also move over immense distances and appear to have attachments to particular places. These movements cannot be described as purely mechanical, instinctive, or lacking in meaningful sequences. Humpback whales, for instance, mark the passage of time by changing their songs from year to year.[43] This would hardly be possible if they lived "entirely in the Here and Now."

As far back as the 1930s the biologist Jakob von Uexküll demonstrated that many animals actively interpret their surroundings, creating their own experiential worlds.[44] This idea has long been

anathema to those who believe that it is a cardinal error to attribute human qualities to animals. But, as Eileen Crist has so per-
suasively shown in her book *Images of Animals: Anthropomorphism
and Animal Mind*, to rigorously avoid anthropomorphism is only
to risk falling into the related fallacy of mechanomorphism—the
assumption that animals are machine-like creatures that cannot,
in principle, be endowed with minds or interpretive faculties.[45]

In short, there are many good reasons to conclude, as Donna
Haraway does, that "storying cannot any longer be put into the
box of human exceptionalism."[46] The anthropologist Thom van
Dooren goes further. In a fascinating study of a flock of penguins
who doggedly return, year after year, to the shores of a Sydney
suburb, he concludes that the birds' attachment to the place arises
out of "storying." He writes: "Experiencing beings like penguins
'represent' the world to themselves, too: they do not just take in
sensory data as unfiltered and meaningless phenomena, but weave
meaning out of experiences, so that they, like humans, 'inhabit an
endlessly storied world.'"[47]

It would seem then that the idea that humans are the only storytelling animal is by no means an unproblematic reflection of reality. It is something that some people like to believe, just as some
once believed that most humans were brutes and thus incapable
of making meaning. It is, in other words, a construct, one that is
intimately connected with structures of power and with the forceful repression of the awareness of nonhuman forms of agency and
expression. Not surprisingly, in this matter, too, the hand of power
has often fallen hardest on Indigenous people.

When we think of the suppression of stories today, our minds
leap immediately to dissident literature and authoritarian regimes.
Yet there were other kinds of stories that were also suppressed, or
repressed, for quite different reasons over much longer spans of
time—for example, the hummah-hah narratives of the Laguna
Pueblo. In Leslie Marmon Silko's words, these stories are about the
conversations that "coyotes, crows and buzzards used to have with
human beings." In her memoir, *The Turquoise Ledge*, Silko recalls
how, in her childhood, hummah-hah stories could not be mentioned in certain public spaces because they revealed the "Laguna

spiritual outlook towards animals, plants and spirit beings."[48] The stories existed in the shadows, as a secret lore.

It is perfectly possible, then, that far from being an exclusively human attribute, the narrative faculty is the most *animal* of human abilities, a product of one of the traits that humans indisputably share with animals and many other beings—attachments to place. Perhaps, then, storytelling, far from setting humans apart from animals, is actually the most important residue of our formerly wild selves. This would explain why stories, above all, are quintessentially the domain of human imaginative life in which nonhumans had voices, and where nonhuman agency was fully recognized and even celebrated. To make this leap may be difficult in other, more prosaic domains of thought, but it was by no means a stretch in the world of storytelling, where anything is possible.

The shrinking of the possibilities of this domain, and the consequent erasure of nonhuman voices from "serious" literature, has played no small part in creating that blindness to other beings that is so marked a feature of official modernity. It follows, then, that if those nonhuman voices are to be restored to their proper place, then it must be, in the first instance, through the medium of stories.

This is the great burden that now rests upon writers, artists, filmmakers, and everyone else who is involved in the telling of stories: to us falls the task of imaginatively restoring agency and voice to nonhumans. As with all the most important artistic endeavors in human history, this is a task that is at once aesthetic and political—and because of the magnitude of the crisis that besets the planet, it is now freighted with the most pressing moral urgency.

16

"The Falling Sky"

What does it mean to live on Earth as though it were Gaia—that is to say, a living, vital entity in which many kinds of beings tell stories? And how does the planetary crisis appear when seen from that perspective?

It is perhaps impossible to regain an intuitive feeling for the Earth's vitality once it has been lost; or if it has been suppressed, through education and indoctrination. Even to retrieve a sense of it from the documentary record is very difficult, because written accounts of Gaian conceptions of the world are rare—simply because those who are most powerfully aware of nonhuman vitality have largely been silenced, marginalized, or simply exterminated by the unfolding of the very processes that lie behind the planetary crisis. Yet, from time to time, Indigenous thinkers and visionaries have succeeded, even while living through the devastation of their own life-worlds, in producing written records of their beliefs. One such testament is a 620-page text called *The Falling Sky: Words of a Yanomami Shaman.* Originally published in French in 2012, the book is the product of a decades-long collaboration between the Yanomami shaman and leader Davi Kopenawa and the French anthropologist and activist Bruce Albert. At once a political memoir, polemic, autobiography, and compendium of knowledge, *The Falling Sky* is all the more remarkable for being a direct response to the acceleration of the planetary crisis within the very theater that holds the Earth's fate in the balance—the Amazon basin.

DAVI KOPENAWA WAS born deep in the interior of Brazil's Amazonas province, not far from the Venezuelan border, and his early childhood was spent in a Yanomami communal house. It was his stepfather who recognized his gifts and introduced him to shamanism. But his initiation was repeatedly interrupted by lethal epidemics that killed most of his relatives, and by invasions of Yanomami territories by settlers and gold prospectors.[1] At one point, after losing many of his closest kin, Kopenawa left home and tried for a while, by his own account, "to become a white man." But after a few years away he returned and completed his induction into shamanism under the tutelage of his wife's father.

Through this time the territories of the Yanomami were ravaged again and again by disease and settler invasions. For Kopenawa, the gouging of the rain forest by gold prospectors became a call to political action, because "a shaman's work is to protect the earth."[2] Kopenawa had known Bruce Albert since the 1970s, and he now enlisted Albert's help in resisting the forces that were ravaging the forest and killing its Indigenous peoples. Together Kopenawa and Albert produced recordings that had a significant impact on public opinion in Brazil and Europe.

This happened to coincide with the period of reform, starting in 1985, that followed the end of the military dictatorship that had governed Brazil since 1964. Long-suppressed concerns about the environment came to the fore at this time, and the new constitution that was adopted in 1988 enshrined many protections for Indigenous peoples.[3] Over the ensuing decades successive governments enacted several measures for the protection of the Amazon. The laws did not always work as intended, but they were still remarkably effective: between 2005 and 2012, deforestation was brought down by as much as 80 percent.[4]

It was against this background that the Yanomami started a campaign to gain legal recognition for their territorial claims. Their political struggle met with partial success in 1992, when their right to a part of Amazonia was legally recognized at the Earth Summit in Rio de Janeiro. After the summit, Kopenawa rose to prominence, nationally and internationally, as the Yanomami's best-known spokesman.

BY CHOOSING TO become a shaman Kopenawa was undertaking a profoundly political act of resistance; his choice was in itself a rebellion against the processes of muting that accompany colonization and resource extraction. His familiarity with those processes went back to his early childhood when Christian missionaries had tried to stamp out the Yanomami's beliefs and rituals. "They kept telling [the] shamans," he writes, "that they were evil and that their chests were dirty. They called them ignorant. They threatened them: 'Stop making your forest spirits dance, it is evil! They are demons.'" Words like these, "repeated unceasingly, finally frightened all the shamans. . . . They also became mute."

The Falling Sky is Kopenawa's unmuting of himself: "All these words have accumulated in me since I have known the white people. Yet today I am no longer satisfied with keeping them deep inside my chest, as I did when I was younger. I want them to be heard in their cities, everywhere they can be. . . . This is why I want to speak to white people!"

The phrase "the white people," which recurs often in the book, must be read as a metaphor that designates a project rather than a specific group of people. For, of course, this project has now been adopted by a great many people who are not "white," in the sense of being Euro-descended: indeed, the most voracious agents of extractivist capitalism today are probably those who came late to settler colonialism, like the elites of many Asian and African countries.

It was in order to address the modern world in its entirety that Kopenawa decided to expand his collaboration with Albert into the book that became *The Falling Sky*. One of Kopenawa's most important reasons for writing the book was to send a warning to future generations, to let them know that the settler-colonial holocaust that has devoured so many Native American life-worlds will one day engulf the entirety of the planet.

This is why *The Falling Sky* is so important. Not only has Kopenawa had to deal with the planetary crisis since his earliest childhood; his training as a shaman has allowed him to observe it from a perspective that is not centered on humans. He is one of the few living people who can give us a sense of how the planetary crisis appears when viewed with nonhuman eyes.

KOPENAWA'S AWARENESS of the other-than-human world started early; he was one of a small number of children who would see "strange and frightening beings" in his dreams: "the other children grew up without ever knowing what scared us so much."

Images of these spirit beings would come to Kopenawa at night, as he lay sleeping in his mother's hammock. The spirits, or *xapiri*, that revealed themselves to him were beautiful but terrifying: "They really wanted to dance for me, yet I was scared of them. These dreams lasted throughout the time of my childhood, until I became a teenager. First I would see the glimmering light of the *xapiri* approaching, then they would take hold of me and take me into the sky's chest."

An important element of Kopenawa's initiation was learning to use a snuff-like powder called *yãkoana*, a mind-altering substance whose principal ingredient is extracted from the bark of the *yãkoana hi* tree. It is through this interspecies collaboration, between humans and a tree, that Yanomami shamans gain the ability to "become a ghost" and enter the world of *xapiri* spirits: "You can only really know the *xapiri* after drinking the *yãkoana* for a long time. Once you have reached that point, they no longer leave your dream. This is how one truly becomes a spirit being in one's own right!"

It was by mastering the techniques of becoming a "spirit being" himself that Kopenawa was able to enter a realm where *all* beings are spirits—humans, animals, trees, water, plants. In this realm there is no difference between beings; it is only in the earthly realm that they differ, and there too the difference lies not in their spirit selves but in their bodies.

Because of his knowledge of the spirit world, Kopenawa's perspective on the forest is completely different from that of contemporary nature lovers and ecologists. He makes this point repeatedly in *The Falling Sky*: "The white people, they find the forest beautiful without knowing why. On the contrary, we know that what they call 'nature' is the forest as well as all the *xapiri* who live in it. . . . But these are words that the white people do not understand. They think that the forest is dead and empty, that 'nature' is there for no reason and that it is mute."

For many contemporary nature lovers, the beauty of the forest lies in the wonders revealed by scientists; this is why "nature writing" is often studded with the binomial names of the Linnean system. For Kopenawa, on the other hand, the forest far exceeds human comprehension; a name given by humans to a tree would not even begin to exhaust its presence in the world, because the tree, and the forest itself, also exists as an image, and it is this that keeps it alive: "For us the *xapiri* are the true owners of 'nature,' not human beings."

Not all *xapiri* are beautiful; some are dangerous and threatening. One cuts up children with his sharp machete; another gives children fevers and devours them. In Kopenawa's description this is a realm that teems with beings that are every bit as beautiful and as ugly, as nurturing and as malign, as potent and as dangerous, as are humans: in this realm invisible threats lurk everywhere and life can be extinguished at any moment.

In no way does this realm resemble the orderly, mechanistic universe conjured up by the term "nature"; this world, in its uncanniness, is much more akin to the reality unveiled by the plague year of 2020.

FOR KOPENAWA, the *xapiri* are not endemic to Amazonia; they often reveal themselves to him when he is far from home. Describing a journey to Europe, he writes: "Today's white people know nothing about the *xapiri* who inhabit their land and they never even think about them. Yet they always existed, long before the white people themselves were created. Their spirits are truly numerous there!"

During this trip to Europe, Kopenawa often slept in a "ghost state" after eating unfamiliar food. One day the *xapiri* of the bees appeared to him in his dreams and told him that the forests they lived in were being so mistreated that they could no longer make honey and were in danger of perishing. "You who know how to become spirit," they pleaded, "speak firmly to the outsiders who will listen to you! The white people truly lack wisdom!"

The next day Kopenawa revealed his vision at a public meeting and entreated the audience to listen to the bees. "You do not see their images dance and you do not hear their songs in your dreams. Yet we shamans, we know how to listen to the bees' distress, and they are asking us to speak to you so your people will stop eating the forest."

In 2017 a German study confirmed that there had been a massive decline in the population of flying insects in Europe: their numbers had fallen by 75 percent over a period of twenty-seven years.[5] The bees are indeed now in danger of perishing.

FOR KOPENAWA, the failure of the modern gaze to "truly see" the forest is a result of its inability to perceive the spirits that reveal themselves to him. "The white people," he writes, "know nothing of the things of the forest, for they cannot really see them. . . . [They] never stop setting their eyes on the drawings of their speech, which they circulate among themselves pasted on paper skins. This way they just stare at their own thought and only end up knowing what is already inside their minds. Their paper skins do not speak and do not think. They are simply there, inert, with their black drawings and their lies."[6]

In Kopenawa's view, then, it is the written word that is inert: marks on paper are lifeless and function as blinders, enclosing humans entirely within the thoughts and perceptions of their own species. This view finds a distant, and unlikely, echo in the words of the primatologist Jane Goodall: "It is all but impossible to describe the new awareness that comes when words are abandoned. . . . Words are a part of our rational selves, and to abandon them for a while is to give freer reign to our intuitive selves."[7]

There are striking similarities also between Kopenawa's views on literacy and those of David Abram, an American environmentalist and philosopher, who (not incidentally, perhaps) has had a long connection with James Lovelock and Lynn Margulis. In his book *The Spell of the Sensuous: Perception and Language in a More-Than-Human World*,[8] Abram argues that literacy, especially alphabetic literacy, creates a different way of seeing and thinking, abstracted from the nonhuman world. This is because *"the letters of the alphabet, like the Platonic Ideas, do not exist in the world of ordinary vision.* The letters, and the written words that they present, are not subject to the flux of growth and decay, to the perturbations and cyclical changes common to other visible things; they seem to hover, as it were, in another, strangely timeless dimension."

Interesting as these observations are, there is one respect in which, in my view, Abram's insights are clouded by a kind of technological determinism. He presents alphabetical literacy as a technology that can achieve certain effects on its own, almost passively. What this ignores is the enmeshment of literacy in historical processes, particularly those that were intended to snuff out certain forms of awareness: for example, the violent suppression of the rituals and belief systems of Indigenous peoples like the Yanomami.

Those processes are still at work. In the early 1980s, when I lived in a Muslim village in Egypt's Nile Delta, I quickly discovered that the lives of the villagers, especially those of women, were intimately enmeshed with beings of many kinds, ranging from communicative animals to long-departed Sufi saints and spirits like jinns. But even back then, young Salafi-influenced Islamists were doing their best to stamp out these enmeshments by forbidding certain rituals and practices on the grounds that they were "superstitious" or "idolatrous." The fervor of these Islamists was not unlike that of sixteenth- and seventeenth-century Protestants in Europe, who had also been intent on stamping out conceptions of vitality, which they often identified with women and witchcraft.[9] The same could be said of important strains of contemporary Hindu fundamentalism, which have also tried to rationalize and "reform" traditional beliefs in order to fit them into the mechanistic modes of thought that are currently dominant.[10]

In short: The awareness of a Gaia-like Earth did not wither away of itself because of literacy; it was systematically exterminated, through orgies of bloodletting that did not spare Europe, although its violence was directed most powerfully at the Indigenous peoples of the Americas. Yet, not only has that awareness survived among the Indigenous people of the Americas; many of them also credit their perceptions of the Earth with having made their own survival possible, in the face of exterminatory violence. Never have these perceptions of the Earth mattered more than at this moment when the mechanistically ordered world of modernity is disintegrating before our very eyes.

IT WAS ON ANOTHER TRIP, to New York City this time, that Kopenawa gained fresh insights into the connections between the predicament of the Yanomami and the long history of settler colonialism in the Americas: "While I was staying in this city, I also told myself that the white people who had built it had mistreated these regions' first inhabitants the same way those in Brazil do with us today. . . . They probably told themselves: 'We're going to do away with these dirty, lazy Indians. We're going to take their place on this land. We will be the real Americans because we are white.'"[11]

Kopenawa's intuition was confirmed when he went to visit an Onondaga reservation in northern New York State. When his hosts took him on a tour of the reservation, he saw that the Onondaga were "encircled on a little patch of land." The sight shocked him, because it made him realize: "This is what the white people also want to do with us and all the other inhabitants of Brazil's forest! This is what they have always done. They will kill all the game, the fish, and the trees. They will soil all the rivers and lakes, and they will finally take over what is left of our lands. They won't leave anything alive!"

Those processes, as Kopenawa has repeatedly pointed out, tie the current predicament of the Yanomami directly to a Pan-American history of colonialism. In 2019, for example, when asked to comment on Brazil's president, Jair Bolsonaro, Kopenawa said: "He wants to kill my people, he wants to get rid of our forest, he wants to destroy our health. A lot of that came from the US, and the Brazilian government is using it like a copy."[12]

A desire to copy the United States, especially in the manner of its westward expansion, is indeed central to Bolsonaro's program. In 1998, he even remarked: "It's a shame that the Brazilian cavalry hasn't been as efficient as the Americans who exterminated the Indians."[13]

This statement is deeply disingenuous: Brazil is second to none in the rate at which it has exterminated Indigenous peoples. It is estimated that when the Portuguese first arrived, in 1500, the region that is now Brazil had a population of 11 million Indigenous people, divided among some two thousand tribes. By the mid-twentieth century that number had dwindled to around 70,000, and tribes were dying out at the rate of one per year.[14]

Where Bolsonaro is right, however, is that a large part of Brazil has so far escaped the fate of the interior of North America: it has not yet been terraformed into a neo-Europe, like, say, the American Midwest. But that is exactly what Bolsonaro's government intends to change: the goal is to complete the project of colonial terraforming by replacing vast swaths of the rain forest with cattle ranches, mines, and soya and sugarcane monocultures. All that stands in the way is the set of protective measures that were put in place by earlier, left-leaning governments.

That regulatory structure came under fire immediately after Bolsonaro's election, when he slashed the funding of Brazil's National Indian Foundation (FUNAI) and took steps to dismantle regulations on mining and energy corporations.[15] Emboldened by his actions, settlers began to occupy large swaths of the forest after clearing them with deliberately set "wildfires."[16] As a result, Brazil's rate of deforestation soared. In 2019 the country's National Institute for Space Research reported an 84 percent year-to-year increase in wildfires in Amazonia. Bolsonaro's response to the news was to fire the head of the institute.[17]

Grim though these developments are, it is important to recognize that in Bolsonaro's Brazil, as in the United States under Trump, attempts to eliminate environmental safeguards were not entirely successful. In Brazil the judicial system presented stiff opposition to Bolsonaro, and in the US many banks and investors withdrew from extractive projects because of pressure from activists and organizations like 350.org, which has spearheaded a rapidly growing movement for divestment from fossil fuels. In short, one of the more hopeful lessons of this period is that activism and public pressure can be extremely effective in resisting environmental deregulation.

AMAZONIA'S CURRENT CONDITION could be regarded as an instance of the deepening crises of a new era, the Anthropocene.[18] Yet, nothing about it is new except the dates: what is happening there is actually a replication of centuries-old patterns in the settler-colonial history of the Americas.

The Covid pandemic, for instance, has played out in Brazil as an uncanny reprisal of earlier episodes in the settling of the Americas. By mid-June 2020, the mortality rate for Covid-infected people in the general population of Brazil was 5.7 percent—but for Indigenous people, the rate of mortality was 9.7 percent. On July 11 a federal judge described the pandemic's impact on Indigenous and Black communities as a genocide, suggesting that legal consequences may await Bolsonaro and his government.[19]

This too was a disaster unleashed by inaction. From the start of the pandemic, Bolsonaro took the position that Covid-19 was nothing but a mild fever, and he did little to contain its spread, effectively allowing it to play out as a "default genocide."[20] Yet his government did not neglect to seize upon the pandemic as an opportunity to push its long-term agenda of opening up the Amazon. In February 2020, Brazil's environment minister, no less, said in a recorded speech that the government should "take advantage of the fact that the attention of the press is on the pandemic to approve infra-legal reforms of deregulation of the environment."[21] Once again the rate of deforestation in the Amazon soared, with an area the size of the Netherlands being cleared of its tree cover.[22]

In short, the Amazon basin, the last ecological redoubt of the pre-Columbian Americas, is living through a delayed version of the settler-colonial history that began in the sixteenth and seventeenth centuries.

Scientists have been warning for years that the Amazon rain forest is nearing a catastrophic tipping point. The rain forest sustains
its own climate; its greenery generates 20 to 30 percent of the rainfall on which the ecosystem depends.[23] Beyond a certain point,
the loss of greenery will trigger a series of feedback loops that will
destroy the Amazon basin's capacity to regenerate and sustain
itself: it will then turn into degraded savannah and bushlands.
"Once there is more dry area," says Thomas Lovejoy, an ecologist
who has studied the Amazon for decades, "you get more fire and it
begins to be cumulative."[24]

The fallout of such a transition, from rain forest to degraded
bushland, would be catastrophic for the entire planet, because the
Amazon, which has long been one of the world's most important
carbon sinks, would then become a major source of carbon emissions.[25] This is not a distant prospect. "We are scientists who have
been studying the Amazon and all its wondrous assets for many
decades," write Thomas Lovejoy and Carlos Nobre, Brazil's most
eminent climatologist. "Today, we stand exactly in a moment of
destiny: The tipping point is here, it is now. The peoples and leaders of the Amazon countries together have the power, the science,
and the tools to avoid a continental-scale, indeed, a global environmental disaster."[26]

In Brazil today we can see, with absolute clarity, how colonial
terraforming lies at the heart of the planetary crisis.

· · ·

I WAS WRITING these paragraphs in mid-August 2020, when my
mother, in Kolkata, took a turn for the worse and stopped eating. Tests were done, and it was confirmed that she did not have
Covid-19, or indeed any ailment other than the respiratory problems that had plagued her for the last few years. It was just that
the will to thrive, which had not been strong in her for a while, now
seemed to be vanishing altogether.

From the start of the pandemic I had been haunted by the possibility of not being able to travel to Kolkata in the event of a sudden
decline in my mother's health. And now here it was, the nightmare
prospect that haunts every migrant and exile, staring me full in
the face.

On August 23 I was on the phone with my sister almost until the minute we lost our mother: it was then 8:53 a.m. in Brooklyn.

Once again, the thought that was uppermost in my mind was that with so many people dying in hospitals, beyond the reach of their loved ones, my mother had been fortunate to be at home, in her own bed, lovingly cared for by her daughter and granddaughter, and ensconced within a household that had done everything possible to ensure her comfort.

Through the rest of that interminable day my mind kept going back to something that had happened a year and a half before, in December 2018, when my mother had last been hospitalized because of complications brought on by her respiratory problems. Debbie and I were in Kolkata then, and we were sitting by her bedside one afternoon, when she suddenly reached for our hands and squeezed them as if to say goodbye. Then, abruptly, she went into a kind of trance, tossing her head from side to side, showing the whites of her eyes, and mumbling to herself. Listening to her, I realized that she was describing a vision as it unfolded before her eyes; she was seeing a brightly lit scene with figures coming toward her, as if to welcome her into their midst. There was something wrapped around her, she said, a creature that was holding her in a protective embrace, so that no harm could come to her— a snake. This was astonishing to hear, for she had had a great terror of snakes all her life. But strangely, she wasn't at all afraid; she kept saying, "*Kono bhoy nei*—there's nothing to be afraid of, I feel no fear, I am not afraid."

Then doctors and nurses came rushing in, and an infusion of potassium dispelled the trance. But no sooner had she floated to the surface again than she began to say, disconsolately, "Why didn't you let me go? Why did you hold on to me? Why did you keep me here?"

It was clear that whatever she had seen on the other side had inspired not dread, but longing.

I felt then, as I do now, a strange envy that she had been granted this vision. But I felt also a sense of reassurance, thinking that she, who had always been a little bit shamanic, would make sure that when my own time came I too would be granted such a vision.

17
Utopias

In the seventeenth century, even as conquered territories like the Bandas were being violently emptied of their inhabitants, it was becoming fashionable for intellectuals in Europe to imagine perfect societies, or Utopias. This early form of science fiction was another companion genre of colonialism, in that it imagined alternative worlds built on supposedly "empty" spaces. In Francis Bacon's *New Atlantis*, published just five years after the Banda massacre, that alternative world was an island kingdom of "generosity and enlightenment," centered upon an institution of learning that might be interpreted as an early avatar of the modern research university.

The irony of these utopian imaginings is that they date back to a time when Europeans were actively engaged in constructing new societies, in lands where the native populations had been effectively eliminated. Jan Coen, for instance (unlike his contemporary, Francis Bacon), actually had an opportunity to create a new civilization, on the islands that he had emptied with the massacre of 1621. But Coen and his subordinates were practical men rather than philosophers, and they had no interest in creating a Utopia in the Bandas; indeed, the system they put in place was, for the great majority of its inhabitants, a grim dystopia, especially in its early years.

This system did not come about by chance; indeed, it is clear, as the historian Vincent C. Loth has noted, that those who built it knew "exactly what they were up to."[1] What they created was a structure that was an instance of "racial capitalism"—that is to say, an early form of industrial agriculture, enveloped within a racially stratified society in which a small number of Euro-descended planters ruled over a majority population of enslaved workers.[2]

What the Bandas witnessed, then, in the decades after the massacre of 1621 was a fast-forwarded version of a history that would unfold at a slower pace in many other parts of the world. The global hierarchies that were then put in place persisted well into modern times, and were in many ways constitutive of modernity. While Coen and his colleagues may not have been philosophers, they were certainly visionaries, and they clearly understood the Western project far better than the celebrated thinkers of their time.

The first step in creating a new social order in the Bandas was the repopulating of the islands. This was done from the top down, starting with the handing over of sixty-eight newly created nutmeg estates to Dutch-descended *perkeniers* (planters).[3] Next came the workforce, for which indentured laborers, convicts, migrants, and enslaved people were brought in from many distant places: "Gujerat, Malabar, Coromandel, the Malay peninsula, Java, Borneo, coastal China, Bouton, several parts of Maluku, Kai, and Aru."[4] A number of the enslaved workers were Christian converts, many of them of South Asian origin; and a significant proportion, as much as 13 percent, consisted of recently enslaved Bandanese—in a horrifying instance of enforced transfer of technology, 530 captives were brought back, not as the original owners of the land, but as enslaved people, to teach the art of nutmeg cultivation to the very settlers with whom they had been replaced.[5]

In the early decades of the conquest, so many enslaved people died due to "poor treatment, harsh conditions, illness (especially beriberi), and sheer misery" that the VOC was hard put to keep the nutmeg planters supplied with workers.[6] But the Company persevered for centuries, ensuring "a continuous stream of slaves"—as many as 5,000 to 7,700 annually—for its nutmeg estates.[7] Throughout this period, the majority of the population of the Bandas, from two-thirds to three-quarters, consisted of enslaved people.[8]

What kind of culture could have emerged out of these dystopic conditions, with a medley of people from far-flung places being shipped in to replace the eliminated natives?

It might be thought that a population as unrooted and heterogenous as this would end up being utterly estranged from the land. And it might also be thought that if any semblance of order were to emerge within this disparate population, it would be the result of some kind of social contract, as envisaged by Western philosophers.

But that is not what happened. In time a vibrant, deeply rooted culture came into being in the Bandas, and this was due neither to contractual abstractions, nor to the invention of myths of primordial connections with the land. Instead it was the vitality of the landscape itself that helped to forge a sense of rootedness among the people.

Phillip Winn, an anthropologist who has written extensively about the Banda Islands, did his fieldwork on Lonthor in the 1990s. By his account the islanders completely disclaimed any suggestion of ancestral connections with the land: not only did they accept that they all had roots elsewhere, but they insisted that they were a hybrid group, or *orang campur*, "mixed people." Very rarely did anyone claim Indigenous Bandanese ancestry.[9]

Yet for this new population too, Muslims and Christians alike, the islands were a "sacred territory" (*tanah berkat*) anchored by the spirits of "founder-figures," or *datu-datu*, who were thought to have arisen from the land.[10] Since these unseen beings were linked to particular locations, their presence could not be extinguished. Even after the islands' original population had been mostly eliminated, they continued to animate the land, living on as "emplaced spirit forms, maintaining a watchful presence and exerting a powerful influence over their original territory."[11]

These spirits of place became once again an integral part of Bandanese culture, associated with legends and rituals. Christian Bandanese participated in these rituals along with their Muslim neighbors, thereby effectively "elevating identification with place beyond religious affiliation."[12] Sites associated with the *datu-datu* were dotted across the islands, and people were always aware of their presence as they moved across the landscape.[13] "One elderly ritual specialist," writes Winn, "literally feels the presence of these beings when she visits these places. Her body shivers, her skin forms goose bumps, her hair stands on end. She describes this as pleasure rather than fear — it is evidence of her relation to the *datu-datu*, and their interest in her. More than once on returning from such a place she would turn to me, proffering her goose-bumpy arm, exclaiming that the particular spirit-personage associated with the site was following us home."[14]

The fact that the Banda landscape, and its spirits, remained vividly alive for the islands' inhabitants until contemporary times is a sign that this landscape was capable of making its own meanings, and of narrating its own stories. This is completely different from a situation in which humans create a cultural construction of a place, investing it with myths and meanings of their own invention. Circumstances of this latter kind have never been more neatly summed up than by Richard Eburne, a seventeenth-century English settler in the Americas: "It be the people," he wrote, "that makes the land English, not the land the people."[15] The Four Corners Monument, which marks an intersection imagined by humans, is an instantiation of this dictum: here the terrain is an empty, Euclidean space that has been invested with a particular meaning by a group of occupants. That meaning would be no different if the monument were located on a snowy mountaintop or a verdant valley instead of a dusty plain.

For the Bandanese, on the other hand, as for the Diné, it was the landscape, and its vitality, that created meanings and thereby connected them with its autochthonous spirits. This is a form of emplacement in which the landscape, and its hidden forces, are active, vital participants: they are by no means subordinate to humans.[16] It is as if the islands had turned Eburne's dictum on its head, crying out: "It be the land that makes the people Bandanese; not the people the land."

The fact that an extremely diverse group, like the new Bandanese, could interact with their surroundings in this fashion, gives the lie to the idea that powerful connections to a place, or beliefs in the vitality of a landscape, are necessarily rooted in racial homogeneity, as blood-and-soil nationalists have claimed since the nineteenth century. For those who experience the Earth as Gaia, as a living, vital entity, a landscape doesn't spring to life because its inhabitants happen to share a common origin. It is, rather, the vitality of the place itself that creates commonalities between the people who dwell in it, no matter what their origin.

This may well have been the primordial process through which humans were indigenized and assimilated into landscapes everywhere around the planet—for after all, except for one small part of Africa, nowhere on Earth can people be said to be truly native, in the sense of having come into being on that soil.

THE CONNECTIONS CRAFTED by the land were powerful enough to hold the Bandanese together until well into the 1990s. But at the turn of the millennium, when rumors sparked by gangland conflicts in distant Jakarta spread across Maluku on cell phone networks, setting Muslims against Christians, the Banda Islands did not escape the ensuing violence. At the start of the riots some Ambonese Christians fled to the Bandas, thinking that they would be safer there. But the violence followed them: on Banda Naira, where most of the islands' Christians lived, churches and Christian houses were set on fire. When the art historian Julie Hochstrasser visited the Bandas in 2006, the old Dutch church was a charred ruin. "All that survived within the blackened shell of the structure," she writes, "were the massive granite stones still paving the floor. . . . Yet my memory is more about the children: Ambonese Christian refugees who had taken shelter here in the churchyard since their own homes were likewise put to the torch during the outbreak. Their laundry was strung about the charred walls; their mothers quietly retreated upon my arrival, but the children slowly gathered around me, curious as anywhere, as I inspected the gravestones set into the church floor."[17]

The direct result of the violence in the Bandas, writes Phillip Winn, "was the departure of nearly all of the island's Christian minority population." Most were resettled in government-built settlements in Ambon.[18] By the time of my visit in 2016, the old Dutch church in Banda Naira had been carefully restored, but the charred remains of other structures still bore witness to the violence that had extinguished the Christian presence in the Bandas. It was as if the curse of the nutmeg had struck the Bandas once again, with a new iteration of the logic of elimination.

That centuries-old ties could disintegrate so suddenly, in a place as sleepy and inaccessible as the Banda Islands, is an indication of the depth and complexity of the crisis that now grips the planet. It is a crisis that is all-pervasive and omnipresent, in which geopolitics; capitalism; climate change; and racial, ethnic, and religious divides interlock, each amplifying and accelerating the other. In these upheavals the residues of human history interact with nonhuman entities and agencies in ways that no one would have thought possible even a few years ago.

It should not come as a surprise that algorithms and communications technologies are a major contributing factor in these upheavals.[19] Even as I write this, on September 12, 2020, the media are reporting that Portland, Oregon, where months-long Black Lives Matter protests have led to lethal violence between Left and Far Right activists, is besieged by "staggering" and unprecedented waves of wildfires. Yet, in the midst of this conflagration, some of the people who were most directly threatened by the fires refused to evacuate because of digitally disseminated rumors about antifascist looters roaming the streets. The fires, the rumors, and the confrontations are all, in different ways, residues of human history interacting with each other in a widening spiral of catastrophe.

SO EXPLOSIVE ARE the tensions and uncertainties of this era that it becomes imperative to ask: Is a "politics of vitality" at all possible, or desirable, at this advanced stage of the planetary crisis? After all, the very idea of nonhuman vitality could be regarded as dangerous by those who believe that humans are the only beings endowed with souls, minds, language, and agency. And if this axiom is taken to be a defining feature of rationality itself, then it follows that to think otherwise is to be irrational, superstitious, or "mystical." The votaries of such a definition of rationality might allow for the toleration of superstition or mysticism in private affairs, but they would strongly object to their presence in the public sphere, most of all in politics—which is, in the post-Enlightenment view, the paradigm of a domain that ought to be guided by reason, and reason alone. From this point of view, the thinking of a Davi Kopenawa—and indeed the very idea of what I have described as a "shamanic" or "vitalist" politics—would appear at best a contradiction in terms, and at worst a notion that holds the potential for unleashing all of humanity's worst, most destructive, and most barbaric instincts.

This line of reasoning demands careful consideration; for there now exists a large body of historical research to show that it is solidly grounded, especially in relation to certain strains of right-wing ecological thought. One of the best-known works on this subject is the excellent 1995 study *Ecofascism Revisited: Lessons from the German Experience*, by Janet Biehl and Peter Staudenmaier.[20] This book is especially important because it was written as a response to the rise of neo-fascism in post-unification Germany.

In Germany exclusivist beliefs about the environment are founded on the idea that there is a mystical connection between people of Germanic blood and the soil of the lands they inhabit. Biehl and Staudenmaier trace this mystique of "blood and soil" back to the nineteenth-century German writer Ernst Moritz Arndt, who is believed to be "the earliest example of 'ecological' thinking in the modern sense." They go on to explain, however, that Arndt's environmentalism "was inextricably bound up with virulently xenophobic nationalism. His eloquent and prescient appeals for ecological sensitivity were couched always in terms of the well-being of the *German* soil and the *German* people, and his repeated lunatic polemics against miscegenation, demands for Teutonic racial purity, and epithets against the French, Slavs, and Jews marked every aspect of his thought. At the very outset of the nineteenth century the deadly connection between love of land and militant racist nationalism was firmly set in place."

Arndt's ideas were developed by his disciples and eventually grew into the *völkisch* movement, which "preached a return to the land, to the simplicity and wholeness of a life attuned to nature's purity." It was against this backdrop that the German zoologist Ernst Haeckel coined the term "ecology" in 1867. Haeckel

224 · CHAPTER SEVENTEEN

was also the "chief popularizer of Darwin's evolutionary theory in the German-speaking world," which meant that from the very moment of its birth a connection was established between ecological thought and social Darwinism: "Haeckel believed in Nordic racial superiority, strenuously opposed race mixing and enthusiastically supported racial eugenics. . . . From its very beginnings, then, ecology was bound up in an intensely reactionary political framework." The defining characteristic of this ideological complex is "the direct, unmediated application of biological categories to the social realm."

Many of these ideas were absorbed by the *Wandervögel* ("wandering free spirits"), a German youth movement inspired by "a hodgepodge of countercultural elements, blending neo-Romanticism, Eastern philosophies, nature mysticism, hostility to reason, and a strong communal impulse in a confused but no less ardent search for authentic, non-alienated social relations." In the 1930s the *Wandervögel* went over to the Nazis in their thousands, a tendency that Biehl and Staudenmeier ascribe to the fact that the movement's primary emphasis was on the "improvement of the individual" rather than on politics.

One reason National Socialism appealed to so many young German nature lovers was that strains of ecological thought were also woven into Nazism, and even found their way into Hitler's own writing and personal habits: "Hitler and Himmler were both strict vegetarians and animal lovers, attracted to nature mysticism and homeopathic cures, and staunchly opposed to vivisection and cruelty to animals. . . . Hitler, at times, could sound like a veritable Green utopian, discussing authoritatively and in detail various renewable energy sources (including appropriate hydropower and producing natural gas from sludge) as alternatives to coal, and declaring 'water, winds and tides' the energy path of the future."

The fact that ecofascistic ideas took root in German culture at a time when the country led the world in many sciences, including forestry, ensured that their influence would extend far beyond Europe. In the nineteenth century many of the top forestry officials in the British Empire were either German or German-trained, and through them colonial forestry policies came to be imbued with enduring prejudices against Indigenous and forest-dwelling peoples. These biases continue to influence administrative practices in Africa and Asia to this day.

German environmental thought also landed on fertile soil in North America: some of the founding figures of American conservationism, such as John Muir and Henry Fairfield Osborn, held White supremacist views and wrote derogatorily about Native Americans and African Americans.[21] Madison Grant, one of the founders of the Bronx Zoo and an advocate for Glacier National Park, was also the author of *The Passing of the Great Race; or, The Racial Basis of European History* (1916), which has been described as "the most influential eugenicist tract ever penned."[22] This history has shaped the ethos of some of America's oldest conservation groups, burdening them with a residue of institutionalized racism with which they have only recently begun to contend. This is yet another realm in which Black Lives Matter has made a significant difference: it was at the height of the protests, in July 2020, that the Sierra Club publicly addressed the question of institutional racism within its own organization. "As defenders of Black life pull down Confederate monuments across the country," wrote the club's executive director, "we must also take this moment to reexamine our past and our substantial role in perpetuating white supremacy."[23]

But the damaging effects of this history can perhaps never be truly undone—for American environmentalism has had a powerful influence far beyond the borders of the United States, leaving a poisoned legacy of elitist, anti-Indigenous prejudice in conservation organizations around the world.[24] Little wonder then that Western environmentalists are often regarded with deep suspicion and resentment by the poor and disadvantaged. On occasion those attitudes have even led to open conflict, as happened in the Galápagos Islands in 1993 and 1994, when local fishermen burned in effigy an official of the Darwin Foundation, and later attacked a colony of tortoises, killing thirty-one and injuring another.[25]

On the very day that I was typing the above paragraph, October 8, 2020, news broke that a World Wildlife Fund employee was the top official at Salonga National Park in the Democratic Republic of Congo, where many incidents of murder, rape, and torture have been documented (including the gang rape of four women in 2015 by forest rangers). Commenting on this, the director of Survival International, an advocacy group for the rights of Indigenous people, said: "WWF and other big conservation NGOs have been well aware of their responsibility for gross human rights violations for decades. Survival first pointed them out over 30 years ago. Over the last half century I've personally confronted dozens of corporations and governments about their abuse of tribal peoples' rights. None have been as duplicitous as these big conservation NGOs. These violations ultimately damage our world too. They destroy the planet's best defenders."[26]

WITH THE INTENSIFICATION of the planetary crisis, exclusivist conservationism has already begun to take an even more sinister turn, with extreme right-wing groups in North America, Europe, and the antipodes using ecofascistic ideas to attack immigrants and people of color.[27] The White supremacist who attacked the Al Noor mosque in Christchurch, New Zealand on March 15, 2019, killing fifty people and injuring forty-nine, explicitly identified as an "ethno-nationalist eco-fascist."[28] Writing about this massacre, Naomi Klein notes: "My fear is that, unless something significant changes in how our societies rise to the ecological crisis, we are going to see this kind of white power eco-fascism emerge with much greater frequency, as a ferocious rationalization for refusing to live up to our collective climate responsibilities."[29]

For these reasons and more, Biehl and Staudenmaier's warnings about the blood-and-soil mystique deserve the most careful attention. But to acknowledge this does not necessarily lead to any clear conclusion on the relationship between "mysticism" and ecofascist thought. There is, first of all, the glaring fact that none of the key figures named by Biehl and Staudenmaier were "mystics" in any recognizable sense; many of them were, in fact, scientists of one kind or another. Haeckel, for example, was a zoologist, and his students and acolytes were all scientifically trained, many of them in the discipline that he had founded, "scientific ecology." One of the most influential among them, Willibald Hentschel, had a doctorate in biology, and went on to earn a vast fortune by inventing an indigo dye. Indeed, many of the most important ideas in ecofascism were borrowed from science, as Biehl and Staudenmaier themselves acknowledge when they identify "the direct, unmediated application of biological categories to the social realm" as the central feature of this ideological complex. So if mystical irrationality is to be blamed for ecofascism, then it is hard to see how "rational" scientific thought can be exonerated, since it seems to have played an even greater role in this complex of ideas. Nor can it be said that ecofascism's central ideas were "pseudoscientific": "The scientists who gave scientific racism its credibility and respectability were often first-rate scientists struggling to understand what appeared to them to be deeply puzzling problems of biology and human society. To dismiss their work as merely 'pseudoscientific' would mean missing an opportunity to explore something important about the nature of scientific inquiry itself."[30]

On examination, then, it would appear that ultimately Western ecofascist thought derives not (or not just) from "mysticism," but also from various forms of "scientism," like social Darwinism, eugenicism, exterminationism, and so on—all of which are ultimately products of deeply rooted beliefs about race. What makes ecofascism especially dangerous, however, is that its biological motifs lend themselves very easily to contemporary forms of scientism.

But the fact that certain kinds of scientific reasoning are integral to ecofascism does not, of course, imply that every branch of the sciences should be suspect. Nor should the fact that the founder of ecology was a Far Right, racist thinker cast an indelible stain on all of ecology; the truth is that most contemporary ecologists are keenly aware of issues of justice. Indeed, it is misleading to speak of "science" as though it were a monolith in this regard: the field is vast, and it now includes a whole range of anti-colonial, justice-oriented sciences.[31] In relation to ecofascism, it would seem that it is biology—rather than, say, atmospheric physics—that plays a special role. That being the case, what should serve as a warning signal for incipient ecofascism is, exactly as Biehl and Stauden-meier suggest, the application of biological metaphors and categories to social life.

It remains true, nonetheless, that "dominant science" has a long history of reinforcing militarism and colonialism, and that it tends, generally speaking, to produce outcomes that favor the world's ruling classes and nations.[32] Elements of this legacy can be discerned even today in the enthusiasm for geo-engineering that is already being evinced by some elite scientific and technological institutions.[33]

That being said, there is no reason why those who oppose eco-fascism should be wary of "science" in general. So far as atmospheric physics and the climate sciences are concerned, it is clearly essential for climate activists to collaborate with scientists. It is important to note that environmentalism too has undergone major changes in recent years, with many leading organizations disowning past practices and creating alliances with Indigenous peoples. The emergence of an increasingly vocal environmental justice movement in the US shows that there exist many common-alities between the concerns of poor and Indigenous Americans and their counterparts in other parts of the world—commonalities that were long obscured by elite environmentalism.

What is of the utmost urgency at this time is to find points of convergence on Earth-related issues between people whose concerns, approaches, life experiences, and identities may otherwise be completely different. This is not a project that can be left to credentialed experts, who are by definition a tiny group of highly educated people. At the same time, there can be no doubt that experts and scientists have a great deal to offer, and it would clearly be self-defeating to suggest that they have no role to play in confronting a crisis that science has itself, in no small part, been responsible for creating. But it would be similarly self-defeating to reject the political ideas of someone like Davi Kopenawa merely because they are not founded on the mechanistic paradigms of of-ficial modernity, and may therefore offer the temptation (to those who subscribe to linear conceptions of time) to brush them aside as "primitivist" or "romantic" or "atavistic." But the planetary crisis has done away with those linear conceptions of time; it is evident today that humanity is in an era where many different axes of time interpenetrate and exist alongside each other. Thus Kopenawa, like many others who are actively resisting the onslaught of extractive industries in remote forests, may in many ways be more "advanced" in his understanding of the planetary crisis than an academic in a tranquil Western university town. Nor is there anything remotely romantic about Kopenawa's story: it is a narrative of loss that conveys the violence and conflict of the environmental struggles of our time more accurately than many academic papers and journalistic reports.

In the end, every approach, no matter whether technological, technocratic, or political, needs to be scrutinized with the greatest care—because, as the recent religious violence in Maluku so clearly demonstrates, we are now in an era when intersections of technology and politics can destabilize and pervert even the most deeply rooted vitalist conceptions. And there could be no better example of this than contemporary India.

IT MIGHT BE IMAGINED that India, with its pantheistic traditions and its history of colonization and resistance, would be a country where vitalist conceptions of the Earth would have a powerful impact on political life. This was indeed the case through a significant part of the twentieth century, when the influence of Mahatma Gandhi, whose beliefs were profoundly anti-mechanistic, was felt in every aspect of the subcontinent's social and spiritual life. But Gandhi's influence began to decline soon after India's independence, and has now waned almost to nothingness, especially within the political class.

The waning of anti-mechanistic, vitalist ideas as a potent force in Indian politics is due in large part to the caste system, which ensures that the people whose lives are most closely tied to the land's soils and rivers, forests and coasts, are relegated to the farthest margins of the power structure. This outcome is the product of the very logic of caste, in which those who deal with certain organic substances that are regarded by upper castes as impure—

manure, meat, leather, bodily wastes, and so on—are consigned to the lowest ranks of the hierarchy.[34]

This logic ensures that Dalit and Adivasi (Indigenous) communities that make their living by farming, fishing, hunting, leather-curing, herding livestock, making pottery, and so on are systemically marginalized, oppressed, and excluded from the mainstream. Yet it is precisely the traditions of Dalits and Adivasis that are most similar to those of Indigenous peoples elsewhere, in that they foreground relations with nonhumans and with the land. Writing about Dalit groups in western Odisha, Mukul Sharma, an environmental historian, notes: "In Dalit narratives here, earth is where the souls of forefathers live; the earth is alive and powerful and must be treated with respect and care. In every Dalit house, at an earthy sacred place, lives Duma, their forefather."[35]

The logic of caste thus counteracts, and effectively negates, the elements of vitalism that are present in Indian belief systems. What recent experience shows, rather, is that upper-caste conceptions of sacredness are dangerously susceptible to political appropriation and manipulation. In a detailed study of three quite different Indian environmental movements, Mukul Sharma has shown that Hindu fundamentalists were able to take over all three by mixing the language of green activism with upper-caste ideas about diet, purity, and sacred spaces. Environmentalism has thus served, in a classically ecofascistic fashion, to strengthen the grip of dominant urban groups while marginalizing Dalits, Adivasis, and poor Muslims. Sharma notes: "with its political discourse the Hindu right has also shown that it has the power to absorb, co-opt and re-orient the political trajectory of an environmental movement."[36]

The utter hollowness and hypocrisy of this kind of right-wing environmentalism is evident in the startling speed with which the BJP's current leadership has dismantled long-standing environmental restrictions and regulations for the benefit of mining, energy, and construction corporations—all behind the cover of torrents of greenwashing rhetoric.[37]

In many respects, therefore, India's recent history is a cautionary tale about the very real dangers that "mysticism" can present when it is mixed with exclusionary right-wing politics. Nor is this coincidental: the ideologues who laid the foundations of Hindu fundamentalism explicitly embraced fascistic theories of race, Aryanism, and so on. They may have invoked ancient symbols and images in their writings, but their ideas were very much products of colonial modernity, which is why they have now morphed so easily into an ideology of rapaciously extractivist nationalism.

But India's drift toward a full-scale extractivist economy cannot be blamed solely on the weaponization of "mysticism" by the right wing; it was set in motion by the self-professedly secular Congress Party a long time ago.[38] Nor did the parties of the Left prove to be a bulwark against this trend. Between 2006 and 2008 the West Bengal wing of the CPI(M) (Communist Party of India [Marxist]) embarked on a massive program of enclosures, attempting to take over thousands of hectares of agricultural lands from small farmers for the benefit of two giant multinational corporations, one of which planned to build a Special Economic Zone, and the other a car factory. The resulting resistance and repression led to the virtual erasure of the CPI(M) in West Bengal, where it had dominated the political scene for many decades.

The upshot is that India, where the historic model of colonialism was very different from that of the settler colonies, is now striving to remake itself in the image of settler colonialism. As in the Americas and Australia, those who stand most conspicuously in the way of this ambition are forest-dwelling Adivasis, who happen, by their very presence, to occupy the lands and forests that contain "resources." In India, as elsewhere, colonialism is "first, foremost and always" about land.[39]

Legal protections for Adivasis were never very strong in India; since colonial times, officially designated forest lands—which cover no less than a fifth of the country's surface area—have formed an internal "state of exception" where the normal functioning of the laws of the land are suspended. This realm is controlled by the Forest Department (an immense bureaucracy with vast powers) and an army of forest guards that functions like a paramilitary force. This department bears a more than passing resemblance to the settler-colonial bureaucracies that dealt with

Indigenous affairs in North America and Australia: like them, it has proved to be an effective instrument in helping corporate interests penetrate deeper and deeper into regions that were once protected by their remoteness. As in North America and Africa, the policing of reserve forests has often resulted in what amounts to ethnic cleansing, with Indigenous peoples being evicted from their homelands for the benefit of the tourism industry and its urban, middle-class clients. Displaced Adivasis are often forced to relocate to settlements that bear a strong resemblance to reservations.

The parallels abound: as with the "Indian boarding schools" of North America, privately owned institutions are now reeducating Adivasi children; in consonance with settler-colonial practice, the material basis of Adivasi life is being steadily undermined by restricting access to traditional foraging grounds and the banning of certain kinds of hunting and gathering.[40] As in the Americas and Australia, mines and extractive industries are being sited on mountains and other locations that are sacred for Adivasis. Completing the parallels are the long-simmering, decades-long "irregular wars," fought between government forces and tribal insurgents in central, eastern, and northeastern India.[41]

But within this grim and steadily darkening picture, there are also a few points of light, emanating mainly from grassroots resistance movements—and it is no coincidence that some of them exemplify the possibilities of vitalist forms of politics. One of the most notable of these was the Chipko movement of the mountain region of Uttarakhand. Starting in early 1973, groups of villagers, most of them women, began to literally embrace trees in order to protect them from timber merchants. Folk poetry played a major part in inspiring the protesters and their movement, which eventually attracted so much support that the regional government was forced to enact protective legislation.[42] The movement also inspired others around the world, and tree-hugging became a global tactic of protest. Similarly, in the Niyamgiri region of Odisha, Adivasis have made the sacredness of their mountains the basis of their resistance to bauxite mining, and have been able to gain some significant court victories on those grounds. These are just two instances of a form of resistance that remains widespread among India's marginalized peoples.[43] Ultimately, as Mukul Sharma notes, the strength of the Indian environmental movement lies in its heterogeneity: "In their practical political activities, many environmental groups and movements have been at the forefront of efforts to democratize state institutions, as well as in the creation of more democratic and accountable forms of environmental decision-making."[44]

All of this conforms to what appears to be a consistent pattern in the relationship between vitalist ideas and politics: almost always, beliefs in the Earth's sacredness and the vitality of trees, rivers, and mountains are signs of an authentic commitment to the defense of nonhumans when they are associated with what Ramachandra Guha calls "livelihood environmentalism"—that is to say, movements that are initiated and led by people who are intimately connected with the specificities of particular landscapes. By the same token, such ideas must always be distrusted and discounted when they are espoused by elitist conservationists, avaricious gurus and godmen, right-wing cults, and most of all political parties: in each of these manifestations they are likely to be signs of exactly the kind of "mysticism" that lends itself to co-optation by exclusivist right-wingers and fascists.

This is not to say that a vitalist politics will always and necessarily be benevolent in intent: that is very far from being the case (ecofascism does not lack for shamans). In the end, *all* approaches to the planetary crisis, no matter whether technocratic or vitalist, must be judged by the same criteria, which have never been better summed up than by Pope Francis, in his 2016 encyclical, *Laudato Si*: "A true ecological approach always becomes a social approach; it must integrate questions of justice in debates on the environment, so as to hear both the cry of the earth and the cry of the poor."

18

A Vitalist Politics

The idea of a vitalist politics may seem improbable at first, but it takes only a moment's reflection to realize that some of the most effective political movements of modern times have derived their energy from vitalist sources. The decades-long struggle led by Mahatma Gandhi is a case in point.

Even though Gandhi's political arena was India, his thought and his political strategies were nourished by the old and powerful countercurrents that have continued to flow around the planet, like a subterranean river, throughout the time in which the mechanistic metaphysic was rising to dominance.[1] Through the centuries this current has surfaced again and again, even in the very heartlands of European modernity, manifesting itself in anti-enclosure movements, peasant revolts, and sometimes even more stridently vitalist forms of protest such as those associated with the Diggers, Ranters, and Levellers of the seventeenth century. These were all revolts against the project of reducing the Earth to a clockwork mechanism in which every kind of being was brutishly mute, except for European elites and Euro-descended colonists.

Nowhere did the project of muting and subduing the Earth unleash more violence than in the Americas, so it is hardly surprising that it is in the traditions of Amerindians and African Americans that the possible contours of a vitalist, anti-mechanistic politics can most clearly be seen. In South America the European conquest was followed by innumerable uprisings, many of which were led by shamans whose beliefs about the connections between humans and the more-than-human world mirrored those of Davi Kopenawa. One instance of this was the Taqui Ongo movement that began in Peru in 1565, and ended only after the execution of the last Inca of Vilcabamba, Tupac Amaru, in 1572. Shamans played a major part in this movement, and its rituals included "resurrection ceremonies" for the *huacas* (spirits) who dwelt in rocks, streams, and lakes.[2] These and innumerable similar movements in South and Central America mounted a much tougher resistance to Spanish rule "than traditional historiography has always allowed."[3] In North America, similarly, there were many shaman-led uprisings, culminating in the Ghost Dance mass movement inspired by the Paiute prophet Wovoka.[4]

African American traditions of resistance also draw upon resources that are completely different from those of official modernity. This, precisely, is the import of Cedric Robinson's portrayal of the Black radical tradition: by his account resistance to slavery in the Americas was not merely political in the usual sense; it was metaphysical in that it contested the White enslaver's fundamental conceptions of the world by imaginatively re-creating an earlier metaphysic. The raw material of the Black radical tradition, Robinson argues, was "a shared philosophy developed in the African past and transmitted as culture, from which revolutionary consciousness was realized and the ideology of struggle formed."[5] Often, when open rebellion was impossible, "people prepared themselves through *obeah*, voodoo, Islam, and Black Christianity . . . hardening themselves and their young with beliefs, myths, and messianic visions that would allow them, someday, to attempt the impossible."

This aspect of Black militancy was incomprehensible to European enslavers, who saw Black resistance as a reversion to savagery "under the influence of satanic madmen." But colonial masters weren't alone in being confounded by this idiom of resistance: this was true also of Western radicals, including some Black intellectuals who saw themselves as belonging to that tradition. They too had to work their way slowly toward the realization that contrary to mainstream Marxist theory, the working classes of Europe and

America, far from mounting a sustained challenge to bourgeois society, had proved all too susceptible to nationalism and racism. Belying the expectations of Western radicals, the major challenges to the capitalist and imperialist order had come not from "advanced" nations but rather from peasants and farm workers in regions that were considered peripheral to history—Asia, Africa, and Latin America. Nor had their fervor arisen out of "the proletarian consciousness that was a presumption of Marx's theory of revolution"; it had come instead from what W. E. B. Du Bois described as "part legend, part whimsy, part art."

EVEN MORE INSISTENTLY vitalist are Native American movements of resistance which have long been based on an ethic that foregrounds the familial instinct to protect "all our relatives"— that is to say, the entire spectrum of nonhuman kin, including rivers, mountains, animals, and the spirits of the land.[6]

This approach is essentially spiritual or religious, yet it has been surprisingly effective. In her book *All Our Relations*, the author and activist Winona LaDuke writes: "Despite our meager resources we are winning many hard-fought victories on the local level. We have faced down huge waste dumps and multinational mining, lumber, and oil companies. And throughout the Native nations, people continue to fight to protect Mother Earth for future generations."[7]

In its simplicity and power the idea of protecting "all our relatives" may well be the key to creating bridges between people across the globe. An important indication of this lies in the many significant legal victories that Indigenous peoples around the world have won in recent years, precisely on vitalist grounds, by underscoring the sacredness of mountains, rivers, and forests, and by highlighting the ties of kinship by which they are bound to humans. To cite just one example, the Sarayakus, a tiny Kichwa group in the Ecuadorian Amazon, won a historic victory in 2012, when the Inter-American Court of Human Rights ruled that the government of Ecuador had violated their rights by permitting an energy company to prospect for oil on their land without prior consultation. The turning point in the case came with the testimony of the Sarayaku's most important shaman, 92-year-old Don Sabino Gualinga, who told the court that the explosives used by the company's prospectors had driven away the beings who maintained the forest.[8] Similarly, a Maori tribe won a major victory in 2017, when the Whanganui River in New Zealand's North Island was granted the legal rights of a human being by a court. The tribe's chief negotiator said, on that occasion: "The reason we have taken this approach is because we consider the river an ancestor and always have."[9] Indigenous groups have won similar cases in Australia, Canada, and India.

What is astonishing about these victories is that the judges who granted them would probably, in their personal capacities, find the notion of a sacred mountain no less preposterous than the thought that a river might be their ancestor. Yet they were willing to grant legal standing to such ideas, something that could not have been imagined even a couple of decades ago. This is a profoundly hopeful development, because it indicates that even courtrooms, which are among the most redoubtable citadels of official modernity, are increasingly susceptible to the influence of that subterranean river of vitalism, which, after having been driven underground for centuries, is now once again rising powerfully to the surface around the world.

A PARTICULARLY IMPRESSIVE example of the effectiveness of vitalist forms of politics is the long and sustained protest movement directed at the Dakota Access Pipeline. The campaign against the pipeline has scored several significant victories despite intense and often violent attempts at repression by energy corporations and their security forces.

The campaign against the pipeline, which originates in the Bakken shale oil fields of North Dakota and cuts across the territory of the Standing Rock Sioux Reservation, began in 2015, and was galvanized by what was seen to be at once a desecration of a sacred landscape and an attack upon the more-than-human relationships of Indigenous people.[10] Through this framing, the campaign became much more than an environmental protest: it became a means of laying claim to the land, and of foregrounding the historic injustices that colonialism had imposed on the terrain as well as on all the beings who inhabit it.[11] In this sense, to use the words of the scholar and activist Edward Valandra, the struggle was "fundamentally a culture or paradigm war."[12]

The paradigm shift extended to the movement's practices, which were completely different from those of "politics as usual": they included storytelling, sweat lodges, and rituals involving the river and other features of the landscape. These practices, in turn, were founded on an alternative conception of dwelling, in the literal sense of creating a site of habitation, in the form of an encampment, that at one point housed several thousand people—enough to make it the fourth largest settlement in South Dakota. In the process of creating procedures for the camp's kitchens, eating spaces, child care centers, medical facilities, and so on, the participants also reconnected with ancestral ways of inhabiting a landscape without building permanent structures.[13]

In the sense that the movement became synonymous with a place—Standing Rock—it could be said that its political energy was generated in large part by the landscape itself. In the words of a group of activists, "Standing Rock emerged as a 'prayer camp' because the grounds in question are sacred, a site of ceremony and ancestral knowledge."[14]

But the movement's insistence on the particularity of a specific landscape did not, in any way, limit its appeal; to the contrary, Standing Rock became a magnet for people from many countries and faith traditions. "There were Iraqi people there; there were Egyptian people there," says an activist. "You had many people from different European countries that came to Standing Rock. Different walks of life. Filipinos. You have every walk of life there." He adds: "After a while it didn't matter what race or color you were. You were there to protect each other."[15]

This again gives the lie to ecofascistic ideas of intrinsic linkages between blood and soil. The non-Indigenous people who came to Standing Rock had no difficulty in understanding the vitality of the landscape: indeed, that was *why* they were drawn to it. This is possible because of that capacity for empathy that exists in humans

radically uncertain, nothing works—insurance, share prices, credit, dividends, even money (which is, after all, a promissory note that someone must redeem).

"Capitalism can avoid extinction," writes Dupuy, "only by persuading economic agents that an indefinitely long future stretches before them. If the future were to be closed off, a reverse domino effect would abolish all economic activity from the moment its end point became known. With the approach of the end, trust would be impossible since there would no longer be any time to come in which debts could be repaid, and money would lose all value since no one would accept it in payment of outstanding obligations."[19] No one understands this better than the billionaires who stand atop the pyramid of global capitalism—hence the panicked rush to escape to Mars, or, for the somewhat less wealthy, to buy bunkers and underground safehouses. "These immensely powerful people," writes Dupuy, "in their heart of hearts, no longer believe in the future."

THE INTENSIFYING GLOBAL connectivity of the last decades has had many damaging and disruptive effects, but it has also created new opportunities for addressing the planetary crisis through broad and inclusive transcontinental alliances. This is of crucial importance, for the magnitude of this crisis is such that it cannot be addressed by any one nation, or even by a loose grouping of nations such as "the West"—simply because the trajectory of the carbon economy is no longer being decided in the West. While it is certainly true that the West bears much of the responsibility for global warming, that does not mean that it can, at this juncture, address—much less solve—the planetary crisis without the active and willing participation of the great majority of the world's population. A necessary first step toward finding solutions is to find a common idiom and a shared story—a narrative of humility in which humans acknowledge their mutual dependence not just on each other, but on "all our relatives."

The acceptance of such a narrative would of course require a seismic shift in consciousness for those who remain wedded to the conception that humans are the only ensouled beings and that the Earth is an inert entity that exists in order to provide its rulers with resources. But the intensification of the planetary crisis has made the old mechanistic ideologies of conquest increasingly difficult to cling to: it would seem that the mounting violence of Gaia's stirrings is indeed beginning to bring about a major shift in consciousness in the West by breathing fresh spirit into a growing number of "nature religions." That is certainly the inference of Bron Taylor's book *Dark Green Religion*, which describes the growing popularity, in the West, of many kinds of countercultural, biocentric belief systems: their adherents range from neo-pagans, New Agers, soul-surfers, pantheists, Wiccans, and neo-animists to Gaia-loving post-Darwinians.

In other parts of the world, where the mechanistic metaphysic of modernity was never completely hegemonic, vitalist beliefs have always been integrated into grassroots, livelihood-oriented environmental movements. These too are now growing rapidly, in Latin America, Africa, and Asia. Perhaps the most hopeful sign, as Prasenjit Duara shows in his book *The Crisis of Global Modernity: Asian Traditions and a Sustainable Future*, is that many middle-class Asians, who have for the last three decades been totally absorbed in the headlong pursuit of consumerism, are now increasingly susceptible to the appeal of Earth-oriented movements that draw their strength from "pan-Asian ideas of sacred forests, lands and waters." China, for instance, is often (and rightly) castigated for its environmental depredations; yet, in recent years environmental groups have burgeoned in China, and activists have scored some major successes by invoking the sacredness of lands and forests. "Local ideas of sacred place and nature," writes Duara, "continue to abound across Asia and many other parts of the global south; and while they are susceptible to denial and abuse . . . they remain an important source for regenerating nature."[20]

Also of enormous significance is the fact that the Catholic Church, under the influence of a pontiff who has taken his papal name from the most shamanic of Christian saints, has significantly revised its doctrines in relation to the Earth. Pope Francis speaks directly to more than a billion people, and has already done more, perhaps, to awaken the world to the planetary crisis than any other person on Earth.

If these admittedly disparate groups can find common ground in an Earth-centered mass movement, then it is not impossible, as Taylor suggests, that they could start a "social epidemic" that would bring about "wide-scale political, economic and ecological changes, even in the face of ambivalence and hostility."[21] Taylor bolsters her argument by citing the fable of the Hundredth Monkey: if an isolated group of monkeys living on an island learns a new behavior, goes the story, there will come a point when, if enough of them adopt that behavior, then other monkey populations on other nearby islands will also follow suit.

What the story highlights is the faculty of empathy, which humans share with many kinds of animals, and which may even, in the end, provide us with a path to salvation. The lesson, in any event, is "that everyone must optimistically and continually do their part to promote the needed spiritual, ecological, and political changes, because one never knows who the decisive monkey will be."

Is this magical thinking? Perhaps—but no more so than the idea of colonizing Mars; or the belief, now enshrined in the Paris Agreement, that a new technology for removing vast amounts of carbon from the atmosphere will magically appear in the not-too-distant future.

The difference is that a vitalist mass movement, because it depends not on billionaires or technology, but on the proven resources of the human spirit, may actually be magical enough to change hearts and minds across the world.

19

Hidden Forces

To this day Banda Naira is instantly recognizable, even from the deck of a ferry, as a minuscule "neo-Europe."

The island's main jetty is overlooked by the frowning, turreted ramparts of a four-hundred-year-old Dutch citadel, Fort Belgica. The old town sits huddled below, its streets lined with the verandas of decaying colonial-era mansions.

A short distance from the jetty, facing Gunung Api across a narrow channel, is the Maulana Hotel, which was built by Des Alwi, the Bandanese writer and conservationist. Alwi, whose ancestors included "Arabs, Chinese, Javanese, Manadonese, and Sumatrans," personified the islands' hybrid cosmopolitanism.[1] His book *Friends and Exiles: A Memoir of the Nutmeg Isles and the Indonesian Nationalist Movement* is a story of growing up in Banda Naira in the 1930s and 1940s, in the midst of a population so varied that within the Chinese community alone "there were three categories." The dominant minority, however, consisted of a small group of Euro-descended planters. But no matter what their background, "all were considered Bandanese if they followed Bandanese customs and spoke the Bandanese-Malay dialect."[2]

An essential element of this hybrid Bandanese identity, Alwi explains, was a belief in *foe-foe*, or Banda magic, and "*orang halus* [ghosts], the invisible protectors of Banda."[3] Apart from this, Alwi has little to say about the unseen beings of the Bandas, which is unfortunate because he was evidently a gifted storyteller. In the

FIGURE 5. Gunung Api seen from Lonthor Island. Photograph by the author.

1940s, in Jakarta, Alwi was befriended by the celebrated Indonesian poet Chairil Anwar. The poet was so captivated by Alwi's stories that he wrote a poem in the voice of a legendary Malukan figure, Pattiradjawane:[4]

> I am Pattiradjawane, guarding the
>   nutmeg groves.
> I am fire on the shore. Whoever comes
>   near
> Must call my name three times.
>
> In the night time quiet,
>   seaweed dances
> To the sound of my drum,
> Nutmeg trees become maidens'
>   bodies
> And live till dawn.

DES ALWI DIED in 2010, six years before my visit to the island. It was his daughter Tanya, a rosy-cheeked, cheerful woman in her six-

FIGURE 6. Memorial to forty Bandanese executed by the Dutch on May 8, 1621. Photograph by the author.

ties, who led me to the well where the remains of the slaughtered Bandanese headmen were deposited after their execution in 1621; it is now the site of a modest memorial, built by Des Alwi.

Behind the well, mounted on a wall, is a plaque that lists the names of those who were killed that day. The inscription begins: "Here, on the morning of the 8th of May, 1621, 40 great sons of the Banda Islands were executed on the orders of the governor-general Jan Pieterszoon Coen. They were patriots who fought to defend their sovereignty, and resist the invaders who had forced a nutmeg monopoly on the Banda Islands."

Looking into that well, it is impossible not to imagine the presence of ghosts; the air seems to seethe with the voices of silenced beings.

. . .

ALSO NEARBY, ONLY a few minutes' walk from the well, lie the sprawling, pillared mansions in which the VOC's officials lived. They too have been restored by Alwi's foundation.

The mansions' palatial rooms are totally empty, of people as well as furniture. When you step on the tiled floor of a ballroom the sound echoes desolately between the walls, like a trapped bird looking for a means of escape.

Many stories are told about these empty buildings, and about the *hantus* (spirits) and *orang halus* who haunt them. In one mansion, there is a room where a French verse has been inscribed on a windowpane: it is said to be the work of a Dutch official who later committed suicide. Translated, the inscribed lines read:

> When will come the time that will form my happiness?
> When will the bell strike the hour,
> The moment I will see again the shores of my country,
> The bosom of my family that I love and bless?[5]

It isn't hard to see why a resident of that mansion would want to be gone from the Bandas; living in that house, your eyes would be constantly drawn to the well where the bones of the slaughtered Bandanese headmen lie buried.

Looking out of that window, I couldn't help wondering what had possessed the VOC to choose this macabre location for the residences of its top local officials. It is as if slaughtering the headmen wasn't enough; it was necessary also to keep an eye on their ghosts.

·   ·   ·

AFTER SHOWING ME the inscribed window, Tanya Alwi stepped out for a minute, leaving me alone in the empty, echoing room. I was stooping to take a picture of the inscribed windowpane, when I felt a cold breeze blowing through. Perhaps a door had been left open, I thought, but I looked around and saw that this was not the case.

On turning back to the window again, I was suddenly seized by a sensation like that which makes us turn our heads while walking down a street—because we feel that a stranger is staring at us. I looked over my shoulder, but there was nobody there. Yet I had an uncanny sense that someone, or something, was in the room with me—a presence that was a shadow of something human and yet nonhuman.

I left the house with a feeling of being haunted—not only by my encounter with that presence, but also by a dim recollection of a book, a novel set in an old colonial house like the one I had just stepped out of. I couldn't immediately recall its name, and it did not come back to me until the night before my departure from Banda Naira, when I was suddenly roused from my sleep by a loud crash.

The date was November 9, 2016: it is seared into my memory, because on the other side of the planet, fifteen hours away, the polls had opened for the US presidential elections. Considering the circumstances, it is perhaps a little surprising that I had been able to fall asleep at all. But so I had, and now, on being abruptly awakened, I sat up and switched on a light. Looking around the room, I saw that, not far from my bed, a lamp had tipped over on a desk and fallen to the ground.

I was staring at the wreckage when I remembered the name of the novel that I had thought of after visiting that old, empty house: it was *The Hidden Force*, by the Dutch writer Louis Couperus.[6]

LOUIS COUPERUS IS a towering figure in the Dutch literary canon, and *The Hidden Force*, which was published in 1900, is regarded by many as his finest work, a classic. In my view it is the most insightful of all European colonial novels.

The main character in *The Hidden Force* is Otto Van Oudijk, a middle-aged colonial official who presides over a small town in Java. Van Oudijk is a stolid, unimaginative, hardworking man, not at all given to flights of fancy; he is, so to speak, an archetypal representative of colonial modernity. But his wife's infidelities and his own clashes with a Javanese aristocrat lead to a series of mysterious manifestations inside his official residence. The cries and moans of children are heard at odd hours; stones come pelting down from no identifiable source; people find themselves inexplicably spattered with blood.

Van Oudijk pays no heed at first; he is, after all, a representative of a European power that has imposed a certain kind of order, political as well as epistemic, on the East Indies: "It was not in his nature to believe in supernatural events, nor did he do so. He was secretly enraged at being unable to discover the culprits, or an explanation. But he refused to believe. He did not believe when he found his bed soiled. . . . He did not believe when the glass he lifted broke into slivers. He did not believe when he heard a constant irritating hammering overhead."[7]

Then, just as inexplicably as they had begun, the manifestations stop. For a while Van Oudijk thinks that he has triumphed, "that he had been too strong for the hidden force, because of his simple courage, as an official, as a Hollander, and as a man."

But the mysterious happenings leave behind a "hatred that arose everywhere like the demoniacal bloom of that strange secret."[8] Van Oudijk's domestic and official life disintegrates and he,

> who had never been superstitious, who had worked on, coolly and calmly in his lonely house, with the incomprehensible witchcraft all about him, who had read reports while the hammering went on above his head and his whisky soda ochred in his glass; Van Oudijk for the first time in his life . . . became superstitious, believing in a hidden force that lurked, he knew not where. . . . And when he noticed this superstition within himself, something so new to him, the practical man, something so strange and incredible to him, a man of ordinary masculine simplicity, he was afraid of himself, as of insipient insanity, which he began to perceive deep down within himself. . . . It had never occurred to him that somewhere, deeply hidden in life, there might be things that were stronger than the power of the human will and intellect.[9]

Van Oudijk's crisis is not just personal; he is forced, rather, to confront the *epistemic* violence of colonialism. He, who believes himself to be in a place that has been subjugated and brought to order long ago, now finds himself dealing with forces that he can neither control nor understand. He is unable, despite his best efforts, to mute the voices that are making themselves heard around him.

Those voices come vividly to life also in a novel by another Dutch writer, Maria Dermoût: *The Ten Thousand Things*, which was published in 1958.[10] Dermoût, who was twenty-five years younger than Couperus, was born in Java, and spent a part of her childhood there. As an adult she spent some time in Maluku, and it is there that *The Ten Thousand Things* is set, on an island that is never named but is probably Ambon. The novel's main character, Felicia, "an old woman beyond fifty now," lives in a bayside spice garden that has come down to her as the "last of an old Dutch line of spice growers."

Felicia's tutelary spirit is none other than Rumphius, the seventeenth-century naturalist whose work helped to launch the European project of cataloging all things, human and nonhuman. But Felicia's interest lies not so much in Rumphius's botanical classifications as in his *Ambonese Curiosity Cabinet*, a book that describes a vast spectrum of rarities that are native to Maluku. Inspired by Rumphius, Felicia creates her own cabinet of curiosities, and through those objects, and their stories, she becomes aware of the vitality of everything that surrounds her, including the spirits of the dead. One of those spirits is that of her own son, a colonial soldier who was killed on a neighboring island.

Once every month Felicia makes sure she is completely alone in her spice garden, and then she waits for her son, and the spirits of others who have been murdered, to visit her. And when they do, she opens her cabinet of curiosities, and they become, in unison, the ten thousand things of the novel's title: "They weren't a hundred things but much more than a hundred, and not only hers; a hundred times 'a hundred things,' next to each other, separate from each other, touching, here and there flowing into each other, without any link anywhere, and at the same time linked forever."[11]

In Felicia's world, everything is a spirit, everything has a soul.[12]

IN BOTH NOVELS the vitality of the setting manifests itself in the domain of the uncanny, as the frontier where colonial power meets a limit beyond which lies something unfathomable, an abyss that cannot be made to submit to the colonist's will to impose order. In *The Hidden Force*, Van Oudijk grudgingly accepts the epistemic limits of his power; in *The Ten Thousand Things*, Felicia steps beyond that limit and embraces the abyss.

Both Van Oudijk and Felicia belong to the modern world. Neither of them is a foot soldier of empire, armed with guns and swords; their experience is of a late stage of colonialism, when a centuries-old history is lurching toward its end. If they are able to accept, or embrace, the hidden forces of the land, it is because they are not directly threatened by them: it is neither possible nor necessary for them to respond by shooting into the darkness—as would almost certainly have been the first impulse of those who were in the advance guard of empire, men like John Mason, John Underhill, and indeed Jan Coen and his subordinate Martijn Sonck.

And that, perhaps, is what happened in Selamon on the night of April 21, 1621, at that fateful moment when a lamp came crashing down in the *bale-bale* where Sonck and his colleagues were quartered. Sonck would certainly have known that the villagers, although outwardly quiescent, were seething with anger and resentment: if there were ever a night when a hidden force would stalk the land, then that was surely it.

This was a time when many Europeans were all too ready to jump to such conclusions. Their home continent was then in the grip of a witch craze; everything from bad weather to dead livestock was being blamed on witches. Every Dutch member of the Banda expedition, including Sonck and Coen, would have come of age in the peak period of witch-hunting—that is to say, the years between 1560 and 1630.[13] Coen himself was from Hoorn, which, like many other Dutch cities, had a public "weigh house," where suspects were weighed to determine whether they were unnaturally light, as witches were thought to be. Archival records show that the Dutch were less extreme in their pursuit of witches than their neighbors in Denmark and Germany; yet, just eight years before the Banda massacre, in 1613, sixty-three women and one man were burned at the stake in the mainly Dutch-speaking town of Roermond.[14] This was the largest ever witch-burning in the Low Countries. The supposed witches were said to have killed six hundred children, four hundred old people, and over six thousand animals.

It was customary, through much of the twentieth century, to treat Western witch hunts as remnants of the Dark Ages, aberrations in the story of progress that led to the Enlightenment and the triumph of rationality and humanism. But recent scholarship has demonstrated that this was very far from being the case: there were no large-scale witch-burnings in Europe in the Middle Ages. The phenomenon was specific to the early modern era, and it occurred in the context of many other developments that were distinctive of the time: religious upheavals; the formation of centralized states; the circulation of printed texts; the consolidation of new forms of patriarchy; the colonization of the Americas; and, not least, the severe environmental disruptions of the Little Ice Age.[15] It was in the midst of these multiple crises that new forms of thought began to take shape among Europe's educated elites, ideas of witchcraft among them.[16] These ideas may have intersected with peasant notions of natural vitality, but they were also different, in that they formed a highly elaborated body of doctrine, articulated by some of the leading intellectuals of the time. As the historian Brian Levack notes: "Witch beliefs . . . were mainly the property of the literate and ruling elites, and not the common people. . . . In order for the intensive hunting of witches to take place, it was necessary for ruling elites to believe that the crime was of the greatest magnitude and that it was being committed on a large scale and in a conspiratorial manner."[17] Coen and Sonck, both educated men, would have shared — or at least been aware of — these beliefs.

This background wraps another layer of mystery around the events of that night in Selamon. What was it that Sonck and his counselors really feared when they leapt out of their beds and began firing indiscriminately into the darkness? Why did Sonck instantly assume that the incident denoted a "conspiracy," and why was Coen so easily convinced that this was the case?[18] Why did Coen pursue the matter of the conspiracy to such extreme lengths, not only torturing the headmen, but having their bodies dismembered in a macabre execution?

The concept of "conspiracy" provides a clue. To the contemporary mind that word suggests a plot between human conspirators. But in the seventeenth century the word was also used in the context of witchcraft, to refer to pacts between witches and the Devil.[19] Witchcraft trials typically focused on the unearthing of these pacts, and in the Netherlands, as elsewhere in Europe, torture was sometimes used to obtain confessions about such compacts.[20] Even though the majority of witchcraft accusations were directed at women, those charges were also leveled at many men; and in the Netherlands, male witchcraft suspects, unlike women, tended to be well-to-do—a profile that fits the *orang-kaya*.[21]

"Extermination" is another word that occurs frequently in the context of witchcraft. In this too there is a connection with the processes of colonization that were under way at the time: it was in the Americas that Europeans came to believe that entire tribes could be witches, and needed to be wiped out *en masse*. Often demands for the extermination of witches were premised on the belief that witches had the power to create disorder not just in society, but also in the weather and other ecological conditions.[22] Thus, in the German city of Trier, the site of some of the largest witch hunts of the time, a late sixteenth-century chronicler wrote: "Because everyone generally believed that crop failures over many years had been brought on by witches and malefactors out of dev-ilish hatred, the whole land rose up to exterminate them."[23]

Could it be that the falling of the lamp in Selamon triggered associations of this kind? Could it be that the reason Coen and Sonck became so fixated on the incident was that it indicated to them that they were dealing with forms of disorder that were not merely social or political but also natural—or rather, unnatural? That would certainly explain the obsessive need to obtain proof of a "conspiracy" to justify the ritualized elimination, not just of the supposed ringleaders, but of *all* the *orang-kaya*.

The torturing of the *orang-kaya* also begs many questions. It is striking that they were tortured *after* Coen had already obtained the "confession" he wanted. Once he had that document in hand, the executions were clearly a foregone conclusion. What then was to be achieved by torturing them as well? Moreover, the fact that one of the headmen was able to break free and jump overboard suggests that the torturing was done not below deck, in the bowels of the *Dragon*, but on an upper deck—that is to say, in full public view.[24] That in turn suggests that what happened was not just tor-ture but also a ritualized *performance* of torture.

In her seminal book, *The Death of Nature* (1980), Carolyn Merchant argues that the torturing of witches was a powerful metaphor for an emerging philosophy of science in which nature was seen as an essentially feminine domain of disorder that had to be conquered, subjugated, and indeed tortured in order to extract her secrets.[25] Thus she writes of Francis Bacon, believed by many to be the founding philosopher of science: "Much of the imagery he used in delineating his new scientific objectives and methods derives from the courtroom, and, because it treats nature as a female to be tortured through mechanical inventions, strongly suggests the interrogations of the witch trials and the mechanical devices used to torture witches."[26] The implication of this is that the torturing (or "vexing") of witches' bodies furnished a metaphor that was crucial to the emergence of mechanistic conceptions of nature.[27] These in turn "legitimated the exploitation of natural resources."[28]

The fashion in which the *orang-kaya* were tortured suggests that there was more at stake than just revenge, or punishment, or any practical goal. It is as if the pain inflicted on the headmen were a means of subjugating not just a group of humans but also the landscape they inhabited. It is as if the islands themselves were being exorcised so that no ghosts would remain to hinder the efficiency of the future nutmeg-producing machine.

It would seem, then, that Coen's plan for the Bandas anticipated elements of the mechanistic philosophies that were being articulated by the philosophers of his time. But it was surely not through philosophy that the mechanistic paradigm came to be reflected in his plans: they were the product, rather, of historical processes of colonization and conflict.

Despite the long and tortured birth pangs of the mechanistic metaphysic, its rise to dominance was such that it would eventually claim a place of pride amongst the horsemen who are now driving humanity toward apocalypse. Yet that metaphysic has never been able to entirely swallow the remnants of its nemesis, vitalism, which has remained forever stuck in its gullet.[29] This source of torment is still capable of producing spasms of violence. So it happens that even today, cries as simple as "water is sacred" and "honor the earth" can enrage the armed security forces that guard oil pipelines.[30] Where does this rage reside if not in the repressed awareness of earthly vitality?

This too was presaged in the Bandas. If the Dutchmen's responses to the falling of the lamp were indeed triggered by the suspicion of a conspiracy between the *orang-kaya* and some nonhuman power, would that not imply that what they feared most was that the hidden forces of the landscape were being turned against them? Their annihilatory rage was fueled, perhaps, by their own terror-filled awareness of the Bandas' vitality.

From fears like these arose that distrust and suspicion of conquered landscapes that sometimes haunted European settlers.[31] Thus the urgency of terraforming conquered terrain, of ridding the land of its hidden forces, of transforming it into a tame and familiar repository of resources. Yet paradoxically, that annihilatory impulse hides within itself an implicit recognition of something that cannot be explicitly acknowledged by the colonist: that Indigenous people were right all along, that landscapes are neither inert nor mute, but imbued with vitality.

. . . .

THE HIDDEN FORCE was written at a time when European empires seemed indestructible and Anglo-American writers were busy celebrating colonialism. Couperus, on the other hand, depicts the colonial project as an epistemic failure, and he does so by making claims that would not for a moment have been publicly defended by respectable people, much less those who defined the borders of European literary canons. So why then did Couperus's educated Dutch contemporaries receive his book with acclaim? Why did they come to regard it as a literary classic? Could it be that even at a moment when colonial modernity seemed triumphant and unstoppable, even within a society as Protestant, capitalist, and technologically confident as Holland's, there existed a lurking suspicion that behind all the agreed-upon certainties of modernity there lay something elusive, something that could not be muted even though it gave the appearance of being silent?

In any event, it is now increasingly evident that Van Oudijk's predicament is emblematic of the plight of all of humanity, as it faces the planetary crisis. Much, if not most, of humanity today lives as colonialists once did—viewing the Earth as though it were an inert entity that exists primarily to be exploited and profited from, with the aid of technology and science. Yet even the sciences are now struggling to keep pace with the hidden forces that are manifesting themselves in climatic events of unprecedented and uncanny violence.

And as these events intensify, they add ever greater resonance to voices like that of Davi Kopenawa, voices that have stubbornly continued to insist, in the face of unrelenting, apocalyptic violence, that nonhumans can, do, and *must* speak. It is essential now, as the prospect of planetary catastrophe comes ever closer, that those nonhuman voices be restored to our stories.

The fate of humans, and all our relatives, depends on it.

Acknowledgments

I was able to travel to Maluku in 2016 thanks to the Explore Indonesia program of the Indonesian Ministry of Education and Culture. I am grateful to Dr. Hilmar Farid, Director General of Culture, and his colleagues Nadjamuddin Ramly and Restu Gunawan for this opportunity. I am indebted particularly to Gentur Adiutama and I Gusti Gede Irawan Putra, of the Directorate for Heritage and Cultural Diplomacy, for accompanying me on my travels in Maluku. I owe them many thanks for their help with the logistics, and for being diligent, patient, and good-humored travel companions and translators.

John H. McGlynn, of the Lontar Foundation in Jakarta, has long been a tireless advocate for contemporary Indonesian literature. I owe him a very special word of thanks for putting me in touch with the Explore Indonesia program. Many friends in Jakarta were generous with their advice and support: I am grateful particularly to Goenawan Mohammad, Nirwan Dewanto, and Leila Chudori. Nukila Amal, being Malukan herself, was a fount of information on the region; I owe her many thanks. It was fortunate for me that my friends Nengcha Lhouvum and Gautam Mukhopadhaya were in Jakarta at that time—my thanks to them for their hospitality. In Banda Naira, Tanya Des Alwi was immensely generous with her time; I owe her a great debt of gratitude.

For his help with Dutch sources, I am deeply grateful to Professor Dirk H. A. Kolff of Leiden University. I have long admired his work and was fortunate to be able to draw on his vast erudition. For their help with sources, I am grateful to Joseph R. Klein and Jesse Rumsey-Merlan.

For their help with my research on migration in Italy, I would like to thank Annalisa Camilli, Luca Ciabarri, Mauro Van Aken, Roberto Beneduce, Shail Jha, Stefano Liberti, Sara Scarafia, Antonio Fraschilla, Mara Matta, Fausto Melluso, Gianfranco Benello, Alessandro Triulzi, Paola Splendore, Shaul Bassi, and most particularly, Hasna Hena Mamataz.

The three anonymous readers who reviewed the manuscript for the University of Chicago Press had many useful suggestions; I thank them all. My old friend Chris (now Sir Christopher) Clark read the manuscript with the most painstaking attention despite all his other commitments; I am deeply in his debt for his comments and suggestions.

I was immensely fortunate to be able to rely on the support of Rahul Srivastava and his team at urbz.net: I am grateful in particular to Partha Shrungarpure for his help. My editors, Meru Gokhale and Jocasta Hamilton, provided much encouragement and many useful suggestions; and Alan Thomas of the University of Chicago Press was, as always, a rock to lean on. I am indebted to all of them.

This book has been enriched by conversations with many friends, old and new. To name them all would be impossible, but I would be remiss if I did not mention Julia Adeney Thomas, Debjani Ganguly, Donna Haraway, James Clifford, Susan Harding, and Annu Jalais. A final word of thanks to Debbie, for her careful readings of the manuscript, and for her unfailing support, without which it would have been impossible to write a book during a year of unprecedented loss, anxiety, and uncertainty. My gratitude to her is beyond measure.

Brooklyn
October 26, 2020

Notes

CHAPTER ONE

1   The name "Banda" is thought to derive from a Persian word, "bandar," meaning harbor or emporium. Cf. Roy Ellen, *On the Edge of the Banda Zone: Past and Present in the Social Organization of a Moluccan Trading Network* (Honolulu: University of Hawaii Press, 2003), 65.

2   The island's name is also sometimes spelled "Lonthoir"; see Phillip Winn, "Graves, Groves and Gardens: Place and Identity—Central Maluku, Indonesia," *Asia-Pacific Journal of Anthropology* 2, no. 1 (2001): 24–44.

3   H. G. Aveling, "Seventeenth Century Bandanese Society in Fact and Fiction: 'Tambera' Assessed," *Bijdragen tet de Taal-, Land- en Volkenkunde* 123, no. 3 (1967): 351.

4   The following account is based on a narrative compiled by J. A. van der Chijs (*De Vestiging van het Nederlandsche Gezag over de Banda-Eilanden (1599–1621)* [Batavia: Albrecht & Co., 1886]), based on Dutch East India Company documents. The only account in English is Willard A. Hanna's *Indonesian Banda: Colonialism and Its Aftermath in the Nutmeg Islands* (reprint, Banda Naira: Yayasan Warisan da Budaya, 1991). Hanna's account also appears to be based largely on Van der Chijs's, but there are many discrepancies between the two narratives. Hanna, for instance, spells Sonck as 't Sonck. Where the accounts diverge, I have followed Van der Chijs's text. The rest of this section and the next section are based entirely on Van der Chijs, *De Vestiging*, 139–43.

5   Cf. Frans S. Watuseke, "The Name Moluccas, Maluku," *Asian Profile*, June 1977.

6   Leonard Y. Andaya, "Local Trade Networks in Maluku in the 16th, 17th, and 18th Centuries," *Cakalele* 2, no. 2 (1991): 79.

7   Cf. Thomas J. Zumbroich, "From Mouth Fresheners to Erotic Perfumes: The Evolving Socio-Cultural Significance of Nutmeg, Mace and Cloves in South Asia," *eJournal of Indian Medicine* 5 (2012): 37–97.

8   Cf. Ken Stark and Kyle Latinis, "The Response of Early Ambonese Foragers to the Maluku Spice Trade: The Archaeological Evidence," *Cakalele* 7 (1996): 51–67.

9   For a concise account of these trade networks, see Anthony Reid, *A History of Southeast Asia: Critical Crossroads* (Malden, MA: Blackwell, 2015), 62–63.

10 Cf. Ellen, *On the Edge of the Banda Zone*, 54.

11 George Masselman, *The Money Trees: The Spice Trade* (New York: McGraw-Hill, 1967), 36. See also Alison Games, *Inventing the English Massacre: Amboyna in History and Memory* (New York: Oxford University Press, 2020), 19.

12 Giles Milton, *Nathaniel's Nutmeg, or, the True and Incredible Adventures of the Spice Trader Who Changed the Course of History* (New York: Penguin, 1999), 1–8.

13 Cf. Rajani Sudan, *The Alchemy of Empire: Abject Materials and the Technologies of Colonialism* (New York: Fordham University Press, 2016), 59–60; and Milton, *Nathaniel's Nutmeg*, 3.

14 Jean-Pierre Dupuy, *The Mark of the Sacred*, trans. M. B. DeBevoise (Stanford, CA: Stanford University Press, 2013), 153.

15 Cf. Reid, *A History of Southeast Asia*, 70.

16 Peter Hulme, *Colonial Encounters; Europe and the Native Caribbean, 1492–1797* (New York: Methuen, 1986), 35.

17 Cf. Timothy Morton, *The Poetics of Spice: Romantic Consumerism and the Exotic* (Cambridge: Cambridge University Press, 2000), 8.

18 Peter V. Lape, "Political Dynamics and Religious Change in the Late Pre-Colonial Banda Islands, Eastern Indonesia," *World Archaeology* 32, no. 1 (2000): 139.

19 Masselman, *The Money Trees*, 122.

20 C. R. Boxer, *The Dutch Seaborne Empire, 1600–1800* (London: Penguin, 1990), 110.

21 Harold J. Cook, *Matters of Exchange: Commerce, Medicine, and Science in the Dutch Golden Age* (New Haven, CT: Yale University Press, 2007), 182.

22 George Masselman, *The Cradle of Colonialism* (New Haven, CT: Yale University Press, 1963), 261.

23 Vincent C. Loth, "Pioneers and Perkeniers: The Banda Islands in the 17th Century," *Cakalele* 6 (1995): 17.

24 Vincent C. Loth, "Armed Incidents and Unpaid Bills: Anglo-Dutch Rivalry in the Banda Islands in the Seventeenth Century," *Modern Asian Studies* 29, no. 4 (October 1995): 711.

25 Andaya, "Local Trade Networks in Maluku," 82. See also Hans Derks, *History of the Opium Problem: The Assault on the East, ca. 1600–1950* (Leiden: Brill, 2012), chaps. 10, 12.

26 On the Portuguese (and European) desire to impose monopolies on the spice trade, see Jack Turner, *Spice: The History of a Temptation* (New York: Vintage Books, 2004), Kindle book, loc. 639 of 6701; Michael Krondl, *The Taste of Conquest: The Rise and Fall of the Three Great Cities of Spice* (New York: Ballantine, 2008), Kindle book, locs. 2051 and 2054 of 4689; and *The Rise of Merchant Empires: Long Distance Trade in the Early Modern World*, ed. James D. Tracy (Cambridge: Cambridge University Press, 1990), 28. For the contrasting Indian Ocean approach to trade see Reid, *A History of Southeast Asia*, 63, 136 (and also chapter 3, section "The East Asian Trading System of 1280–1500," 65–69).

27 Games, *Inventing the English Massacre*, 20.

28 Cf. Ellen, *On the Edge of the Banda Zone*, 64: "Although most nutmeg (*Myristica fragrans*) came from Banda, Banda itself was dependent for its subsistence upon its periphery."

29 The most comprehensive study of Bandanese trading networks is Ellen, *On the Edge of the Banda Zone.*

30 Cf. Sudan, *The Alchemy of Empire*, 35.

31 Cf. Muridan Widjojo, *The Revolt of Prince Nuku: Cross-Cultural Alliance-Making in Maluku, c. 1780–1810* (Leiden: Brill, 2009), 29.

32 Adam Clulow, "The Art of Claiming: Possession and Resistance in Early Modern Asia," *American Historical Review* 121, no. 1 (February 2016): 27.

33 João de Barros in the *Decadas*. This quote is taken from Albert S. Bickmore, *Travels in the East Indian Archipelago* (London: John Murray, 1868), 211, who took it from Crawfurd's *Dictionary of the India Islands.*

34 Lape, "Political Dynamics and Religious Change in the Late Pre-Colonial Banda Islands," 147.

35 See Aveling, "Seventeenth Century Bandanese Society in Fact and Fiction," 347–65, for a detailed account of what can be learned about Bandanese society from early European sources.

36 Ellen, *On the Edge of the Banda Zone*, 78.

37 Timo Kaartinen, *Songs of Travel and Stories of Place: Poetics of Absence in an Eastern Indonesian Society* (Helsinki: Academia Scientiarum Fennica, 2010), 37; Widjojo, *The Revolt of Prince Nuku*, 16; and Cook, *Matters of Exchange*, 182.

38 Andaya, "Local Trade Networks in Maluku," 80; Loth, "Armed Incidents and Unpaid Bills," 709.

39 Andaya, "Local Trade Networks in Maluku," 82; Gerrit J. Knaap, "Crisis and Failure: War and Revolt in the Ambon Islands, 1636–1637," *Cakalele* 3 (1992): 2.

40 For an account of Bandanese relations with the English, see Loth, "Armed Incidents and Unpaid Bills," 705–40; and Clulow, "The Art of Claiming," 30–34.

41 Aveling, "Seventeenth Century Bandanese Society in Fact and Fiction," 352.

42 Loth, "Armed Incidents and Unpaid Bills," 710: "To this day it remains unclear whether the Bandanese did not understand these western-style documents." See also Clulow, "The Art of Claiming," 28–30.

43 Cook, *Matters of Exchange*, 182.

44 Cf. Donna Merwick, *The Shame and the Sorrow: Dutch-Amerindian Encounters in New Netherland* (Philadelphia: University of Pennsylvania Press, 2006), loc. 1537.

45 "By 1612," writes Harold Cook, "Coen and others had forced the Heren XVII to recognize that in pursuing large profits negotiated by treaties that were imbalanced to their advantage they would have to enforce the agreements with military power, despite the financial and other costs. He firmly believed that to be financially secure the VOC needed to acquire a monopoly over the spice trade and to enforce it, which would require coercion against rival merchants and sometimes against the suppliers." Cook, *Matters of Exchange*, 183.

46 "The English tended to appear on the scene and follow the Dutch wherever they went, but without ever displaying signs of having any overall strategy." Widjojo, *The Revolt of Prince Nuku*, 13. For accounts of Anglo-Dutch rivalry in Maluku in the seventeenth century, see also Masselman, *The Cradle of Colonialism*, 266–389; and Milton, *Nathaniel's Nutmeg.*

47 Lucas Kiers, *Coen Op Banda: Del Conqueste Getoest aan het Recht van den Tijd* (Utrecht: Oosthoek, 1943), 156. I am grateful to the eminent historian Dirk Kolff for translating this and other passages where I have quoted directly from Dutch texts.

48 Games, *Inventing the English Massacre*, 24.

49 The historian Vincent C. Loth writes: "Banda has been curiously neglected. It would not be true to say that the history of these islands has been completely ignored, or that it remains unknown to this day, but a comprehensive history based on a detailed analysis of the sources from a modern viewpoint has yet to be written." Loth, "Pioneers and Perkeniers," 13–35.

50 "Omstreeks middernacht van den 21sten op den 22sten April viel eene lamp in de bale-bale, waar Sonck met zijne raadslieden sliepen, welk onbeduidend voorval genoeg was om onder de overal en altijd verraad ziende Europeanen eene paniek te verwekken." Van der Chijs, *De Vestiging*, 140.

51 I am grateful to Vincent Loth for this information. In a personal communication, he writes: "As to what we have now: Van der Chijs is still the closest we can get to the firsthand reports of the conquest, in my opinion. Almost every author (contemporary or of later date) based him- of herself on his work. There are a few eye-witness testimonies of VOC-personnel who were present as soldiers, but they do not give an overview presentation of the happenings as Van der Chijs does."

52 Cf. Juan Moreno Cruz and M. Scott Taylor, "A Spatial Approach to Energy Economics," Working Paper 18908, National Bureau of Economic Research, March 2013, 2, http://www.nber.org/papers/w18908.

CHAPTER TWO

1 The numbers given for the Japanese mercenaries tend to vary, but Van der Chijs says unambiguously that there were two companies of forty each. Since Japanese who left Japan at that time were not allowed to return, it seems likely that these swordsmen were renegades of some sort, very likely pirates. (I am grateful to Julia Adeney Thomas for this suggestion.)

2 Lucas Kiers, *Coen Op Banda: Del Conqueste Getoest aan het Recht van den Tijd* (Utrecht: Oosthoek, 1943), 157.

3 "Tuan Derek Kalengbakar," in the Maluku dialect: Cf. Nikodemus Yudho Sulistyo, "The Half-Blood Hero in Y. B. Mangunwijaya's Ikan-Ikan Hiu, Ido, Homa and James Cameron's *Avatar*," *Spectral: Jurnal Ilmiah* 3, no. 2 (June 2017): 34.

4 J. A. van der Chijs, *De Vestiging van het Nederlandsche Gezag over de Banda-Eilanden (1599–1621)* (Batavia: Albrecht & Co., 1886), 147.

5 Van der Chijs, 148.

6 Vincent C. Loth, "Pioneers and Perkeniers: The Banda Islands in the 17th Century," *Cakalele* 6 (1995): 18.

7 Cf. Donna Merwick, *The Shame and the Sorrow: Dutch-Amerindian Encounters in New Netherland* (Philadelphia: University of Pennsylvania Press, 2006), loc. 1780.

8 Alison Games, *Inventing the English Massacre: Amboyna in History and Memory* (New York: Oxford University Press, 2020), 7.

9   Barry O'Connell, *On Our Own Ground: The Complete Writings of William Apess, a Pequot* (Amherst: University of Massachusetts Press, 1992), xxv.

10   Cf. Merwick, *The Shame and the Sorrow*, loc. 2240.

11   John Mason, *A Brief History of the Pequot War: Especially of the memorable Taking of their Fort at Mistick in Connecticut in 1637* (Boston, 1736), 8–9. Dutch armies of this period relied heavily on foreign mercenaries; see C. R. Boxer, *The Dutch Seaborne Empire, 1600–1800* (London: Penguin, 1990), 88.

12   John Underhill, *Newes from America; or, A New and Experimentall Discoverie of New England* (1638), 34–36. I have modernized some of the spellings in this passage and the next.

13   Neal Salisbury, *Manitou and Providence: Indians, Europeans and the Making of New England, 1500–1643* (New York: Oxford University Press, 1982), loc. 3381.

14   One of the clauses of the Treaty of Hartford, which ended the Pequot War, dictates that the 200 Pequot who had survived would be distributed among other tribes, and that they "shall no more be called Pequots but Narragansetts and Mohegans." "The Hartford Treaty, 1638, Signifying the Close of the Pequot War," http://pequotwar.org/wp-content/uploads/2014/11/Grade-8-Treaty-of-Hartford-Guiding-Questions-Avery.pdf. See also Salisbury, *Manitou and Providence*, loc. 2284; and Katherine A. Grandjean, "The Long Wake of the Pequot War," *Early American Studies* 9, no. 2 (Spring 2011): 391.

15   O'Connell, *On Our Own Ground*, xxv.

16   Francis Bacon, *An Advertisement Touching an Holy War*, 30–33, https://sites.duke.edu/conversions/files/2014/09/Manion_Bacon-on-Holy-War.pdf.

17   Elizabeth A. Fenn, "Biological Warfare in Eighteenth-Century North America: Beyond Jeffery Amherst," *Journal of American History*, March 2000, 1574.

18   Peter Linebaugh and Marcus Rediker, *The Many-Headed Hydra: Sailors, Slaves, Commoners, and the Hidden History of the Revolutionary Atlantic* (Boston: Beacon Press, 2000), 40.

19   Rozengin (or Rosengain, now Pulao Hatta) is an island in the archipelago. Coen also notes that the only island that the Dutch had not occupied was Pulao Run, which "we left alone as they kept quiet." In fact, Run was left alone because there was an English base there. Van der Chijs, *De Vestiging*, 149.

20   Harold J. Cook, *Matters of Exchange: Commerce, Medicine, and Science in the Dutch Golden Age* (New Haven, CT: Yale University Press, 2007), 188.

21   Loth states that 48 headmen were killed: Loth, "Pioneers and Perkeniers," 18. Others put the figure at 40. I have used Van der Chijs's figure of 44.

22   Cf. Loth, 18.

23   Adam Clulow, "The Art of Claiming: Possession and Resistance in Early Modern Asia," *American Historical Review* 121, no. 1 (February 2016): 36.

CHAPTER THREE

1   Cf. Leonard Y. Andaya, "Centers and Peripheries in Maluku," *Cakalele* 4 (1993): 1–21.

2   Cf. Heather Builth et al., "Environmental and Cultural Change on the Mt. Eccles Lava-Flow Landscapes of Southwest Victoria, Australia," *Holocene* 18, no. 3 (2008): 413–24; and Erin L. Matchan et al., "Early Human Occupation

of Southeastern Australia: New Insights from 40Ar/39Ar Dating of Young Volcanoes," *Geology* 20, no. 20 (2019).

3 Heather Builth, "Mt. Eccles Lava Flow and the Gunditjmara Connection: A Landform for All Seasons," *Proceedings of the Royal Society of Victoria*, November 2004, 168.

4 For the dating of the eruption, see Matchan et al., "Early Human Occupation of Southeastern Australia."

5 Colin Barras, "Is an Aboriginal Tale of an Ancient Volcano the Oldest Story Ever Told?" *Science*, February 11, 2020, https://www.sciencemag.org/news /2020/02/aboriginal-tale-ancient-volcano-oldest-story-ever-told. See also Duane W. Hamacher and Ray P. Norris, "Australian Aboriginal Geomythology: Eyewitness Accounts of Cosmic Impacts?" Paper submitted to *Archaeoastronomy: The Journal of Astronomy in Culture*, September 22, 2010. https:// arxiv.org/abs/1009.4251.

. 6 Cf. Jessica K. Weir, *The Gunditjmara Land Justice Story* (Australian Institute of Aboriginal and Torres Strait Islander Studies, 2009).

7 Nils Bubandt, "Haunted Geologies: Spirits, Stones and the Necropolitics of the Anthropocene," in *Arts of Living on a Damaged Planet*, ed. Ana Tsing et al. (Minneapolis: University of Minnesota Press, 2017), 131.

8 Valentin R. Troll et al., "Ancient Oral Tradition Describes Volcano-Earthquake Interaction at Merapi Volcano, Indonesia," *Geografiska Annaler: Series A, Physical Geography* 97, no. 1 (2015): 140.

9 Troll et al., 141.

10 Nukila Amal, *The Original Dream*, trans. Linda Owens (Seattle: Amazon-Crossing, 2017), 53.

11 The Bandanese language, *turwandan*, is now spoken only by a few thousand people, mainly on the Ai islands. Timo Kaartinen, *Songs of Travel and Stories of Place: Poetics of Absence in an Eastern Indonesian Society* (Helsinki: Academia Scientiarum Fennica, 2010), 13, 57.

12 Vine Deloria Jr., *God Is Red: A Native View of Religion* (Golden, CO: North American Press, 1992), loc. 2879. The quotations in the next two paragraphs are also from this book: locs. 1341, 1677.

13 Keith H. Basso, *Wisdom Sits in Places: Landscape and Language among the Western Apache* (Albuquerque: University of New Mexico Press, 1996), loc. 723.

14 Roy Ellen, *On the Edge of the Banda Zone: Past and Present in the Social Organization of a Moluccan Trading Network* (Honolulu: University of Hawaii Press, 2003), 61.

15 Kaartinen, *Songs of Travel and Stories of Place*, 113–14.

16 Max Liboiron, *Pollution Is Colonialism* (Durham, NC: Duke University Press, 2021), 7.

17 For a comprehensive account of the rise of new philosophies of nature in seventeenth-century Holland, see Harold J. Cook, *Matters of Exchange: Commerce, Medicine, and Science in the Dutch Golden Age* (New Haven, CT: Yale University Press, 2007).

18 Akeel Bilgrami, *Secularism, Identity, and Enchantment* (Cambridge, MA: Harvard University Press, 2014), 296.

19 Carolyn Merchant, *The Death of Nature: Women, Ecology and the Scientific Revolution* (San Francisco: Harper and Row, 1983), 226.

20 Cf. Jesse Goldstein, "Terra Economica: Waste and the Production of Enclosed Nature," *Antipode* 45, no. 2 (2013): 357–75.

21 Cf. Roxanne Dunbar-Ortiz, *An Indigenous Peoples' History of the United States* (Boston: Beacon Press, 2014), 34.

22 Charles Zika, "Cannibalism and Witchcraft in Early Modern Europe: Reading the Visual Images," *History Workshop Journal*, no. 44 (1997): 89.

23 W. Arens, *The Man-Eating Myth: Anthropology and Anthropophagy* (New York: Oxford University Press, 1979), 179. See also Zika, "Cannibalism and Witchcraft in Early Modern Europe," 101: "As the atrocities committed by Christian against Christian in sixteenth century Europe increase, as do those committed by Christian upon non-Christian in the Americas, they begin to be projected more intensively upon the traditional and more recent enemies of Christian society."

24 Cf. Bilgrami, *Secularism, Identity, and Enchantment*, 300.

25 See, for example the work of the Italian anthropologist Ernesto de Martino on *tarantismo* in Puglia, or the work of Jeanne Favret-Saada on witchcraft practices among farmers in the Mayenne, in northwest France.

26 Jeffrey J. Kripal, *Authors of the Impossible: The Paranormal and the Sacred* (Chicago: University of Chicago Press, 2010), 28.

27 Cf. J. P. S. Uberoi, *The Other Mind of Europe: Goethe as a Scientist* (New Delhi: Oxford University Press, 1984).

28 Ben Ehrenreich, *Desert Notebooks: A Road Map for the End of Time* (Berkeley, CA: Counterpoint, 2020), 76.

29 Masselman, *The Cradle of Colonialism* (New Haven, CT: Yale University Press, 1963), 437.

30 C. R. Boxer, *The Dutch Seaborne Empire, 1600–1800* (London: Penguin, 1990), 5.

31 Quoted in Julie Berger Hochstrasser, "The Conquest of Spice and the Dutch Colonial Imaginary: Seen and Unseen in the Visual Culture of Trade," in *Colonial Botany: Science, Commerce, and Politics in the Early Modern World*, ed. Londa Schiebinger and Claudia Swan (Philadelphia: University of Pennsylvania Press, 2007), 171–72.

32 Boxer, *The Dutch Seaborne Empire*, 25. See also Hochstrasser, "The Conquest of Spice and the Dutch Colonial Imaginary," 173.

33 Hochstrasser, "The Conquest of Spice and the Dutch Colonial Imaginary," 169.

34 Hochstrasser, 182.

35 Albert S. Bickmore, *Travels in the East Indian Archipelago* (London: John Murray, 1868), 217.

36 Cf. Vincent C. Loth, "Pioneers and Perkeniers: The Banda Islands in the 17th Century," *Cakalele* 6 (1995): 25.

37 Quoted in Hochstrasser, "The Conquest of Spice and the Dutch Colonial Imaginary," 174.

38 Phillip Winn estimates that about a thousand Bandanese survived; see Winn, "Graves, Groves and Gardens: Place and Identity—Central Maluku, Indonesia," *Asia-Pacific Journal of Anthropology* 2, no. 1 (2001): 25n5.

39 Cf. Donna Merwick, *The Shame and the Sorrow: Dutch-Amerindian Encounters in New Netherland* (Philadelphia: University of Pennsylvania Press, 2006), loc. 2403.

40 George Masselman, an American, writes of Coen: "It will be difficult to find, in the historiography of nations, a similar example of censure of a national figure by his own countrymen." Masselman, *The Cradle of Colonialism* (New Haven, CT: Yale University Press, 1963), 421. It is telling that Masselman did not think the censure of Coen was justified because "Banda was only one in a long series of similar events in the age of capitalistic colonialism, when indigenous peoples found themselves in the way of the self-imposed rights of vigorous nations seeking to exploit their resources" (422).

41 Quoted in Masselman, 421.

42 Bart Luttikhuis and A. Dirk Moses, "Mass Violence and the End of the Dutch Colonial Empire in Indonesia," *Journal of Genocide Research* 14, nos. 3–4 (2012).

43 Boxer, *The Dutch Seaborne Empire*, 107.

44 Cf. Russell Shorto, *The Island at the Center of the World* (New York: Vintage, 2005), 61.

45 Cook, *Matters of Exchange*, 187.

46 Chapter 11, in Giles Milton, *Nathaniel's Nutmeg, or, the True and Incredible Adventures of the Spice Trader Who Changed the Course of History* (New York: Penguin, 1999), locs. 4023–4314 of 5052, is a comprehensive account of the massacre of Amboyna.

47 Cook, *Matters of Exchange*, 188.

48 Alison Games, *Inventing the English Massacre: Amboyna in History and Memory* (New York: Oxford University Press, 2020), 6. The quotations in the rest of this section are all from this book: 85, 10, 3, 79, 111, 80, 6, 194, 190–91, 140, 6, 172, 194, 10.

49 Games, 3. The next few citations of Games will be given by page number in the text.

50 Games, 10.

51 Cf. Jon Goss, "Understanding the 'Maluku Wars': Overview of Sources of Communal Conflict and Prospects for Peace," *Cakalele* 11 (2000): 7–39.

52 Amal, *The Original Dream*, loc. 3023.

CHAPTER FOUR

1 Richard Drinnon, *Facing West: The Metaphysics of Indian-Hating and Empire-Building* (Minneapolis: University of Minnesota Press, 1980), 55.

2 Jennifer Nez Denetdale, *Reclaiming Diné History: The Legacies of Navajo Chief Manuelito and Juanita* (Tucson: University of Arizona Press, 2007), loc. 859.

3 These words are from an article I wrote in 1988 titled "The Four Corners." It was published in *Granta*.

4 Robert S. McPherson, *Sacred Land, Sacred View: Navajo Perceptions of the Four Corner Region* (Salt Lake City, UT: Brigham Young University Press, 1992), 1–2.

5 The historian Robert S. McPherson writes: "Just as stained glass windows of the cathedrals built in the Middle Ages served the illiterate as a picture book of the tenets of Christianity, so do landforms for the Diné. The land serves as a mnemonic device that jogs the memory into remembering events and lessons associated with it. . . . Just as another religion might insist that reading the scriptures, going to a church or temple, or meditating in a certain

place increases the chances of inspiration or supernatural aid, so does the land serve a similar purpose for the Navajo people." McPherson, 73.

6   Donna J. Haraway, *Staying with the Trouble: Making Kin in the Chthulucene* (Durham, NC: Duke University Press, 2016), 93.

7   Nick Estes, *Our History Is the Future: Standing Rock versus the Dakota Access Pipeline, and the Long Tradition of Indigenous Resistance* (New York: Verso, 2019), 102.

8   *Treaty Between the United States of America and the Navajo Tribe of Indians: With a Record of the Discussions That Led to Its Signing* (Flagstaff, AZ: K. C. Publications, 1968), 2.

9   "American Indians," writes Vine Deloria Jr., "hold their lands—places—as having the highest possible meaning, and all their statements are made with this reference point in mind." Deloria, *God Is Red: A Native View of Religion* (Golden, CO: North American Press, 1992), 60.

10 Deloria, loc. 1596.

11 Edwin L. Sabin, *Kit Carson Days, 1809–1868: "Adventures in the Path of Empire,"* vol. 2 (Lincoln: University of Nebraska Press, 1995), 656.

12 James W. M. Newlin, *Proposed Indian Policy* (1881), 43.

13 Alfred Crosby, *Ecological Imperialism: The Biological Expansion of Europe, 900–1900* (Cambridge: Cambridge University Press, 1986; e-book edition, 2015), loc. 97.

14 Cf. Simon L. Lewis and Mark A. Maslin, "Defining the Anthropocene," *Nature* 1519 (March 12, 2015): 175.

15 David S. Jones, "Virgin Soils Revisited," *William and Mary Quarterly* 60, no. 4 (October 2003): 703. See also David E. Stannard, *American Holocaust: The Conquest of the New World* (Oxford: Oxford University Press, 1992), 72; Neal Salisbury, *Manitou and Providence: Indians, Europeans and the Making of New England, 1500–1643* (New York: Oxford University Press, 1982), locs. 95, 237, 1066; and Michael Williams, *Deforesting the Earth: From Prehistory to Global Crisis* (Chicago: University of Chicago Press, 2006), 194.

16 For a critique, see Dagomar Degroot, "Did Colonialism Cause Global Cooling? Revisiting an Old Controversy," *Historical Climatology*, February 22, 2019, https://www.historicalclimatology.com/features/did-colonialism-cause-global-cooling-revisiting-an-old-controversy.

17 Christopher M. Clark, "This Is a Reality, Not a Threat," *New York Review of Books*, November 22, 2018.

18 The concept of "settler colonialism" has been theorized by Lorenzo Veracini in his book *Settler Colonialism: A Theoretical Overview* (London: Palgrave Macmillan, 2010). Veracini suggests that "transforming the environment to suit the colonizing project" is one of the defining features of settler colonialism that distinguishes it from other forms of colonialism (22).

19 Quoted in Silvia Federici, *Caliban and the Witch: Women, the Body and Primitive Accumulation*, 2nd ed. (Brooklyn: Automedia, 2014), 219.

20 Alexis de Tocqueville, *Democracy in America and Two Essays on America*, trans. Gerald E. Bevan (New York: Penguin, 2003), 378–79.

21 John Grenier, *The First Way of War: American War Making on the Frontier, 1607–1814* (New York: Cambridge University Press, 2005), 12. The quotations and references in the next three paragraphs are also from this book, 27, 28, 43.

22 Grenier, 27–29.

23   Jill Lepore, *The Name of War: King Philip's War and the Origins of American Identity* (New York: Vintage, 1998), loc. 148.

24   "This way of war," writes Roxanne Dunbar-Ortiz, "forged in the first century of colonization—destroying Indigenous villages and fields, killing civilians, ranging, and scalp hunting—became the basis for the wars against the Indigenous across the continent into the late nineteenth century." Dunbar-Ortiz, *An Indigenous Peoples' History of the United States* (Boston: Beacon Press, 2014), 65.

25   Dunbar-Ortiz, loc. 226.

26   Dunbar-Ortiz, loc. 169.

27   Richard Grove, *Ecology, Climate and Empire: Colonialism and Global Environmental History, 1400–1940* (Cambridge: White Horse Press, 1997), 183.

28   Joyce E. Chaplin, *Subject Matter: Technology, the Body, and Science on the Anglo-American Frontier, 1500–1676* (Cambridge, MA: Harvard University Press, 2001), locs. 96–106.

29   Cf. Dunbar-Ortiz, *An Indigenous Peoples' History of the United States*, 39.

30   Jones, "Virgin Soils Revisited," 707.

31   Jones, 718. See also Paul Kelton, *Epidemics and Enslavement: Biological Catastrophe in the Native Southeast, 1492–1715* (Lincoln: University of Nebraska Press, 2007), 44.

32   Dunbar-Ortiz, *An Indigenous Peoples' History of the United States*, 40.

33   Sam White, *A Cold Welcome: The Little Ice Age and Europe's Encounter with North America* (Cambridge, MA: Harvard University Press, 2017), 110.

34   White, 742.

35   Kelton, *Epidemics and Enslavement*, xviii.

36   Jones, "Virgin Soils Revisited," 712.

37   Jones, 734.

38   Chaplin, *Subject Matter*, loc. 356. See also Kelton, *Epidemics and Enslavement*, 78.

39   Elizabeth A. Fenn, "Biological Warfare in Eighteenth-Century North America: Beyond Jeffery Amherst," *Journal of American History*, March 2000, 1566.

40   Fenn, 1567.

41   Crosby, *Ecological Imperialism*, loc. 3220.

42   Fenn, "Biological Warfare in Eighteenth-Century North America," 1557. The quotations in the next two paragraphs are also from this article, 1555, 1556–57, 1558, 1564.

43   Fenn, 1577–79.

44   Quoted in Estes, *Our History Is the Future*, 86.

CHAPTER FIVE

1   Jill Lepore, *The Name of War: King Philip's War and the Origins of American Identity* (New York: Vintage, 1998), 76.

2   This doctrine was formalized by philosophers like John Locke: cf. Jesse Goldstein, "Terra Economica: Waste and the Production of Enclosed Nature," *Antipode* 45, no. 2 (2013): 13.

3   Michael Williams, *Deforesting the Earth: From Prehistory to Global Crisis* (Chicago: University of Chicago Press, 2006), 147.

4   "If English visitors to New England thought it a paradox," writes William Cronon, "that Indians seemed to live like paupers in a landscape of great natural wealth, then the problem lay with English eyesight rather than with any real Indian poverty." Cronon, *Changes in the Land: Indians, Colonists and the Ecology of New England* (New York: Hill and Wang, 1983), 53–54.

5   Cronon, 51, 53.

6   Quoted in Bron Taylor, *Dark Green Religion: Nature, Spirituality and the Planetary Future* (Berkeley: University of California Press, 2010), 43. See also Williams, *Deforesting the Earth*, 147.

7   Cf. Williams, *Deforesting the Earth*, 150–90.

8   Cronon, *Changes in the Land*, 5.

9   Thomas Yellowtail, *Yellowtail, Crow Medicine Man and Sun Dance Chief: An Autobiography*, as told to Michael Oren Fitzgerald (Norman: University of Oklahoma Press, 1991), 49.

10 Robin Wall Kimmerer, *Braiding Sweetgrass: Indigenous Wisdom, Scientific Knowledge, and the Teaching of Plants* (Minneapolis: Milkweed Editions, 2013), 7.

11 Cronon, *Changes in the Land*, 82.

12 Neal Salisbury, *Manitou and Providence: Indians, Europeans and the Making of New England, 1500–1643* (New York: Oxford University Press, 1982), loc. 128.

13 Virginia DeJohn Anderson, *Creatures of Empire: How Domestic Animals Transformed Early America* (New York: Oxford University Press, 2004), 5. The following quotes are from the same book, 8, 9, 224. For a similar argument, see Williams, *Deforesting the Earth*, 195–96.

14 Anderson, *Creatures of Empire*, 206.

15 Salisbury, *Manitou and Providence*, loc. 148.

16 Lepore, *The Name of War*, 74.

17 Anderson, *Creatures of Empire*, 178.

18 Lepore, *The Name of War*, 71.

19 Anderson, *Creatures of Empire*, 236.

20 John Grenier, *The First Way of War: American War Making on the Frontier, 1607–1814* (New York: Cambridge University Press, 2005), 46. The quotations and references in the next three paragraphs are also from this book, 12, 27, 28, 43.

21 Davi Kopenawa and Bruce Albert, *The Falling Sky: Words of a Yanomami Shaman*, trans. Nicholas Elliott and Alison Dundy (Cambridge, MA: Belknap Press, 2013), 307–8.

22 Roxanne Dunbar-Ortiz, *An Indigenous Peoples' History of the United States* (Boston: Beacon Press, 2014), 142.

23 Nick Estes, *Our History Is the Future: Standing Rock versus the Dakota Access Pipeline, and the Long Tradition of Indigenous Resistance* (New York: Verso, 2019), 110.

24 Peter Nabokov, *Native American Testimony: An Anthology of Indian and White Relations, First Encounter to Dispossession* (New York: Harper and Row, 1978), 221.

25 Dina Gilio-Whitaker, *As Long as Grass Grows: The Indigenous Fight for Environmental Justice, from Colonization to Standing Rock* (Boston: Beacon, 2019), 48.

26 Estes, *Our History Is the Future*, 133–38.

27 Quoted in Estes, 139.

28 Patrick Wolfe, "Settler Colonialism and the Elimination of the Native," *Journal of Genocide Research* 8, no. 4 (2006): 387–409, DOI: 10.1080/14623520601056240.

29 Gregory Hooks and Chad L. Smith, "The Treadmill of Destruction: National Sacrifice Areas and Native Americans," *American Sociological Review* 69 (2004): 565.

30 LaDuke, Winona, *All Our Relations: Native Struggles for Land and Life*, Chicago: Haymarket Books, 1999, 2.

31 Gregory Hooks and Chad L. Smith, "Treadmills of Production and Destruction: Threats to the Environment Posed by Militarism," *Organization & Environment* 18, no. 1 (March 2005): 26.

32 Doug Brugge, Timothy Benally, and Esther Yazzie-Lewis, eds., *The Navajo People and Uranium Mining* (Albuquerque: University of New Mexico Press, 2006), xv.

33 Leslie Marmon Silko, *The Turquoise Ledge* (New York: Viking, 2010), 69.

34 Hooks and Smith, "The Treadmill of Destruction," 560.

35 See Cody Nelson, "Navajo Nation Faces Twin Threats as Wildfires Spread during Pandemic," *Guardian*, July 6, 2020, https://www.theguardian.com/us-news/2020/jul/06/arizona-wildfires-coronavirus-navajo-nation.

36 Nabokov, *Native American Testimony*, 108.

37 Nabokov, 232.

CHAPTER SIX

1 Cf. Jason W. Moore, "The Rise of Cheap Nature," in *Anthropocene or Capitalocene? Nature, History and the Crisis of Capitalism*, ed. Jason W. Moore (Oakland, CA: PM Press, 2016).

2 For a detailed treatment of this, see Thomas Walter Laqueur, *Solitary Sex: A Cultural History of Masturbation* (New York: Zone Books, 2003).

3 Timothy Morton, *The Poetics of Spice: Romantic Consumerism and the Exotic* (Cambridge: Cambridge University Press, 2000), 95.

4 Leonard Y. Andaya, *The World of Maluku: Eastern Indonesia in the Early Modern Period* (Honolulu: University of Hawaii Press, 1993), 201.

5 Cf. Roy Ellen, *On the Edge of the Banda Zone: Past and Present in the Social Organization of a Moluccan Trading Network* (Honolulu: University of Hawaii Press, 2003), 87.

6 Andaya, *The World of Maluku*, 167.

7 Muridan Widjojo, *The Revolt of Prince Nuku: Cross-Cultural Alliance-Making in Maluku, c. 1780–1810* (Leiden: Brill, 2009), 44.

8 Andaya, *The World of Maluku*, 203–4.

9 Cf. Vincent C. Loth, "Armed Incidents and Unpaid Bills: Anglo-Dutch Rivalry in the Banda Islands in the Seventeenth Century," *Modern Asian Studies* 29, no. 4 (October 1995): 707.

10 Pedro de Cieza de León, *The Incas*, quoted in David E. Stannard, *American Holocaust: The Conquest of the New World* (Oxford: Oxford University Press, 1992), 87.

11 Andaya, *The World of Maluku*, 208.

12 Cf. Leo Akveld and Els M. Jacobs, eds., *The Colourful World of the VOC: National Anniversary Book, VOC 1602–2002* (Bussum, Neth.: THOTH Publishers, 2002), 22; Widjojo, *The Revolt of Prince Nuku*, 37; George Masselman, *The Cradle of Colonialism* (New Haven, CT: Yale University Press, 1963), 460–72;

C. R. Boxer, *The Dutch Seaborne Empire, 1600–1800* (London: Penguin, 1990), 315–31.

13　Greg Grandin, *The End of the Myth: From the Frontier to the Border Wall in the Mind of America* (New York: Metropolitan Books, 2019), 40.

14　Cf. Rupa Marya and Raj Patel, *Inflamed: Deep Medicine and the Anatomy of Injustice* (New York: Farrar, Straus and Giroux, 2021), 247.

15　Charles Darwin, *The Descent of Man and Selection in Relation to Sex* (New York, 1871), 193.

16　Suman Seth, "Darwin and the Ethnologists: Liberal Racialism and the Geological Analogy," *Historical Studies in the Natural Sciences* 46, no. 4 (2016): 526.

17　Banu Subramaniam writes: "While Darwin himself was deeply steeped in ideas of gender, race, and nation of his time, Darwinism opened evolutionary biology and the development of theories of evolution to the powerful forces of social Darwinism and the politics of gender, race, class, nation and sexuality of nineteenth-century Britain." Subramaniam, *Ghost Stories for Darwin: The Science of Variation and the Politics of Diversity* (Urbana: University of Illinois Press, 2014), 12–13.

18　As Suman Seth points out: "Among the most basic points to glean from this division is the fact that racialism—a term I use to indicate that these men all considered race a meaningful category of analysis for understanding human civilization and development—was a position shared across the political spectrum. Too often, scientific racialism has been read as a simple cover for and/or instantiation of odious political and social views. Even more problematically, this connection is often implicitly read in reverse, suggesting that only those with such odious views could be racialists. Hence the import of Darwin's abolitionism as inoculation against a more detailed treatment of the racialist views that litter his work." Suman, 495n12.

19　As Elizabeth Strakosch and Alissa Macoun have observed, colonialism doesn't just take place in time; it creates its own narratives of time. Strakosch and Macoun, "The Vanishing Endpoint of Settler Colonialism," *Arena Journal*, nos. 37/38 (2012): 49.

20　Benjamin Noys, *Malign Velocities: Accelerationism and Capitalism* (Washington, DC: Zero Books, 2014), 63.

21　Cf. Bron Taylor, *Dark Green Religion: Nature, Spirituality and the Planetary Future* (Berkeley: University of California Press, 2010), 153–54. See also Melissa Nursey-Bray et al., "Old Ways for New Days: Australian Indigenous Peoples and Climate Change," *Local Environment* 24, no. 5 (2019): 479; and Max Liboiron, *Pollution Is Colonialism* (Durham, NC: Duke University Press, 2021), 53n46.

CHAPTER SEVEN

1　James Lovelock, "What Is Gaia?" http://www.ecolo.org/lovelock/what_is _Gaia.html.

2　Bron Taylor, a scholar of religion, defines animism as "perceptions that natural entities, forces, and nonhuman life-forms have one or more of the following: a soul or vital lifeforce or spirit, personhood (an affective life and personal intentions), and consciousness, often but not always including special spiritual intelligence of powers." Taylor, *Dark Green Religion: Nature,*

Spirituality and the Planetary Future (Berkeley: University of California Press, 2010), 15.

3   "As an inanimate object of inquiry": Joyce E. Chaplin, *Subject Matter: Technology, the Body, and Science on the Anglo-American Frontier, 1500–1676* (Cambridge, MA: Harvard University Press, 2001), loc. 3635. For the Algonquian concept of "Manitou," see also Neal Salisbury, *Manitou and Providence: Indians, Europeans and the Making of New England, 1500–1643* (New York: Oxford University Press, 1982), loc. 398.

4   Chaplin, *Subject Matter*, locs. 3644, 3654.

5   Ben Ehrenreich, *Desert Notebooks: A Road Map for the End of Time* (Berkeley, CA: Counterpoint, 2020), 76.

6   Tamara Pico, "The Darker Side of John Wesley Powell," *Scientific American*, September 9, 2019, https://blogs.scientificamerican.com/voices/the-darker -side-of-john-wesley-powell/.

7   Cf. Dennis Zotigh, "Native Perspectives on the 40th Anniversary of the American Indian Religious Freedom Act," *Smithsonian Magazine*, November 30, 2018.

8   Nick Estes, *Our History Is the Future: Standing Rock versus the Dakota Access Pipeline, and the Long Tradition of Indigenous Resistance* (New York: Verso, 2019), 18.

9   For a detailed treatment of Lovelock's vitalism, see Taylor, *Dark Green Religion*, 35–41.

10   Cf. José Gualinga and Bethany Pitts, "The Border of Life: A Response to the Pandemic from the Amazon," *Resilience*, May 18, 2020, https://www .resilience.org/stories/2020-05-18/the-border-of-life-a-response-to-the -pandemic-from-the-amazon/.

11   The Greek word is πελώρη, *pelore*, "monstrous." I am grateful to Jonathan Hall of the University of Chicago for his help with this.

12   These words, and all the following quotations, are from William Blake Tyrell's translation of the *Theogony*.

13   Bartolomé Leonardo de Argensola, *The Discovery and Conquest of the Molucca and Philippine Islands &c.*, trans. John Stevens (London, 1708).

14   Hans Derks, *History of the Opium Problem: The Assault on the East, ca. 1600–1950* (Leiden: Brill, 2012), 248.

15   Under Dutch rule there was a huge increase in the use of opium in Maluku. "By the mid nineteenth century opium smoking had become a major social problem . . . and trade in opium in the Moluccas had become very important. In 1851 the value of the opium trade in Ternate exceeded that of all other categories of goods . . . it was also widespread on Gorom, as well as on Banda." Roy Ellen, *On the Edge of the Banda Zone: Past and Present in the Social Organization of a Moluccan Trading Network* (Honolulu: University of Hawaii Press, 2003), 115.

16   See, for instance, Jacques M. Downs and Frederic D. Grant Jr., *The Golden Ghetto: The American Commercial Community at Canton and the Shaping of American China Policy, 1784–1844* (Hong Kong: Hong Kong University Press, 2014).

17   The words are those of Andy Coop, a professor of pharmaceutical sciences; quoted in Sam Quinones, *Dreamland: The True Tale of America's Opiate Epidemic* (New York: Bloomsbury, 2015), 39.

18   Robin Wall Kimmerer, *Braiding Sweetgrass: Indigenous Wisdom, Scientific Knowledge, and the Teaching of Plants* (Minneapolis, MN: Milkweed Editions, 2013), 208.

19   Harold J. Cook, *Matters of Exchange: Commerce, Medicine, and Science in the Dutch Golden Age* (New Haven, CT: Yale University Press, 2007), 413. The word "scientist" was not invented until 1834; see Banu Subramaniam, *Ghost Stories for Darwin: The Science of Variation and the Politics of Diversity* (Urbana: University of Illinois Press, 2014), 19.

20   Antonio Lafuente and Nuria Valverde, "Linnaean Botany and Spanish Imperial Biopolitics," in *Colonial Botany: Science, Commerce, and Politics in the Early Modern World*, ed. Londa Schiebinger and Claudia Swan (Philadelphia: University of Pennsylvania Press, 2007), 134.

21   Cf. Pieter Baas and Jan Frits Veldkamp, "Dutch Pre-Colonial Botany and Rumphius's Ambonese Herbal," *Allertonia* 13 (January 2014): 9–19.

22   Cook, *Matters of Exchange*, 329–32.

23   Anthony Reid, *A History of Southeast Asia: Critical Crossroads* (Malden, MA: Blackwell, 2015), 129. See also Cook, *Matters of Exchange*, 176, 202–4.

24   Baas and Veldkamp, "Dutch Pre-Colonial Botany and Rumphius's Ambonese Herbal," 12.

25   Baas and Veldkamp, 13.

26   Cf. E. M. Beekman, ed. and trans., *The Poison Tree: Selected Writings of Rumphius on the Natural History of the Indies* (Amherst: University of Massachusetts Press, 1981), 8.

27   Baas and Veldkamp, "Dutch Pre-Colonial Botany and Rumphius's Ambonese Herbal," 12.

28   Cf. Bradley C. Bennett, "Thoughts on Rumphius and His Plants: Parallels with Neotropical Ethnobotany," *Allertonia* 13 (January 2014): 72–80.

29   Beekman, *The Poison Tree*, 16.

30   Cf. Lafuente and Valverde, "Linnaean Botany and Spanish Imperial Biopolitics."

31   Lafuente and Valverde, 135.

32   Cf. Cook, *Matters of Exchange*, 412. See also Rupa Marya and Raj Patel, *Inflamed: Deep Medicine and the Anatomy of Injustice* (New York: Farrar, Straus and Giroux, 2021), 136.

33   Ellen, *On the Edge of the Banda Zone*, 64.

34   Cf. E. C. Spary, "Of Nutmegs and Botanists: The Colonial Cultivation of Botanical Identity," in *Colonial Botany: Science, Commerce, and Politics in the Early Modern World*, ed. Londa Schiebinger and Claudia Swan (Philadelphia: University of Pennsylvania Press, 2007), 187–203.

35   Cf. Dorit Brixius, "A Hard Nut to Crack: Nutmeg Cultivation and the Application of Natural History between the Maluku Islands and Isle de France (1750s–1780s)," *British Journal for the History of Science* 51, Special Issue 4 (Science and Islands in Indo-Pacific Worlds) (December 2018): 585–606.

36   Ashis Nandy, *Alternative Sciences: Creativity and Authenticity in Two Indian Scientists* (New Delhi: Oxford University Press, 1995), 99.

37   Kimmerer, *Braiding Sweetgrass*, 43.

38   Kimmerer, 345.

39   Kimmerer, 6. The quote in the following paragraph is from p. 9 of the same source.

40   Thomas J. Zumbroich, "From Mouth Fresheners to Erotic Perfumes: The Evolving Socio-Cultural Significance of Nutmeg, Mace and Cloves in South Asia," *eJournal of Indian Medicine* 5 (2012): 39.

CHAPTER EIGHT

1   Cf. Naomi Oreskes and Eric Conway, *Merchants of Doubt: The Denial of Global Warming* (New York: Bloomsbury, 2010).

2   Cf. Nathaniel Rich, *Losing Earth: A Recent History* (New York: Farrar, Straus and Giroux, 2019).

3   Cf. Naomi Klein, *This Changes Everything: Capitalism vs. the Climate* (New York: Knopf, 2014), 64–95.

4   Andreas Malm, *Fossil Capital: The Rise of Steam Power and the Roots of Global Warming* (London: Verso, 2016), 66.

5   Cf. Timothy Mitchell, *Carbon Democracy: Political Power in the Age of Oil* (London: Verso, 2011).

6   Malm, *Fossil Capital*, 12.

7   Malm,, 55.

8   The words are from Louis C. Hunter's *A History of Industrial Power in the United States, 1780–1930*, vol. 1, quoted by Malm, *Fossil Capital*, 64.

9   Hunter, quoted by Malm, 63.

10 Malm, 63.

CHAPTER NINE

1   Andreas Malm, *Fossil Capital: The Rise of Steam Power and the Roots of Global Warming* (London: Verso, 2016), 543.

2   Malm, 539.

3   W. G. Jensen, "The Importance of Energy in the First and Second World Wars," *Historical Journal* 11, no. 3 (1968): 552. See also Eric Dean Wilson, *After Cooling: On Freon, Global Warming, and the Terrible Cost of Comfort* (New York: Simon and Schuster, 2021), 156.

4   James Bradley, *The China Mirage: The Hidden History of American Disaster in Asia* (New York: Little, Brown, 2015), 208–10.

5   Elizabeth DeLoughrey, "Toward a Critical Ocean Studies for the Anthropocene," *English Language Notes* 57, no. 1 (April 2019): 24.

6   Michael T. Klare, "Garrisoning the Global Gas Station," *TomDispatch*, June 12, 2008, https://www.globalpolicy.org/component/content/article /154-general/25938.html.

7   Cf. William R. Clark, *Petrodollar Warfare: Oil, Iraq and the Future of the Dollar* (Gabriola Island, British Columbia: New Society Publishers, 2005), 28; and David E. Spiro, *The Hidden Hand of American Hegemony: Petrodollar Recycling and International Markets* (Ithaca, NY: Cornell University Press, 1999). The references in the next two paragraphs are also to this book, unless otherwise indicated: 107, 147.

8   Clark, *Petrodollar Warfare*, 28.

9   Daniel Yergin, *The Quest: Energy, Security and the Remaking of the Modern World* (New York: Penguin, 2012), 286.

10 The term is Chalmers Johnson's, quoted in Clark, *Petrodollar Warfare*, 13.

11 For China's "Melaka dilemma," see Sunil S. Amrith, *Crossing the Bay of Bengal: The Furies of Nature and the Fortunes of Migrants* (Cambridge, MA: Harvard University Press, 2015), 255.

12 Timothy Morton, *The Poetics of Spice: Romantic Consumerism and the Exotic* (Cambridge: Cambridge University Press, 2000), 51.

13 Tiny Ternate has no less than fourteen fortifications dotted around its circumference; cf. Muridan Widjojo, *The Revolt of Prince Nuku: Cross-Cultural Alliance-Making in Maluku, c. 1780–1810* (Leiden: Brill, 2009), map 3.

14 Zorawar Daulet Singh, *Powershift: India-China Relations in a Multipolar World* (New Delhi: Macmillan, 2020), 231.

15 Deborah Cowen, *The Deadly Life of Logistics: Mapping Violence in Global Trade* (Minneapolis: University of Minnesota Press, 2014). The figures and quotes in the following paragraphs are all from the digital edition of this book: locs. 1133, 1392, 3069–118, 1337, 2331.

16 See, for instance, Armed Conflict Location & Event Data Project (ACLED), "Global Conflict and Disorder Patterns, 2020," https://acleddata.com/2020/02/14/global-conflict-and-disorder-patterns-2020/.

17 Jean-Pierre Dupuy, *Economy and the Future: A Crisis of Faith*, trans. M. B. DeBevoise (East Lansing: Michigan State University Press, 2014), loc. 213.

18 Déborah Danowski and Eduardo Viveiros de Castro, *The Ends of the World*, trans. Rodrigo Nunes (New York: Polity Press, 2017), loc. 2692.

19 Priya Satia, *Empire of Guns: The Violent Making of the Industrial Revolution* (Stanford, CA: Stanford University Press, 2019), 154.

20 Satia, 2.

21 Satia, 12.

22 Cedric J. Robinson, *Black Marxism: The Making of the Black Radical Tradition* (Chapel Hill: University of North Carolina Press, 1983), 116.

23 Cf. Ruth Wilson Gilmore's foreword to *On Racial Capitalism, Black Internationalism, and Cultures of Resistance*, by Cedric J. Robinson, ed. H. L. T. Quan (London: Pluto Press, 2019).

24 George Masselman, *The Cradle of Colonialism* (New Haven, CT: Yale University Press, 1963), 148.

25 Vincent C. Loth, "Pioneers and Perkeniers: The Banda Islands in the 17th Century," *Cakalele* 6 (1995): 32.

26 However, many people remained in virtual servitude in the Bandas long after the banning of slavery. Cf. Hanna Rambé, *Mirah of Banda*, trans. Toni Pollard (Jakarta: Lontar, 2010).

27 Robinson, *Black Marxism*, 68, 308.

28 "All else, it seems, is derivative. (On this score the preoccupation of Western radicalism with capitalism as a system has served the same purpose . . .)." Robinson, 68.

29 The words are usually attributed to the literary critic Fredric Jameson.

CHAPTER TEN

1 Cf. Andrew K. Jorgenson, Brett Clark, and Jennifer E. Givens, "The Environmental Impacts of Militarization in Comparative Perspective: An Overlooked Relationship," *Nature and Culture* 7, no. 3 (2012): 314–37.

2 W. G. Jensen, "The Importance of Energy in the First and Second World Wars," *Historical Journal* 11, no. 3 (1968): 538.

3   Michael T. Klare, *Rising Powers, Shrinking Planet: The New Geopolitics of Energy* (New York: Metropolitan Books, 2008), 11.

4   Andrew K. Jorgenson, Brett Clark, and Jeffrey Kentor, "Militarization and the Environment: A Panel Study of Carbon Dioxide Emissions and the Ecological Footprints of Nations, 1970–2000," *Global Environmental Politics* 10, no. 1 (February 2010): 11.

5   Andrew K. Jorgenson and Brett Clark, "The Temporal Stability and Developmental Differences in the Environmental Impacts of Militarism: The Treadmill of Destruction and Consumption-Based Carbon Emissions," *Sustainability Science* 11 (2016): 507.

6   Joseph Masco, *The Theater of Operations: National Security Affect from the Cold War to the War on Terror* (Durham, NC: Duke University Press, 2014), 28; Brett Clark, Andrew K. Jorgenson, and Jeffrey Kentor, "Militarization and Energy Consumption: A Test of Treadmill of Destruction Theory in Comparative Perspective," *International Journal of Sociology* 40, no. 2 (Summer 2010): 27.

7   V. Smil, "Energy in the Twentieth Century: Resources, Conversions, Costs, Uses, and Consequences," *Annual Review of Energy and the Environment* 25 (2000): 38, quoted in Jorgenson, Clark, and Givens, "Environmental Impacts," 314–37.

8   Jorgenson, Clark, and Kentor, "Militarization and the Environment," 9.

9   Jorgenson and Clark, "The Temporal Stability and Developmental Differences in the Environmental Impacts of Militarism," 507.

10   Sophie Yeo, "Where Climate Cash Is Flowing and Why It's Not Enough," *Nature*, October 19, 2019, https://www.nature.com/articles/d41586-019-02712-3.

11   Stockholm International Peace Research Institute, "Global Military Expenditure Sees Largest Annual Increase in a Decade—Says SIPRI—Reaching $1917 Billion in 2019," April 27, 2020, https://www.sipri.org/media/press-release/2020/global-military-expenditure-sees-largest-annual-increase-decade-says-sipri-reaching-1917-billion.

12   Neta C. Crawford, "United States Budgetary Costs and Obligations of Post-9/11 Wars through FY2020: $6.4 Trillion," Watson Institute, Brown University, November 13, 2019.

13   Kenneth A. Gould, "The Ecological Costs of Militarization," *Peace Review: A Journal of Social Justice* 19 (2007): 331.

14   Jorgenson, Clark, and Kentor, "Militarization and the Environment," 8.

15   See, for instance, Jorgenson and Clark's article "The Temporal Stability and Developmental Differences in the Environmental Impacts of Militarism."

16   "While the economy and military are interlinked," write Jorgenson and Clark, "treadmill of destruction scholars note that the latter has its own independent expansionary dynamics that contribute to distinct environmental problems." Jorgenson and Clark, "The Temporal Stability and Developmental Differences in the Environmental Impacts of Militarism," 506. Two other scholars of this school write: "we are not suggesting that the treadmill of destruction is the dominant treadmill, and we do not believe that the treadmill of destruction is insulated from the treadmill of production. However, we believe that arms races and wartime mobilizations are fundamentally distinct from the treadmill dynamics at work in commercial activities." Gregory Hooks and Chad L. Smith, "Treadmills of Production and

Destruction: Threats to the Environment Posed by Militarism," *Organization & Environment* 18, no. 1 (March 2005): 23.

17   Jairus Grove, *Savage Ecologies: War and Geopolitics at the End of the World* (Durham, NC: Duke University Press, 2019), loc. 200; "1992 World Scientists' Warning to Humanity," July 16, 1992, Union of Concerned Scientists, https://www.ucsusa.org/about/1992-world-scientists.html; "World Scientists' Warning to Humanity: A Second Notice," https://scientistswarning.forestry.oregonstate.edu/sites/sw/files/Warning_article_with_supp_11-13-17.pdf.

18   For a list of such reports and assessments, see Emily Gilbert, "The Militarization of Climate Change," *ACME: An International Journal for Critical Geographies* 11, no. 1 (2012): 2.

19   Joseph Masco, "Bad Weather: The Time of Planetary Crisis," in *Times of Security, Ethnographies of Fear: Protest and the Future*, ed. Martin Holbraad and Morten Axel Pedersen (London: Routledge, 2013), 171–72.

20   Michael T. Klare, *All Hell Breaking Loose: The Pentagon's Perspective on Climate Change* (New York: Henry Holt, 2019), 184. The figures and quotation in the next paragraph are also from this book, 197, 187.

21   Neta C. Crawford, "Pentagon Fuel Use, Climate Change, and the Costs of War," Watson Institute, Brown University, updated and revised November 13, 2019, 27–28.

22   Crawford, 8.

23   George Kennan, document PPS 23, in *Foreign Relations of the United States, 1948*, vol. 1, 509–29, quoted in William R. Clark, *Petrodollar Warfare: Oil, Iraq and the Future of the Dollar* (Gabriola Island, British Columbia: New Society Publishers, 2005), 24.

24   Joseph Masco, "The Crisis in Crisis," *Current Anthropology* 58, supp. 15 (February 2017): 566. See also Simon Dalby, "The Geopolitics of Climate Change," *Political Geography* 37 (2013): 41.

25   Jorgenson, Clark, and Kentor, "Militarization and the Environment," 9.

26   See, for example, Kurt M. Campbell et al., *The Age of Consequences: The Foreign Policy and National Security Implications of Global Climate Change* (Washington, DC: Center for Strategic and International Studies, 2007); CNA Corporation, *National Security and the Threat of Climate Change*, 2007, https://www.cna.org/cna_files/pdf/national%20security%20and%20the%20threat%20of%20climate%20change.pdf; and Department of Defense, *National Security Implications of Climate-Related Risks and a Changing Climate*, 2015, https://archive.defense.gov/pubs/150724-congressional-report-on-national-implications-of-climate-change.pdf.

27   Cf. François Gemenne et al., "Climate and Security: Evidence, Emerging Risks, and a New Agenda," *Climatic Change* 123 (2014): 1–9; and Solomon M. Hsiang and Marshall Burke, "Climate, Conflict, and Social Stability: What Does the Evidence Say?," *Climatic Change* 123 (2014): 39–55.

28   Sanjay Chaturvedi and Timothy Doyle, *Climate Terror: A Critical Geopolitics of Climate Change* (London: Palgrave Macmillan, 2015), 148.

29   See, for example, Kathy E. Ferguson, "The Sublime Object of Militarism," *New Political Science* 31, no. 4 (December 2009).

30   Joseph Masco, "Bad Weather: The Time of Planetary Crisis," in *Times of Security, Ethnographies of Fear: Protest and the Future*, ed. Martin Holbraad and Morten Axel Pedersen (London: Routledge, 2013), 186–87.

CHAPTER ELEVEN

1 Cf. K. Jones et al., "Global Trends in Emerging Infectious Diseases," *Nature* 451 (2008): 990–93, https://doi.org/10.1038/nature06536.

2 "GDP per Capita," Worldometer, https://www.worldometers.info/gdp/gdp -per-capita/.

3 Indi Samarajiva, "COVID Underdogs: Sri Lanka; Like New Zealand Except Better," *Medium*, June 24, 2020, https://medium.com/indica/covid -underdogs-sri-lanka-db6eca164a35.

4 Norimitsu Onishi and Constant Méheut, "Pandemic Shakes France's Faith in a Cornerstone: Strong Central Government," *New York Times*, April 29, 2020, https://www.nytimes.com/2020/04/29/world/europe/coronavirus-france -masks.html. In July 2020 the *New York Times* would publish an article that described in detail how arrogance and hubris had led to the mishandling of the pandemic in Europe and the United States. Its headline was: "Europe Said It Was Pandemic Ready. Pride Was Its Downfall." "Pride," however, is clearly a euphemism: David D. Kirkpatrick, Matt Apuzzo, and Selam Gebrekidan, "Europe Said It Was Pandemic Ready: Pride Was Its Downfall," *New York Times*, July 20, 2020.

5 Anuradha Sengupta, "Tired of Running from the River: Adapting to Climate Change on India's Disappearing Islands," *Yes!*, June 2, 2016, https://www .yesmagazine.org/environment/2016/06/02/tired-of-running-from-the -river-adapting-to-climate-change-on-indias-disappearing-islands/.

6 Cf. Mitra Srijana Das, "Over-Consumption Underlies Cyclone Amphan and Covid-19," *Times of India*, May 22, 2020, https://timesofindia.indiatimes.com /over-consumption-underlies-cyclone-amphan-and-covid-19/articleshow /75880597.cms.

7 Annu Jalais and Amites Mukhopadhyay, "Of Pandemics and Storms in the Sundarbans," in "Intersecting Crises," ed. Calynn Dowler, *American Ethnolo-gist*, October 12, 2020, https://americanethnologist.org/features/pandemic -diaries/introduction-intersecting-crises/of-pandemics-and-storms-in -the-sundarbans.

8 *Foreign Policy* magazine's "Covid Response Index" had Senegal in second place globally. FP Analytics, "Covid-19 Global Response Index," *Foreign Policy*, September 4, 2020.

9 Caleb Okereke and Kelsey Nielsen, "The Problem with Predicting Corona-virus Apocalypse in Africa," *Al Jazeera*, May 7, 2020, https://www.aljazeera .com/indepth/opinion/problem-predicting-coronavirus-apocalypse-africa -200505103847843.html.

10 Cf. Simon Dalby, "Anthropocene Geopolitics: Globalisation, Empire, Envi-ronment and Critique," *Geography Compass* 1, no. 1 (2007): 104, 109.

11 "Racial Data Dashboard," Covid Tracking Project, https://covidtracking.com /race/dashboard.

12 Ibram X. Kendi, "We're Still Living and Dying in the Slaveholders' Republic," *Atlantic*, May 4, 2020.

13 Julian Brave NoiseCat, "How to Survive an Apocalypse and Keep Dreaming," *Nation*, June 2, 2020, https://www.thenation.com/article/society/native -american-postapocalypse/.

14 NoiseCat.

15   Cf. Creede Newton, "Why Has Navajo Nation Been Hit So Hard by the Corona-
      virus?," *Al Jazeera*, May 27, 2020, https://www.aljazeera.com/news/2020/05
      /navajo-nation-hit-hard-coronavirus-200526171504037.html.

16   Adam Serwer, "The Coronavirus Was an Emergency until Trump Found Out
      Who Was Dying," *Atlantic*, May 8, 2020, https://www.theatlantic.com/ideas
      /archive/2020/05/americas-racial-contract-showing/611389/.

17   Serwer.

18   Maggie McGrath, "63% of Americans Don't Have Enough Savings to Cover
      a $500 Emergency," *Forbes*, January 6, 2016, https://www.forbes.com/sites
      /maggiemcgrath/2016/01/06/63-of-americans-dont-have-enough-savings
      -to-cover-a-500-emergency/.

19   Cf. Naomi Klein, *Battle for Paradise: Puerto Rico Takes on the Disaster Capitalists*
      (Chicago: Haymarket, 2018).

20   Stefano Liberti, *Terra Bruciata: Come la crisi ambientale sta cambiando l'Italia e
      la nostra vita* (Rome: Rizzoli, 2020), 166.

21   Steve Horn, "Arizona Reels as Three of the Biggest Wildfires in Its His-
      tory Ravage State," *Guardian*, July 2, 2020, https://amp.theguardian.com
      /environment/2020/jul/02/arizona-wildfires.

22   *Global Health and Security Index*, Center for Health and Security, Bloomberg
      School of Public Health, Johns Hopkins University, 2019, https://www
      .ghsindex.org/wp-content/uploads/2020/04/2019-Global-Health-Security
      -Index.pdf. See also David Elliott, "These Are the Countries Best Prepared for
      Health Emergencies," *World Economic Forum*, February 12, 2020, https://www
      .weforum.org/agenda/2020/02/these-are-the-countries-best-prepared-for
      -health-emergencies/.

23   Joseph Masco, "The Crisis in Crisis," *Current Anthropology* 58, supp. 15 (Febru-
      ary 2017): 565.

CHAPTER TWELVE

1   Joseph Masco, *The Theater of Operations: National Security Affect from the Cold
      War to the War on Terror* (Durham, NC: Duke University Press, 2014), 199.

2   Neta C. Crawford, "Pentagon Fuel Use, Climate Change, and the Costs of
      War," Watson Institute, Brown University, updated and revised, Novem-
      ber 13, 2019, 12.

3   Geoffrey Parker, *Global Crisis: War, Climate Change and Catastrophe in the
      Seventeenth Century* (New Haven, CT: Yale University Press, 2013), chap. 16:
      "Getting It Right: Early Tokugawa Japan." See also Julia Adeney Thomas,
      "Practicing Hope in Anthropocene History," AHR Anthropocene Workshop,
      Position Paper, April 28, 2019.

4   Quoted in Parker, *Global Crisis*, loc. 782.

5   Melissa Nursey-Bray et al., "Old Ways for New Days: Australian Indigenous
      Peoples and Climate Change," *Local Environment* 24, no. 5 (2019): 478.

6   Keith H. Basso, *Wisdom Sits in Places: Landscape and Language among the West-
      ern Apache* (Albuquerque: University of New Mexico Press, 1996), loc. 377.

7   Basso, loc. 395.

8   G. Supran and Naomi Oreskes, personal communication; see also Julie
      Doyle, "Where Has All the Oil Gone? BP Branding and the Discursive Elim-

ination of Climate Change Risk," January 2011, https://www.researchgate
.net/publication/305209345_Where_has_all_the_oil_gone_BP_branding
_and_the_discursive_elimination_of_climate_change_risk.

9   Paul Sabin, "'The Ultimate Environmental Dilemma': Making a Place for
Historians in the Climate Change and Energy Debates," *Environmental History* 15, no. 1 (2010): 78.

10 See, for example, the epilogue to Parker, *Global Crisis*.

11 Cf. Jan Zalasiewicz et al., "A Formal Anthropocene Is Compatible with but
Distinct from Its Diachronous Anthropogenic Counterparts: A Response to
W. F. Ruddiman's 'Three-Flaws in Defining a Formal Anthropocene,'" *Progress
in Physical Geography* (2019): 1–15.

12 UNHCR, "Refugees and Migrants Arrivals to Europe in 2017."

13 Kaushik Basu, "Why Is Bangladesh Booming?" *Project Syndicate*, April 23,
2018, https://www.project-syndicate.org/commentary/bangladesh-sources
-of-economic-growth-by-kaushik-basu-2018-04.

14 Stefano Liberti, *Terra Bruciata: Come la crisi ambientale sta cambiando l'Italia e
la nostra vita* (Rome: Rizzoli, 2020), 75.

15 Sunil S. Amrith, *Crossing the Bay of Bengal: The Furies of Nature and the Fortunes
of Migrants* (Cambridge, MA: Harvard University Press, 2015), 265.

16 Thomas J. Zumbroich, "From Mouth Fresheners to Erotic Perfumes: The
Evolving Socio-Cultural Significance of Nutmeg, Mace and Cloves in South
Asia," *eJournal of Indian Medicine* 5 (2012): 39.

CHAPTER THIRTEEN

1   *Prothom Alo*, "26 Bangladeshis Killed in Libya," May 28, 2020, https://
en.prothomalo.com/bangladesh/bangladesh-in-world-media/26
-bangladeshis-killed-in-libya.

2   Shehab Sumon, "Human Traffickers Kill 26 Bangladeshis in Libya," *Arab
News*, May 30, 2020, https://www.arabnews.com/node/1681906/world.

3   Global Security.org, "Libyan Civil War 2020," https://www.globalsecurity
.org/military/world/war/libya-civil-war-2020.htm.

4   Cf. Emina Osmandzikovic, "How Conflicts Turned the Middle East into an
Organ-Trafficking Hotspot," *Arab News*, July 8, 2020, https://www.arabnews
.com/node/1701871/middle-east.

5   I am following Rob Nixon's usage of the phrase "slow violence." Cf. Nixon,
Slow Violence and the Environmentalism of the Poor (Cambridge, MA: Harvard
University Press, 2013).

6   Alexis de Tocqueville, *Democracy in America and Two Essays on America*, trans.
Gerald E. Bevan (New York: Penguin, 2003), 378.

7   Virginia DeJohn Anderson, *Creatures of Empire: How Domestic Animals Transformed Early America* (New York: Oxford University Press, 2004), 80.

8   David S. Jones, "Virgin Soils Revisited," *William and Mary Quarterly* 60, no. 4
(October 2003): 737.

9   See, for instance, Roxanne Dunbar-Ortiz, "What White Supremacists Know,"
Boston Review, November 20, 2020.

10 See, for instance, Julian Brave NoiseCat, "How to Survive an Apocalypse and

Keep Dreaming," *Nation*, June 2, 2020, https://www.thenation.com/article
/society/native-american-postapocalypse/.

11   Australian Prime Minister Scott Morrison, for instance, has responded to
epic wildfires "by cautioning 'against raising the anxieties of children.' And
when, in November, hundreds of homes were destroyed and four people
killed by bushfires in New South Wales and Queensland, he told the ABC
there was 'no evidence' that Australia's emissions had any role in it and
that 'we're doing our bit' to tackle climate change." James Plested, "How the
Rich Plan to Rule a Burning Planet," *The Bullet*, December 23, 2019, https://
socialistproject.ca/bullet/about/. And the Trump administration promoted
fossil fuels even at climate conferences: Lisa Friedman, "Trump Team to
Promote Fossil Fuels and Nuclear Power at Bonn Climate Talks," *New York
Times*, November 2, 2017, https://www.nytimes.com/2017/11/02/climate
/trump-coal-cop23-bonn.html.

12   Joyce E. Chaplin, *Subject Matter: Technology, the Body, and Science on the Anglo-
American Frontier, 1500–1676* (Cambridge, MA: Harvard University Press,
2001), loc. 118.

13   Chaplin, loc. 96.

14   Chaplin, loc. 103.

15   J. T. Walton, "The Comparative Mortality of the White and Colored Races in
the South," *Charlotte Medical Journal* 10 (1897): 291–94, quoted in Jim Downs,
*Sick from Freedom: African-American Illness and Suffering during the Civil War and
Reconstruction* (New York: Oxford University Press, 2012), 102.

16   The historian Jim Downs writes: "Medical authorities, journalists, and even
researchers who later studied the high rates of mortality during the postwar
period, consistently used arguments about biological differences between
the races as an explanation for the large number of freedpeople's deaths."
Downs, *Sick from Freedom*, 102.

17   Downs, 102.

18   Cf. Dipesh Chakrabarty, "The Politics of Climate Change Is More than the
Politics of Capitalism," *Theory, Culture & Society*, Special Issue: Geosocial Formations and the Anthropocene (2017): d6.

CHAPTER FOURTEEN

1   Cf. Douglas Rushkoff, "Survival of the Richest: The Wealthy Are Plotting
to Leave Us Behind," *Medium*, July 5, 2018, https://onezero.medium.com
/survival-of-the-richest-9ef6cdddocc1.

2   Cf. Benjamin Noys, *Malign Velocities: Accelerationism and Capitalism* (Washington, DC: Zero Books, 2014), 63.

3   "We no longer hear advocated among really civilized men," wrote the US
Board of Indian Commissioners in 1880, "the theory of extermination, a the-
ory that would disgrace the wildest savage." From *Twelfth Annual Report of the
Board of Indian Commissioners* (1880), 7–9, reprinted in Francis Paul Prucha,
ed., *Americanizing the American Indians: Writings by the "Friends of the Indian"*
(Lincoln: University of Nebraska Press, 1978), 193.

4   Roxanne Dunbar-Ortiz, *An Indigenous Peoples' History of the United States* (Boston: Beacon Press, 2014), 9.

5   Cf. "L. Frank Baum's Editorials on the Sioux Nation," https://warwick.ac.uk/fac/arts/english/currentstudents/undergraduate/modules/fulllist/second/en213/term1/l_frank_baum.pdf.

6   Merrill E. Gates, "Addresses at the Mohonk Conferences," from *Proceedings of the Fourteenth Annual Meeting of the Lake Mohonk Conferences of Friends of the Indian*, reprinted in Prucha, *Americanizing the American Indians*, 334.

7   Naomi Klein, *On Fire: The (Burning) Case for a Green New Deal* (New York: Simon and Schuster, 2019), 47.

8   Garrett Hardin, "Living on a Lifeboat: A Reprint from *Bioscience*, October 1974," *Social Contract*, Fall 2001, 36.

9   Hardin, 37.

10 Hardin, 38. Cf. Garrett Hardin, "The Tragedy of the Commons," *Science* 162 (1968): 1243–48.

11 Carolyn Merchant, *The Death of Nature: Women, Ecology and the Scientific Revolution* (San Francisco: Harper and Row, 1983), 47.

12 See, for instance, David Sloan Wilson, "The Tragedy of the Commons: How Elinor Ostrom Solved One of Life's Greatest Dilemmas," *Evonomics*, October 29, 2016, https://evonomics.com/tragedy-of-the-commons-elinor-ostrom/; and Mukul Sharma, *Caste and Nature: Dalits and Indian Environmental Politics* (New Delhi: Oxford University Press, 2018), 204–16. For the evolutionary advantages of cooperation, see Roberto Cazzolla Gatti, "A Conceptual Model of New Hypothesis on the Evolution of Biodiversity," *Biologia* 71, no. 3 (2016).

13 Robert H. Frank, Thomas Gilovich, and Dennis T. Regan, "Does Studying Economics Inhibit Cooperation?," *Journal of Economic Perspectives* 7, no. 2 (Spring 1993): 159–71. I am grateful to an anonymous reader of the manuscript for pointing me to this article.

14 Rutger Bregman, "The Real Lord of the Flies: What Happened When Six Boys Were Shipwrecked for 15 Months," *Guardian*, May 9, 2020, https://www.theguardian.com/books/2020/may/09/the-real-lord-of-the-flies-what-happened-when-six-boys-were-shipwrecked-for-15-months.

15 My book *In an Antique Land* (1992) describes the travels of a twelfth-century Jewish merchant from North Africa who spent nearly two decades in India's Malabar Coast, and even had a family there, before returning to Cairo. See also Sebouh Aslanian, "'The Salt in a Merchant's Letter': The Culture of Julfan Correspondence in the Indian Ocean and the Mediterranean," *Journal of World History* 19, no. 2 (2008): 127–88.

16 I was introduced to the concepts of "circulatory migration" and "circulatory urbanism" through the work of Rahul Srivastava and Matias Echanove. Cf. Srivastava and Echanove, "The Misunderstood Paradigm: Circulatory Urbanism in India," *Uncube*, July 2015, https://www.uncubemagazine.com/blog/15799893; and Echanove and Srivastava, "Circulatory Urbanism," *Broken Nature*, 2019, http://www.brokennature.org/circulatory-urbanism/. But there now exists a substantial literature on the subject. See, for example, Patrick Weil, "Circulatory Migration vs. Sedentary Immigration," Migration Policy Centre, CARIM-South, CARIM

Analytic and Synthetic Notes, 2011/36, https://cadmus.eui.eu/handle /1814/16209, retrieved from Cadmus, European University Institute Research Repository, http://hdl.handle.net/1814/16209; and Klaus F. Zimmermann, "Circular Migration: Why Restricting Labor Mobility Can Be Counterproductive," *IZA World of Labor* (2014), DOI: 10.15185/izawol.1| wol .iza.org.

17 Zimmermann, "Circular Migration."

18 Sven Lindqvist, *"Exterminate All the Brutes": One Man's Odyssey into the Heart of Darkness and the Origins of European Genocide* (New York: New Press, 1992), 8.

CHAPTER FIFTEEN

1 Sven Lindqvist, *Terra Nullius: A Journey through No One's Land* (London: Granta, 2007).

2 Lindqvist, 83.

3 Sven Lindqvist, *"Exterminate All the Brutes": One Man's Odyssey into the Heart of Darkness and the Origins of European Genocide* (New York: New Press, 1992), 26.

4 Lindqvist, 62.

5 Lindqvist, 132.

6 Lindqvist, 140.

7 Thaddeus Mason Harris, "A Discourse Delivered at Plymouth, December 22d 1808, at the ANNIVERSARY COMMEMORATION of the Landing of Our Ancestors at that Place" (Boston, 1808), 25.

8 Cf. the website of the Underhill Society of America (https://underhillsociety .org/cpage.php?pt=15) and the Wikipedia entries of "Underhill Burying Ground" (https://en.wikipedia.org/wiki/Underhill_Burying_Ground) and "John Underhill (Captain)" (https://en.wikipedia.org/wiki/John_Underhill _(captain)). For the adoption, see E. Tuck and K. W. Yang, "Decolonization Is Not a Metaphor," *Decolonization: Indigeneity, Education and Society* 1, no. 1 (2012): 14.

9 Elizabeth A. Fenn, "Biological Warfare in Eighteenth-Century North America: Beyond Jeffery Amherst," *Journal of American History*, March 2000, 1579.

10 Lindqvist, *"Exterminate All the Brutes,"* 9.

11 Cf. Chinua Achebe, "An Image of Africa: Racism in Conrad's Heart of Darkness," in *Hopes and Impediments: Selected Essays* (New York: Doubleday, 1988).

12 Déborah Danowski and Eduardo Viveiros de Castro, *The Ends of the World*, trans. Rodrigo Nunes (New York: Polity Press, 2017), loc. 2692.

13 Danowski and Viveiros de Castro, 9.

14 Immanuel Wallerstein, "The Albatross of Racism," *London Review of Books* 22, no. 10 (May 18, 2000).

15 Julia Adeney Thomas, "The Present Climate of Economics and History," in *Economic Development and Environmental History in the Anthropocene: Perspectives on Asia and Africa*, ed. Gareth Austin (London: Bloomsbury, 2017), 291.

16 Charlotte H. Bruner, "The Meaning of Caliban in Black Literature Today," *Comparative Literature Studies* 13, no. 3 (1976): 242. See also Peter Hulme, *Colonial Encounters: Europe and the Native Caribbean, 1492–1797* (New York: Methuen, 1986), 107.

17   Hulme, *Colonial Encounters*, 19. On the unlikelihood of cannibalism among
     the Carib, see W. Arens, *The Man-Eating Myth: Anthropology and Anthropoph-
     agy* (New York: Oxford University Press, 1979).

18   William Shakespeare, *The Works of William Shakespeare*, ed. William George
     Clark and John Glover, vol. 1 (Cambridge: Macmillan, 1863), 19.

19   Akeel Bilgrami, *Secularism, Identity, and Enchantment* (Cambridge, MA: Har-
     vard University Press, 2014), 152.

20   David E. Stannard, *American Holocaust: The Conquest of the New World* (Oxford:
     Oxford University Press, 1992), 69.

21   Stannard, 69.

22   Stannard, 69–70.

23   Daniel Nass, "Shootings Are a Glaring Exception to the Coronavirus
     Crime Drop," *The Trace*, April 29, 2020, https://www.thetrace.org/2020/04
     /coronavirus-gun-violence-stay-at-home-orders/.

24   Nayanika Mathur, "What I Learned at the 'Rhodes Must Fall' Protest at
     Oxford," *The Wire*, May 11, 2020, https://thewire.in/world/cecil-rhodes
     -oxford-protest-george-floyd.

25   George W. Hartmann, "The 'Black Hole' of Calcutta: Fact or Fiction?," *Journal
     of Social Psychology* 27 (1948): 21.

26   Cf. Partha Chatterjee, *The Black Hole of Empire: History of a Global Practice of
     Power* (Ranikhet: Permanent Black, 2012), 160.

27   Hartmann, "The 'Black Hole' of Calcutta," 17.

28   Chatterjee, *The Black Hole of Empire*, 268.

29   Chatterjee, 335.

30   Priya Satia, *Time's Monster: How History Makes History* (Cambridge, MA: Har-
     vard University Press, 2020), 6.

31   Assumptions about race, for instance, are deeply embedded in the pedagogy
     of economics. Cf. Matthew Watson, "Crusoe, Friday and the Raced Market
     Frame of Orthodox Economics Textbooks," *New Political Economy* 23, no. 5
     (2018): 544–59. See also Banu Subramaniam, *Ghost Stories for Darwin: The
     Science of Variation and the Politics of Diversity* (Urbana: University of Illinois
     Press, 2014), 55. "The scientific 'truth' of eugenic doctrine came to dominate
     economics, shifting economics from assumptions of human homogene-
     ity in the classical period to ideas of foundational differences among and
     within races of people in postclassical economics."

32   Cf. Malavika Gupta and Felix Padel, "Confronting a Pedagogy of Assimi-
     lation: The Evolution of Large-Scale Schools for Tribal Children in India,"
     Journal of the Anthropological Society of Oxford, n.s., 10, no. 1 (2018).

33   For efforts to communicate with whales, see Alexandra Morton, *Listening to
     Whales: What the Orcas Have Taught Us* (New York: Ballantine, 2002), 22–32.
     See also Bron Taylor, *Dark Green Religion: Nature, Spirituality and the Planetary
     Future* (Berkeley: University of California Press, 2010), 23: "Katy Payne, an
     acoustic biologist has scrutinized elephant communication and concluded
     that attentive humans can communicate with elephants. Increasing num-
     bers of scientists are arriving at similar conclusions, finding communicative
     and affective similarities between humans and other animals."

34   Quoted in Taylor, *Dark Green Religion*, 25.

35   Subramaniam, *Ghost Stories*, 38.

36   Robin Wall Kimmerer, *Braiding Sweetgrass: Indigenous Wisdom, Scientific*

Knowledge, and the Teaching of Plants (Minneapolis, MN: Milkweed Editions, 2013), 19.

37 Donna J. Haraway, *Staying with the Trouble: Making Kin in the Chthulucene* (Durham, NC: Duke University Press, 2016), 67.

38 Julia Adeney Thomas, "History and Biology in the Anthropocene: Problems of Scale, Problems of Value," AHR Roundtable, *American Historical Review* (2014): 1594. See also Rupa Marya and Raj Patel, *Inflamed: Deep Medicine and the Anatomy of Injustice* (New York: Farrar, Straus and Giroux, 2021), 114–15.

39 Quoted in Ana Tsing, *The Mushroom at the End of the World: On the Possibility of Life in Capitalist Ruins* (Princeton, NJ: Princeton University Press, 2015), 141.

40 Haraway, *Staying with the Trouble*, 66.

41 Dalai Lama, XIVth (Bhikshu Tenzin Gyatso), *The Sheltering Tree of Interdependence: A Buddhist Monk's Reflections on Ecological Responsibility*, transcreated in English by Amit Jayaram, 1993.

42 William Cronon, "A Place for Stories: Nature, History, and Narrative," *Journal of American History* 78, no. 4 (1992): 1367.

43 Cf. Morton, *Listening to Whales*, 308.

44 Thom van Dooren and Deborah Bird Rose, "Storied-Places in a Multispecies City," *Humanimalia* 3, no. 2 (2012): 3.

45 Eileen Crist, *Images of Animals: Anthropomorphism and Animal Mind* (Philadelphia: Temple University Press, 1999), 203–4.

46 Haraway, *Staying with the Trouble*, 39.

47 Thom van Dooren, *Flightways: Life and Loss at the Edge of Extinction* (New York: Columbia University Press, 2014), 78. See also van Dooren and Rose, "Storied-Places in a Multispecies City."

48 Leslie Marmon Silko, *The Turquoise Ledge* (New York: Viking, 2010), 43. See also Leslie Marmon Silko, "Landscape, History, and the Pueblo Imagination," in *The Ecocriticism Reader: Landmarks in Literary Ecology*, ed. Cheryll Glotfelty and Harold Fromm (Athens: University of Georgia Press, 1996), 268.

CHAPTER SIXTEEN

1 This account of Kopenawa's early life is based on Davi Kopenawa and Bruce Albert, *The Falling Sky: Words of a Yanomami Shaman*, trans. Nicholas Elliott and Alison Dundy (Cambridge, MA: Belknap Press, 2013), 2–4.

2 Kopenawa and Albert, 152.

3 Cf. Jean-Pierre Leroy, "Markets or the Commons? The Role of Indigenous Peoples, Traditional Communities and Sectors of the Peasantry in the Environmental Crisis," in *Brazil in the Anthropocene: Conflicts between Predatory Development and Environmental Politics*, ed. Liz-Rejane Issberner and Philippe Léna (New York: Routledge, 2017), 105.

4 Cf. José Augusto Padua, "Brazil in the History of the Anthropocene," in *Brazil in the Anthropocene: Conflicts between Predatory Development and Environmental Politics*, ed. Liz-Rejane Issberner and Philippe Léna (New York: Routledge, 2017), 37; and Pablo Correa, "Brazil Drives Increase in Worldwide Forest Loss," *SciDevNet*, June 12, 2020, https://www.scidev.net/global/news/brazil -drives-increase-in-worldwide-forest-loss/.

5   Casper Hallmann et al., "More than 75 Percent Decline over 27 Years in Total Flying Insect Biomass in Protected Areas," *PLOS One*, October 18, 2017, https://doi.org/10.1371/journal.pone.0185809.

6   Kopenawa and Albert, *The Falling Sky*, 370–71.

7   Quoted in Bron Taylor, *Dark Green Religion: Nature, Spirituality and the Planetary Future* (Berkeley: University of California Press, 2010), 25.

8   David Abram, *The Spell of the Sensuous: Perception and Language in a More-than-Human World* (New York: Vintage, 1997). The following quotes are from the e-book edition, locs. 2026, 1921, 1941, 2107.

9   Jesse Goldstein, "Terra Economica: Waste and the Production of Enclosed Nature," *Antipode* 45, no. 2 (2013): 3. See also Silvia Federici, "The Great Witch Hunt," *Maine Scholar* 1 (1988): 31.

10 For a detailed treatment of this, see Bithika Mukerji, *Neo-Vedanta and Modernity* (Varanasi: Ashutosh Prakashan Sansthan, 1983).

11 Kopenawa and Albert, *The Falling Sky*, 352.

12 "Democracy Now," December 4, 2019, https://www.youtube.com/watch?v=uoqkzNPzYag.

13 Fiona Watson, "Bolsonaro's Election Is Catastrophic News for Brazil's Indigenous Tribes," *Guardian*, October 31, 2018.

14 Survival International, "Brazil's Indians," https://www.survivalinternational.org/tribes/brazilian.

15 Cf. Philippe Léna and Liz-Rejane Issberner, "Anthropocene in Brazil: An Inquiry into Development Obsession and Policy Limits," in *Brazil in the Anthropocene*, ed. Issberner and Léna, 8.

16 Ernesto Londoño and Letícia Casado, "As Bolsonaro Keeps Amazon Vows, Brazil's Indigenous Fear 'Ethnocide,'" *New York Times*, April 19, 2020.

17 Shanna Hanbury, "'The Tipping Point Is Here, It Is Now,' Top Amazon Scientists Warn," *Mongabay*, December 20, 2019, https://news.mongabay.com/2019/12/the-tipping-point-is-here-it-is-now-top-amazon-scientists-warn/.

18 Cf. Issberner and Léna, eds., *Brazil in the Anthropocene*.

19 Elian Brum, "Hay indicios significativos para que autoridades brasileñas, incluido Bolsonaro, sean investigadas por genocidio," *El Pais*, July 25, 2020, https://elpais.com/internacional/2020-07-25/hay-indicios-significativos-para-que-autoridades-brasilenas-incluido-bolsonaro-sean-investigadas-por-genocidio.html.

20 The phrase "genocide by default" probably originated with an award-winning Yale epidemiologist, Gregg Gonsalves, who had tweeted on May 6, 2020: "This is getting awfully close to genocide by default. What else do you call mass death by public policy?" Cf. Lee Moran, "Epidemiologist Slams U.S. Coronavirus Response: 'Close to Genocide by Default,'" *Huffpost*, May 6, 2020, https://www.huffpost.com/entry/epidemiologist-coronavirus-genocide-by-default_n_5eb2a5ebc5b63e6bd96f5d81.

21 Open Democracy, "As the Pandemic Continues to Accelerate, So Does the Deforestation of the Amazon," June 1, 2020, https://www.opendemocracy.net/en/democraciaabierta/se-acelera-la-pandemia-y-se-acelera-la-deforestacion-del-amazonas-en/.

22 Open Democracy.

23 Open Democracy, "The Survival of the Amazon Is at Stake," July 24, 2020,

https://www.opendemocracy.net/en/democraciaabierta/survival-amazon
-stake/.

24 Hanbury, "'The Tipping Point Is Here, It Is Now.'"

25 Hanbury.

26 Thomas E. Lovejoy and Carlos Nobre, "Amazon Tipping Point: Last Chance for Action," *Science Advances* 5, no. 12 (December 20, 2019).

CHAPTER SEVENTEEN

1 Vincent C. Loth, "Pioneers and Perkeniers: The Banda Islands in the 17th Century," *Cakalele* 6 (1995): 30.

2 "The nutmeg estates of the Banda Islands . . . provide a rare unequivocal example of a slave mode of production in Southeast Asia, and its sole instance in an agricultural context." Phillip Winn, "Slavery and Cultural Creativity in the Banda Islands," *Journal of Southeast Asian Studies* 41, no. 3 (2020): 365.

3 Harold J. Cook, *Matters of Exchange: Commerce, Medicine, and Science in the Dutch Golden Age* (New Haven, CT: Yale University Press, 2007), 187.

4 Loth, "Pioneers and Perkeniers," 24.

5 Winn, "Slavery and Cultural Creativity in the Banda Islands," 371.

6 Loth, "Pioneers and Perkeniers," 24.

7 Winn, "Slavery and Cultural Creativity in the Banda Islands," 385; and Alison Games, *Inventing the English Massacre: Amboyna in History and Memory* (New York: Oxford University Press, 2020), 56.

8 Winn, "Slavery and Cultural Creativity in the Banda Islands," 371.

9 Phillip Winn, "'Banda Is the Blessed Land': Sacred Practice and Identity in the Banda Islands, Maluku," *Antropologi Indonesia* 57 (1998): 73. See also Winn, "Slavery and Cultural Creativity in the Banda Islands," 20.

10 Phillip Winn, "'Everyone Searches, Everyone Finds': Moral Discourse and Resource Use in an Indonesian Muslim Community," *Oceania* 72 (2002): 278. See also Phillip Winn Graves, "Graves, Groves and Gardens: Place and Identity—Central Maluku, Indonesia," *Asia-Pacific Journal of Anthropology* 2, no. 1 (2001): 28.

11 Winn, "'Everyone Searches, Everyone Finds,'" 278.

12 Winn, "Slavery and Cultural Creativity in the Banda Islands," 383.

13 Cf. Philip Winn, "Tanah Berkat (Blessed Land): The Source of the Local in the Banda Islands, Central Maluku," in *Sharing the Earth, Dividing the land: Land and Territory in the Austronesian World*, ed. Thomas Reuter (Canberra: ANU Press, 2006), 125.

14 Winn, "'Everyone Searches, Everyone Finds,'" 278.

15 Quoted in Joyce E. Chaplin, *Subject Matter: Technology, the Body, and Science on the Anglo-American Frontier, 1500–1676* (Cambridge, MA: Harvard University Press, 2001), loc. 1944.

16 Winn writes: "While it could be argued that it is the current population [of the Bandas] who wholly animate place through their contemporary conceptualizing and reading of their environment, it would be a serious distortion of local perspectives to represent agency as residing entirely with human individuals in this way. Place itself is also conceived as exerting agency, both

through shaping daily lived practices . . . and particularly in local understand-ings of the islands as a sacred territory (*tanah berkat*) inhabited by active autochthonous spirit figures." Winn, "Graves, Groves and Gardens," 26.

17 Julie Berger Hochstrasser, "The Bones in Banda: Vision, Art, and Memory in Maluku," *Midwestern Arcadia: Essays in Honor of Alison Kettering* (2015): 157, DOI:10.18277/makf.2015.14.

18 Winn, "Slavery and Cultural Creativity in the Banda Islands," 383n114.

19 For more on these interactions between humans and contemporary com-munications technologies, see N. Katherine Hayles, "Cognitive Assemblages: Technical Agency and Human Interactions," *Critical Inquiry* 43 (Autumn 2016): 32–55. I am grateful to Debjani Ganguly for bringing this article to my attention.

20 Janet Biehl and Peter Staudenmaier, *Ecofascism Revisited: Lessons from the German Experience* (Porsgrunn, Norway: New Compass Press, 1995). The quo-tations and references in the next five paragraphs are also to this book: 7, 11, 12, 12–13, 14–15, 16, 21–22.

21 Cf. Alex Fox, "Sierra Club Grapples with Founder John Muir's Racism," *Smith-sonian Magazine*, July 24, 2020, https://www.smithsonianmag.com/smart-news/sierra-club-grapples-founder-john-muirs-racism-180975404/. See also Rupa Marya and Raj Patel, *Inflamed: Deep Medicine and the Anatomy of Injustice* (New York: Farrar, Straus and Giroux, 2021), 176.

22 Nils Gilman, "The Coming Avocado Politics: What Happens When the Ethno-Nationalist Right Gets Serious about the Climate Emergency?," *Break-through Institute*, February 7, 2020, https://thebreakthrough.org/journal/no-12-winter-2020/avocado-politics.

23 Michael Brune, "Pulling Down Our Monuments," *Sierra*, July 22, 2020, https://www.sierraclub.org/michael-brune/2020/07/john-muir-early-history-sierra-club. See also: Hop Hopkins, "Racism Is Killing the Planet," *Sierra*, June 8, 2020, https://www.sierraclub.org/sierra/racism-killing-planet.

24 For a detailed treatment of this subject, see Raymond Bonner, *At the Hand of Man: Peril and Hope for Africa's Wildlife* (New York: Vintage, 1993). Rama-chandra Guha has also addressed these issues in many of his writings—for example, "Radical American Environmentalism and Wilderness Preser-vation: A Third World Critique," *Environmental Ethics* 11, no.1 (1989): 71–83; and "Toward a Cross-Cultural Environmental Ethic," *Alternatives* 15 (1990): 431–47.

25 Ramachandra Guha and J. Martinez-Alier, eds., *Varieties of Environmentalism: Essays North and South* (London: Earthscan, 1997), xvi.

26 Survival International, "WWF's Secret War," October 7, 2020, https://www.sixdegreesnews.org/archives/29331/leaked-report-us-halts-funding-to-wwf-wcs-and-other-conservation-ngos-over-abuses.

27 See, for example, Alex Amend, "Blood and Vanishing Topsoil: American Eco-fascism Past, Present, and in the Coming Climate Crisis," *Political Research Associates*, July 9, 2020, http://politicalresearch.org/2020/07/09/blood-and-vanishing-topsoil; Kate Aronoff, "The European Far Right's Environmen-tal Turn," *Dissent*, May 31, 2019, https://www.dissentmagazine.org/online_articles/the-european-far-rights-environmental-turn; and Eric Levitz,

"Far-Right Climate Denial Is Scary: Far-Right Climate Acceptance Might Be Scarier," *New York Magazine*, March 6, 2019, https://nymag.com/intelligencer/2019/03/climate-science-invites-liberal-solutions-or-fascist-ones.html.

28 Stephen Corry, "It's Time to Clean Ecofascism Out of Environmentalism," *Counterpunch*, April 2, 2020, https://www.counterpunch.org/2020/04/02/its-time-to-clean-ecofascism-out-of-environmentalism/. See also Marya and Patel, *Inflamed*, 169.

29 Naomi Klein, "Only a Green New Deal Can Douse the Fires of Eco-Fascism," *The Intercept*, September 16, 2019.

30 Nancy Stepan, quoted in Banu Subramaniam, *Ghost Stories for Darwin: The Science of Variation and the Politics of Diversity* (Urbana: University of Illinois Press, 2014), 4.

31 Max Liboiron writes: "Even within dominant science, there are many anti-colonial sciences: queer science, abolitionist science, Zapatista science, feminist science, anarchist science, slow science, anticapitalist and communitarian science, sciences from below, among others." Liboiron, *Pollution Is Colonialism* (Durham, NC: Duke University Press, 2021), 130–31.

32 There is now a vast literature on the many ways in which European empires buttressed and were buttressed by science. See, for example, Rohan Deb Roy, *Malarial Subjects: Empire, Medicine and Nonhumans in British India, 1820–1909* (Cambridge: Cambridge University Press, 2017); and Subramaniam, *Ghost Stories*, 18. See also Marya and Patel, *Inflamed*, 241.

33 Cf. Simon Dalby, "Anthropocene Geopolitics: Globalisation, Empire, Environment and Critique," *Geography Compass* 1, no. 1 (2007): 103–18; and N. Clark, "Geo-Politics and the Disaster of the Anthropocene," *Sociological Review* 62, no. 1 suppl. (2014): 19–37.

34 Mukul Sharma, *Green and Saffron: Hindu Nationalism and Indian Environmental Politics* (Ranikhet: Permanent Black, 2012), 17.

35 Mukul Sharma, *Caste and Nature: Dalits and Indian Environmental Politics* (New Delhi: Oxford University Press, 2018), 75.

36 Sharma, *Green and Saffron*, 20.

37 For an account of the BJP's environmental moves during the pandemic, see Ashish Kothari, "India Needs a Rainbow Recovery Plan," *The Hindu*, October 6, 2020; Ashish Kothari, "No Atma, Lots of Nirbharta: The Socio-Ecological Bankruptcy of Modi's Self-Reliance Stimulus," *The Wire*, September 28, 2020, https://m.thewire.in/article/government/india-atmanirbhar-economic-package-environment-coal-mining/amp?__twitter_impression=true&s=03; and Akshay Deshmane, "Documents Show How Javadekar and Harsh Vardhan Diluted India's Green Law," *Huffpost*, July 3, 2020, https://www.huffingtonpost.in/entry/environment-news-india-narendra-modi-government_in_5efe08c6c5b6acab284cf0a1.

38 As far back as 1995, Ramachandra Guha observed, citing Gandhi's famous remark uttered in 1928—"God forbid that India should ever take to industrialization in the manner of the West"—that "in the last few decades we have attempted precisely to 'make India like England and America.' Without the access to resources and markets enjoyed by those two nations when they began to industrialize, India has had perforce to rely on the exploitation of

its own people and environment." Guha, "Mahatma Gandhi and the Environmental Movement in India," *Capitalism Nature Socialism* 6, no. 3 (1995): 49.

39 Liboiron, *Pollution Is Colonialism*, 10.

40 For more on Adivasis and boarding schools, see Malavika Gupta and Felix Padel, "Confronting a Pedagogy of Assimilation: The Evolution of Large-Scale Schools for Tribal Children in India," *Journal of the Anthropological Society of Oxford*, n.s., 10, no. 1 (2018), https://www.anthro.ox.ac.uk/files/jaso1012018pdf. For the criminalization of Adivasi lifestyles and diet, see Madhu Ramnath, *Woodsmoke and Leafcups* (New Delhi: HarperCollins, 2015).

41 For an authoritative account of the wars in central India, see Nandini Sundar, *The Burning Forest: India's War in Bastar* (New Delhi: Juggernaut, 2016).

42 There is a vast literature on the Chipko movement. The most complete treatment of the subject is in Ramachandra Guha, *The Unquiet Woods: Ecological Change and Peasant Resistance in the Himalaya* (New Delhi: Oxford University Press, 1989); see also Vandana Shiva and J. Bandyopadhyay, "The Evolution, Structure, and Impact of the Chipko Movement," *Mountain Research and Development* 6, no. 2 (May 1986): 133–42.

43 For a detailed treatment of this movement, see Samarendra Das and Felix Padel, *Out of This Earth: East India Adivasis and the Aluminium Cartel* (Hyderabad: OrientBlackSwan, 2010), esp. chapters 20 and 212.

44 Sharma, *Green and Saffron*, 262.

CHAPTER EIGHTEEN

1 Cf. Ashis Nandy, "From Outside the Imperium: Gandhi's Cultural Critique of the 'West,'" *Alternatives: Global, Local, Political* 7 (1981): 171, http://alt.sagepub.com/content/7/2/171.

2 Nathan Wachtel, *The Vision of the Vanquished: The Spanish Conquest of Peru through Indian Eyes, 1530–1570*, trans. Ben and Siân Reynolds (Sussex: Harvester Press, 1977), 180–82.

3 Wachtel, 186.

4 Cf. Roxanne Dunbar-Ortiz, *An Indigenous Peoples' History of the United States* (Boston: Beacon Press, 2014), 152–54. See also Nick Estes, *Our History Is the Future: Standing Rock versus the Dakota Access Pipeline, and the Long Tradition of Indigenous Resistance* (New York: Verso, 2019), 122–25.

5 Cedric J. Robinson, *Black Marxism: The Making of the Black Radical Tradition* (Chapel Hill: University of North Carolina Press, 1983), 309. The quotations in the following paragraphs are all from this book: 310, 308, 240, 240, 237, 275, 239.

6 In the words of Vine Deloria Jr.: "The phrase 'all my relatives' is frequently invoked by Indians performing ceremonies and this phrase is used to invite all other forms of life to participate as well as to inform them that the ceremony is being done on their behalf." Deloria, *God Is Red: A Native View of Religion* (Golden, CO: North American Press, 1992), 83.

7 Winona LaDuke, *All Our Relations: Native Struggles for Land and Life* (Chicago: Haymarket Books, 1999), 4.

8 Beth Pitts, "Voice of the Living Forest: Interview with Indigenous Resis-

tance Leader José Gualinga," *Extinction Rebellion*, October 8, 2020, https://writersrebel.com/voice-of-the-living-forest-interview-with-indigenous-resistance-leader-jose-gualinga/.

9   Eleanor Ainge Roy, "New Zealand River Granted Same Legal Rights as Human Being," *Guardian*, March 16, 2017, https://www.theguardian.com/world/2017/mar/16/new-zealand-river-granted-same-legal-rights-as-human-being.

10   In the words of Kim Tallbear: "The tied oppressions and fates of Indigenous peoples and our other-than-human relations is a key ethic undergirding both Standing Rock's and Idle No More's actions." TallBear, "Badass Indigenous Women Caretake Relations: #Standingrock, #Idlenomore, #BlackLivesMatter," in *Standing with Standing Rock: Voices from the #noDAPL Movement*, ed. Nick Estes and Jaskiran Dhillon (Minneapolis: University of Minnesota Press, 2019), 30.

11   "The #NoDAPL struggle," write Nick Estes and Jaskiran Dhillon, "is a continuation of the Indian wars of extermination." Estes and Dhillon, eds., *Standing with Standing Rock*, 13.

12   Edward Valandra, "Mni Wiconi; Water Is [More Than] Life," in *Standing with Standing Rock*, ed. Estes and Dhillon, 104.

13   Elizabeth Ellis, "Centering Sovereignty: How Standing Rock Changed the Conversation," in *Standing with Standing Rock*, ed. Estes and Dhillon, 245.

14   Sandy Grande et al., "Red Praxis: Lessons from Mashantucket to Standing Rock," in *Standing with Standing Rock*, ed. Estes and Dhillon, loc. 5892.

15   Nick Estes, "Traditional Leadership and the Oceti Sakowin: An Interview with Lewis Grassrope," in *Standing with Standing Rock*, ed. Estes and Dhillon, 51–52.

16   There is enough evidence of nonhuman "storying" that, as Donna Haraway writes, it "cannot any longer be put into the box of human exceptionalism." Haraway, *Staying with the Trouble: Making Kin in the Chthulucene* (Durham, NC: Duke University Press, 2016), 39.

17   For a critique from an Indigenous perspective, see E. Tuck and K. W. Yang, "Decolonization Is Not a Metaphor," *Decolonization: Indigeneity, Education and Society* 1, no. 1 (2012): 23–35.

18   Asher Moses, "'Collapse of Civilisation Is the Most Likely Outcome': Top Climate Scientists," *Resilience*, June 8, 2020, https://www.resilience.org/stories/2020-06-08/collapse-of-civilisation-is-the-most-likely-outcome-top-climate-scientists/. See also Marlowe Hood, "Scientists Warn Multiple Overlapping Crises Could Trigger 'Global Systemic Collapse,'" *ScienceAlert*, February 5, 2020, https://www.sciencealert.com/hundreds-of-top-scientists-warn-combined-environmental-crises-will-cause-global-collapse.

19   Jean-Pierre Dupuy, *Economy and the Future: A Crisis of Faith*, trans. M. B. DeBevoise (East Lansing: Michigan State University Press), 65. The next quotation is from loc. 333 of the same book.

20   Prasenjit Duara, *The Crisis of Global Modernity: Asian Traditions and a Sustainable Future* (Cambridge: Cambridge University Press, 2015), 287, 280.

21   Bron Taylor, *Dark Green Religion: Nature, Spirituality and the Planetary Future* (Berkeley: University of California Press, 2010), 207, 208.

CHAPTER NINETEEN

1   Barbara S. Harvey, Introduction to *Friends and Exiles: A Memoir of the Nutmeg Isles and the Indonesian Nationalist Movement,* by Des Alwi, ed. Barbara S. Harvey, Southeast Asia Program Publications (Ithaca, NY: Cornell University Press, 2008), 2.

2   Des Alwi, *Friends and Exiles,* 9–10.

3   Alwi, 9–10.

4   Alwi, 128.

5   The lines are taken from Julie Berger Hochstrasser, "The Bones in Banda: Vision, Art, and Memory in Maluku," *Midwestern Arcadia: Essays in Honor of Alison Kettering* (2015), DOI:10.18277/makf.2015.14.

6   Louis Couperus, *The Hidden Force,* trans. Alexander Teixeira De Mattos, ed. E. M. Beekman, Paperback Library of the Indies English (Amherst: University of Massachusetts Press, 1990).

7   Couperus, 187.

8   Couperus, 198.

9   Couperus, 198–200.

10   Maria Dermoût, *The Ten Thousand Things,* trans. Hans Koning (New York: New York Review Books, 2002).

11   Dermoût, 208.

12   The novel's translator, Hans Koning, writes in his introduction that in Felicia's world "everyone and everything in it has a role and a fate, has in a sense a soul of its own." Dermoût, ix.

13   The years between 1570 and 1630 were the peak period of Europe's witch hunts. Cf. Brian P. Levack, *The Witch-Hunt in Early Modern Europe* (New York: Routledge, 2016), 207–9. See also Wolfgang Behringer, "Weather, Hunger and Fear: Origins of the European Witch-Hunts in Climate, Society and Mentality," in *The Witchcraft Reader,* ed. Darrin Oldridge (New York: Routledge, 2019), 71. See also Robin Briggs, "'Many Reasons Why': Witchcraft and the Problem of Multiple Explanation," in *Witchcraft in Early Modern Europe: Studies in Culture and Belief,* ed. Jonathan Barry, Marianne Hester, and Gareth Roberts (Cambridge: Cambridge University Press, 1996), 54.

14   Willem de Blécourt, "The Making of the Female Witch: Reflections on Witchcraft and Gender in the Early Modern Period," *Gender and History* 12, no. 2 (2000): 296. For Dutch tolerance of witchcraft, see Levack, *The Witch-Hunt in Early Modern Europe,* 196.

15   Robin Briggs discusses several "explanations" of witchcraft in her article "'Many Reasons Why': Witchcraft and the Problem of Multiple Explanation." The connections between witch-hunting and climate have been examined by Behringer, "Weather, Hunger and Fear"; the relationship between witch-hunting and state-building is analyzed by Brian P. Levack in "State-Building and Witch Hunting in Early Modern Europe," in *Witchcraft in Early Modern Europe,* ed. Barry, Hester, and Roberts, 96–117. There is an extensive literature on witchcraft and patriarchy. See, for example, Christina Larner, *Enemies of God: The Witch Hunt in Scotland* (Baltimore, MD: Johns Hopkins University Press, 1981).

16   Behringer, "Weather, Hunger and Fear," 82. See also Jonathan Barry, "Intro-

duction," in *Witchcraft in Early Modern Europe*, ed. Barry, Hester, and Roberts, 15.

17 Levack, *The Witch-Hunt in Early Modern Europe*, 28–29.

18 Lyndal Roper observes: "all phenomena in the early modern world, natural and fantastic, had a kind of hyper-reality which resided in their significance. Circumstantial details were ransacked for their meaning for the individual, and for what they might reveal about causation and destiny." Roper, "Witchcraft and Fantasy in Early Modern Germany," in *Witchcraft in Early Modern Europe*, ed. Barry, Hester, and Roberts, 211.

19 For notions of diabolical conspiracy in relation to witchcraft, see Levack, *The Witch-Hunt in Early Modern Europe*, 67, 224; and Gary K. Waite, "'Man Is a Devil to Himself': David Joris and the Rise of a Sceptical Tradition towards the Devil in the Early Modern Netherlands, 1540–1600," *Dutch Review of Church History* 75, no. 1 (1995): 2.

20 Brian Levack argues that "it is valid to claim that torture in a certain sense 'created' witchcraft." Levack, *The Witch-Hunt in Early Modern Europe*, 15. See also Blécourt, "The Making of the Female Witch," 301; for the personal participation of King James VI of Scotland (later James I of England) in the torture of witches, see Carolyn Merchant, "The Scientific Revolution and *The Death of Nature*," *Isis* 97 (2006): 522–23.

21 Blécourt, "The Making of the Female Witch," 298, 300. See also Wolfgang Behringer, "Witchcraft Studies in Austria, Germany and Switzerland," in *Witchcraft in Early Modern Europe*, ed. Barry, Hester, and Roberts, 94.

22 "In all major witchcraft persecutions involving action by entire communities, weather magic played at least a catalytic role." Behringer, "Witchcraft Studies in Austria, Germany and Switzerland," 92.

23 Behringer, "Weather, Hunger and Fear," 71.

24 For the use of torture in witch-hunting, see Roper, "Witchcraft and Fantasy in Early Modern Germany," 213–18.

25 Merchant, *The Death of Nature*, 168. Merchant further elaborated on these issues in her 2006 article "The Scientific Revolution and *The Death of Nature*."

26 Merchant, *The Death of Nature*, 168.

27 For the nuances of the word "vexation" in this context, see Merchant, "The Scientific Revolution and *The Death of Nature*," 528–29.

28 Merchant, *The Death of Nature*, 189.

29 For an account of European vitalism, see Merchant, 99–148.

30 Elizabeth Ellis, "Centering Sovereignty: How Standing Rock Changed the Conversation," in *Standing with Standing Rock: Voices from the #noDAPL Movement*, ed. Nick Estes and Jaskiran Dhillon (Minneapolis: University of Minnesota Press, 2019), loc. 4290.

31 Cf. Francis Jennings, *The Invasion of America; Indians, Colonialism and the Cant of Conquest* (New York: Norton, 1975), 33; Jill Lepore, *The Name of War: King Philip's War and the Origins of American Identity* (New York: Vintage, 1998), 85–86; and Bron Taylor, *Dark Green Religion: Nature, Spirituality and the Planetary Future* (Berkeley: University of California Press, 2010), 43.

Bibliography

Abram, David. *The Spell of the Sensuous: Perception and Language in a More-than-Human World*. New York: Vintage, 1997.

Achebe, Chinua. "An Image of Africa: Racism in Conrad's Heart of Darkness." In *Hopes and Impediments: Selected Essays*. New York: Doubleday, 1988.

Akveld, Leo, and Els M. Jacobs, eds. *The Colourful World of the VOC: National Anniversary Book, VOC 1602–2002*. Bussum, Neth.: THOTH Publishers, 2002.

Albert, Bruce. "Covid-19: Lessons from the Yanomami." *New York Times*, April 27, 2020.

Alwi, Des. *Friends and Exiles: A Memoir of the Nutmeg Isles and the Indonesian Nationalist Movement*. Edited by Barbara S. Harvey. Southeast Asia Program Publications. Ithaca, NY: Cornell University Press, 2008.

Amal, Nukila. *The Original Dream*. Translated by Linda Owens. Seattle: AmazonCrossing, 2017.

Amend, Alex. "Blood and Vanishing Topsoil: American Ecofascism Past, Present, and in the Coming Climate Crisis." *Political Research Associates*, July 9, 2020. http://politicalresearch.org/2020/07/09/blood-and-vanishing-topsoil.

Amrith, Sunil S. *Crossing the Bay of Bengal: The Furies of Nature and the Fortunes of Migrants*. Cambridge, MA: Harvard University Press, 2015.

Andaya, Leonard Y. "Centers and Peripheries in Maluku." *Cakalele* 4 (1993): 1–21.

Andaya, Leonard Y. "Local Trade Networks in Maluku in the 16th, 17th, and 18th Centuries." *Cakalele* 2, no. 2 (1991): 71–96.

Andaya, Leonard Y. *The World of Maluku: Eastern Indonesia in the Early Modern Period.* Honolulu: University of Hawaii Press, 1993.

Anderson, Virginia DeJohn. *Creatures of Empire: How Domestic Animals Transformed Early America.* New York: Oxford University Press, 2004.

Arens, W. *The Man-Eating Myth: Anthropology and Anthropophagy.* New York: Oxford University Press, 1979.

Argensola, Bartolomé Leonardo de. *The Discovery and Conquest of the Molucca and Philippine Islands &c.* Translated by John Stevens. London, 1708.

Armed Conflict Location & Event Data Project (ACLED). "Global Conflict and Disorder Patterns, 2020." https://acleddata.com/2020/02/14 /global-conflict-and-disorder-patterns-2020/.

Aronoff, Kate. "The European Far Right's Environmental Turn." *Dissent,* May 31, 2019. https://www.dissentmagazine.org/online_articles/the -european-far-rights-environmental-turn.

Aslanian, Sebouh. "'The Salt in a Merchant's Letter': The Culture of Julfan Correspondence in the Indian Ocean and the Mediterranean." *Journal of World History* 19, no. 2 (2008): 127–88.

Aveling, H. G. "Seventeenth Century Bandanese Society in Fact and Fiction: 'Tambera' Assessed." *Bijdragen tet de Taal-, Land- en Volkenkunde* 123, no. 3 (1967): 347–65.

Baas, Pieter, and Jan Frits Veldkamp. "Dutch Pre-Colonial Botany and Rumphius's Ambonese Herbal." *Allertonia* 13 (January 2014): 9–19.

Bacon, Francis. *An Advertisement Touching an Holy War.* https://sites.duke .edu/conversions/files/2014/09/Manion_Bacon-on-Holy-War.pdf.

Barras, Colin. "Is an Aboriginal Tale of an Ancient Volcano the Oldest Story Ever Told?" *Science,* February 11, 2020. https://www.sciencemag.org /news/2020/02/aboriginal-tale-ancient-volcano-oldest-story-ever-told.

Barry, Jonathan. "Introduction." In *Witchcraft in Early Modern Europe: Studies in Culture and Belief,* edited by Jonathan Barry, Marianne Hester, and Gareth Roberts. Cambridge: Cambridge University Press, 1996.

Barry, Jonathan, Marianne Hester, and Gareth Roberts, eds. *Witchcraft in Early Modern Europe: Studies in Culture and Belief.* Cambridge: Cambridge University Press, 1996.

Basso, Keith H. *Wisdom Sits in Places: Landscape and Language among the Western Apache*. Albuquerque: University of New Mexico Press, 1996.

Basu, Kaushik. "Why Is Bangladesh Booming?" *Project Syndicate*, April 23, 2018. https://www.project-syndicate.org/commentary/bangladesh-sources-of-economic-growth-by-kaushik-basu-2018-04?barrier=accesspaylog.

Basu, Miharika. "Arctic Circle May Have Recorded Its Highest-Ever Temperature as Siberian Town Hits 100.4°F." Meaww.com. https://meaww.com/arctic-circle-highest-temperature-100-degree-siberian-town-verkhoyansk-may-hottest-month.

BBC News Report. "Amazon Fires Increase by 84% in One Year." October 21, 2019. https://www.bbc.com/news/world-latin-america-49415973.

Beekman, E. M., ed. and trans. *The Poison Tree: Selected Writings of Rumphius on the Natural History of the Indies*. Amherst: University of Massachusetts Press, 1981.

Behringer, Wolfgang. "Witchcraft Studies in Austria, Germany and Switzerland." In *Witchcraft in Early Modern Europe: Studies in Culture and Belief*, edited by Jonathan Barry, Marianne Hester, and Gareth Roberts, 64–95. Cambridge: Cambridge University Press, 1996.

Behringer, Wolfgang. "Weather, Hunger and Fear: Origins of the European Witch-Hunts in Climate, Society and Mentality." In *The Witchcraft Reader*, edited by Darrin Oldridge. New York: Routledge, 2019.

Bennett, Bradley C. "Thoughts on Rumphius and His Plants: Parallels with Neotropical Ethnobotany." *Allertonia* 13 (January 2014): 72–80.

Bennett, Jane. *Vibrant Matter: A Political Ecology of Things*. Durham, NC: Duke University Press, 2010.

Benzoni, Girolamo. *History of the New World; Shewing His Travels in America from A.D. 1541 to 1556, with Some Particulars of the Island of Canary*. Translated by W. H. Smyth. London: Hakluyt Society, 1857.

Bickmore, Albert S. *Travels in the East Indian Archipelago*. London: John Murray, 1868.

Biehl, Janet, and Peter Staudenmaier. *Ecofascism Revisited: Lessons from the German Experience*. Porsgrunn, Norway: New Compass Press, 1995.

Bilgrami, Akeel. *Secularism, Identity, and Enchantment*. Cambridge, MA: Harvard University Press, 2014.

Blécourt, Willem de. "The Making of the Female Witch: Reflections on

Witchcraft and Gender in the Early Modern Period." *Gender and History* 12, no. 2 (2000): 287–309.

Bonner, Raymond. *At the Hand of Man: Peril and Hope for Africa's Wildlife.* New York: Vintage, 1993.

Boxer, C. R. *The Dutch Seaborne Empire, 1600–1800.* London: Penguin, 1990.

Bradley, James. *The China Mirage: The Hidden History of American Disaster in Asia.* New York: Little, Brown, 2015.

Bregman, Rutger. "The Real Lord of the Flies: What Happened When Six Boys Were Shipwrecked for 15 Months." *Guardian*, May 9, 2020. https://www.theguardian.com/books/2020/may/09/the-real-lord-of-the-flies-what-happened-when-six-boys-were-shipwrecked-for-15-months.

Briggs, Robin. "'Many Reasons Why': Witchcraft and the Problem of Multiple Explanation." In *Witchcraft in Early Modern Europe: Studies in Culture and Belief*, edited by Jonathan Barry, Marianne Hester, and Gareth Roberts, 49–63. Cambridge: Cambridge University Press, 1996.

Brixius, Dorit. "A Hard Nut to Crack: Nutmeg Cultivation and the Application of Natural History between the Maluku islands and Isle de France (1750s–1780s)." *British Journal for the History of Science* 51, Special Issue 4 (Science and Islands in Indo-Pacific Worlds) (December 2018): 585–606. doi:10.1017/S0007087418000754.

Brugge, Doug, Timothy Benally, and Esther Yazzie-Lewis, eds. *The Navajo People and Uranium Mining.* Albuquerque: University of New Mexico Press, 2006.

Brum, Elian. "Hay indicios significativos para que autoridades brasileñas, incluido Bolsonaro, sean investigadas por genocidio." *El País*, July 25, 2020. https://elpais.com/internacional/2020-07-25/hay-indicios-significativos-para-que-autoridades-brasilenas-incluido-bolsonaro-sean-investigadas-por-genocidio.html.

Brune, Michael. "Pulling Down Our Monuments." *Sierra*, July 22, 2020. https://www.sierraclub.org/michael-brune/2020/07/john-muir-early-history-sierra-club.

Bruner, Charlotte H. "The Meaning of Caliban in Black Literature Today." *Comparative Literature Studies* 13, no. 3 (1976): 240–53.

Bubandt, Nils. "Haunted Geologies: Spirits, Stones and the Necropolitics of the Anthropocene." In *Arts of Living on a Damaged Planet*, edited by Ana Tsing et al. Minneapolis: University of Minnesota Press, 2017.

Builth, Heather. "Mt. Eccles Lava Flow and the Gunditjmara Connection:

A Landform for All Seasons." *Proceedings of the Royal Society of Victoria*, November 2004, 165–84.

Builth, Heather, Peter Kershaw, Chris White, Anna Roach, Lee Hartney, Merna McKenzie, Tara Lewis, and Geraldine Jacobsen. "Environmental and Cultural Change on the Mt. Eccles Lava-Flow Landscapes of Southwest Victoria, Australia." *Holocene* 18, no. 3 (2008): 413–24.

Campbell, Kurt M., Jay Gulledge, J. R. McNeill, John Podesta, Peter Ogden, Leon Fuerth, R. James Woolsey, Alexander T. J. Lennon, Julianne Smith, Richard Weitz, and Derek Mix. *The Age of Consequences: The Foreign Policy and National Security Implications of Global Climate Change*. Washington, DC: Center for Strategic and International Studies, 2007.

Cederlöf, Gunnel, and K. Sivaramakrishnan, eds. *Ecological Nationalisms: Nature, Livelihoods, and Identities in South Asia*. Ranikhet: Permanent Black, 2006.

Chakrabarty, Dipesh. "Climate and Capital: On Conjoined Histories." *Critical Inquiry* 41, no. 1 (2014): 1–23.

Chakrabarty, Dipesh. "The Politics of Climate Change Is More than the Politics of Capitalism." *Theory, Culture & Society*, Special Issue: Geosocial Formations and the Anthropocene (2017).

Chaplin, Joyce E. *Subject Matter: Technology, the Body, and Science on the Anglo-American Frontier, 1500–1676*. Cambridge, MA: Harvard University Press, 2001.

Chatterjee, Partha. *The Black Hole of Empire: History of a Global Practice of Power*. Ranikhet: Permanent Black, 2012.

Chaturvedi, Sanjay, and Timothy Doyle. *Climate Terror: A Critical Geopolitics of Climate Change*. London: Palgrave Macmillan, 2015.

Chuter, Andrew. "UK to Boost Defense Budget by $21.9 Billion." *DefenseNews*, November 11, 2020. https://www.defensenews.com/global/europe/2020/11/19/uk-to-boost-defense-budget-by-219-billion-heres-who-benefits-and-loses-out/.

Clark, Brett, Andrew K. Jorgenson, and Jeffrey Kentor. "Militarization and Energy Consumption: A Test of Treadmill of Destruction Theory in Comparative Perspective." *International Journal of Sociology* 40, no. 2 (Summer 2010): 23–43.

Clark, Christopher M. "This Is a Reality, Not a Threat." *New York Review of Books*, November 22, 2018.

Clark, N. "Geo-Politics and the Disaster of the Anthropocene." *Sociological Review* 62, no. 1 suppl. (2014): 19–37. doi:10.1111/1467-954X.12122.

Clark, William R. *Petrodollar Warfare: Oil, Iraq and the Future of the Dollar.* Gabriola Island, British Columbia: New Society Publishers, 2005.

Clement, Charles R., et al. "The Domestication of Amazonia before European Conquest." *Proceedings of the Royal Society B: Biological Sciences* 282, no. 1812 (August 7, 2015). https://www.ncbi.nlm.nih.gov/pmc/articles/PMC4528512/.

Clulow, Adam. "The Art of Claiming: Possession and Resistance in Early Modern Asia." *American Historical Review* 121, no. 1 (February 2016): 17–38. https://doi.org/10.1093/ahr/121.1.17.

CNA Corporation. *National Security and the Threat of Climate Change.* 2007. https://www.cna.org/cna_files/pdf/national%20security%20and%20the%20threat%20of%20climate%20change.pdf.

Cook, Harold J. *Matters of Exchange: Commerce, Medicine, and Science in the Dutch Golden Age.* New Haven, CT: Yale University Press, 2007.

Correa, Pablo. "Brazil Drives Increase in Worldwide Forest Loss." *SciDevNet*, June 12, 2020. https://www.scidev.net/global/news/brazil-drives-increase-in-worldwide-forest-loss/.

Corry, Stephen. "It's Time to Clean Ecofascism Out of Environmentalism." *Counterpunch*, April 2, 2020. https://www.counterpunch.org/2020/04/02/its-time-to-clean-ecofascism-out-of-environmentalism/.

Couperus, Louis. *The Hidden Force.* Edited by E. M. Beekman. Translated by Alexander Teixeira De Mattos. Paperback Library of the Indies English. Amherst: University of Massachusetts Press, 1990.

Cowen, Deborah. *The Deadly Life of Logistics: Mapping Violence in Global Trade.* Minneapolis: University of Minnesota Press, 2014.

Crawford, Neta C. "Pentagon Fuel Use, Climate Change, and the Costs of War." Watson Institute, Brown University, updated and revised, November 13, 2019.

Crawford, Neta C., "United States Budgetary Costs and Obligations of Post-9/11 Wars through FY2020: $6.4 Trillion." Watson Institute, Brown University, November 13, 2019.

Crist, Eileen. *Images of Animals: Anthropomorphism and Animal Mind.* Philadelphia: Temple University Press, 1999.

Cronon, William. *Changes in the Land: Indians, Colonists and the Ecology of New England.* New York: Hill and Wang, 1983.

Cronon, William. "A Place for Stories: Nature, History, and Narrative." *Journal of American History* 78, no. 4 (1992): 1347–76.

Crosby, Alfred. *Ecological Imperialism: The Biological Expansion of Europe, 900–1900*. Cambridge: Cambridge University Press, 1986; e-book edition, 2015.

Cruz, Juan Moreno, and M. Scott Taylor. "A Spatial Approach to Energy Economics." Working Paper 18908, National Bureau of Economic Research, March 2013. http://www.nber.org/papers/w18908.

Dalai Lama, XIVth (Bhikshu Tenzin Gyatso). *The Sheltering Tree of Interdependence: A Buddhist Monk's Reflections on Ecological Responsibility*. Transcreated in English by Amit Jayaram. New York: Tibet House, 1993.

Dalby, Simon. "Anthropocene Geopolitics: Globalisation, Empire, Environment and Critique." *Geography Compass* 1, no. 1 (2007): 103–18.

Dalby, Simon. "The Geopolitics of Climate Change." *Political Geography* 37 (2013): 38–47.

Danowski, Déborah, and Eduardo Viveiros de Castro. *The Ends of the World*. Translated by Rodrigo Nunes. New York: Polity Press, 2017.

Darwin, Charles. *The Descent of Man and Selection in Relation to Sex*. New York, 1871.

Das, Mitra Srijana. "Over-Consumption Underlies Cyclone Amphan and Covid-19." *Times of India*, May 22, 2020. https://timesofindia .indiatimes.com/over-consumption-underlies-cyclone-amphan-and -covid-19/articleshow/75880597.cms.

Das, Samarendra, and Felix Padel. *Out of This Earth: East India Adivasis and the Aluminium Cartel*. Hyderabad: OrientBlackSwan, 2010.

Deb Roy, Rohan. *Malarial Subjects: Empire, Medicine and Nonhumans in British India, 1820–1909*. Cambridge: Cambridge University Press, 2017.

Degroot, Dagomar. "Did Colonialism Cause Global Cooling? Revisiting an Old Controversy." *Historical Climatology*, February 22, 2019. https:// www.historicalclimatology.com/features/did-colonialism-cause -global-cooling-revisiting-an-old-controversy.

Deloria, Vine, Jr. *God Is Red: A Native View of Religion*. Golden, CO: North American Press, 1992.

DeLoughrey, Elizabeth. "Toward a Critical Ocean Studies for the Anthropocene." *English Language Notes* 57, no. 1 (April 2019).

Denetdale, Jennifer Nez. *Reclaiming Diné History: The Legacies of Navajo Chief Manuelito and Juanita*. Tucson: University of Arizona Press, 2007.

Department of Defense. *National Security Implications of Climate-Related*

Risks and a Changing Climate. 2015. https://archive.defense.gov/pubs /150724-congressional-report-on-national-implications-of-climate -change.pdf.

Derks, Hans. *History of the Opium Problem: The Assault on the East, ca. 1600– 1950.* Leiden: Brill, 2012.

Dermoût, Maria. *The Ten Thousand Things.* Translated by Hans Koning. New York: New York Review Books, 2002.

Deshmane, Akshay. "Documents Show How Javadekar and Harsh Vard-han Diluted India's Green Law." *Huffpost,* July 3, 2020. https://www .huffingtonpost.in/entry/environment-news-india-narendra-modi -government_in_5efe08c6c5b6acab284cf0a1.

Diniz Alves, José Eustáquio, and George Martine. "Population, Devel-opment and Environmental degradation in Brazil." In *Brazil in the Anthropocene: Conflicts between Predatory Development and Environmental Politics,* edited by Liz-Rejane Issberner and Philippe Léna. New York: Routledge, 2017.

Downs, Jacques M., and Frederic D. Grant, Jr. *The Golden Ghetto: The American Commercial Community at Canton and the Shaping of American China Policy, 1784–1844.* Hong Kong: Hong Kong University Press, 2014.

Downs, Jim. *Sick from Freedom: African-American Illness and Suffering during the Civil War and Reconstruction.* New York: Oxford University Press, 2012.

Doyle, Julie. "Where Has All the Oil Gone? BP Branding and the Discur-sive Elimination of Climate Change Risk." January 2011. https://www .researchgate.net/publication/305209345_Where_has_all_the_oil _gone_BP_branding_and_the_discursive_elimination_of_climate _change_risk.

Drinnon, Richard. *Facing West: The Metaphysics of Indian-Hating and Empire-Building.* Minneapolis: University of Minnesota Press, 1980.

Dryden, John. *Amboyna: The State of Innocence.* In *The Works of John Dryden,* Vol. 5, edited by Walter Scott; EBook #16208, 2005.

Duara, Prasenjit. *The Crisis of Global Modernity: Asian Traditions and a Sustainable Future.* Cambridge: Cambridge University Press, 2015.

Dunbar-Ortiz, Roxanne. *An Indigenous Peoples' History of the United States.* Boston: Beacon Press, 2014.

Dunbar-Ortiz, Roxanne. "What White Supremacists Know." *Boston Review,* November 20, 2020.

Dupuy, Jeans-Pierre. *The Mark of the Sacred*. Translated by M. B. DeBevoise. Stanford, CA: Stanford University Press, 2013.

Dupuy, Jean-Pierre. *Economy and the Future: A Crisis of Faith*. Translated by M. B. DeBevoise. East Lansing: Michigan State University Press, 2014.

Echanove, Matias, and Rahul Srivastava. "Circulatory Urbanism." *Broken Nature*, 2019. http://www.brokennature.org/circulatory-urbanism/.

Ehrenreich, Ben. *Desert Notebooks: A Road Map for the End of Time*. Berkeley, CA: Counterpoint, 2020.

Ellen, Roy. *On the Edge of the Banda Zone: Past and Present in the Social Organization of a Moluccan Trading Network*. Honolulu: University of Hawaii Press, 2003.

Elliott, David. "These Are the Countries Best Prepared for Health Emergencies." *World Economic Forum*, February 12, 2020. https://www.weforum.org/agenda/2020/02/these-are-the-countries-best-prepared-for-health-emergencies/.

Ellis, Elizabeth. "Centering Sovereignty: How Standing Rock Changed the Conversation." In *Standing with Standing Rock: Voices from the #noDAPL Movement*, edited by Nick Estes and Jaskiran Dhillon. Minneapolis: University of Minnesota Press, 2019.

Estes, Nick. *Our History Is the Future: Standing Rock versus the Dakota Access Pipeline, and the Long Tradition of Indigenous Resistance*. New York: Verso, 2019.

Estes, Nick. "'They Took Our Footprint Out of the Ground': An Interview with Ladonna Bravebull Allard." In *Standing with Standing Rock: Voices from the #noDAPL Movement*, edited by Nick Estes and Jaskiran Dhillon. Minneapolis: University of Minnesota Press, 2019.

Estes, Nick. "Traditional Leadership and the Oceti Sakowin: An Interview with Lewis Grassrope." In *Standing with Standing Rock: Voices from the #noDAPL Movement*, edited by Nick Estes and Jaskiran Dhillon. Minneapolis: University of Minnesota Press, 2019.

Estes, Nick, and Jaskiran Dhillon, eds. *Standing with Standing Rock: Voices from the #noDAPL Movement*. Minneapolis: University of Minnesota Press, 2019.

Federici, Silvia. *Caliban and the Witch: Women, the Body and Primitive Accumulation*. 2nd ed. Brooklyn: Automedia, 2014.

Federici, Silvia. "The Great Witch Hunt." *Maine Scholar* 1 (1988): 31–52.

Fearnside, Philip. "How a Dam Building Boom Is Transforming the

Brazilian Amazon." *Yale Environment 360*, September 26, 2017. https://
e360.yale.edu/features/how-a-dam-building-boom-is-transforming
-the-brazilian-amazon.

Fenn, Elizabeth A. "Biological Warfare in Eighteenth-Century North
America: Beyond Jeffery Amherst." *Journal of American History*, March
2000, 1552–80.

Ferguson, Kathy E. "The Sublime Object of Militarism." *New Political
Science* 31, no. 4 (December 2009).

Figueiredo, Patrícia. "Number of Deaths of Indigenous Leaders in 2019
Is the Highest in at Least 11 Years, Says Pastoral da Terra." Globo
.com, October 12, 2019. https://g1.globo.com/natureza/noticia/2019
/12/10/mortes-de-liderancas-indigenas-batem-recorde-em-2019-diz
-pastoral-da-terra.ghtml.

Fox, Alex. "Sierra Club Grapples with Founder John Muir's Racism."
Smithsonian Magazine, July 24, 2020. https://www.smithsonianmag
.com/smart-news/sierra-club-grapples-founder-john-muirs-racism
-180975404/.

Fox, Justin. "Why the Missouri River Is Just Going to Keep on Flooding:
Viewpoint." *Insurance Journal*, April 30, 2019.

FP Analytics. "Covid-19 Global Response Index." *Foreign Policy*, September 4, 2020.

Frank, Robert H., Thomas Gilovich, and Dennis T. Regan. "Does Studying
Economics Inhibit Cooperation?" *Journal of Economic Perspectives* 7, no.
2 (Spring 1993): 159–71.

Friedman, Lisa. "Trump Team to Promote Fossil Fuels and Nuclear Power
at Bonn Climate Talks." *New York Times*, November 2, 2017. https://www
.nytimes.com/2017/11/02/climate/trump-coal-cop23-bonn.html?_r=0.

Games, Alison. *Inventing the English Massacre: Amboyna in History and
Memory*. New York: Oxford University Press, 2020.

Garcia, Claude A., and J.-P. Pascal. "Sacred Forests of Kodagu: Ecological
Value and Social Role." In *Ecological Nationalisms: Nature, Livelihoods,
and Identities in South Asia*, edited by Gunnel Cederlöf and K. Sivaramakrishnan, 199–229. Ranikhet: Permanent Black, 2006.

Gatti, Roberto Cazzolla. "A Conceptual Model of New Hypothesis on the
Evolution of Biodiversity." *Biologia* 71, no. 3 (2016). DOI: 10.1515/biolog-
2016-0032.

Gemenne, François, Jon Barnett, W. Neil Adger, and Geoffrey D. Dabelko.

"Climate and Security: Evidence, Emerging Risks, and a New Agenda."
Climatic Change 123 (2014): 1–9.

Gilbert, Emily. "The Militarization of Climate Change." *ACME: An International Journal for Critical Geographies* 11, no. 1 (2012): 1–14.

Gilio-Whitaker, Dina. *As Long as Grass Grows: The Indigenous Fight for Environmental Justice, from Colonization to Standing Rock.* Boston: Beacon Press, 2019.

Gilman, Nils. "The Coming Avocado Politics: What Happens When the Ethno-Nationalist Right Gets Serious about the Climate Emergency?" *Breakthrough Institute*, February 7, 2020. https://thebreakthrough.org /journal/no-12-winter-2020/avocado-politics.

Gilmore, Ruth Wilson. Foreword to *On Racial Capitalism, Black Internationalism, and Cultures of Resistance*, by Cedric J. Robinson, edited by H. L. T. Quan. London: Pluto Press, 2019.

Global Health and Security Index. Center for Health and Security, Bloomberg School of Public Health, Johns Hopkins University, 2019. https://www.ghsindex.org/wp-content/uploads/2020/04/2019 -Global-Health-Security-Index.pdf.

Global Security.org. "Libyan Civil War 2020." https://www.globalsecurity .org/military/world/war/libya-civil-war-2020.htm.

Glotfelty, Cheryll, and Harold Fromm, eds. *The Ecocriticism Reader: Landmarks in Literary Ecology.* Athens: University of Georgia Press, 1996.

Goldstein, Jesse. "Terra Economica: Waste and the Production of Enclosed Nature." *Antipode* 45, no. 2 (2013): 357–75.

Goss, Jon. "Understanding the 'Maluku Wars': Overview of Sources of Communal Conflict and Prospects for Peace." *Cakalele* 11 (2000): 7–39.

Gould, Kenneth A. "The Ecological Costs of Militarization." *Peace Review: A Journal of Social Justice* 19 (2007): 331–34.

Grande, Sandy, et al. "Red Praxis: Lessons from Mashantucket to Standing Rock." In *Standing with Standing Rock: Voices from the #noDAPL Movement*, edited by Nick Estes and Jaskiran Dhillon. Minneapolis: University of Minnesota Press, 2019.

Grandin, Greg. *The End of the Myth: From the Frontier to the Border Wall in the Mind of America.* New York: Metropolitan, 2019.

Grandjean, Katherine A. "The Long Wake of the Pequot War." *Early American Studies* 9, no. 2 (Spring 2011): 379–411.

Grenier, John. *The First Way of War: American War Making on the Frontier, 1607–1814.* New York: Cambridge University Press, 2005.

Grove, Jairus. *Savage Ecologies: War and Geopolitics at the End of the World.* Durham, NC: Duke University Press, 2019.

Grove, Richard. *Ecology, Climate and Empire: Colonialism and Global Environmental History, 1400–1940.* Cambridge: White Horse Press, 1997.

Gualinga, José, and Bethany Pitts. "The Border of Life: A Response to the Pandemic from the Amazon." *Resilience,* May 18, 2020. https://www.resilience.org/stories/2020-05-18/the-border-of-life-a-response-to-the-pandemic-from-the-amazon/.

Guha, Ramachandra. "Mahatma Gandhi and the Environmental Movement in India." *Capitalism Nature Socialism* 6, no. 3 (1995): 47–61. DOI: 10.1080/10455759509358641.

Guha, Ramachandra. "Radical American Environmentalism and Wilderness Preservation: A Third World Critique." *Environmental Ethics* 11, no. 1 (1989): 71–83.

Guha, Ramachandra. "Toward a Cross-Cultural Environmental Ethic." *Alternatives* 25 (1990): 431–47.

Guha, Ramachandra. *The Unquiet Woods: Ecological Change and Peasant Resistance in the Himalaya.* New Delhi: Oxford University Press, 1989.

Guha, Ramachandra, and J. Martinez-Alier, eds. *Varieties of Environmentalism: Essays North and South.* London: Earthscan, 1997.

Gupta, Malavika, and Felix Padel. "Confronting a Pedagogy of Assimilation: The Evolution of Large-Scale Schools for Tribal Children in India." *Journal of the Anthropological Society of Oxford,* n.s., 10, no. 1 (2018). https://www.anthro.ox.ac.uk/files/jaso1012018pdf.

Hallmann, Caspar A., et al. "More than 75 Percent Decline over 27 Years in Total Flying Insect Biomass in Protected Areas." *PLOS One,* October 18, 2017. https://doi.org/10.1371/journal.pone.0185809.

Hamacher, Duane W., and Ray P. Norris. "Australian Aboriginal Geomythology: Eyewitness Accounts of Cosmic Impacts?" Paper submitted to *Archaeoastronomy: The Journal of Astronomy in Culture,* September 22, 2010. https://arxiv.org/abs/1009.4251.

Hanbury, Shanna. "'The Tipping Point Is Here, It Is Now,' Top Amazon Scientists Warn." *Mongabay,* December 20, 2019. https://news.mongabay.com/2019/12/the-tipping-point-is-here-it-is-now-top-amazon-scientists-warn/.

Hanna, Willard A. *Indonesian Banda: Colonialism and Its Aftermath in the Nutmeg Islands.* Reprint, Banda Naira: Yayasan Warisan da Budaya, 1991.

Haraway, Donna J. *Staying with the Trouble: Making Kin in the Chthulucene.* Durham, NC: Duke University Press, 2016.

Hardin, Garrett. "Living on a Lifeboat: A Reprint from *Bioscience*, October 1974." *Social Contract*, Fall 2001, 36–47.

Hardin, Garrett. "The Tragedy of the Commons." *Science* 162 (1968): 1243–48.

Harris, Thaddeus Mason. "A Discourse Delivered at Plymouth, December 22d 1808, at the ANNIVERSARY COMMEMORATION of the Landing of Our Ancestors at that Place." Boston, 1808.

"The Hartford Treaty, 1638, Signifying the Close of the Pequot War." http://pequotwar.org/wp-content/uploads/2014/11/Grade-8-Treaty-of -Hartford-Guiding-Questions-Avery.pdf.

Hartmann, George W. "The 'Black Hole' of Calcutta: Fact or Fiction?" *Journal of Social Psychology* 27 (1948): 17–35.

Hayles, N. Katherine. "Cognitive Assemblages: Technical Agency and Human Interactions." *Critical Inquiry* 43 (Autumn 2016): 32–55.

Hochstrasser, Julie Berger. "The Bones in Banda: Vision, Art, and Memory in Maluku." *Midwestern Arcadia: Essays in Honor of Alison Kettering.* 2015. DOI:10.18277/makf.2015.14.

Hochstrasser, Julie Berger. "The Conquest of Spice and the Dutch Colonial Imaginary: Seen and Unseen in the Visual Culture of Trade." In *Colonial Botany: Science, Commerce, and Politics in the Early Modern World,* edited by Londa Schiebinger and Claudia Swan, 169–86. Philadelphia: University of Pennsylvania Press, 2007.

Hood, Marlowe. "Scientists Warn Multiple Overlapping Crises Could Trigger 'Global Systemic Collapse.'" *ScienceAlert*, February 5, 2020. https://www.sciencealert.com/hundreds-of-top-scientists-warn -combined-environmental-crises-will-cause-global-collapse.

Hooks, Gregory, and Chad L. Smith. "The Treadmill of Destruction: National Sacrifice Areas and Native Americans." *American Sociological Review* 69 (2004): 558–75.

Hooks, Gregory, and Chad L. Smith. "Treadmills of Production and Destruction: Threats to the Environment Posed by Militarism." *Organization & Environment* 18, no. 1 (March 2005): 19–37.

Hopkins, Hop. "Racism Is Killing the Planet." *Sierra*, June 8, 2020. https://

www.sierraclub.org/sierra/racism-killing-planet?amp&__twitter
_impression=true.

Horn, Steve. "Arizona Reels as Three of the Biggest Wildfires in Its
History Ravage State." *Guardian*, July 2, 2020. https://amp.theguardian
.com/environment/2020/jul/02/arizona-wildfires?__twitter
_impression=true.

Horne, Gerald. *The Apocalypse of Settler Colonialism: The Roots of Slavery,
White Supremacy, and Capitalism in Seventeenth-Century North America
and the Caribbean*. New York: Monthly Review Press, 2017.

Hsiang, Solomon M., and Marshall Burke. "Climate, Conflict, and Social
Stability: What Does the Evidence Say?" *Climatic Change* 123 (2014):
39–55.

Hulme, Peter. *Colonial Encounters: Europe and the Native Caribbean, 1492–
1797*. New York: Methuen, 1986.

Issberner, Liz-Rejane, and Philippe Léna, eds. *Brazil in the Anthropocene:
Conflicts between Predatory Development and Environmental Politics*. New
York: Routledge, 2017.

Jalais, Annu, and Amites Mukhopadhyay. "Of Pandemics and Storms
in the Sundarbans." In "Intersecting Crises," edited by Calynn
Dowler. Special issue, *American Ethnologist*, October 12, 2020. https://
americanethnologist.org/features/pandemic-diaries/introduction
-intersecting-crises/of-pandemics-and-storms-in-the-sundarbans.

Jennings, Francis. *The Invasion of America: Indians, Colonialism and the Cant
of Conquest*. New York: Norton, 1975.

Jensen, W. G. "The Importance of Energy in the First and Second World
Wars." *Historical Journal* 11, no. 3 (1968): 538–54.

Jones, David S. "Virgin Soils Revisited." *William and Mary Quarterly* 60, no.
4 (October 2003): 703–42.

Jones, K., N. Patel, M. Levy et al. "Global Trends in Emerging Infectious
Diseases." *Nature* 451 (2008): 990–93. https://doi.org/10.1038/nature
06536.

Jorgenson, Andrew K., and Brett Clark. "The Temporal Stability and
Developmental Differences in the Environmental Impacts of Milita-
rism: The Treadmill of Destruction and Consumption-Based Carbon
Emissions." *Sustainability Science* 11 (2016): 505–14.

Jorgenson, Andrew K., Brett Clark, and Jennifer E. Givens. "The Environmental Impacts of Militarization in Comparative Perspective: An Overlooked Relationship." *Nature and Culture* 7, no. 3 (2012): 314–37.

Jorgenson, Andrew K., Brett Clark, and Jeffrey Kentor. "Militarization and the Environment: A Panel Study of Carbon Dioxide Emissions and the Ecological Footprints of Nations, 1970–2000." *Global Environmental Politics* 10, no. 1 (February 2010): 7–29.

Kaartinen, Timo. *Songs of Travel and Stories of Place: Poetics of Absence in an Eastern Indonesian Society*. Helsinki: Academia Scientiarum Fennica, 2010.

Kelton, Paul. *Epidemics and Enslavement: Biological Catastrophe in the Native Southeast, 1492–1715*. Lincoln: University of Nebraska Press, 2007.

Kendi, Ibram X. "We're Still Living and Dying in the Slaveholders' Republic." *Atlantic*, May 4, 2020.

Kiers, Lucas. *Coen Op Banda: Del Conqueste Getoest aan het Recht van den Tijd*. Utrecht: Oosthoek, 1943.

Kimmerer, Robin Wall. *Braiding Sweetgrass: Indigenous Wisdom, Scientific Knowledge, and the Teaching of Plants*. Minneapolis: Milkweed Editions, 2013.

Kirkpatrick, David D., Matt Apuzzo, and Selam Gebrekidan. "Europe Said It Was Pandemic Ready: Pride Was Its Downfall." *New York Times*, July 20, 2020.

Klare, Michael T. *All Hell Breaking Loose: The Pentagon's Perspective on Climate Change* (New York: Henry Holt, 2019).

Klare, Michael T. "Garrisoning the Global Gas Station." *TomDispatch*, June 12, 2008. https://www.globalpolicy.org/component/content/article/154-general/25938.html.

Klare, Michael T. *Rising Powers, Shrinking Planet: The New Geopolitics of Energy*. New York: Metropolitan Books, 2008.

Klein, Naomi. *Battle for Paradise: Puerto Rico Takes on the Disaster Capitalists*. Chicago: Haymarket Books, 2018.

Klein, Naomi. *On Fire: The (Burning) Case for a Green New Deal*. New York: Simon and Schuster, 2019.

Klein, Naomi. "Only a Green New Deal Can Douse the Fires of Eco-Fascism." *The Intercept*, September 16, 2019.

Klein, Naomi. *This Changes Everything: Capitalism vs. the Climate*. New York: Knopf, 2014.

Knaap, Gerrit J. "Crisis and Failure: War and Revolt in the Ambon Islands, 1636–1637." *Cakalele* 3 (1992): 1–26.

Kopenawa, Davi, and Bruce Albert. *The Falling Sky: Words of a Yanomami Shaman*. Translated by Nicholas Elliott and Alison Dundy. Cambridge, MA: Belknap Press, 2013.

Kothari, Ashish. "India Needs a Rainbow Recovery Plan." *The Hindu*, October 6, 2020.

Kothari, Ashish. "No Atma, Lots of Nirbharta: The Socio-Ecological Bankruptcy of Modi's Self-Reliance Stimulus." *The Wire*, September 28, 2020. https://m.thewire.in/article/government/india-atmanirbhar -economic-package-environment-coal-mining/amp?__twitter _impression=true&s=03.

Kripal, Jeffrey J. *Authors of the Impossible: The Paranormal and the Sacred*. Chicago: University of Chicago Press, 2010.

Krondl, Michael. *The Taste of Conquest: The Rise and Fall of the Three Great Cities of Spice*. New York: Ballantine, 2008.

LaDuke, Winona. *All Our Relations: Native Struggles for Land and Life*. Chicago: Haymarket Books, 1999.

Lafuente, Antonio, and Nuria Valverde. "Linnaean Botany and Spanish Imperial Biopolitics." In *Colonial Botany: Science, Commerce, and Politics in the Early Modern World*, edited by Londa Schiebinger and Claudia Swan. Philadelphia: University of Pennsylvania Press, 2007.

Lape, Peter V. "Political Dynamics and Religious Change in the Late Pre-Colonial Banda Islands, Eastern Indonesia." *World Archaeology* 32, no. 1 (2000): 138–55.

Laqueur, Thomas Walter. *Solitary Sex: A Cultural History of Masturbation*. New York: Zone Books, 2003.

Larner, Christina. *Enemies of God: The Witch Hunt in Scotland*. Baltimore, MD: Johns Hopkins University Press, 1981.

Léna, Philippe, and Liz-Rejane Issberner. "Anthropocene in Brazil: An Inquiry into Development Obsession and Policy Limits." In *Brazil in the Anthropocene: Conflicts between Predatory Development and Environmental Politics*, edited by Liz-Rejane Issberner and Philippe Léna. New York: Routledge, 2017.

Lem, Stanislaw. *Solaris*. Translated by Joanna Kilmartin and Steve Cox. 1970. Reprint, New York: Faber & Faber, 2016.

Lepore, Jill. *The Name of War: King Philip's War and the Origins of American Identity*. New York: Vintage, 1998.

Leroy, Jean-Pierre. "Markets or the Commons? The Role of Indigenous Peoples, Traditional Communities and Sectors of the Peasantry in the Environmental Crisis." In *Brazil in the Anthropocene: Conflicts between Predatory Development and Environmental Politics*, edited by Liz-Rejane Issberner and Philippe Léna. New York: Routledge, 2017.

Levack, Brian P. "State-Building and Witch Hunting in Early Modern Europe." In *Witchcraft in Early Modern Europe: Studies in Culture and Belief*, edited by Jonathan Barry, Marianne Hester, and Gareth Roberts, 96–117. Cambridge: Cambridge University Press, 1996.

Levack, Brian P. *The Witch-Hunt in Early Modern Europe*. New York: Routledge, 2016.

Levitz, Eric. "Far-Right Climate Denial Is Scary: Far-Right Climate Acceptance Might Be Scarier." *New York Magazine*, March 6, 2019. https://nymag.com/intelligencer/2019/03/climate-science-invites-liberal-solutions-or-fascist-ones.html.

Lewis, Simon L., and Mark A. Maslin. "Defining the Anthropocene." *Nature* 1519 (March 12, 2015).

Liberti, Stefano. *Terra Bruciata: Come la crisi ambientale sta cambiando l'Italia e la nostra vita*. Rome: Rizzoli, 2020.

Liboiron, Max. *Pollution Is Colonialism*. Durham, NC: Duke University Press, 2021.

Lindqvist, Sven. *"Exterminate All the Brutes": One Man's Odyssey into the Heart of Darkness and the Origins of European Genocide*. New York: New Press, 1992.

Lindqvist, Sven. *Terra Nullius: A Journey through No One's Land*. London: Granta, 2007.

Linebaugh, Peter, and Marcus Rediker. *The Many-Headed Hydra: Sailors, Slaves, Commoners, and the Hidden History of the Revolutionary Atlantic*. Boston: Beacon Press, 2000.

Londoño, Ernesto, and Letícia Casado. "As Bolsonaro Keeps Amazon Vows, Brazil's Indigenous Fear 'Ethnocide.'" *New York Times*, April 19, 2020.

Loth, Vincent C. "Armed Incidents and Unpaid Bills: Anglo-Dutch Rivalry in the Banda Islands in the Seventeenth Century." *Modern Asian Studies* 29, no. 4 (October 1995): 705–40.

Loth, Vincent C. "Pioneers and Perkeniers: The Banda Islands in the 17th Century." *Cakalele* 6 (1995): 13–35.

Loureiro, Violeta Refkalefsky. "The Amazon before the Brazilian Environmental Issue." In *Brazil in the Anthropocene: Conflicts between Predatory Development and Environmental Politics*, edited by Liz-Rejane Issberner and Philippe Léna. New York: Routledge, 2017.

Lovejoy, Thomas E., and Carlos Nobre. "Amazon Tipping Point: Last Chance for Action." *Science Advances* 5, no. 12 (December 20, 2019).

Lovelock, James. "What Is Gaia?" ecolo.org/lovelock/what_is_Gaia.html.

Luttikhuis, Bart, and A. Dirk Moses. "Mass Violence and the End of the Dutch Colonial Empire in Indonesia." *Journal of Genocide Research* 14, nos. 3–4 (2012).

Malm, Andreas. *Fossil Capital: The Rise of Steam Power and the Roots of Global Warming.* London: Verso, 2016.

Marya, Rupa, and Raj Patel. *Inflamed: Deep Medicine and the Anatomy of Injustice.* New York: Farrar, Straus and Giroux, 2021.

Masco, Joseph. "Bad Weather: The Time of Planetary Crisis." In *Times of Security, Ethnographies of Fear: Protest and the Future*, edited by Martin Holbraad and Morten Axel Pedersen, 163–97. London: Routledge, 2013.

Masco, Joseph, "The Crisis in Crisis." *Current Anthropology* 58, supp. 15 (February 2017): 565–76.

Masco, Joseph. *The Theater of Operations: National Security Affect from the Cold War to the War on Terror.* Durham, NC: Duke University Press, 2014.

Mason, John. *A Brief History of the Pequot War: Especially of the memorable Taking of their Fort at Mistick in Connecticut in 1637.* Boston, 1736.

Masselman, George. *The Cradle of Colonialism.* New Haven, CT: Yale University Press, 1963.

Masselman, George. *The Money Trees: The Spice Trade.* New York: McGraw-Hill, 1967.

Matchan, Erin L., David Phillips, Fred Jourdan, and Korien Oostingh. "Early Human Occupation of Southeastern Australia: New Insights from 40Ar/39Ar Dating of Young Volcanoes." *Geology* 20, no. 20 (2019).

Mathur, Nayanika. "What I Learned at the 'Rhodes Must Fall' Protest at Oxford." *The Wire*, May 11, 2020. https://thewire.in/world/cecil-rhodes-oxford-protest-george-floyd.

Mbembe, Achille. *Necropolitics*. Translated by Steven Corcoran. Durham, NC: Duke University Press, 2019.

McGreal, Chris. *American Overdose: The Opioid Tragedy in Three Acts*. New York: Public Affairs, 2018.

McGrath, Maggie. "63% of Americans Don't Have Enough Savings to Cover a $500 Emergency." *Forbes*, January 6, 2016. https://www.forbes .com/sites/maggiemcgrath/2016/01/06/63-of-americans-dont-have -enough-savings-to-cover-a-500-emergency/?sh=787dadfb4e0d.

McPherson, Robert S. *Sacred Land, Sacred View: Navajo Perceptions of the Four Corner Region*. Salt Lake City, UT: Brigham Young University Press, 1992.

Merchant, Carolyn. *The Death of Nature: Women, Ecology and the Scientific Revolution*. San Francisco: Harper and Row, 1983.

Merchant, Carolyn. "The Scientific Revolution and *The Death of Nature*." *Isis* 97 (2006): 513–33.

Merchant, Carolyn. "'The Violence of Impediments': Francis Bacon and the Origins of Experimentation." *Isis* 99 (2008): 731–60.

Merwick, Donna. *The Shame and the Sorrow: Dutch-Amerindian Encounters in New Netherland*. Philadelphia: University of Pennsylvania Press, 2006.

Milton, Giles. *Nathaniel's Nutmeg, or, the True and Incredible Adventures of the Spice Trader Who Changed the Course of History*. New York: Penguin, 1999.

Mitchell, Timothy. *Carbon Democracy: Political Power in the Age of Oil*. London: Verso, 2011.

Moran, Lee. "Epidemiologist Slams U.S. Coronavirus Response: 'Close to Genocide by Default.'" *Huffpost*, May 6, 2020. https://www.huffpost .com/entry/epidemiologist-coronavirus-genocide-by-default_n _5eb2a5ebc5b63e6bd96f5d81.

Moore, Jason W. "The Rise of Cheap Nature." In *Anthropocene or Capitalocene? Nature, History and the Crisis of Capitalism*, edited by Jason W. Moore, 78–115. Oakland: PM Press, 2016.

Morton, Alexandra. *Listening to Whales: What the Orcas Have Taught Us*. New York: Ballantine, 2002.

Morton, Timothy. *The Poetics of Spice: Romantic Consumerism and the Exotic*. Cambridge: Cambridge University Press, 2000.

Moses, Asher. "'Collapse of Civilisation Is the Most Likely Outcome': Top Climate Scientists." *Resilience*, June 8, 2020. https://www.resilience

.org/stories/2020-06-08/collapse-of-civilisation-is-the-most-likely
-outcome-top-climate-scientists/.

Mukerji, Bithika. *Neo-Vedanta and Modernity*. Varanasi: Ashutosh
Prakashan Sansthan, 1983.

Muneta, Ben. "The American Global Frontiers: Tribal Armies and Herbi-
cides." *Akwesasne Notes* (Early Summer 1974): 26–28.

Nabokov, Peter. *Native American Testimony: An Anthology of Indian and
White Relations, First Encounter to Dispossession*. New York: Harper and
Row, 1978.

Naipaul, V. S. *The Overcrowded Barracoon and Other Articles*. New York:
Knopf, 1973.

Nandy, Ashis. *Alternative Sciences: Creativity and Authenticity in Two Indian
Scientists*. New Delhi: Oxford University Press, 1995.

Nandy, Ashis. "From Outside the Imperium: Gandhi's Cultural Critique
of the 'West.'" *Alternatives: Global, Local, Political* 7 (1981): 171. http://alt
.sagepub.com/content/7/2/171.

Nass, Daniel. "Shootings Are a Glaring Exception to the Coronavirus
Crime Drop." *The Trace*, April 29, 2020. https://www.thetrace.org/2020
/04/coronavirus-gun-violence-stay-at-home-orders/.

Neihardt, John G. *Black Elk Speaks: The Complete Edition*. Lincoln: University of Nebraska Press, 2014.

Nelson, Cody. "Navajo Nation Faces Twin Threats as Wildfires Spread
during Pandemic." *Guardian*, July 6, 2020. https://www.theguardian
.com/us-news/2020/jul/06/arizona-wildfires-coronavirus-navajo
-nation.

Newlin, James W. M. *Proposed Indian Policy*. 1881.

Newton, Creede. "Why Has Navajo Nation Been Hit So Hard by the Coronavirus?" *Al Jazeera*, May 27, 2020. https://www.aljazeera.com/news
/2020/05/navajo-nation-hit-hard-coronavirus-200526171504037
.html.

Nixon, Rob. *Slow Violence and the Environmentalism of the Poor*. Cambridge,
MA: Harvard University Press, 2013.

NoiseCat, Julian Brave. "How to Survive an Apocalypse and Keep Dreaming." *Nation*, June 2, 2020. https://www.thenation.com/article/society
/native-american-postapocalypse/.

Noys, Benjamin. *Malign Velocities: Accelerationism and Capitalism*. Washington, DC: Zero Books, 2014.

Nursey-Bray, Melissa, R. Palmer, T. F. Smith, and P. Rist. "Old Ways for New Days: Australian Indigenous Peoples and Climate Change." *Local Environment* 24, no. 5 (2019): 473–86.

O'Connell, Barry. *On Our Own Ground: The Complete Writings of William Apess, a Pequot.* Amherst: University of Massachusetts Press, 1992.

Okereke, Caleb, and Kelsey Nielsen. "The Problem with Predicting Coronavirus Apocalypse in Africa." *Al Jazeera*, May 7, 2020. https://www .aljazeera.com/indepth/opinion/problem-predicting-coronavirus -apocalypse-africa-200505103847843.html.

Onishi, Norimitsu, and Constant Méheut. "Pandemic Shakes France's Faith in a Cornerstone: Strong Central Government." *New York Times*, April 29, 2020. https://www.nytimes.com/2020/04/29/world /europe/coronavirus-france-masks.html?action=click&module=Top %20Stories&pgtype=Homepage.

Open Democracy. "Covid-19 Has Already Affected 93 Different Indigenous Nations." June 12, 2020. https://www.opendemocracy.net /en/democraciaabierta/la-covid-19-ya-afecta-a-93-nacionalidades -indigenas-en/.

Open Democracy. "As the Pandemic Continues to Accelerate, So Does the Deforestation of the Amazon." June 1, 2020. https://www .opendemocracy.net/en/democraciaabierta/se-acelera-la-pandemia -y-se-acelera-la-deforestacion-del-amazonas-en/?source=in-article -related-story.

Open Democracy. "The Survival of the Amazon Is at Stake." July 24, 2020. https://www.opendemocracy.net/en/democraciaabierta/survival -amazon-stake/.

Oreskes, Naomi, and Eric Conway. *Merchants of Doubt: The Denial of Global Warming.* New York: Bloomsbury, 2010.

Osmandzikovic, Emina. "How Conflicts Turned the Middle East into an Organ-Trafficking Hotspot." *Arab News*, July 8, 2020. https://www .arabnews.com/node/1701871/middle-east.

Ostler, Jeffrey. "The Shameful Final Grievance of the Declaration of Independence." *Atlantic*, February 8, 2020.

Padua, José Augusto. "Brazil in the History of the Anthropocene." In *Brazil in the Anthropocene: Conflicts between Predatory Development and Environmental Politics*, edited by Liz-Rejane Issberner and Philippe Léna. New York: Routledge, 2017.

Parker, Geoffrey. *Global Crisis: War, Climate Change and Catastrophe in the Seventeenth Century.* New Haven, CT: Yale University Press, 2013.

Pico, Tamara. "The Darker Side of John Wesley Powell." *Scientific American,* September 9, 2019. https://blogs.scientificamerican.com/voices/the-darker-side-of-john-wesley-powell/.

Pitts, Beth. "Voice of the Living Forest: Interview with Indigenous Resistance Leader José Gualinga." *Extinction Rebellion,* October 8, 2020. https://writersrebel.com/voice-of-the-living-forest-interview-with-indigenous-resistance-leader-jose-gualinga/.

Plested, James. "How the Rich Plan to Rule a Burning Planet." *The Bullet,* December 23, 2019. https://socialistproject.ca/bullet/about/.

Prothom Alo. "26 Bangladeshis Killed in Libya." May 28, 2020. https://en.prothomalo.com/bangladesh/bangladesh-in-world-media/26-bangladeshis-killed-in-libya.

Prucha, Francis Paul, ed. *Americanizing the American Indians: Writings by the "Friends of the Indian."* Lincoln: University of Nebraska Press, 1978.

Quinones, Sam. *Dreamland: The True Tale of America's Opiate Epidemic.* New York: Bloomsbury, 2015.

Ramanujan, A. K. "Is There an Indian Way of Thinking? An Informal Essay." *Contributions to Indian Sociology* 23, no. 1 (1989): 41–58.

Rambé, Hanna. *Mirah of Banda.* Trans. Toni Pollard. Jakarta: Lontar, 2010.

Ramnath, Madhu. *Woodsmoke and Leafcups.* New Delhi: HarperCollins, 2015.

Reid, Anthony. *A History of Southeast Asia: Critical Crossroads.* Malden, MA: Blackwell, 2015.

Rich, Nathaniel. *Losing Earth: A Recent History.* New York: Farrar, Straus and Giroux, 2019.

Robinson, Cedric J. *Black Marxism: The Making of the Black Radical Tradition.* Chapel Hill: University of North Carolina Press, 1983.

Robinson, Cedric J. *On Racial Capitalism, Black Internationalism, and Cultures of Resistance.* Edited by H. L. T. Quan. London: Pluto Press, 2019.

Roper, Lyndal. "Witchcraft and Fantasy in Early Modern Germany." In *Witchcraft in Early Modern Europe: Studies in Culture and Belief,* edited by Jonathan Barry, Marianne Hester, and Gareth Roberts, 207–35. Cambridge: Cambridge University Press, 1996.

Roy, Eleanor Ainge. "New Zealand River Granted Same Legal Rights as Human Being." *Guardian,* March 16, 2017. https://www.theguardian

.com/world/2017/mar/16/new-zealand-river-granted-same-legal
-rights-as-human-being.

"Rules Governing the Court of Indian Offenses." Department of the
Interior, Office of Indian Affairs, Washington, DC, March 30, 1883.
https://rclinton.files.wordpress.com/2007/11/code-of-indian-offenses
.pdf.

Rushkoff, Douglas. "Survival of the Richest: The Wealthy Are Plotting to
Leave Us Behind." *Medium*, July 5, 2018. https://onezero.medium.com
/survival-of-the-richest-9ef6cdddocc1.

Sabin, Edwin L. *Kit Carson Days, 1809–1868, "Adventures in the Path of
Empire."* Vol. 2. Lincoln: University of Nebraska Press, 1995.

Sabin, Paul. "'The Ultimate Environmental Dilemma': Making a Place for
Historians in the Climate Change and Energy Debates." *Environmental
History* 15, no. 1 (2010): 76–93.

Salisbury, Neal. *Manitou and Providence: Indians, Europeans and the Making
of New England, 1500–1643.* New York: Oxford University Press, 1982.

Samarajiva, Indi. "COVID Underdogs: Sri Lanka: Like New Zealand
Except Better." *Medium*, June 24, 2020. https://medium.com/indica
/covid-underdogs-sri-lanka-db6eca164a35.

Satia, Priya. *Empire of Guns: The Violent Making of the Industrial Revolution.*
Stanford, CA: Stanford University Press, 2019.

Satia, Priya. *Time's Monster: How History Makes History.* Cambridge, MA:
Harvard University Press, 2020.

Schiebinger, Londa, and Claudia Swan, eds. *Colonial Botany: Science, Commerce, and Politics in the Early Modern World.* Philadelphia: University of
Pennsylvania Press, 2007.

Sengupta, Anuradha. "Tired of Running from the River: Adapting to
Climate Change on India's Disappearing Islands." *Yes!*, June 2, 2016.
https://www.yesmagazine.org/environment/2016/06/02/tired-of
-running-from-the-river-adapting-to-climate-change-on-indias
-disappearing-islands/?utm_content=bufferd7286&utm_medium=
social&utm_source=twitter.com&utm_campaign=buffer.

Serwer, Adam. "The Coronavirus Was an Emergency until Trump Found
Out Who Was Dying." *Atlantic*, May 8, 2020. https://www.theatlantic
.com/ideas/archive/2020/05/americas-racial-contract-showing
/611389/.

Seth, Suman. "Darwin and the Ethnologists: Liberal Racialism and the

Geological Analogy." *Historical Studies in the Natural Sciences* 46, no. 4 (2016): 490–527.

Shakespeare, William. *The Works of William Shakespeare*. Edited by William George Clark and John Glover. Vol. 1. Cambridge: Macmillan and Co., 1863.

Shiva, Vandana, and J. Bandyopadhyay. "The Evolution, Structure, and Impact of the Chipko Movement." *Mountain Research and Development* 6, no. 2 (May 1986): 133–42.

Silko, Leslie Marmon. "Landscape, History, and the Pueblo Imagination." In *The Ecocriticism Reader: Landmarks in Literary Ecology*, edited by Cheryll Glotfelty and Harold Fromm, 264–75. Athens: University of Georgia Press, 1996.

Silko, Leslie Marmon. *The Turquoise Ledge*. New York: Viking, 2010.

Singh, Zorawar Daulet. *Powershift: India-China Relations in a Multipolar World*. New Delhi: Macmillan, 2020.

Sharma, Mukul. *Caste and Nature: Dalits and Indian Environmental Politics*. New Delhi: Oxford University Press, 2018.

Sharma, Mukul. *Green and Saffron: Hindu Nationalism and Indian Environmental Politics*. Ranikhet: Permanent Black, 2012.

Shorto, Russell. *The Island at the Center of the World*. New York: Vintage, 2005.

Skafish, Peter. "The Metaphysics of Extra-Moderns: On the Decolonization of Thought: A Conversation with Eduardo Viveiros de Castro." *Common Knowledge* 22, no. 3 (2016).

Spary, E. C. "Of Nutmegs and Botanists: The Colonial Cultivation of Botanical Identity." In *Colonial Botany: Science, Commerce, and Politics in the Early Modern World*, edited by Londa Schiebinger and Claudia Swan, 187–203. Philadelphia: University of Pennsylvania Press, 2007.

Spiro, David E. *The Hidden Hand of American Hegemony: Petrodollar Recycling and International Markets*. Ithaca, NY: Cornell University Press, 1999.

Srivastava, Rahul, and Matias Echanove. "The Misunderstood Paradigm: Circulatory Urbanism in India." *Uncube*, July 2015. https://www.uncubemagazine.com/blog/15799893.

Stannard, David E. *American Holocaust: The Conquest of the New World*. Oxford: Oxford University Press, 1992.

Stark, Ken, and Kyle Latinis. "The Response of Early Ambonese Foragers to the Maluku Spice Trade: The Archaeological Evidence." *Cakalele* 7 (1996): 51–67.

Stockholm International Peace Research Institute. "Global Military Expenditure Sees Largest Annual Increase in a Decade — Says SIPRI — Reaching $1917 Billion in 2019." April 27, 2020. https://www.sipri.org /media/press-release/2020/global-military-expenditure-sees-largest -annual-increase-decade-says-sipri-reaching-1917-billion.

Strakosch, Elizabeth, and Alissa Macoun. "The Vanishing Endpoint of Settler Colonialism." *Arena Journal* nos. 37/38 (2012).

Subramaniam, Banu. *Ghost Stories for Darwin: The Science of Variation and the Politics of Diversity.* Urbana: University of Illinois Press, 2014.

Sudan, Rajani. *The Alchemy of Empire: Abject Materials and the Technologies of Colonialism.* New York: Fordham University Press, 2016.

Sulistyo, Nikodemus Yudho. "The Half-Blood Hero in Y. B. Mangun-wijaya's *Ikan-Ikan Hiu, Ido, Homa* and James Cameron's *Avatar.*" *Spectral: Jurnal Ilmiah* 3, no. 2 (June 2017).

Sumon, Shehab. "Human Traffickers Kill 26 Bangladeshis in Libya." *Arab News*, May 30, 2020. https://www.arabnews.com/node/1681906/world.

Sundar, Nandini. *The Burning Forest: India's War in Bastar.* New Delhi: Juggernaut, 2016.

Survival International. "Brazil's Indians." https://www .survivalinternational.org/tribes/brazilian.

Survival International. "WWF's Secret War." October 7, 2020. https:// www.sixdegreesnews.org/archives/29331/leaked-report-us-halts -funding-to-wwf-wcs-and-other-conservation-ngos-over-abuses.

Takaki, Ronald. "The Tempest in the Wilderness: The Racialization of Savagery." *Journal of American History* 79, no. 3 (December 1992): 892–912.

TallBear, Kim. "Badass Indigenous Women Caretake Relations: #Stand-ingrock, #Idlenomore, #BlackLivesMatter." In *Standing with Standing Rock: Voices from the #noDAPL Movement*, edited by Nick Estes and Jaskiran Dhillon. Minneapolis: University of Minnesota Press, 2019.

Taylor, Bron. *Dark Green Religion: Nature, Spirituality and the Planetary Future.* Berkeley: University of California Press, 2010.

Thomas, Julia Adeney. "The Cage of Nature: Modernity's History in Japan." *History and Theory* 40, no. 1. (February 2001): 16–36.

Thomas, Julia Adeney. "History and Biology in the Anthropocene: Problems of Scale, Problems of Value." AHR Roundtable, *American Historical Review*, 2014.

Thomas, Julia Adeney. "Practicing Hope in Anthropocene History." AHR Anthropocene Workshop, Position Paper, April 28, 2019.

Thomas, Julia Adeney. "The Present Climate of Economics and History." In *Economic Development and Environmental History in the Anthropocene: Perspectives on Asia and Africa*, edited by Gareth Austin, 291–312. London: Bloomsbury, 2017.

Tocqueville, Alexis de. *Democracy in America and Two Essays on America*. Translated by Gerald E. Bevan. New York: Penguin, 2003.

Tracy, James D., ed. *The Rise of Merchant Empires: Long Distance Trade in the Early Modern World*. Cambridge: Cambridge University Press, 1990.

Treaty Between the United States of America and the Navajo Tribe of Indians: With a Record of the Discussions That Led to Its Signing. K. C. Publications, 1968.

Troll, Valentin R., Frances M. Deegan, Ester M. Jolis, David A. Budd, Börje Dahren, and Lothar M. Schwarzkopf. "Ancient Oral Tradition Describes Volcano-Earthquake Interaction at Merapi Volcano, Indonesia." *Geografiska Annaler*: Series A, *Physical Geography* 97, no. 1 (2015): 137–66. DOI: 10.1111/geoa.12099.

Tsing, Ana. *The Mushroom at the End of the World: On the Possibility of Life in Capitalist Ruins*. Princeton, NJ: Princeton University Press, 2015.

Tuck, E., and K. W. Yang. "Decolonization Is Not a Metaphor." *Decolonization: Indigeneity, Education and Society* 1, no. 1 (2012): 1–40.

Turner, Jack. *Spice: The History of a Temptation*. New York: Vintage Books, 2004.

Tyrrell, Wm. Blake. *Theogony*. https://msu.edu/~tyrrell/theogon.pdf.

Uberoi, J. P. S. *The Other Mind of Europe: Goethe as a Scientist*. New Delhi: Oxford University Press, 1984.

Underhill, John. *Newes from America; or, A New and Experimentall Discoverie of New England* (1638). Edited by Paul Royster. DigitalCommons@University of Nebraska–Lincoln; Electronic Texts in American Studies, 37.

UNHCR. "Refugees and Migrants Arrivals to Europe in 2017."

United Nations. *Review of Maritime Transport 2019*. https://unctad.org/en/PublicationsLibrary/rmt2019_en.pdf.

Valandra, Edward. "Mni Wiconi: Water Is [More Than] Life." In *Standing with Standing Rock: Voices from the #noDAPL Movement*, edited by Nick

Estes and Jaskiran Dhillon. Minneapolis: University of Minnesota Press, 2019.

van der Chijs, J. A. *De Vestiging van het Nederlandsche Gezag over de Banda-Eilanden (1599–1621)*. Batavia: Albrecht & Co., 1886.

van Dooren, Thom. *Flightways: Life and Loss at the Edge of Extinction*. New York: Columbia University Press, 2014.

van Dooren, Thom, and Deborah Bird Rose. "Storied-Places in a Multi-species City." *Humanimalia* 3, no. 2 (2012).

Veracini, Lorenzo. *Settler Colonialism: A Theoretical Overview*. London: Palgrave Macmillan, 2010.

Villiers, John. "Trade and Society in the Banda Islands in the Sixteenth Century." *Modern Asian Studies* 15, no. 4 (1981): 723–50.

Wachtel, Nathan. *The Vision of the Vanquished: The Spanish Conquest of Peru through Indian Eyes, 1530–1570*. Translated by Ben and Siân Reynolds. Sussex: Harvester Press, 1977.

Waite, Gary K. "'Man Is a Devil to Himself': David Joris and the Rise of a Sceptical Tradition towards the Devil in the Early Modern Netherlands, 1540–1600." *Dutch Review of Church History* 75, no. 1 (1995): 1–30.

Wallace, Alfred Russel. *The Malay Archipelago: The Land of the Orang-Utan and the Bird of Paradise: A Narrative of Travel with Studies of Man and Nature*. London: Macmillan, 1890.

Wallerstein, Immanuel. "The Albatross of Racism." *London Review of Books* 22, no. 10 (May 18, 2000).

Watson, Fiona. "Bolsonaro's Election Is Catastrophic News for Brazil's Indigenous Tribes." *Guardian*, October 31, 2018.

Watson, Matthew. "Crusoe, Friday and the Raced Market Frame of Orthodox Economics Textbooks." *New Political Economy* 23, no. 5 (2018): 544–59.

Watuseke, Frans S. "The Name Moluccas, Maluku." *Asian Profile*, June 1977.

Weil, Patrick. "Circulatory Migration vs. Sedentary Immigration." Migration Policy Centre, CARIM-South, CARIM Analytic and Synthetic Notes, 2011/36. https://cadmus.eui.eu/handle/1814/16209. Retrieved from Cadmus, European University Institute Research Repository, http://hdl.handle.net/1814/16209.

Weir, Jessica K. *The Gunditjmara Land Justice Story*. Australian Institute of Aboriginal and Torres Strait Islander Studies, 2009.

White, Sam. *A Cold Welcome: The Little Ice Age and Europe's Encounter with North America*. Cambridge, MA: Harvard University Press, 2017.

Widjojo, Muridan. *The Revolt of Prince Nuku: Cross-Cultural Alliance-Making in Maluku, c. 1780–1810*. Leiden: Brill, 2009.

Williams, Michael. *Deforesting the Earth: From Prehistory to Global Crisis*. Chicago: University of Chicago Press, 2006.

Wilson, David Sloan. "The Tragedy of the Commons: How Elinor Ostrom Solved One of Life's Greatest Dilemmas." *Evonomics*, October 29, 2016. https://evonomics.com/tragedy-of-the-commons-elinor-ostrom/.

Wilson, Eric Dean. *After Cooling: On Freon, Global Warming, and the Terrible Cost of Comfort*. New York: Simon and Schuster, 2021.

Winn, Phillip. "'Banda Is the Blessed Land': Sacred Practice and Identity in the Banda Islands, Maluku." *Antropologi Indonesia* 57 (1998): 71–79.

Winn, Phillip. "'Everyone Searches, Everyone Finds': Moral Discourse and Resource Use in an Indonesia Muslim Community." *Oceania* 72, no. 4 (June 2002).

Winn, Phillip. "Graves, Groves and Gardens: Place and Identity — Central Maluku, Indonesia." *Asia-Pacific Journal of Anthropology* 2, no. 1 (2001): 24–44.

Winn, Phillip. "Slavery and Cultural Creativity in the Banda Islands." *Journal of Southeast Asian Studies* 41, no. 3 (2020): 365–89.

Winn, Phillip. "Tanah Berkat (Blessed Land): The Source of the Local in the Banda Islands, Central Maluku." In *Sharing the Earth, Dividing the Land: Land and Territory in the Austronesian World*, edited by Thomas Reuter. Canberra: ANU Press, 2006.

Winter, Brian. "Jair Bolsonaro's Guru." *Americas Quarterly*, December 17, 2018. https://www.americasquarterly.org/article/jair-bolsonaros-guru/.

Wolfe, Patrick. "Settler Colonialism and the Elimination of the Native." *Journal of Genocide Research* 8, no. 4 (2006): 387–409. DOI: 10.1080/14623520601056240.

Yellowtail, Thomas. *Yellowtail, Crow Medicine Man and Sun Dance Chief: An Autobiography*. As told to Michael Oren Fitzgerald. Norman: University of Oklahoma Press, 1991.

Yeo, Sophie. "Where Climate Cash Is Flowing and Why It's Not Enough." *Nature*, October 19, 2019. https://www.nature.com/articles/d41586-019-02712-3.

Yergin, Daniel. *The Quest: Energy, Security and the Remaking of the Modern World*. New York: Penguin, 2012.

Zalasiewicz, Jan, et al. "A Formal Anthropocene Is Compatible with but Distinct from Its Diachronous Anthropogenic Counterparts: A Response to W. F. Ruddiman's 'Three-Flaws in Defining a Formal Anthropocene.'" *Progress in Physical Geography* (2019): 1–15.

Zika, Charles. "Cannibalism and Witchcraft in Early Modern Europe: Reading the Visual Images." *History Workshop Journal* no. 44 (1997): 77–105.

Zimmermann, Klaus F. "Circular Migration: Why Restricting Labor Mobility Can Be Counterproductive." *IZA World of Labor* (2014). DOI: 10.15185/izawol.1| wol.iza.org.

Zotigh, Dennis. "Native Perspectives on the 40th Anniversary of the American Indian Religious Freedom Act." *Smithsonian Magazine*, November 30, 2018.

Zumbroich, Thomas J. "From Mouth Fresheners to Erotic Perfumes: The Evolving Socio-Cultural Significance of Nutmeg, Mace and Cloves in South Asia." *eJournal of Indian Medicine* 5 (2012): 37–97.

Index

Abram, David, 211
Abu Ghraib, 115
Aden, 108–9
Adivasi community, 230–32
Advertisement Touching an Holy War, An
   (Bacon), 26
Afghanistan, 122, 125, 154, 164
Africa, 9, 57, 108, 118–19, 142, 144, 154, 180, 188,
   207, 221, 225, 232, 237, 243; "COVID Apoca-
   lypse," prediction of, 138
African Americans, 70, 192, 225, 235; epidemics,
   disproportionate numbers affected by, 169;
   resistance of, 236
Agamben, Giorgio, 111
agency: human and nonhuman forms of, 14,
   59, 80, 165–66, 201, 203–4; and inaction,
   167; of landscape, 34–35; and place, 289n16
Ai Islands, 266n11
Alabama, 140
Albert, Bruce, 205–7
Algonquians, 65–66
Alwi, Des, 14–15, 245, 246–47
Alwi, Tanya, 246–48
Amal Nukila, 33, 46
Amazon, 205–6, 214–15; deforestation of, 67
Amazonia, 206–7, 209, 213–14; virgin soil
   populations of, 59
Ambon (Maluku), 42–43, 46, 93–94, 221, 251.
   See also Amboyna
Amboyna (Maluku), 194; as company town,
   42–43; English conspiracy against, 43–45;
   Japanese *ronin*, 43–44; myth of, and fake
   news, 45. *See also* Ambon
Amboyna; the State of Innocence (Dryden), 44

American Indian Religious Freedom Act, 87
American Indians, 38, 70–71, 269n9
American Midwest, 83, 213
American Revolution, 185
Amerindians, 53, 59–60, 118–19, 165, 187–88,
   235; genocide of, 116
Americas, 44, 52–54, 62–63, 86, 116, 118, 168,
   231–32, 235, 267n23; colonization of, 166,
   253; conquest of, 187; desire to destroy
   everything, impulse of, 75; Great Dyings
   of, 38; influenza, introduction to, 191;
   remaking of, 49; repopulation of, 37;
   settler colonialism of, 212, 214; slavery, re-
   sistance to, 236; terraforming of, 67; tribes,
   as witches, 254
Amherst, Jeffrey, 61–62, 185
Amherst, Massachusetts, 185
Amherst College, 185
Amsterdam, 74
Andaya, Leonard, 75
Anglo-Dutch rivalries, 25, 30
Anglosphere, 42, 44, 110, 130, 174–75
animism, 86, 273–74n2
Anthropocene, 116, 153, 214
anthropomorphism, 203
Anwar, Chairil, 245–46
Apache, 35, 150
Aphrodite, 90
Argensola, Bartolomé Leonardo de, 90–91
Arizona, 35, 49, 87, 143, 150
Arndt, Ernst Moritz, 223
Aryanism, 231
Asia, 17, 30, 40, 43, 57, 90, 115, 142, 154–55, 179–
   80, 182, 207, 225, 237, 243, 289n2

Athena, 90

Australia, 32, 52, 83, 128, 144, 150, 165, 168, 175, 183, 231–32, 238; transportation policy, 179; wildfires in, 282–83n11

Bacon, Francis, 26, 37, 187, 217, 255
Baker, Barbara, 16
Baker, Deborah, 16, 161–62, 216
Balkans, 154
Banda Islands, 8, 11–13, 18–19, 22, 24–25, 32, 34, 43, 51, 73–74, 84, 118, 159, 217, 240, 248, 252, 256, 261n1, 262n28, 264n49, 268n40, 274n15, 289n16; burning of, 23, 27, 41–42; conspiracy, 28–29; deportation, 21; destruction of, 27, 41; elimination from, 29–31, 39, 42; enslaving of, 23, 27; expulsion, campaign of, 21; extermination of, 40, 42, 52; genocide, 40–42, 191; killing of elders, 39; lamp, falling of, 5, 7, 14–17, 27–30; and landscape, 36; nutmeg, 247, 255; nutmeg, curse of, 222; nutmeg, and lost homeland, 76; nutmeg, as object of horticulture and commerce to, 35; nutmeg estates, creating of, 218, 289n2; as nutmeg-producing factory, 36; racial capitalism, 119; repopulating of, 218–20; resistance, 27, 29; songs and stories of, 35–36, 70, 183; unrest in, 221
Banda massacre, 26–27, 34–35, 42, 44–45, 93, 118, 217, 247, 252; survivors of, 40–41, 267n38
Banda Naira, 11–12, 28, 221–22; as neo-Europe, 245
Bangalore, 135
Bangladesh, 122–23, 128, 136, 154–57, 174–75
Barbados, as Nutmeg Island, 75–76
Barboncito, 50
Bartolomeo de las Casas, 187
Basra Logistics City, 114–15
Basso, Keith H., 35, 150
Battle of Britain, 105
Baum, L. Frank, 174
Behringer, Wolfgang, 294n15
Belgium, 134, 185
Bengal, 137, 154–55, 181
Benteng (Fort) Kastella, 111
Benzoni, Girolamo, 55
Bhima, 91
Bickmore, Albert, 40, 52
Biehl, Janet, 223–24, 226–28
Big Coal, 100
Big Oil, 100
Bilgrami, Akeel, 190
biopolitical warfare, 58, 166, 191; of colonization, 171; refugees of, 164–65

Black Hole of Calcutta, 45, 193–94
Black Lives Matter, 161, 170, 192–93, 222, 225, 241; police brutality, 190–91
Black Radical Tradition, 117
Blake, William, 38
blood and soil, 239–40; mystique of, 226
Board of Indian Commissioners, 283n3
Bolsonaro, Jair, 170–71, 212–14
Bose, Jagadis Chandra, 197
Boston Brahmins, 92
Boulton, Matthew, 117
Bouquet, Henry, 61–62
Boyle, Robert, 37
brandschattingen, 23–24
Brazil, 67, 168, 212; Amazonas province, 206; Covid-19 mortality rate, 214; deforestation of, 213; Indigenous peoples, 206, 213; inequity of, 141–42; terraforming, 215
Briggs, Robin, 294n15
Bristol, England, 191
British Empire, 43, 45, 121, 224–25
British Petroleum (BP), 152
Bronx Zoo, 225
Brunei, 103–4
brutalization: brutality, as word, 191; "brute" v. human, 195, 203; meaning making, 203; and non-Whites, 197; unbruting of middle classes of non-West, 196; as word, 190
Buchenwald, 186
Buddha, 199
Budj Bim, 32–33
Builth, Heather, 32
Bush, George W., 129

Calcutta, 45, 162. See also Kolkata
California, 83, 144
Callenbacker, Joncker Dirck, 22, 28–29
Camões, Luis de, 111
Camp Bucca, 115
Canada, 168, 238
Canary Islands, 52, 54
capitalism, 100–101, 147–48, 222, 242; climate change, 116; colonial conquest, race, and slavery, as essential to, 117–19; and colonialism, 117; extractivist, 207, 241; free trade, 119; and geopolitics, 119–20; myths of, 117; neoliberal, 142; planetary crisis, at center of, 120, 142, 160; racial, 118–19, 218; as war economy, 119
carbon footprint, 121, 128, 130–31, 151, 174
Caribbean, 45, 191
Carib tribe, 188–89
Carleton, James H., 51

Carson, Kit, 51
Catholic Church, 243
Cayuse, 51
Centers for Disease Control and Prevention
    (CDC), 144
Central America, 53, 165, 236
Challenger (space shuttle), 77–78
Chaplin, Joyce, 58, 66, 169
Charles, Mark, 141
Charles V, 187
Charlottesville, Virginia, 161
Chatterjee, Partha, 194
Chavez, Hugo, 107
Chile, 7
China, 8, 92, 108–10, 113, 116, 121, 123, 134, 141,
    144, 160, 165, 167, 180, 243; Uighurs, 196
Chinese Empire, 54
Chipko movement, 232, 291–92n42
choke points, 109; and oil, 107–8
Christchurch, New Zealand, 226
circulatory urbanism, 284n16
civil war, Libya, 169
Clark, Brett, 278n16
Clark, Christopher M., 54
climate change, 100, 123, 142–43, 147–50,
    153–55, 157, 168–69, 171, 222, 282–83n11;
    and capitalism, 116; carbon economy,
    defending of, 126; carbon footprint, 151;
    as cognate phenomenon, 133, 158; denial
    of, 58–59, 126, 170; effects of, as threat
    multiplier, 127, 138; as future threat, 152,
    158; global research on, 127; greenhouse
    gas emissions, 127, 167; migrants and refu-
    gees, as security threats, 127–28; military
    assessment of, 145; personal responsibility,
    151; planetary crisis, 158; power, global
    distribution of, 158–59; terraforming, 144;
    US military, understanding of, 124–25; and
    vulnerabilities, 144; as war, 164
climate disasters, 168
climate disruptions, 53, 55, 149, 182
climate justice, 153, 158
climate migration, 153–58
climate refugees, 154–55
cloves, 9, 31–32, 74, 91, 104, 108, 110, 112, 159;
    power of, 111
coal, 102–3, 105
Coen, Jan Pieterszoon, 11–14, 21–23, 27–29,
    36–37, 39, 41–42, 93, 117, 119, 185, 191, 217–18,
    247, 252–55, 263n45, 265n19, 268n40
Cold War, 106, 124, 127
colonialism, 42, 52, 54, 188, 192, 212, 238–
    239, 256, 273n18; brutalization, 196; and

capitalism, 117; and disease, 60; epistemic
    violence of, 250; industrial modernity,
    built on, 116; and land, 231; and militarism,
    228; Utopias, as companion genre of, 217;
    and vitalism, 87
colonization, 18, 54–55, 58, 65, 86, 160, 167,
    169, 229, 270n24; of Americas, 59, 166, 253;
    biopolitical wars of, 171; planetary crisis,
    191; subjugation, as process of, 190
Colorado, 49, 140
Columbus, Christopher, 9, 188, 191–92
Columbus, Fernando, 191
Communist Party of India (CPI), 231
company towns, 115
Congress Party, 231
Connecticut, 24–25, 49, 185; as Nutmeg State,
    75–76
conquest: of Americas, 187; and capital-
    ism, 117–119; ideology of, 39, 63; world-as-
    resource, 76
Conrad, Joseph, 183–84, 186
conservation groups: anti-Indigenous preju-
    dice in, 225; White supremacy, 225
consumerism, 243
Conway, Erik, 100
Cook, Harold, 263n45
Coop, Andy, 274n17
coronavirus, 14, 18. *See also* Covid-19 pandemic
Couperus, Louis, 249–51, 256
Covid-19 pandemic, 15–16, 70, 134, 142, 144, 158,
    161, 163, 177, 209, 215; as cognate phenom-
    enon, 133; as default genocide, 214; gun
    violence, increase in, 192; Hispanic, Black,
    and Native American populations, dispro-
    portionate number among, 140; lockdown,
    relaxing of, 141; meatpacking plants, 141;
    mishandling of, 280n4; planetary crisis,
    178; racial disparities, 141, 169–70; unrest
    and violence, 139–40. *See also* coronavirus
Covid Racial Data Tracker, 140
cowpox, 62
Crist, Eileen, 203
Cronon, William, 63, 201, 271n4
Crosby, Alfred, 52, 83
Cuba, 142, 188
Curzon, Lord, 194
Cyclone Amphan, 136–38, 141

Dakota Access Pipeline, 238
Dalai Lama, 199
Dalit community, 230
Dark Ages, 252, 253
Darwin, Charles, 78–80, 223–24, 273n16, 273n17

Darwin Foundation, 225

Defoe, Daniel, 44

deforestation, 67, 213

Dekker, Eduard Douwes, 42

Deloria, Vine, Jr., 34–35, 69, 269n9, 292n6

DeLoughrey, Elizabeth, 106

Democracy in America (Tocqueville), 55–56

Democratic Republic of Congo, 225–26

Denetdale, Jennifer Nez, 50

Denmark, 252

Dermoût, Maria, 250–51

De Ruyter, Michiel, 121–22

Descartes, René, 37

Descent of Man, The (Darwin), 79

desertification, 165

development studies, 195

Dhillon, Jaskiran, 292–93n11

Diderot, Denis, 39

Diego Garcia, 109, 125

Diggers, 235

Diné, 50, 52, 84, 220, 268–69n5; homeland, attachment to, 51

Dinétah, 84

disaster relief, 128

diseases: as "invisible bullets," 60; as weapons of war, 62

dislocation, 14, 158

displacement, 58, 69, 155, 165; of refugees, 158

doctrines of empire: "savage peoples," exterminating of, 26

Dooren, Thom van, 203

Downs, Jim, 283n16

Dragon (warship), 22, 28, 254

Drake, Francis, 121–22

Draupadi, 91

Dryden, John, 44

Duara, Prasenjit, 243

Dubai, 156

Dubai Logistics City, 114–15

Du Bois, W. E. B., 117, 237

Dunbar-Ortiz, Roxanne, 270n24

Dupuy, Jean, 116, 242

Dutch East India Company. *See* East India Company (VOC)

Dutch East Indies, 106, 119

Dutch Empire, 93

Dutch Golden Age, 40

Earhart, Amelia, 185

Earth, 88, 90–91, 144, 148–49, 173, 197, 205–6, 212, 235, 237; as alive, 7; as bountiful, 65; as dead weight, 82; as exhausted, 76–77; as inanimate, 38; as inert, 37, 83, 87, 242–43; as living entity, 84–86

East India Company (Vereenigde Oostindische Compagnie) (VOC), 11–14, 17, 36, 41–42, 73, 91–93, 119, 218, 247–48, 263n45; Amboyna conspiracy, 43–44; capitalism, as pioneer of, 75, 118; collapse of, 76; nutmeg trees, campaign of extermination against, 74–75; Seventeen Gentlemen, 39; water torture, use of, 27–28

East Indies, 11, 14, 39, 42, 91–92, 94

Eburne, Richard, 220

Echanove, Matias, 284n16

ecocide, 82

ecofascism, 82, 224, 228, 233; blood and soil, 239; and mysticism, 226–27; and scientism, 227

ecology, 227; as term, 223

Ecuador, 237

Egypt, 9, 188; Nile Delta, 211

Ehrenreich, Ben, 39

empathy, 177, 193, 239; stories, nurtured by, 240, 244

energy, 18–19, 101–2; greenhouse gas emissions, 147; renewable, 99–100, 103, 109–10; transitions of, 129–31

England, 9, 64, 117–18, 179, 185, 291n38; enclosure in, 176. *See also* Great Britain

English colonization, 66–67; and nature, 58; superiority of, 169

English East India Company, 39

Enlightenment, 38, 252–53

environmentalism, 225, 230; environmental deregulation, 214; environmental disruptions, 157, 165–66; environmental justice movement, 228; livelihood, 233; xenophobic nationalism, 223

environmental movements, 100, 243; as Earth-centered mass movement, 244; social epidemic, 244

epidemics, 59–60, 169. *See also* Covid-19; pandemics

Eris, 90

Eritrea, 154

Escapes (organization), 155

Estes, Nick, 68, 165, 292–93n11

E.T. (film), 180

ethnic cleansing, 141, 232

eugenics, 224–25, 227; in economics, 286n31

Eurasia, 9

Europe, 8–9, 25, 36–39, 52–53, 57, 64, 83, 90, 93, 108, 111, 116–20, 175–76, 181, 186, 196, 206, 209–12, 217, 224, 226, 236–37, 267n23, 280n4; conquest, ideology of, 63; environment, proper use of, 63; humanism, 188; migration crisis, 153–54; sexuality, anxieties about, 73–74; witches, 253–54, 294n13

European colonization, 59, 167, 190; of Americas, 173, 179; ecological interventions, 63–66, 68; legacy of, 76; pathogens, as allies, 61–62; scale and rapidity of, 54–55; structural violence of, 59

European Union (EU), 175, 182

evolution, 78, 80–81; theory of, 184, 223–24

"Exterminate All Brutes" (Lindquist), 183

exterminationism, 227

extermination policy, 173, 186, 212, 283n3; Western elite culture, as central to, 184–85; and witchcraft, 254

extinction, 87

Extinction Rebellion, 161

Faisal, King, 107

Falling Sky, The: Words of a Yanomami Shaman (Kopenawa), 205–9

Favret-Saada, Jeanne, 267n25

fazendeiros (squatter farmers), 68

Fenn, Elizabeth, 62

First Opium War, 119, 121

Fletcher, John, 111

flooding, 69, 125, 127, 136, 143–44, 150, 154–56, 165

Florida, 83, 125

Floyd, George, 139

fokorndan, 34

forever wars, 57–58, 164–65

Fort Greene Park, 193

Fort Kastella, 112

Fort Pitt, Pennsylvania, 61

forts: states of exception, 111–12

fossil fuels, 18, 99–106, 168, 282–83n11; Anglosphere, strategic hegemony of, 110; war-making, role in, 121–23, 125–26

Four Corners Monument, 49–50, 220

France, 44, 105, 134, 188, 193, 267n25

Francis, Pope, 161, 233, 243–44

Fratelli Tutti (Pope Francis), 161

freedmen's organizations, 169

Gaia, 84–88, 100, 105, 108–9, 162, 171, 177, 205, 212, 221, 243; Golden Apples, 89–90

Galápagos Islands, 225

Games, Alison, 43–44

Gandhi, Mahatma, 229, 235, 240, 291n38

Genoa, 9, 117–18

genocide, 24, 35, 40, 42, 75, 82, 141, 190–91, 214; and divinity, 26; genocide by default, 288n20; industrial modernity, built on, 116; as word, 41

geo-engineering, 168, 228

geopolitics, 111, 114, 116, 126, 129–31, 160; and capitalism, 119–20

Germany, 134, 186, 188, 252; blood and soil, 223; ecofascism, 224–25; neo-fascism, rise of, 223; oil, shortage of, 105–6

Ghost Dance mass movement, 236

Gilio-Whitaker, Dina, 69

Glacier National Park, 225

Glittering World, 50–51, 84

global geopolitics, 111; Indian Ocean, importance of to, 112–13, 115–16; and oil, 106

globalization, planetary crisis, 167

global North, 148

global power, 158–59

global South, 160

global warming, 125–27, 148, 152–53, 156–57, 170, 242

Goa, India, 108, 111

Goethe, Johann Wolfgang von, 38

Golden Apples, 89; Fruit of Knowledge, 90

Golding, William, 85, 177–78

Gonsalves, Gregg, 288n20

Goodall, Jane, 197, 210

Good Life, 160–61

Gorom, 274n15

Grandin, Greg, 76

Grant, Madison, 225

Great Britain, 45–46, 101, 105–6, 134, 143–44, 164, 188, 273n16. See also England

Great Depression, 119

Great Dying, 59–60, 169, 173; planetary crisis, solution to, 174

Great Mystery, 64

Great Plains, 67; buffalo herds, extermination of, 68–69, 71; terraforming of, 69

Greece, 154, 188

green activism, 230

green energy, 103

Greenock, Scotland, 102–3

Greenwich, England, 50

Grenier, John, 56, 67

Gualinga, Sabino, 237, 238

Guam, 109

Guangzhou, 180

Guatama, Siddhartha, 199

Guha, Ramachandra, 233, 291n38, 291–92n42

Gulf War, 122

Gunditjmara, 32–33

Gunung Api, 11, 34, 84, 240, 245

Haeckel, Ernst, 223–24, 226

Haiti, 188

Hakluyt, Richard, 179

Hall, Jonathan, 274n11
Hanna, Willard A., 15
Hanumana, 91
Haraway, Donna, 203, 293n16
Hardin, Garrett: lifeboat ethics, metaphor of, 175–76, 178
Hartmann, George W., 194
Heart of Darkness (Conrad), 185; critique of, 186; "Exterminate all brutes," sentence in, 183–84, 186, 190
Helen of Troy, 90
Henry, Charles, 150
Hentschel, Willibald, 226–27
Hera, 89–90
Heraclitus, 116–17
Hermes, 90
Hesiod, 88–89
Hesperides, 89
Heyer, Heather, 161
Hidden Force, The (Couperus), 249–52, 256–57
"High Flight" (Magee), 77–78
Himmler, Heinrich, 224
Hispaniola, 191
History of the New World (Benzoni), 55
Hitler, Adolf, 224
Hochstrasser, Julie Berger, 40, 221, 294n5
Hölderlin, Friedrich, 38
Homer, 88
Homo sapiens, 79, 199
Hong Kong, 108–9
Hormuz, 108
Houston, Texas, 144; flooding in, 143
Houttuyn, Martinus, 95
Hubbard, William, 57
Hulme, Peter, 189
human exceptionalism, 203, 293n16; belief in, 81
humanism, 186, 188, 252–53
Hundredth Monkey, fable of, 244
Hurricane Andrew, 125
Hurricane Katrina, 128–29
Hurricane Maria, 129, 141–42
Hussein, Saddam, 107

Idle No More, 293n10
Iliad (Homer), 240
Images of Animals: Anthropomorphism and Animal Mind (Crist), 203
imperialism, 42–43, 120; imperial optic, 140
Independence Day (film), 180
India, 8, 47, 57, 92, 108–10, 113, 115, 123, 128, 135, 154, 156, 160, 165, 167, 182, 193–94, 196, 235, 238, 291n38; caste system, 142, 229–30;

extractivist economy, drift toward, 231; internal migrants, 180; resistance movements, 232–33
Indians: Americanization of, 174–75; cattle, conflicts over, 67–68; "Indian problem," as "buffalo problem," 68. *See also* Native Americans
Indigenous peoples, 34, 54–55, 66, 68, 71, 86, 96, 150, 166–68, 203, 205–6, 212, 224, 226, 230–31, 237–38, 256, 268n40, 270n24, 293n10; conservation groups, 225; Covid-19, impact on, 214; destruction of life, 67, 69; diseases, as weapons of war, 62; displacement of, 69–70, 165; ecosystems, understanding of, 83–84; eviction of, 232; extermination of, 213; Great Dying of, 59–60; industrial interventions, 70; landscapes, significance to, 35; medical care, withholding of, 62; settler-colonial treatment of, 196; in state of forever war, 57–58; zones of containment, 69. *See also* Indians; *individual tribes*; Native Americans
individualism, 177–78
Indonesia, 33, 46, 110, 115, 160, 165, 167; Papuans, 196
industrialized agriculture, 118
Industrial Revolution, 116; steam engine, 101–3, 117
In Memoriam (Tennyson), 78–79; "crowning race," 80–81
Inter-American Court of Human Rights, 237
Intergovernmental Panel on Climate Change, 147, 152
Iowa, 140
Iraq, 114–15, 122, 125, 154, 164
Iraq War, 106, 115, 122
Ireland, 54, 117–18
Iroquois, 67
irregular wars, 56, 232
Island Princess, The (Fletcher), 111
Israel, 107
Italy, 134, 139, 142, 157, 162–63, 181, 188; climate refugees, 154–55; "the eye of the cyclone," 143; Puglia, 267n25

Jakarta, 110, 221, 245–46
James VI of Scotland (James I of England), 295n20
Jamestown, Virginia, 59
Japan, 106, 108–9, 149, 264n1
Java, 23, 33, 40
Jefferson, Thomas, 45
Jews, 38, 223

Joan of Arc, 241
Johnson, Edward, 64
Jones, David, 59–60
Jorgenson, Andrew K., 278n16
Journey to the West (Wu Cheng'en), 202

Kai (island), 35
Kashmir, 167
Kei (island), 29
Keir, James, 117
Kelton, Paul, 59–60
Kennan, George, 126
Kimmerer, Robin Wall, 64, 93, 96–97
King Philip's War, 57; domestic animals, tar-
    geting of, 66–67; environmental aspects
    of, 66–67; savagery of, 66
kinship, 15, 81, 183, 237
Kiowa, 61, 68–69
Klare, Michael, 106
Klein, Naomi, 100, 175, 226
Kolff, Dirk, 17, 264n47
Kolkata, 134–36, 162, 215–16. *See also* Calcutta
Kopenawa, Davi, 205–7, 209–13, 223, 228–29,
    236, 257; "spirit being," 208
Krenak, Ailton, 67–68
Kronos, 88–89
Kyoto Protocol, 147

labor movements, and coal, 102
Ladon, 89–90
LaDuke, Winona, 70, 237
Laguna, 70, 203–4
Lake Powell, 87
Lakota, 165
Lakota-Cheyenne-Arapaho alliance, 68
Lampedusa, Italy, 156
land, 97; European and Indian conceptions of,
    differences between, 64; ownership of, 63;
    as savage, notion of, 63
landscape, 37–38, 46, 60, 66, 83–84, 103,
    143–44, 183–84, 190, 233, 255; and agency,
    34–35; as alive, 35–36, 51; as factories, 73;
    in literature, portrayal of, 201; meaning of,
    50–51, 220; metaphysical significance of,
    49–50; as sacred, 238; site of habitation,
    239; as terraformed, 171; terrestrial, 52;
    vitality of, 219–21, 256
Langley, Virginia, 125
Latin America, 237, 243
Laudato Si (Pope Francis), 233
Lem, Stanislaw, 83
Lemkin, Raphael, 41
Lenape, 61

Leopold II, 185
Lepore, Jill, 57
Levack, Brian P., 253, 294n15, 295n20
Levant, 9
Levellers, 235
Lewis and Clark expedition, 62
liberal interventionism, 26; wars of choice,
    justification of, 27
liberal world order, 158
Liberti, Stefano, 143
Liboiron, Max, 36, 290–91n31
Libya, 156, 163–65
Limited Test Ban Treaty, 127
Lindqvist, Sven, 183–84, 186, 190
Linebaugh, Peter, 26
Linnaean system, 94, 98, 209; as monopoly on
    truth, 95
Linnaeus, Carl, 79, 95
Little Ice Age, 52–53, 149, 253
Locke, John, 176, 270n2
logistics: logistics cities, 114–15; logistics
    revolution, 114
Lonthor Island, 5, 10–11, 21, 23, 27, 29, 219
Lord of the Flies (Golding), 85, 177–78
Los Angeles, 143
Loth, Vincent C., 217–18, 264n49, 264n51
Louisiana, 70
Lovejoy, Thomas, 215
Lovelock, James, 85–88, 211
Low Countries, 23, 252
Lusiads, The (Camões), 111
Lyell, Charles, 78

Macau, 108–9
mace, 8, 12–14, 22, 31, 91
Macoun, Alissa, 273n18
Magee, John Gillespie, 77, 81
Magellan, Ferdinand, 12
magical thinking, 244
Mahabharata, 91
Makassar, 110
Malabar Coast, 91–92
Malacca, 108–9
Malay Peninsula, 108–9
Malaysia, 180
Malm, Andreas, 101–3
Maluku, 8–9, 12, 30–33, 35, 41–43, 45–47,
    73–76, 90–91, 93–95, 108, 111, 115, 221, 229,
    251, 274n15
Manado, 110
Mandeville, Bernard, 37
Mann, Michael C., 100
Maoris, 238

Margulies, Lynn, 85, 211
Mars, 76–77, 173, 242, 244
Martino, Ernesto de, 267n25
Marx, Karl, 236–37
Masco, John, 144–45; 147
Mason, John, 24–25, 49, 185, 252
massacre: religious martyrdom, 44; sectarian mass killings, 44; as word, 44
Masselman, George, 268n40
mass shootings, 192
materiality: bruteness, feature of, 187, 197; of nature, 197; of opium, 92–93; of petroleum, 104
Mauritius, 95
Max Havelaar (Multatuli), 42
McPherson, Robert S., 268–69n5
mechanistic paradigm, 255
mechanistic philosophies, 37
mechanomorphism, 203
Médecins sans Frontières, 128
Menelaus, 90
Merchant, Carolyn, 176, 255
metastasis, 174–75
Mexico, 165
Miami, Florida, 143–44
Miantonomi, 66–67
Middle Ages, 9, 19, 188, 253, 268–69n5
Middle East, 106, 109, 122, 130, 180
migration, 175; as circulatory, 180–82, 284n16; coerced, 179; internal, 179–80; international labor, 181; migrants, 127–28, 135, 137–38; migration crisis, 155; migration propaganda, 179; settler colonialism, 178–79; and transportation, 179; work-related reasons, 181
militarism, 128; and colonialism, 228
militarization: as ecologically destructive, 123; treadmill of destruction school of sociology, 123–24
Minneapolis, 139–40
Mississippi, 140
Missouri, 69
Missouri River, 144
Mitchell, Timothy, 102
Mizbah, Libya, 163
Mnuchin, Steven, 141
modernity, 19, 38–39, 77, 87, 116, 118–19, 121, 167, 197, 218, 228, 236, 241, 243, 256
Modi, Narendra, 135
Mohegan, 265n14
Moluccas, 111
Montauk, 66
Morris, William, 38

Morrison, Scott, 282–83n11
Mount Gamalama, 33
Mount Merapi, 33
Muir, John, 225
Multatuli. *See* Dekker, Eduard Douwes
Mumbai, 135, 137, 143–44
Mystic, Connecticut, 24
mysticism, 222–24, 226–27, 230–31, 233

naming, 93–94, 97
Napoleon, 193
Narragansett, 66, 265n14
National Indian Foundation (FUNAI), 213
National Institute for Space Research, 213
nationalism, 236–37; extractivist, 231; racist, 223; xenophobic, 223
National Socialism, 224
Native Americans, 51, 58, 87, 96, 174, 192, 207, 225; Covid-19, 140; diseases, as weapons of war, 60, 62; Earth, as bountiful, 64–65; epidemics, disproportionate numbers affected by, 169; Europeanization of terrain, 66; Great Dying among, 169; killing of, as military tradition, 56; lands of, as nuclear testing sites, 70; resistance movements, 237; Skywoman and Eve, stories of, 64–65; systemic neglect of, 140–41; tending the land, 64; virgin soil theory, 59
natural disasters, 135; inequities, impact of, 141–42; militarism of, 129; military as first responders to, 128
natural laws, 80
nature, 94–95, 187, 209; brutishness of, 188–90, 197; conflicts with Native Americans, role in, 58; disorder, as feminine domain of, 255; Great Mystery, 64; as inert entity, 38–40, 197; materiality of, 197; and plants, 197; power over, settlers attempt of, 76; as subdued and cheap, 73; trees, as communicative, 197–98; as wilderness, 64, 76
nature religions, 243
Nauru, 165
Navajo, 50–51
Navajo Nation, 70, 140–41
Nazism, 224
Nelson, Horatio, 121–22
Nemesis (battleship), 121–22
neo-Europes, 54, 82–83, 245; geo-engineering, 168; as term, 52; as terraformed, 168–69, 213
neo-fascism, 223
neoliberalism, 100–101, 142, 167
neo-Romanticism, 224

New Amsterdam, 24, 30, 43, 45
New Atlantis (Bacon), 217
Netherlands, 23–24, 39–40, 42, 188, 214, 253–54, 256
Nevada, 70
New Delhi, 135, 137
New England, 24, 49, 57, 64, 66–67, 271n4
New London, Connecticut, 49
New Mexico, 49, 51
New Netherland, 24, 30, 45
New Organon (Bacon), 187
New York City, 16, 30, 61, 140, 161, 174, 212; Brooklyn, 14–15, 17–18, 139, 194, 216; Central Park birding incident, 139; Manhattan, 24, 30, 43, 45
New York State, 212
New Zealand, 52, 134, 173, 238
Nielsen, Kelsey, 139
Nixon, Richard M., 107
Nixon, Rob: slow violence, 282n5
Nobre, Carlos, 215
#NoDAPL struggle, 292–93n11
NoiseCat, Julian Brave, 141, 271n13
nonhumans, 58, 65, 68, 196–97, 233, 257; agency of, and storytelling, 204; and humans, communication between, 38, 198–99, 286n33; meaning making, 200–202; planetary crisis, 208; storying, 293n16
Norfolk, Virginia, 125
Norse Sagas, 202
North Africa, 154, 165
North America, 34, 52–53, 55, 76, 108, 115, 182, 188, 213, 215, 226, 231; German environmental thought, influence in, 225; Indian boarding schools, 232; noncombatants, killing of, 57; precolonial wars, as form of ritualized conflict, 56; scalp hunting, 57; shaman-led uprisings, 236
North Dakota, 238
Nukila, 111. *See also* Rainha Buki Raja
nutmeg, 8, 10–14, 18, 22, 31–32, 39, 97, 104, 108, 110, 159, 247, 255, 262n28, 289n2; as commodity, 91; curse of, 35–36, 98, 222; as fetishes, 9; horticulture and commerce, object of, 35; luxury, symbols of, 9; medicinal properties, 9; slaves, 218; songs and stories about, 76, 98
nutmeg tree, 31; extermination of, 74; scientific name of, 95

Oakland, California, 115
Occupy movement, 161, 240; legacy of, 241
Oceti Sakowin (Sioux) peoples, 69–70

Odyssey (Homer), 202
Oglala Lakota, 64
oil, 102, 105; choke points, 107–8; geopolitical architecture of, 106; petrodollar system, 106–7; as unevenly distributed, 107–8
Ojibwa, 61
Okereke, Caleb, 139
Omaha (tribe), 71
Oman, 115–16
omnicide, 75, 82, 168, 190–91
Onandaga, 212
opioid crisis, 92, 144
opium, 91, 274n15; materiality of, 92–93
orang campur (mixed people), 219
orang-halus (ghosts), 245, 248
orang-kaya (men of wealth), 13, 22, 23, 27; conspiracy, suspicion of, 256; torture of, 254–55
Oregon, 51
Oreskes, Naomi, 100
Original Dream, The (Amal), 33
Origin of Species, The (Darwin), 80
Osborn, Henry Fairfield, 225
Ostrom, Elinor, 176
Oxfam, 128
Oxford, 192

Pacific Islanders, 182
Pakistan, 164
pandemics, as threat multiplier, 138. *See also* Covid-19; epidemics
Papua, 167
Paracelsus, 38
Paris (mythology), 90
Paris Agreement, 244
Parma, Italy, 155–56
Pattiradjawane, 246
Payne, Katy, 286n33
Pearl River, 108–9
Peleus, 90
penguins, 203
pepper, 108, 110
Pequot, 24–26, 49, 52, 185, 265n14
Pequot War, 25–26, 56, 265n14; as genocidal, 24
Persia, 188
Peru, 236
petrodollar system, 106–7, 130
petroleum, 104
petro-states, 103–4, 180
Philippines, 128
Phoenix, Arizona, 143–44
Pick-Sloan Plan, 69
Pierce, Franklin, 71

Pine Ridge reservation, 69–70

planetary crisis, 68, 126, 133, 142, 164–65, 182, 198, 205–6, 222, 226, 228–29, 233, 240, 242–44, 257; brute v. human, as core of, 195; and capitalism, 120, 160; climate change, 158; and colonization, 191; Covid-19, 178; Great Dying, 174; globalization, Earth's response to, 167; hierarchies, preserving of, 126; Indian Ocean, as chief theater of, 116; nonhuman eyes, viewed with, 208; past, rooted in, 192; sacrifice zones, 70, 171; settler colonialism, connections between, 139; systemic inequities, 138, 140; terraforming, 144, 215

police: protests against, 192; police brutality, 190–91

politics of vitality, 222; and storytelling, 240

Pontiac's Rebellion, 61

Portland, Oregon, 222

Portugal, 108, 117–18, 213

Potawatomi, 60–61

poverty, 59, 69, 135, 164, 169, 176, 195

Powell, John Wesley, 87

power, 103–4, 116; dual meaning of, 102

Priam, 90

Priestley, Joseph, 117

print, technology of, 45

Prison Ship Martyrs monument, 193; White English victimhood, as tale of, 194–95

protest movements, modes of dwelling, 240

Puerto Rico, 129, 142

Pulao Run, 265n19

Purchas, Samuel, 179

Puritans, 49

Qatar, 130

Qing Empire, 121

racialism, 273n17

racism, 120, 193, 236–37; brute, 188; institutional, 225

Rainha Buki Raja, 111. See also Nukila

Rama, Charles, 95–97

Ramanujan, Srinivasa, 96

Ramayana, 202

Ranters, 235

Rapture, 82

rationality, 75, 222–23; economic, 118; and humanism, 252–53; mystical, 227

Ray, Satyajit, 180

Reagan, Ronald, 77–78

Rediker, Marcus, 26

refugees, 127–28, 153, 163–65; climate change, 154–55; displacement of, 158

remapping, ecological and topographic transformation, 52; "new," use of, 52

renaming, semantic and symbolic violence of, 49

Republic of South Maluku, 46

reverse-greenhouse effect, 53

Revolutionary War, 62

Rheia, 89

Rhodes, Cecil, 192

Rhodes Must Fall movement, 192

Rich, Nathaniel, 100

Robinson, Cedric J., 117–20, 236

Rome, 188

Roosevelt, Theodore, 185

Roper, Lynda, 295n18

Rozengin, 265n19

Rumpf, Georg Eberhard. See Rumphius

Rumpf, Susanna, 94

Rumphius, 93–95, 251

Run (island), 14, 30, 41

Russia, 123. See also Soviet Union

sacrifice zones, 69–70, 171

Salisbury, Lord, 185

Salonga National Park, 225–26

Sarayakus, 237–38

Satia, Priya, 117, 195

Saudi Arabia, 103–4, 107, 115, 123, 130

savagery, 56, 66, 87, 174, 236

Schellnhuber, Hans Joachim, 241

Schopenhauer, Arthur, 38

science: anti-colonial sciences, 290–91n31; scientific ecology, 226; scientism, 227; scientist, as word, 275n19

Seattle, Chief, 71

Selamon, 5–6, 21–22, 253; Selamon's lamp, meaning of, 14–15, 252, 254, 256

Senegal, 138

Seram (island), 29

Serwer, Adam, 141

Seth, Suman, 273n17

settler colonialism, 54, 57, 62, 167–68, 196, 207, 212, 214, 231–32; as concept, 269n18; cutting down trees, 65; domestic animals, 65–68; ecological interventions of, 65; Europeanization of land, 66; improving the land, 63, 65; Indians, conflicts between, 66–67; and migration, 178–79; planetary crisis, connections between, 139; as sources of disequilibrium, 65; terraforming of, 63, 82

Shakespeare, William, 188

shamanism, 206, 233, 235–36

Sharma, Mukul, 230, 233

Shelley, Percy Bysshe, 38, 74
Sherman, William T., 173
shipping containers, invention of, 114
Sicily, 156
Sierra Club, 225
Silko, Leslie Marmon, 70, 203–4
Simon, William, 107
Singapore, 109, 115, 180
Sioux, 62, 173
slavery, 25, 37, 179, 191; banning of, 119; capi-
    talism, as essential to, 117–19; on nutmeg
    estates, 218; resistance to, 236; slave camps,
    164; slave forts, 115
slow violence, 165
smallpox, 60–61; deniability, advantage of, 62;
    as weapon of war, 62
Smith, Adam, 9
Sobel, Adam, 134, 136
social Darwinism, 227, 273n16; ecological
    thought, connection between, 223–24
social movements: co-opting of, by military
    planners, 128
Socotra, 108
Solaris, 171, 198
Solaris (Lem), 83
Somalia, 139, 154, 164
Sonck, Martijn, 5–7, 10–11, 17, 21–22, 28–29, 37,
    252–54
South Africa, 108–9
South America, 52–53, 235–36
South Carolina, 140
South Dakota, 239
Southern Paiute, 70
South Korea, 108, 134
Soviet Union, 106. See also Russia
space, and time, 34, 202
Spain, 134, 143, 188
Spanish Empire, 95
spice islands, 111
spices, 9, 73, 91–92; artwork, underwriting
    of, 40; body, as harmful to, 74; monetary
    returns on, 39–40; rivalry for, 111
Spielberg, Steven, 180
Sri Lanka, 23, 134
Srivastava, Rahul, 284n16
Stalingrad, 106
Standing Bear, 64
Standing Rock Sioux Reservation, 238, 240,
    293n10; as prayer camp, 239
statues, toppling of, 191–92, 225
Staudenmaier, Peter, 223–24, 226–28
St. Bartholomew's Day massacre, 44
Steffen, Will, 241

St. Francis of Assisi, 200
St. Francis Xavier, 111
storying, 203; nonhuman, 293n16
storytelling, 201–203; and empathy, 240, 244;
    narrative faculty, 204; politics of vitality,
    240
Strait of Hormuz, 108–9
Strakosch, Elizabeth, 273n18
subjugation, 37–38, 76; history, as tool of,
    192–93
Subject Matter (Chaplin), 169
Subramaniam, Banu, 197, 273n16
Sudan, 154
sugar, 118
sugarcane, 91
Sulawesi, 110
Sultan of Ternate, 112
Sundarban, 135–38
Survival International, 226
Sweden, 188, 241
Swedenborg, Emanuel, 38
Swift, Graham, 201
Swift, Jonathan, 44
Syria, 154

Taiwan, 108, 134
Tallbear, Kim, 293n10
Taqui Ongo movement, 236
Tasmania, 54
Taylor, Bron, 243–44, 273–74n2
Tempest, The (Shakespeare), 189; colonialism,
    as allegory of, 188
Tennessee, 140
Tennyson, Alfred Lord, 78–82; crowning race,
    vision of, 168
Ten Thousand Things, The (Dermoût), 250–52
Ternate (island), 31, 33, 74, 110–12, 159–60,
    274n15, 277n13
terraforming, 53, 70–71, 82, 256; cattle,
    conflicts over, 67–68; climate change, 144;
    colonial history, as extrapolation from,
    54; European models, reengineering of, 55,
    64–65; exhaustion, as metaphor, 76; geo-
    engineering, 168–69, 171; neo-Europes, 168,
    213; planetary crisis, 144, 215; rivers, diver-
    sion and damming of, 69; settler-colonial
    experience, roots in, 54; settler-colonials,
    82; settler identity, 63; strato-forming, 169;
    as violent process, 168; warfare, as mode
    of, 55; world-as-resource, 73
Terra Nullius (Lindquist), 183
terrestrial landscapes, 52
Theogony (Hesiod), 88

Thetis, 90
Thirty Years' War, 23
Thom, Robert, 102–3
Thoreau, Henry David, 38
Thunberg, Greta, 241
Tidore (island), 31, 110
Titanic (ship), 176
tobacco, 91, 118
Tocqueville, Alexis de, 55–56, 166
Tongans, 178
Traditional Ecological Knowledge (TEK), 84
trans-species encounters, 199–200
treadmill of destruction, 278n16
Treaty of Breda, 30
Treaty of Hartford, 265n14
Trent, William, 61
Trevor-Roper, Hugh, 188
Trier, Germany, 254
Trojan War, 90
Troy, 90
Trump, Donald, 124, 144, 170–71, 213, 282–83n11
Tupac Amaru, 236
Tupinamba, 37–38
Turkey, 123, 164
Turqoise Ledge, The (Silko), 70, 203–4
Tyndall Air Force base, 125
Typhoon Haiyan, 128–29

Uexküll, Jakob von, 202
Umm Qasr, Iraq, 114–15
Underhill, John, 24–25, 185, 252
Union of Concerned Scientists, 124
United Arab Emirates, 130
United Nations (UN), 148; climate summit, 123; convention on genocide, 41; Green Climate Fund, 123
United States, 23, 30, 45–46, 56, 58, 65, 69–70, 105, 110, 116, 125, 128, 130, 134, 143, 145, 147, 162, 164, 169–70, 175, 188, 193, 213–14, 225, 228, 236–37, 280n4, 291n38; choke points, watching over, 109; contemporary policing in, and slave patrols, links between, 139; Covid-19, 144, 192; disparity, maintaining of, 126–27; "Drill, baby, drill!" slogan, 168; Empire of Bases, 109; energy policy, as militarized, 106, 122; environmental organizations, 127; fossil fuels, self-sufficiency in, 106; hazardous waste, and US chemical companies, 123; inequity of, 141–42; mass shootings in, 192; Occupy movement, 240; opioid crisis in, 92; petrodollar, 106–7; post-9/11 wars, cost of, 123; protests in, 139–40; War on Terror, 114
Uranos, 88

US Army, 68
US Department of Defense, 123–24, 126; climate change, 125; global warming, 125
US Department of the Interior, Code of Indian Offenses, 87
US military: carbon footprint, 131; fossil fuels, dependence on, 125–26; global warming, 125; Improvised Explosive Device (IED), 125; sea-level rise, 125
US Navy, 129
Utah, 49, 87
Utopias, 217

Valandra, Edward, 239
Vancouver, British Columbia, 115
van der Chijs, J. A., 16–17, 42, 264n1, 264n51
Vasco da Gama, 9
Vattel, Emer de, 26
Venezuela, 107
Venice, 9, 117–18
Veracini, Lorenzo, 269n18
Vietnam, 133–34, 142
Virginia, 45, 60, 66–67, 127, 191
virgin soil theory, 59–60
vitalism, 38, 86, 94, 105, 230, 232–33, 237–38, 241, 243–44; civilization, as mutually exclusive, 87; and colonialism, 87
vitalist politics, 223, 235, 238; resistance movements, 232–33
volcanoes, 33, 36, 39, 110, 159; Indonesian reverence for, 34
volkisch movement, 223

Wakanda (Great Spirit), 71
Wallace, Alfred Russel, 184
Wallerstein, Immanuel, 187–88, 193
Wandervögel movement, 224
War on Terror, 114
War of the Worlds (film), 180
War of the Worlds (Wells), 53; wars of extermination, 54
wars of extermination, 40, 42, 54, 57
wars of religion, 25
Washington Consensus, 167
Washington, George, 193
Wasteland (Swift), 201
waterboarding, 27
Watt, James, 101, 117
Welles, Orson, 77
Wells, H. G., 53–54
West Bengal, 136
Western Shoshone, 70
White body, belief in biological advantages of, 169

White supremacy, 161, 226; conservation
  groups, 225
Whitman, Walt, 38
wildfires, 70, 83, 125, 143–44, 213, 222
Williamson, Jack, 53
Winn, Phillip, 219–21, 267n38, 289n16
Winthrop, John, 63
Wisconsin, 141
Wisdom Sits in Places (Henry), 150
witchcraft, 267n25; and climate, 294n15;
  conspiracy, association with, 253; and
  extermination, 254; and torture, 253–55,
  295n20; weather magic, 295n22; witch
  burnings, 37–38, 252–53; witch craze, 45;
  witch hunts, 37, 294n13; and women, 211
Wolfe, Patrick, 69
world-as-resource, 73, 75; conquest, as process
  of extraction, 76; loss of meaning, 76–77
World War I, 105, 120, 164
World War II, 41, 46, 77, 105–6, 114, 120, 122,
  133, 164

Worldwatch Institute, 70
World Wildlife Fund (WWF), 225–26
Wounded Knee massacre, 69–70
Wovoka (prophet), 236
Wuhan, 141
Wyoming, 140

xapiri (spirits), 208–10
Xinjiang, 167

Yamasees of Virginia, 67
Yanomami, 206–8, 211–12
Yom Kippur War, 107

Zambia, 184
Zeus, 89–90
Zimmerman, Klaus F., 181
zones of containment, 165; as sacrifice zones,
  69–70
Zuiderzee (warship), 28